BIG CITY MAYORS

The Crisis in Urban Politics

THE CRISIS

EDITED BY

BIG CITY MAYORS

IN URBAN POLITICS

Leonard I. Ruchelman

INDIANA UNIVERSITY PRESS

Bloomington / London

To my mother and father,

SARAH *and* JACOB

CONTENTS

PART III: THE MAYOR AS CHIEF EXECUTIVE

PART IV: THE MAYOR AS CHIEF LEGISLATOR

PART V: THE   MAYOR AS CHIEF OF PARTY

EDITOR'S NOTE

BEFORE WE CAN BEGIN TO COPE EFFECTIVELY WITH THE PROBLEMS OF contemporary urban existence, there must be greater understanding of our cities in all their aspects—social, economic, physical and political. Though useful beginnings have been made through various forms of analyses, very little attention has been directed to urban leadership, especially the mayoralty. From my own perspective, this seems an unforgiveable oversight, for unless we are able to break down old fallacies and myths which surround this subject, attempts to improve the urban condition are likely to fail.

Drawing upon selections which treat different communities, this book analyzes the many roles and responsibilities of the big city mayor more broadly than has heretofore been done. In choosing the readings, care has been taken to present a balanced view of the subject. Any biases that appear are unavoidable and merely reflect the available material.

I should like to record my gratitude to all those who made this book possible. First, I am indebted to Professor Wallace S. Sayre of Columbia University whose scholarship and teaching has been a source of inspiration. The College Center of the Finger Lakes Research Grants-in-Aid Program was generous in supporting my research during the summer of 1968. Mr. Lester H. Cohen very helpfully looked after the many details of constructing a project of this kind. And my long-suffering wife, Diana, was indispensable in overseeing matters of style.

Lehigh University   L. I. RUCHELMAN
Bethlehem, Pennsylvania

In the readings, some material and footnotes have been omitted which were not necessary to the purpose of the present work. Editor's omissions in the text are indicated by five points (. . . . .); where necessary, footnotes have been renumbered for this volume and appear at the end of each article.

The Urban Challenge of the Seventies

There has always been a pessimistic element in accounts of the American city. Thomas Jefferson set the tone in his classic assertion: "The mobs of great cities add just so much to the support of pure government as sores do to the strength of the human body." Others such as Emerson, Thoreau, Hawthorne, Poe, Henry Adams and Henry James followed suit, emphasizing the artificiality of the urban community and its tendency to degrade the human spirit.[1]

If the city was denigrated, so too was its politics. In 1888, the noted Englishman, James Bryce, wrote, "There is no denying that the government of the cities is the one conspicuous failure of the United States."[2] And in the same monograph with Bryce, Frank Goodnow contended, "The old party system still remains and must, in a large city like New York with its great masses of ignorant voters, ever offer a great obstacle to the selection of the best men for office. . . . Many of the evils which the city has experienced in the past may be expected to recur, until such time as its electors are more intelligent, their allegiance to party less strong, and their political leaders more pure."[3] Such anxiety about the viability of the city and its political leadership has persisted to the present. Consider the following excerpts from the United States Riot Commission Report, published in 1968:[4]

> The problem [of racial disorders] has many dimensions—financial, political and institutional. Almost all cities—and particularly the central cities of the largest metropolitan regions—are simply unable to meet the growing need for public services and facilities with traditional sources of municipal revenue. Many cities are structured politically so that great numbers of citizens—particularly minority groups—have little or no representation in the pocesses of government. Finally, many cities lack both the

1

will and the capacity to use effectively the resources that are available to them.

Now, as never before, the American city has need for the personal qualities of strong democratic leadership. Given the difficulties and delays involved in administrative reorganization or institutional change, the best hope for the city in the short run lies in this powerful instrument. In most cities the mayor will have the prime responsibility.

In this context of urgency, then, we now attempt to comprehend the problems and responsibilities of big-city mayors. Attention is directed to the elected executives of America's largest cities, such as New York City, Chicago, Los Angeles, because it is here that the obligations of leadership are most awesome. Not only is the welfare of particular cities at stake, but the national welfare as well. Indeed, urban rioting and racial polarization confronts the American democratic system with one of its toughest domestic challenges since the Civil War.

Surprisingly, despite the crucial role that mayors are expected to play in a nation increasingly troubled by its urban problems, the literature of politics has seldom approached the subject in any definitive way. The present undertaking is intended to help supply this deficiency by treating the many dimensions of mayoralty leadership. As a first step, we shall examine the holders of such office as human beings who have various skills, backgrounds and motivations. Because the nation's biggest cities have traditionally been the home of diverse religious, ethnic, racial and occupational groups, one unavoidable question is: who rules? The Yankees, patricians, and entrepreneurs of old have long since given way to ethnic groups of lower social status.[5] Recent developments in Cleveland, Ohio, and Gary, Indiana, have raised the question: how long before other cities have Negro mayors? In addition, a related concern here is: do certain personality types seem to be attracted to the mayoralty, and, if so, what are the political implications of such attractions?

The first business of a mayor is to get himself elected to office, usually a difficult and costly task. Here, the extensive pluralism of most big cities is especially significant. Many centers of power such as business, labor, and ethnic groups compete for influence in the highest public office in the community. At the same time, any serious contender for the mayoralty must seek the support of many, if not most, of the city's important groups, for this can mean money with which to campaign and votes with which to be elected. In the melting pot politics of a place like New York City or Chicago, a good part of campaign strategy is concerned with ethnic and racial appeals. How to avoid the more subtle possibilities for demagoguery latent in such situations is a nicety not always observed.

Furthermore, where elections are nonpartisan (as they are in eleven of the twenty cities with more than 500,000 population),, the problems of running for office can be especially trying; organizational support tends to be weak and the candidate must himself be well-skilled in the fine art of coalition building.

Upon attaining the city's ranking office, the incumbent becomes the focus of responsibility for all that happens in the life of the community. As Sayre and Kaufman explain in their analysis of New York City, the mayor's office "is the most perceptible, the most impressive; it is taken for granted that he has the most power and thus the capacity to act vigorously in the solution of the city's problems great and small."[6] How well he can fulfill such expectations depends on both the man—i.e., his vision and skills—and on the nature of his office. In many cities, even the most vigorous and able mayor is seriously limited by a governmental structure deliberately created to delimit, if not undermine, the executive power. In Los Angeles, for example, the mayor shares executive authority with an independently elected city attorney and a comptroller. In addition, nineteen of the twenty-eight city departments are responsible to independent boards and commissions whose members, although appointed by the mayor, can be removed by him only with great difficulty. Even in the so-called strong mayor system of Chicago, there is considerable decentralization of formal authority. It is reported that no less than 181 city and county officials (excluding party officials) share governmental responsibility in that city. Mayor Daley has bested this situation through his control of the local Democratic organization as well as through his proficiency as a political broker, but other mayors have not been so fortunate.

Fragmentation of power poses a problem for the chief executive in other ways. Today the public bureaucracies, acting through their associations and unions, exert tremendous pressure not only for improved salaries and working conditions but for autonomy of direction as well. Policemen, firemen, teachers, and transit workers, among others, strive to protect their "professional status" from the "political interference" of mayors, commissioners and other "outsiders." As the number of organized public employees continues to increase, mayoral control is likely to become ever more tenuous—contingent, for the most part, on ability to negotiate and bargain rather than to command.

A mayor must be prepared to take advantage of all available opportunities if he is to perform his job well, and this includes exercising leadership in the legislature. Almost all important programs which emanate from his office—e.g., redevelopment, transportation, welfare, education, public works—depend upon council approval. Furthermore, the mayor's yearly budget, the key to just about everything of importance in the public domain, must be passed by the council. Here skills of negotiation and persuasion as well as the veto and the threat of the veto must be brought into play, and always with discretion as to the degree of delicacy or forcefulness of application. In the weak mayor system where city hall shares a substantial proportion of authority with the council, the mayor's legislative role becomes even more crucial. Moreover, he must usually deal with more than one legislative body: because of limitations of city home rule, he must importune before the state legislature in addition to the city council. The classic illustration is New York City, where the city head treads a well-beaten path to the state capitol in Albany to present "both his most important and his most numerous legislative proposals."[7] Nor can he afford to ignore the federal legislature and its growing influence in urban affairs.

Another role which the big city mayor must not neglect is chief of party. Indeed, if he is to perform his executive and legislative responsibilities effectively, he must be able to use the party organization and its resources. Perhaps most significant here is the use of party to overcome the abuses of decentralization or fragmentation of the governmental structure. Because the Mayor of Chicago is also the Chairman of the Cook County Democratic Committee, he wields power otherwise unavailable to his office. Recalcitrant councilmen, elected executive officers and even judges, who function within the city, can be pressed to "cooperate" by the fear that renomination would be denied or patronage and other favors would be withdrawn. In this way, too, the mayor has a better chance of getting his programs through the council and state legislature. Even the President of the United States is likely to be sympathetic to the city's needs in light of his own electoral dependence on the local machine.

It should be recognized, however, that with the expansion of the civil service and the proliferation of public welfare programs, party has been weakened. Where party is weakened, so also is the mayor who cannot easily find other means to mitigate the liabilities of decentralization. Professor Banfield explains: "When the mayor ceases to be boss, he will not have power to run the city as it should be run, unless—a very unlikely possibility—fundamental changes are made in the constitution. In all probability, his loss of informal control will weaken the city government disastrously."[8]

Finally, because he is in effect the living symbol of his city, the mayor is expected to perform a ceremonial function. In this role he makes speeches, greets celebrities, entertains dignitaries, honors heroes, reviews parades, presides at openings, and serves, within the limits of his time and energy, as all-around master of ceremonies. A politically astute mayor will use such events as a way of consolidating support: he can build up gratitude among the various groups who request his presence, particularly among members of minority groups who tend to prize any public recognition. Crucial to his ceremonial role are the mayor's relations with the mass media, especially the press. For it is through them that he achieves his popular image—an image that can turn sour if the media become hostile. Though the mayor's ceremonial activities may often appear trivial if not ludicrous, they should not be demeaned; for if it is true, as many allege, that mass urban society contributes to individual alienation and to social pathology,[9] then the visible responses of the city's ranking personage assume a special significance. As Mayor Lindsay testifies, walking the hot streets of New York City's ghetto neighborhoods is one way to keep them "cool."

Here, then, are the many ingredients to big-city mayoralty leadership. The mayor cannot afford to emphasize any one role to the point of ignoring another. To the extent that he fails in one area, say as chief of party, his stewardship can be seriously threatened in other areas, e.g., as chief executive or chief legislator. In fulfilling his responsibilities, much depends on the mayor's personal skills and qualities. Old institutional props which have provided some support while leaving room for error are being knocked from under him. The party organization does not give such useful backing as it did formerly. Nor does the bureaucracy necessarily see itself as an agent of the chief executive; it is increasingly protective of its own interests. The city council, usually fragmented and lacking expertise, has rarely been able to provide effective leadership.

Worse still, the nation's biggest cities no longer have sufficient resources to meet their growing problems. With few exceptions, slums, unemployment, obsolescence, squalor, and record tax rates have become typical features of the urban landscape. Perhaps the most troublesome aspect of such developments is that as white middle class persons continue their exodus to the suburbs, they are being replaced primarily by low-income and unskilled individuals who bear the stigma of race. In the face of all this, it is the mayor who must somehow hold things together, although the recent explosiveness of America's urban ghettos gives warning that time is running out.

The following pages attempt to explore in depth those things referred to above in a very general way. For material, we rely not only on the writings of those who have observed mayors at work, but on the comments and observations of the mayors themselves. Different cities, of course, function under varying conditions with divergent problems. Thus, while highlighting New York City, care has been taken to present analyses of other very large cities.[10] But despite the differences, the editor was impressed with the many overriding similarities which comprise the urban challenge of the seventies.

N O T E S

1. See Morton and Lucia White, *The Intellectual Versus the City: From Jefferson to Frank Lloyd Wright* (Cambridge, Mass.: Harvard University and The M.I.T. Press, 1962).

2. *The American Commonwealth* (New York and London: Macmillan, 1888) Vol. I, p. 608.

3. Ibid. (1889), Vol. II, p. 353.

4. *Report of the National Advisory Commission on Civil Disorders* (New York: Bantam Books, 1968), pp. 283, 298.

5. For an interesting treatment of this in New Haven, see Robert Dahl, *Who Governs? Democracy and Power in an American City* (New Haven: Yale University Press, 1961), Book I.

6. Wallace S. Sayre and Herbert Kaufman, *Governing New York City* (New York: Russell Sage Foundation, 1960), p. 657.

7. Ibid., p. 660.

8. Edward C. Banfield, *Political Influence: A New Theory of Urban Politics* (New York: The Free Press, 1961), p. 258.

9. See, for example, Jane Jacobs, *The Death and Life of Great American Cities* (New York: Random House, 1961); Robert C. Angell, "The Moral Integration of American Cities," *American Journal of Sociology*, Vol. 57, July, 1951, part 2.

10. New Haven is the only city with less than 500,000 population which is considered in this book.

PART I

Mayors — What Manner of Men?

Any attempt to comprehend the subtleties of political leadership must begin with the public officeholder as a flesh and blood human being. Like anyone else, a mayor comes from a certain level in the social structure and his behavior is in some degree a reflection of the particular kinds of ethnic, religious, and economic groups from which he springs. His special experiences in life further shape his personality and direct him toward a career in politics as a means of self-fulfillment. They also influence his choice of political roles and his use of power once he has achieved the mayoralty. One of the prime interests of this section is to show the blend of behavioral ingredients in a few selected cases.

Another related focus is the shifting characteristics of political "elites" as a measure of community transformation. In the first article, Donald S. Bradley and Mayer N. Zald categorize Chicago mayors according to social and political traits; as conditions change over time, so do mayoralty types. Thus, we see that leadership is by no means a static concept but is a function of evolving cultural forces intrinsic to the larger society. In the two selections immediately following—"Boss Cermak of Chicago" by Alex Gottfried and "Two Irish Politicians" (Mayors Kennelly and Daley of Chicago) by Edward Levine—there can be found a more definitive analysis of the "political administrator," a type of mayor who is quite relevant, still, to the urban scene.

As large numbers of immigrant people flowed into the cities at the turn of the century, they anticipated the day when their own heroes would replace those of the older, established groups. Needless to say, such changes did not occur without substantial antagonism. For insight into the hostility and vindictiveness which many an ethnic politician directed toward the patricians and entrepreneurs who were previously ascendant, we consider the words of Boston's Mayor James M. Curley in his autobiography; the title, appropriately enough, is, "I'd Do it Again." Finally, a person who cannot be ignored in any assessment of mayoralty leadership is New York's Fiorello H. La Guardia, the archetype of flamboyant stewardship in the nation's largest and most polyglot city. Like Gottfried's critique of Mayor Cermak, Arthur Mann's sensitive portrayal of the "Little Flower" is especially useful in its attempt to trace the interrelationship of personality and politics.

1.

From Commercial Elite
to Political Administrator

DONALD S. BRADLEY *and*
MAYER N. ZALD[1]

THE URBANIZATION AND INDUSTRIALIZATION OF AMERICAN LIFE HAVE
had a profound impact on the operations of political institutions and the
elements of political power. This political transformation has occurred
not only on the national scene but in the structure of local politics as well.
There have been changes in the strength and structure of local political,
social, and economic elites and in the political coin necessary to win
office. While this statement is almost a truism, it is difficult to find valid
data which concisely summarize the changes in social structure, politics,
and the linkages between them. Indexes of political transformation that
reveal underlying changes in community structure and composition are
needed.

Our study follows the lead of R. A. Dahl who uses an analysis of the
salient features of the life histories of mayors in New Haven, Connecticut,
as evidence for shifts in the distribution and differentiation of political
resources from 1789 to 1961.[2]

Dahl finds that the social and occupational backgrounds of New
Haven mayors fall into three main groupings: (1) "the patricians," well-
educated, legally trained men from well-established New Haven families,
who dominated the political field from 1784–1842; (2) "the entrepreneurs," heads of the largest and most prominent New Haven industrial
and commercial firms who, whether or not they had high social standing,
consistently were elected to the office of mayor from 1842–99; and (3) the
"ex-plebes," men from working-class and ethnic backgrounds who capi-

From "From Commercial Elite to Political Administrator: The Recruitment of
the Mayors of Chicago," *American Journal of Sociology*, LXX (September 1965),
pp. 153–167. Copyright © 1965 by the University of Chicago and reprinted by permission of the University of Chicago Press.

talized on an arithmetic of ethnic composition and were able to be the major figures in politics from 1899 on. Dahl sees such a man as Richard Lee, mayor since 1953, as possibly the first of "the New Men"; men who build on an ethnic base but also have a wider base of support through advocating such good-government policies as community redevelopment.

To explain these shifts in recruitment Dahl focuses on the relative advantages and disadvantages possessed by the various groupings within the community for gaining important political positions. He does not deal with the motivation to participate in politics. In order to understand the historical shifts in local political elites it is necessary to deal with changes in both the distribution of the resources of political power and the value of political participation for the various social groups, for these are separate aspects of recruitment to political office.

We have used the social characteristics of Chicago mayors as the basis for an analysis of the changes in the political and social structure of Chicago. As compared with New Haven, Chicago has had a more dynamic and restless growth. While New Haven had an established and cohesive elite at the time of its incorporation as a city, the groups that were to make up Chicago's elite migrated there as it grew into a transportation and trading center; where New Haven grew slowly and incorporated a few major ethnic groups, Chicago grew rapidly and assimilated a multitude of diverse immigrant groups. Thus, we were led to expect a rather different pattern of recruitment to the office of mayor. Our central purpose is to present an analysis of the changes in recruitment in Chicago. In order to highlight the differences between the two communities, comparison with New Haven will be reserved for the conclusions.

From a host of biographical sources we gathered information on the social background and political careers of each of the thirty-nine Chicago mayors. By comparing the backgrounds of each of these individuals, we established patterns of common characteristics. The mayors grouped into four periods, which we have labeled according to their most salient characteristics.[3] Changes in the patterned characteristics from one period to another are interpreted in terms of shifts in the social, economic, and ideological conditions of the city. The names and dates of election of the mayors, arranged by the periods to which we have assigned them, are presented in Table 1. In Table 2 we present summaries of the social and occupational backgrounds and of the political background and careers of the mayors of each period.

I. THE ELITE OF COMMERCIAL EXPANSIONS 1837–68

IN 1830 CHICAGO WAS ONLY A SMALL TRADING POST with a population under 100. As the frontier was pushed further west, Chicago rapidly be-

TABLE 1
Mayors of Chicago and the Years in Which They Were Elected,* by Chronological Periods

Period	Mayors
Commercial elite (1837–68)	Ogden, 1837; Morris, 1838; Raymond, 1839 and 1842; Lloyd, 1840; F. C. Sherman, 1841, 1862, and 1863; Garrett, 1843 and 1845; A. Sherman, 1844; Chapin, 1846; Curtiss, 1847 and 1850; Woodworth, 1848 and 1849; Gurnee, 1851 and 1852; Gray, 1853; Milliken, 1854; Boone, 1855; Dyer, 1856; Wentworth, 1850 and 1860; Haines, 1858 and 1859; Ramsey, 1861; Rice, 1865 and 1867
Transition mayors (1869–75)	Mason, 1869; Medill, 1871; Colvin, 1873; Hoyne, 1875†
Personalized politics versus party machine (1876–1930)	Heath, 1876‡ and 1877; Harrison I, 1879, 1881, 1883, 1885, and 1893;§ Roche, 1887; Cregier, 1889; Washburne, 1891; Hopkins, 1893; Swift, 1885; Harrison II, 1897, 1899, 1901, 1903, and 1911; Dunne, 1905; Busse, 1907; Thompson, 1915, 1919, and 1927; Dever, 1923
Political administrators (1931–65)	Cermak, 1931; Kelly, 1933,‖ 1935, 1939, and 1943; Kennelly, 1947 and 1951; Daley, 1955, 1959, and 1963.

*Terms were for 1 year 1837–62, two years 1863–1905, four years from 1907 on.
† Hoyne never took office. Colvin refused to yield seat because of change in election procedure.
‡ Special election.
§ Harrison assassinated, Hopkins elected at special election.
‖ Cermak assassinated, Kelly elected at special election.

came a transportation and trading center. The businessmen who were most prominent in this economic development commanded respect, prestige, and economic resources; they dominated the political scene and, to some extent, other institutional areas of community life. From 1837, the date of Chicago's incorporation, to 1868 the mayor, whether Whig, native American, Democrat, or Republican, was likely to be a leading businessman, highly active in political affairs and active in the affairs of his religious denomination.

A. *Social, Occupational, and Political Characteristics*

The speculative fever that characterized the economic development of Chicago at this time led most of the leading citizens to participate in several kinds of economic enterprise at the same time. More than half of this

TABLE 2*

SUMMARY OF SOCIAL, OCCUPATIONAL, AND POLITICAL
CHARACTERISTICS, BY CHRONOLOGICAL PERIODS

	Commercial Elite (N = 19)	Transition Mayors (N = 4)	Personalized Politics vs. Party Machine (N = 12)	Political Administrators (N = 4)
Social and occupational background:				
Occupations:				
Multiple occupational practice†	10		1	1
Real estate and building	2		2	
Grain and meat processing and packing, and merchandising	5			
Wholesale and distribution, Chicago area			4	1
Law and judiciary	2	1	3	
Newspaper		1		
Career government service				2
Other		2	2	
Education:				
Less than ten years	5‡			
High school	3§	1	5	3
College	1	2	1	
Legal training	4‖		5	1
No information	6	1	1	
Religion:				
Protestant	17	2	6	
Catholic			3	3
Other				1
No information	2	2	3	
Age at arrival in Chicago:				
0–15	1		1	3
15–29	10	1	7	1
30+	8	3	2	
No information			2	
Membership in social elite of modal mayor# (impressionistic rating)	Yes (social elite not highly organized)	Yes	Yes**	No
Economic standing of modal mayor at time of first election (impressionistic rating)	Highest	A level below the highest	A level below the highest	Medium–medium high
Political background and experience:				
Party affiliation:				
Democrat	11		5	4
Republican	4	2	7	
Whig	3			
Other	1	2		

TABLE 2—*Continued*

	Commercial Elite (N = 19)	Transition Mayors (N = 14)	Personalized Politics vs. Party Machine (N = 12)	Political Adminis-trators (N = 4)
Mean age at election (years)	36	57	48	54
Mean length of residence before election (years)	13	23	28	49
Political experience prior to election:††				
Alderman	9		4	1
Other positions:				
From local system	8	2	9	3
Non-local	2‡‡			
No previous position or no information	5	2	3	
Over-all judgment of prior political experience of modal mayor	High	Low	Moderate	High
Number of mayors serving different lengths in office (including two and more terms):				
1 year	10	§§		
2 years	8	2	6	1
3 years		1	1	
4 years	1		2	
5–7 years				
8 or more years			3	3
Later political office (aside from being re-elected mayor):††				
Alderman	4			
Other local-based elections	10		2	
No information or no other known position	7	4	10	4
Summary judgment: Amount of office-holding after mayoralty	High	Low	Low	Low

*The detailed table which this table summarizes has been deposited as Document No. 8387 with the ADI Auxiliary Publications Project, Photoduplication Service, Library of Congress, Washington 25, D.C. A copy may be secured by citing the document number and remitting $1.25 for photoprints or $1.25 for 35-mm. microfilm. Advance payment is required. Make checks or money orders payable to Chief, Photoduplication Service, Library of Congress.

† These men were involved in several lines at once. Almost all speculated in land, two combined this with banking, one was a medical doctor, a contractor, and in banking. Several were also active in railroads.

‡ Includes "very little," "village school," "district school," and "public school."

§ Includes one "superior education for his time."

‖ Two of these four lawyers were "self-educated."

No social registry before 1880.

** Catholics not in social registry.

†† A mayor could have been both an alderman and held other positions. Therefore, some mayors have been recorded twice.

‡‡ Two of the first group of mayors had been members of their state legislatures before moving to Chicago.

§§ See Table 1, n. †.

first group of mayors was engaged in between two and four occupations. For instance, a man might be a practicing lawyer, a land speculator, and a forwarding agent.

The first nineteen mayors represent the commercial, transportation, and building interests related to the growing economy. Real-estate speculation and investment were sources of income for at least eight of the first nineteen mayors; eight were associated with the merchandising and trading activities of the city; at least six were active in the development of railroads; three were in banking and building; and four were practicing lawyers. Almost all were extremely prominent in the business world. As Pierce observed, "Indeed, only two of the twenty-seven men running for the office between 1848 and 1869—Isaac L. Milliken, a blacksmith [and self-taught lawyer] and Timothy Wait, a barkeeper—had not attained enviable standing in the business life of the city."[4] Like most of the early migrants to Chicago all but three of these nineteen men came from New York or New England and all were born in the United States.[5]

Although we do not have complete information on the religious and educational background of this group, the available evidence indicates that it was almost entirely Protestant or non-religious. Furthermore, several of this group were instrumental in the organization of their denominations in Chicago. Raymond, Lloyd, Sherman, and Boone were either founders or prominent supporters of their respective congregations. By and large these men did not have extended formal education. Only three—Curtiss, Boone, and Wentworth—can indisputably be said to have had a college education. Although Morris and Milliken were qualified lawyers, their educational backgrounds are in doubt, for a college degree was not one of the requirements for admission to the bar.

The political careers of these mayors reveal extensive political participation. As a group, they had held substantially more offices than the group which immediately follows them. All but five of the commercial elite had anywhere from one year (Lloyd) to twelve years (Wentworth) of experience in some type of public office. After the mayoralty all but two (Ramsey and Rice) went on to serve in other positions.

Although these men were active in politics, none dominated the mayoralty for long periods, as we find happening later in the century. Even though there were no legal restrictions on the number of consecutive terms that one could serve, of the nineteen mayors only four held office for two consecutive terms and none for more than that. On the one hand, long terms in office would not have been consonant with the maintenance of economic and other interests. On the other hand, given the size of the community in its early days, the office of mayor may have had mainly honorific rather than central career importance.

The small size of the community also means that most of these men must have had extensive business dealings with each other and have known one another quite well. This homogeneity of background did not always result in a common approach to the policies of city administration. In fact, Dyer and Chapin were members of the same firm, but they ran on opposite party tickets. Although some differences in viewpoint may have existed, in Chicago, as in other new commercial towns,[6] the views of the commercial elite were stamped on the administration of the city.

The evidence presented above suggests that these first mayors were part of a "multi-institutional" elite; active in political office both before and after being mayor, heading the largest economic enterprises, and active in school and religious activities, these mayors were the leading figures in the community. They attained their position, not by virtue of family background, but through economic achievement.

B. *Changes in Community Structure*

The population of Chicago grew from 4,000 in 1837 to 29,000 in 1850 to 120,000 in 1860. As the town grew, forces developed to displace the original commercial elite from their position of both economic and political dominance. Before discussing those forces we must account for a peculiarity in the recruitment of the early mayors: Of the mayors from 1837 until 1870 all but Rice arrived in Chicago between 1833 and 1837. What accounts for the "entrenchment" of these early arrivals?

A partial explanation is found in the depression of 1837, which ruined many of the businessmen who had made fortunes during the preceding speculative era. The "panic" also served to change the character of the people who continued to come to Chicago; the speculator and the bankrupt merchant left—1838 is one of the few years in Chicago's history that reveals a decline in population—and in their place came the laboring immigrant. Those who stayed and consolidated their positions found themselves in economic ascendancy with the return of prosperity; those who came later found themselves competing against an entrenched and active group of commercial leaders who also were active in politics and dominated the political scene.

Several factors led to the eventual economic and political decline of the commercial elite, however. First, the original business leaders were eclipsed by later arrivals who built large industrial, trading, and meat-packing firms. Second, requirements developed that made the office of mayor less desireable for the businessman. Third, political resources became available to other groups within the community.

The original commercial entrepreneurs of the city had a dominant position during the 1840's, but in the 1850's and 1860's they began to be economically obscured by later arrivals.[7] By the end of the 1860's they had lost their position of economic supremacy. Such firms as Wadsworth, Dyer, and Chapin were obscured by the growth in Chicago of Armour and Company; the Chicago Packing and Provision Company; Libby, Mc-Neill, and Libby; and others. The new leaders of business did not replace the old commercial elite in politics, however; in part because they did not choose to run for office.

The office of mayor became a less desirable sideline occupation for a businessman as the scope of competing firms was enlarged and more energy and time were required to maintain a commanding position in the business community. Also, to be mayor in an era when the pioneer work of building the physical plant and establishing an order for the growing city was complete was a less valuable financial investment than it had been in the early days when various city improvements in transportation, sanitation, and waterworks could not but benefit economic interests founded on real-estate and commercial holdings.

At the same time, the growth in the physical size of the city and the expansion of public services made the elected officials responsible for more duties, requiring fulltime attention to public office. The increase in municipal expenditures from approximately $45,000 in 1848–49 to over $6,000,000 in 1868 indicates the tremendous growth in municipal complexity. Duties formerly performed by private enterprises were taken over by the administrative authorities of the city.[8] This extension of city services and the increased responsibility of the mayor for the performance of these functions made the office an all-engaging activity.

Furthermore, the proliferation of public services extended governmental responsibility into areas where it conflicted with the interests of some segments of the business community. The business leader in office found it increasingly difficult to resolve his business interests and his public responsibilities, and businessmen found they could buy advantages from the developing ward bosses of the city council. All of these developments—the increased attention demanded by commercial and public activity, the decreasing necessity for active political involvement, and the conflict of interest between the two roles—tended to make the mayoralty less desirable to the leading business notables.

At the same time there was a decline in the political resources of the economic dominants. Specifically, there was a lower popular estimation of the virtues and attainments of the businessman. The commercial elite had dominated the political scene despite rapid changes in the community composition. The city census of 1843 listed almost 30 per cent of Chicago's population as foreign-born, and by 1850 this figure had risen to

52 per cent. Until 1870, in spite of its numerical superiority and with only minimal residence requirements for voting, the foreign-born population of the city continued to support the Yankee businessman year after year.[9] The only explanation of this support seems to be that they believed they too would be the beneficiaries of the rapidly expanding wealth of the city.[10] The rise of labor consciousness, growing public concern over the extent of graft and spoils in public office, and the growing awareness of a divergence of business and public goals all worked to undercut the ideological legitimation of the commercial elite.

II. TRANSITION MAYORS: 1869–75

IN 1869, WITH THE ELECTION OF ROSEWELL MASON, a change occurred in the social background of the mayors. Supported by radical labor and pledged to the restoration of official morals, Mason no longer typifies the commercial elite. During this short period an interlude occurs between a business-dominated political scene and one controlled by charismatic and party leaders.

This period is characterized by political unorthodoxy, conflict between public moralists and advocates of personal liberty, a high degree of party irregularity, and the formation of successful independent parties. Both the disarray of the regular parties and the need for total unity following the fire of 1871 required men who could build a coalition outside of normal channels. The mayors of this period were generally older men with few local political commitments who had high standing in the community.

The type of individual chosen to serve during this period of transition and political conflict had less commitment to the economic growth of Chicago than did the entrepreneur of the preceding period. It is true that Mason and Colvin represented large transportation concerns, but they were managers rather than owners; all of the nineteen previous mayors had been more or less self-employed. Furthermore, the organizations employing them (Mason was employed by the Illinois Central Railroad and was a well-known civil engineer and Colvin was the resident agent of the United States Express Company) were oriented to a much wider area than just that of Chicago.

That the mayoralty was not the prerogative of the leaders of commerce in this period is also indicated by the election of Joseph Medill (editor and owner of the *Chicago Tribune*) and Thomas Hoyne (lawyer and jurist). Although wealthy, Medill did not hold a position in the commercial, industrial, or financial activities of the city comparable to that of the previous mayors. Wentworth, the figure of the first group of mayors most analogous to Medill, in that he owned a newspaper, was also active in real estate, banking, and railroad development. Medill, on the other hand, was completely committed to managing and editing the *Tribune*. Apparently, Hoyne had no active connection with the business community.

The average age of the transition mayors was older than either the preceding or the following groups of mayors. At the time they became mayor the mean age of the first nineteen mayors was forty-one while that of transition mayors was fifty-seven. Of the first nineteen, only two (Dyer and Rice) exceeded the age of the youngest of the second group (Medill). The transition mayors were older in average age than the subsequent two groups (forty-eight and fifty-four, respectively).

Although these mayors were older than their predecessors they had more limited local political involvements. Hoyne and Medill were active in state and national politics, but neither took the usual route to becoming mayor, that is, via the aldermanic position. Moreover, neither Mason nor Colvin had any prior political experience in the city and at the end of their terms of office they discontinued political participation.

How can we account for the selection of these mayors? The disarray in politics had led to the rise of independent parties such as the reform-minded Citizens' Ticket and the labor and ethnic-based People's Party. The "Union-Fireproof" ticket (headed by Medill) was a response to the fire. For finding a candidate that was acceptable to the diverse parties and elements of the community, who could be more acceptable than highly respected older men who had not become identified with the local political issues?

After the election of 1879 the Republicans were convinced that they could elect one of their own candidates and that a bipartisan coalition was not necessary. Thus, party politics returned to their more usual course; the reform elements of the Citizens' Ticket went over to the Republicans, and many of the ethnic elements of the People's Party returned to the ranks of the Democratic party. The transition period was ended.

III. PERSONAL MACHINE VERSUS PARTY MACHINE: 1876–1930

DISUNITY, SELF-INTEREST, AND APATHY characterized the business, labor, and middleclass elements of Chicago during this period. A lack of clear numerical preponderance and a high degree of social mobility prevented a clear victory by any one class or ethnic group. Whereas in other major cities strong machines developed, political factions controlled the various regions and groups of Chicago. The distribution of political resources in the community was such, however, that when the city-wide office of mayor was at stake it took more than these local allegiances to elect a candidate. Because of its "payoff" in patronage and political influence, the office of mayor was the focal point of activity for the politicians of all factions of both parties.

Given these conditions, there seemed to be two chief routes of ascent to the office of mayor during this period: through long and careful service to the party and through charismatic or vote-getting abilities. On the one hand, a potential mayor could extend the range of his influence until he became head of one of the party factions or he could be chosen because he epitomized party loyalty and respectability in reform periods. On the other hand, there were the two Harrisons and Thompson—upper-class notables who came to power because they could at the same time mobilize party support and, through personal qualities, appeal widely to the diverse groups of the community.

A. *Social, Occupational, and Political Characteristics*

Even though commerce and industry were growing rapidly, the period from 1880 to 1930 did not see the election of any businessman from the major industrial companies, department stores, or banks which came to dominate the Chicago economy. Legal practice, wholesaling, and real-estate management were the major business connections of the twelve mayors elected during this period. A larger proportion of these than of the previous mayors had legal training (five out of twelve as compared to six out of twenty-three); and, whereas many of the first group of mayors had been involved in shipping and milling grain or were in general merchandising, only one of these mayors was a merchant. Three of the mayors in this period were practicing lawyers and judges; five were involved primarily in the distribution of coal, paint and wood, and machinery; three were wealthy real-estate owners and operators; and one, Cregier, was a mechanical engineer and former city engineer. Both real estate and law permit an easy transition to and from public office; thus running for public office was more feasible for many of these men than for the heads of major companies.

Even the men whose businesses demanded much time differ from those who were mayors in previous eras. In several instances the political activities of these businessmen seem to be more important than their business careers. For instance, Hopkins was active in Democratic politics from his arrival in 1880 organizing several annexation movements. He was one of the organizers and early presidents of the Cook County Democratic Club; chairman of the Democratic County Committee in 1889; delegate to the Democratic National Conventions of 1892, 1900, and

1904; and oft-time chairman of the Democratic State Committee. Although he held office for only a short time, he had much more than a passing interest in politics. The same prolonged involvement is true of Busse and Swift. Not only were the mayors of this period not the leaders of the business community but politics and party work were a major part of their lives. Furthermore, five of them were identified with the large Irish and German populations of the city.

All but three of the mayors between 1880 and 1931 had obtained enough social standing and financial success to be listed in the social directories of their periods. Their educational attainment was considerably greater than that of the previous mayors. Of the twelve mayors between 1880 and 1931 six had received college educations, and of the remaining six we know that five graduated from high school. (Of the nineteen mayors of the first period only four had a college education.)

Most of these men had long service in their party, and several were heads of factions. Hopkins, Swift, Busse, and Dunne all worked up to power from unpromising beginnings. Using position in the business world and ethnic communities, each gradually extended the range of his influence over party workers and supporters until each became head of one of the party factions. Once in a position to concoct schemes and negotiate treaties, each was able to parlay his political strength into the mayoralty. The success of these mayors in the party was dependent on political generalship, and their election success was a result of the superior working of their respective party organizations.

Heath, Roche, Cregier, and Dever also spent considerable time in the service of their parties. They differed from the former group, however, in their positions within the parties. None was the head of a party faction; rather each was a party supporter. They were chosen as candidates because of their party loyalty and because of their respectability. They pacified the occasional reform or businessman groups that organized to fight the party bosses.

Although the Yankee businessman and the members of first-generation ethnic groups sought and obtained office, the most successful candidate was the charismatic social leader. During this fifty-five-year period, the two Harrisons and Thompson held the office of mayor for a total of thirty-one years and when not in office were a force to be reckoned with. In a sense the history of the mayoralty of this period is the story of these three individuals. Although quite different in their administration of public office, the Harrisons and Thompson were successful because they could appeal to a wider variety of groups than could their opponents.

Chosen to run initially for minor posts because of their silk-stocking respectability and financial standing, both the senior Harrison and

Thompson showed remarkable ability as campaigners. While Harrison, and especially his son, were less raucously flamboyant than Thompson (and were never as involved in scandals), all three had oratorical skills, a sense of showmanship, and an ability to adapt to their audience. Their personal following enabled them to jump to the top of their parties without serving long apprenticeships. Because of their citywide following they were relatively independent of the political fiefs making up the respective party organizations.

B. *Changes in Community Structure*

Between 1876 and 1931 Chicago developed into a great central manufacturing center and one of the principal agricultural clearing houses in the country. From virtually complete destruction in the fire of 1871, Chicago became the showplace of the 1893 Columbian Exposition. These radical rearrangements in the economic and physical structure were paralleled by extensive migration to the city and a reordering of its population composition. In the 1890's extensive numbers of Poles, Bohemians, Russians, and Italians arrived, following the Germans, Irish, and Scandinavians. By 1920, 70.6 per cent of the population was either foreign-born or of foreign parentage. Finally, in the early 1900's the influx of Negroes increased.[11] The high rate of economic growth, the extent of vertical mobility, and the rapid movement of large numbers of people to and from the city prevented stable political organizations and traditional groupings.[12]

Of the groupings that arose out of this economic development, the most effectively organized and *potentially* the most influential was the business element. Able to control newspapers, campaign funds, propaganda, and the services of political leaders, they could play—when they cared to act together—an important role in the political game. They seldom, however, chose either to act, or, when they did act, to do so in concert. There was conflict between commerce and industry and railroads and real-estate operators and public utilities. There was also conflict within each of these groups and between them and the public, which felt that its interests had been subordinated to narrow economic goals. Both factors, the lack of group solidarity and the lessening of social legitimation, prevented the business elite of the community from exerting control over the political scene.[13]

The numerically most powerful group, labor, was not notably successful in political participation. Organized in the 1870's and 1880's under the pressures of an expanding labor force, recurring unemployment, rising food prices and falling wages, and the injustices of child labor, the labor movement was beset by strife resulting from the issue of radicalism versus trade unionism. General prosperity between 1887 and 1892 brought quiet to the labor front and a degree of rapprochement within the labor movement. The insecurity of this rapprochement led the leaders who feared the effects of politics upon the unity of their trade-union organizations, to discourage union participation in political contests. Even when this policy was abandoned, as it was in the mayoralty campaign of 1919, lack of solidarity made labor's efforts in politics unsuccessful.

At the same time, the very diversity of ethnic groups prohibited any one group from dominating the scene. The cleavages in the ethnic composition of the community presented natural lines along which political power could be organized. Capitalizing on the neighborhood segregation of their countrymen, and their own ethnic identification, political bosses appeared who were supreme in their own bailiwicks. Chicago politics became more and more controlled by several party organizations able to distribute patronage and to obtain large campaign funds.[14]

The diversity in the community structure did not totally exclude businessmen from political participation; the time had passed, however, when an individual could be elected merely on the basis of his standing within the business community. Thus, Harrison was able to defeat a movement in 1881 to nominate in his stead candidates of the highest prestige in the business world, such as Levi Z. Leiter, George L. Dunlap, and Cyrus McCormick, and he defeated the Republican John M. Clark, a leather manufacturer, who had the backing of five hundred leading businessmen.

Although the first-ranking businessmen were not elected, several considerations lead to the conclusion that ethnic identification, while important, was not sufficient to insure election to the office of mayor. Such identification had to be paired with some business success. Roche, Hopkins, Dunne, and Dyer were all only one or two generations removed from Ireland. (Of these four, three were sufficiently wealthy to be listed in the elite directory for the mid-1880's, a precursor to the Social Register.) Busse, an influential leader of the Republican party and quite prosperous, represented the large German population in Chicago. Even when business success was paired with factional strength and ethnic identification, however, the flamboyant appeal of Thompson and the Harrisons could dominate such candidates.

The election of Anton Cermak as mayor in 1931 brought an end to the Thompson era and represented the ascendancy of a party machine that was unparalleled in the history of the city. From a position at the beginning of the depression in which the balance between the two major parties in Chicago was fairly even (seven of the last twelve mayors had been Republicans), the political complexion changed so that by 1936 the Democrats were in complete control of all the governmental agencies within the territorial limits of the city of Chicago. Henceforth, the Democratic party machine was the decisive force in the selection of elected officials. No longer could the competition between the two parties or the divergent factions within them be used as a lever for political success. The route to public office was now limited to ascendancy through the party's ranks.

IV. POLITICAL ADMINISTRATORS: 1931–1965

IN MANY OTHER CITIES the economic crisis and the community disorganization that resulted from the depression led to the introduction of political reforms and the election of rabidly antimachine candidates. In Chicago, however, the effect of the depression was to weld together the political resources of the community into the all-powerful Democratic machine. Thus, at a time when the Tammany Hall machine of New York and the Republican machine of Philadelphia were meeting severe reverses, Chicago was embracing an organization of unparalleled strength.[15] Consequently, that individual able to rise to the top of the organization or chosen by the machine to run for the office was elected to the mayoralty. Under such conditions the mayors of this period had to be, above all else, strongly connected to the local Democratic party structures.

A. *Social, Occupational, and Political Characteristics*

The four men who held office between 1931 and 1965 started from rather modest beginnings. They had little formal education—only Daley had college training; the others had a high school diploma or less—and started near the bottom of the occupational hierarchy—Cermak in the coal mines of Illinois, Kelly as an axeman for the Sanitary Department, Kennelly as a laborer in a warehouse, and Daley as a stockyard cowboy.

With the exception of Kennelly, the mayors after 1931 started fairly low in the party organization and served in a variety of elective positions (Cermak spent thirty-three years in elective office) before becoming mayor. Even Kennelly, who has been characterized as an outsider, had a long history of political involvement as a commissioner to the Lincoln Park Board and as a member of the Chicago Park District.

None of these four mayors was among the top leaders in the industrial, commercial, or financial activities of the city (although Cermak's banking and real-estate holdings placed him at the head of his ethnic community of Lawndale). They were not social notables, and none of them appeared in the elite directory of his time.[16] They had demonstrated administrative and managerial abilities, however. For instance, Kelly had been head of a large public-service agency, president of the South Park

Board of Commissioners, and heir apparent to the machine; Daley had been the Illinois Revenue Director and Clerk of Cook County. All had shown ability to organize and direct large organizational structures. They were political rather than economic entrepreneurs.

The religious and ethnic identification of most of the Democratic mayors from Hopkins on reflects the domination of the party by Irish Catholics. With the exception of the Harrisons and Cermak, all of the Democratic mayors from 1893 to the present have been first- or second-generation Irish Catholics.

Cermak, the only foreign-born Chicago mayor and, besides Busse, the only mayor to fall outside of the old-stock American, English, Scottish, or Irish groups, was able to obtain success as spokesman of the "wet" vote and the other ethnic groups making up the Democratic party. His organization and consolidation of the party, however, enabled the Irish to gain consolidated control after Cermak's death.[17]

A long and intimate participation in the life of Chicago became increasingly important for political success. Each of the ten mayors from Swift to Daley had resided in the city for more than twenty-eight years. Of these, five had been born and raised and a sixth raised in the city. The requisite sensitivity to the issues and social arrangements of the community, the necessity of an extensive network of informal social and business connections, and the lengthy party apprenticeship made residence in Chicago an imperative for political leadership.

B. *Changes in Community Structure*

What led to the rise of the political administrators? We must look at the motives for participating in politics. Judging from the social standing of a number of the aldermen and mayors of the pre-1930 period, political participation was accepted as a legitimate activity for the well-to-do. The activities of the "gray wolves" and the "boodle boys" during the era of the Harrisons, the open protection of a wide-open city during the Thompson period, the breaking of scandal after scandal, and the general circus atmosphere under which the political campaigns were run all led to the destruction of any social prestige that had been attached to office-holding and cast political participation in a negative light.[18] Many social and business leaders refrained from mingling in the rough and tumble of politics. Private welfare and philanthropy offered a much more respectable way of performing one's civic duties.[19] Busily engaged in building up their fortunes, fearful of alienating the populace with an unpopular political stand, and finding it much more profitable to buy the political favors they needed, the business and social elite stood at the sidelines of the political game. Furthermore, movement to the suburbs removed many of them from the political scene.[20]

Even those of the economic and social elite who stayed and wished to participate would have had to do so through the party organization, for the party machine, with its mobilization of the working-class vote, financial resources, and hard core of party workers, could afford to pick its candidate from within the organization.[21] The ward committeemen constituted the core of the party machinery. They controlled the selection of candidates for public office as well as the operation of the election machinery that elects the candidates. In order to become boss of the party one had to have the backing of the principal ward bosses of the inner city. It is not surprising, therefore, to find the ward bosses giving support to a leader whose identifications were with the inner-city wards.

Once chosen and in office, however, the mayor possesed a great deal of the coin upon which the machine is built—patronage. This resource made the mayor independent of the ward bosses and the ward bosses dependent upon him. This partially accounts for the coincidence of the mayor and the party boss being one and the same. The mayor, however, never gained complete independence—witness Kennelly's defeat when he tried to run without the support of the regular party organization in 1955 —but must always have some measure of support from the ward bosses.[22] Faced with the necessity of centralized leadership, the ward bosses have chosen to follow individuals with working-class backgrounds, intimate knowledge of Chicago and the party organization, Irish Catholic identification,[23] and demonstrated administrative ability. The popular and charismatic qualities that had enabled the Harrisons and Thompson to dominate the political scene during the 1890's and 1920's would in 1950 only hinder their political aspirations. The kind of leader produced by the organization was, above all else, a political executive.

V. CONCLUSIONS

OUR CONCLUSIONS CAN BEST BE STATED by comparison and contrast with those presented by Dahl for New Haven:[24]

1. In New Haven a long and settled history prior to incorporation led to the selection of mayors from among the patrician families—families of long and established social standing; these mayors had had legal training and extensive education. In comparison, Chicago's first mayors were drawn from its commercial leaders, regardless of family background, who were caught up in the growth and speculative investment of the community. This came about partly because Chicago's "old" families were al-

most non-existent but also because the commercial elite represented the driving force in the new community.

2. After 1842, New Haven's patricians gave way to the leading entrepreneurs, whether recruited from the commercial or from the industrial elite, who were to hold sway until 1900. Chicago's commercial elite were followed in the 1860's and 1870's by the transition mayors, men picked as a compromise because of the disunity and chaos of party alignments. While not unsuccessful in their occupational or social pursuits, they represented neither the commercial elite nor the local politically active.

3. In New Haven, the entrepreneurs were succeeded around 1900 by the ex-plebes, representatives of the city's recent new arrivals. In Chicago, beginning about 1880, two types of men were recruited, social notables with wide popular following and highly politically involved businessmen: men who had status in the business community, but were not from the largest firms or factories; men who had both business, political, and ethnic (Irish or German) connection. While the "ex-plebe" or at least the ethnic, label might fit some of them, ethnic politics seem not to have been as dominant a feature in their election as in that of New Haven's mayors. The diversity of ethnic groups and of the community prohibited giving the simple label of ex-plebe to these men, or to the period, until 1930.

4. Finally, with Cermak, the dominance of the Democratic party machine began. While the new mayors are "ex-plebe," the driving force in community politics becomes the machine, and the style of the mayor becomes that of the political administrator. The machine and city politics had become a full-time career. While a business career parallel to a political one is not impossible in this era, it becomes more and more unlikely.

Dahl suggests that politics and recruitment to the mayoralty may be in a period of transformation in New Haven. Ethnicity is declining as a major criterion of political success; instead Dahl hypothesizes, the "new men" will be those who, by a concern with the fate of the city, expand their political base to the self-interested downtown businessmen and the social-welfare professional. The "new men" expand their support from ethnic organizations by becoming the leaders and initiators of programs of physical and social city renewal.

The parallel with Chicago is difficult to find. As Banfield notes, in a community as diverse as Chicago there is little development of the conditions for consensus supporting a widespread attack on city problems. In such a situation the mayor is more a referee than a combatant in the resolution of the issues facing a city.

There is a parallel of another sort, however. Even though the patronage available to Chicago mayors allows the machine to function with less concession to reform than in other cities, as in other cities there has been a transformation of the posture of its political administrator. Thus, to quote the political slogan of Mayor Richard J. Daley, "Good government is good politics."

With the assimilation of foreign immigrants, the rise of social-security measures, the introduction of civil service, and the transformation of the occupational and educational structure, the only significant source of political support in the traditional patronage-welfare exchange is the Negroes, and even they are becoming increasingly concerned with the ideological dimensions of politics.

Given this transformation of the urban setting, the present mayor of Chicago, like those in Philadelphia, New Haven, and Detroit, must represent the process of collective betterment and not the process of machine greed. A new ethos of "the good of the community" becomes dominant and shapes the administration of the mayor.

N   O   T   E   S

1. We are indebted to the Center for Social Organization Studies and its director, Morris Janowitz, for criticism and financial support. A small grant from the Social Science Research Committee, Division of Social Sciences, University of Chicago, helped in the early stages of the study. A critical reading by R. W. Hodge was also of great help.

This paper was based on a more detailed manuscript prepared by Donald Bradley (Working Paper No. 10, Center for Social Organization Studies, University of Chicago, 1963 [Mimeographed]).

2. Robert A. Dahl, *Who Governs? Democracy and Power in an American City* (New Haven, Conn.: Yale University Press, 1961), pp. 1–81.

3. We recognize that precise dating of periods is risky, but it helps organize reporting of the shifts in recruitment. More important than the dates are the underlying trends.

4. Bessie L. Pierce, *A History of Chicago* (3 vols.; New York: Alfred A. Knopf, 1937, 1940, 1957), II, 305. This work was an indispensable aid to our study.

5. Ibid., I, 174.

6. See Richard C. Wade, *The Urban Frontier: Pioneer Life in Early Pittsburgh, Cincinnati, Lexington, Louisville, and St. Louis* ("Phoenix Book" [Chicago: University of Chicago Press, 1964]), esp. chap. iii, pp. 72–101.

7. Pierce, op. cit., II, 77–117.

8. Ibid., p. 344.

9. With the incorporation of the city in 1837, in addition to an age requirement and a residence requirement of at least six months, there was a requirement that the voter have the status of householder or have paid a city tax

of not less than three dollars. The property qualifications were eliminated in 1841 and the naturalization requirements were clarified in 1843, when it was explicitly stated that persons could vote whether naturalized citizens or not. This was not changed until 1871 when naturalization was made a condition of registration (A. A. Lavery [ed.], *Smith-Hurd Illinois Annotated Statutes* [Chicago: Bendette Smith, 1944], p. 28).

10. Ethnic politics began to play some role quite early. The charge was made that "the Irish entirely controlled" a local election of 1840 (Ogden to Edwin Crowell, August 31, 1840, *Ogden Letter Books*, II, 494).

11. Helen R. Jeter, *Trends of Population in the Region of Chicago* (Chicago: University of Chicago Press, 1927). See also Paul F. Cressy, "The Succession of Cultural Groups in Chicago" (unpublished Ph.D. dissertation, University of Chicago, 1930); Pierce, op. cit., III, 20–64; Charles E. Merriam, *Chicago: A More Intimate View of Urban Politics* (New York: Macmillan, 1929), pp. 134–77.

12. See Merriam, op. cit., and Lincoln Steffens, *The Autobiography of Lincoln Steffens* (New York: Harcourt Brace, 1931), pp. 422–29, for a description of the political system at this time.

13. There is some evidence to suggest that the Republican party was more influenced by the business element of the city than was the Democratic party. Every one of the Republican mayors elected during this period could be found listed in the executive directory of their time, in contrast to the Democratic candidates, only one of whom was listed.

14. Merriam, op. cit., pp. 97–98.

15. Harold F. Gosnell accounts for the ascendancy of the Chicago machine by referring to an "unfavorable press situation, a lack of leadership, and the character of the party division at the beginning of the depression" (*Machine Politics: Chicago Model* [Chicago: University of Chicago Press, 1937]).

16. This lack of representation of the "silk stocking" element is also reflected in the city council. Of the thirty-four aldermen on the council in 1900, five were listed in the *Chicago Social Directory* for that year. By 1935, of the fifty men who sat on the council, not one was listed. This lack of representation of the "better class" has continued so that in 1965 there is still no alderman to be found in the listed elite of Chicago.

17. Alex Gottfried, *Boss Cermak of Chicago: A Study of Political Leadership* (Seattle: University of Washington Press, 1962). See following article.

18. The following volumes give colorful, if at times overly journalistic, accounts of the history of Chicago's political and social reputation: John Bright, *Hizzoner Big Bill Thompson, an Idyll of Chicago* (New York: J. Cape & H. Smith, 1930); Fletcher Dobyns, *The Underworld of American Politics* (New York: privately printed, 1932); Lloyd Lewis and Henry Smith, *Chicago: The History of Its Reputation* (New York: Harcourt Brace, 1929); Merriam, op. cit.; William H. Stuart, *The Twenty Incredible Years* (Chicago: M. A. Donahue, 1935).

19. Much of the motivation dynamics operating in Chicago is similar to that found by Lynd and Merrill in Middletown (Robert S. Lynd and Helen

Merrill, *Middletown: A Study in Modern American Culture* [New York: Harcourt Brace, 1929], p. 421).

20. William R. Gable, "The Chicago City Council: A Study of Urban Politics and Legislation" (unpublished Ph.D. dissertation, University of Chicago, 1953), p. 10.

21. It should be noted that, while the socially and economically advantaged moved out of the city and into the suburbs, their places were taken by the migrants from the agrarian areas of the North and South (chiefly southern Negroes and whites), immigrants from Puerto Rico and other Latin American countries, and occasional immigrants from Europe. Thus the often-predicted changing class character of urban politics and the resulting decline in machine dominance has been postponed in Chicago. See Part V of Edward C. Banfield (ed.), *Urban Government: A Reader in Administration and Politics* (Glencoe, Ill.: Free Press, 1961); especially relevant in this regard are Samuel Lubell, "The New Middle Class" (pp. 301–8) and Frank J. Sorauf, "The Silent Revolution in Patronage" (pp. 308–17).

22. Our analysis draws heavily on Edward C. Banfield's *Political Influence* (Glencoe, Ill.: Free Press, 1961). [See page 247 in this volume—Ed.]

23. A comment on the success of the Irish: both in the city council and in the party hierarchy, the religious similarity between the Irish and the other nationality groups (the principal ethnic groups in the Democratic party, in descending order of importance, were the Poles, Italians, Bohemians, Lithuanians, Slovaks, and Greeks) and the fact that in a city which has no one single ethnic group in a clear majority, the Irish upset the community balance least, made the Irish Catholics the most logical and acceptable candidates. As one investigator quotes a politician: "A Lithuanian won't vote for a Pole, and a Pole won't vote for a Lithuanian. A German won't vote for either of them, but all three will vote for a 'Turkey' [Irishman]" (Martin Meyerson and E. C. Banfield, "A Machine at Work," in Banfield [ed.], op. cit., p. 136).

24. Dahl, op. cit., pp. 11–64.

2.

Boss Cermak of Chicago

ALEX GOTTFRIED

ANTON JOSEPH CERMAK'S SUCCESS AS A POLITICAL LEADER WAS A FUNC-tion of the interaction of his personality, his membership in a particular ethnic group, general social and cultural factors operative in the larger society, certain social and political institutions, a given choice of political roles, and certain situational and chance factors.

The most important basic facet of Cermak's personality for our pur-poses is that he was, as the biographical material illustrates clearly, a power seeker. His entire life effort was dedicated to his career. He appears to have had no other powerful needs or desires outside of gaining, main-taining, and expanding his political power and prestige. When persons interviewed compared him to contemporary or past political figures, they invariably assessed Cermak as being, in their experience, the figure with the fewest soft spots, the fewest extraneous demands on his time and energies, the fewest interests outside the realm of political power. From the first Cermak had to seek power; it was never thrust upon him. He continually fought for position and control in the party and for public offices of increasing prestige and responsibility. On at least two separate occasions in Cermak's career, events seemed to pose objectively desirable alternatives to continued active party work and office holding. In neither instance did Cermak give evidence of seriously or sincerely considering the alternatives, although on both these occasions he was extremely ill, and on one of them his wife was dying.

Cermak fits perfectly into the pattern of Harold Lasswell's construct of the political power seeker.

> The notion of a political type is that of a developmental type who passes through a distinctive career line in which the power opportunities of each

situation are selected in preference to other opportunities. As such a person moves from infancy through maturity, he becomes progressively predisposed to respond to the power-shaping and power-sharing possibilities in each situation in which he finds himself.[1]

Lasswell, in company with numbers of psychologists seeking to discover the reasons for the formation of the power-seeking personality, suggests that the power urge is a "compensatory reaction against low estimates of the self."[2] Certain infantile experiences are of importance in the generation of this feeling of inferiority. Although we cannot reconstruct Cermak's infancy, we do know that he later suffered from colitis, a psychosomatic dysfunction in which the basic conflict is that of the ego seeking to overcome extreme inner demands for inactivity, dependence, love, help, and care, to which the ego reacts with feelings of guilt and inferiority.[3] As a result of this conflict, the individual often strives to overcompensate by being overly aggressive, independent, dominant, and active.[4]

Whatever Cermak's infantile experiences, it is certain that the social conditions of his childhood and youth were not of the sort to allay existing fears, doubts, and insecurities. The poverty of the family; the eventual recognition of low social status; the presence of the more assimilated Irish groups in the Braidwood community—all of these were sufficient to force comparisons in which Cermak's youthful self-estimate may well have suffered. The behavior of his adolescence was marked to an extreme degree by the sort of compensatory mechanisms likely to appear as the result of this conflict; he was a bully, a fighter, a "tough," apparently unable to win feminine affection or to form relationships in any but the dominance-subservience pattern.

Cermak's status in Chicago as towboy and kindlingwood peddler was not much improved in the early days . . . . . over what it had been in Braidwood. Eager to assert himself, what fields lay open to him? His poverty excluded him from any endeavor requiring training or education. But both politics and business might be entered without formal training; and both were, moreover, among the acceptable prestige vocations, both in the American ethos and in the estimate of the American-Czech community. Cermak entered the two fields simultaneously.

Although nominally Cermak remained a businessman to the end of his life and even rationalized his political activity in terms of his business welfare, ultimately he sacrificed the latter to the former. His choice seems to have been determined in the main (1) by his own personality and (2) by the social and cultural environment.

For an aggressive egocentric like Cermak politics was the preferred choice because it offered more direct satisfactions of the power demand. Within the structure of government there were opportunities for the exercise of as nearly naked power as is sanctioned in modern society. It has often been pointed out that government in modern urban society enjoys the monopoly of legally sanctioned coercion.

As a poor, young, semiliterate Czech-American in the urban setting, Cermak had the best chance—perhaps the only chance—for gaining power and prestige through politics. The evidence was there before his eyes. Pilsen had few successful businessmen beyond the level of saloon-keeper or shop owner—no merchant princes, no utilities moguls, no meat-packer magnates. But there were some Czechs in politics who enjoyed both power and prestige.

Cermak's own ethnic group, moreover, set an unusually high premium upon political power, in part no doubt because of their history of forcible detention from political participation in the old country.

> Politics and political leadership and aspiration have suppressed all other aims and achievements and . . . during the past thirty years the Czechs of Chicago have made of their political highlights a matter of hero-worship.
> . . . the glamour of politics . . . in the community of Chicago's Czechs . . . has dimmed all other accomplishments.[5]

So Cermak made his choice, in part an unconsciously conditioned one, in part consciously determined by foreseeable rewards.

Just as Cermak's ethnic group was influential in determining his final choice of politics as an outlet, so was it instrumental in his achievement of success as a political leader. His first contact with the preordained Democratic organization was through the Czechs; his first party superiors were Czechs; his superiors in early appointive patronage jobs were Czechs. His Czech contacts, especially business contacts, as well as his connection with the ward Democratic organization were responsible for his first nomination to elective office.

By this time the population of Lawndale and the senatorial district of which it was part were changing. The Czechs were overtaking the Germans in the ward, and the Germans, Poles, and Irish in the senatorial district. Thus, by the time of Cermak's first nomination, although the ward boss was a German, Cermak had already attained the position of chairman of the ward organization. It was the pressure of the populace which caused Cermak and the Zoldaks to demand a place on the ticket in 1902, and which was responsible for the Irish leadership's acquiescence to the demand.

Cermak continued to use the Czechs as a vehicle in his rise to power and prestige. By 1908 he was ward boss of the predominantly Czech

Twelfth Ward. This position was to remain the anchor of his power to the end of his life. The control of this Czech ward not only was responsible for giving him a preferred place in the Democratic party hierarchy but was also an important factor in his repeated successes in quest of elective office. His ward retained him as ward committeeman for well over twenty years. It elected him alderman five times. Its votes were largely responsible for his four terms as state representative. The Czechs in adjacent wards and their ward leaders soon acknowledged Cermak's position as the spokesman for all the Czechs, increasing his influence in party councils. His role as Czech boss also gave him control of a sizable and relatively dependable body of votes in his search for city and county-wide offices.

From the first, the Czechs admired Cermak; "The Czechs would go to him."[6] The male proletariat as well as Czechs of the lower middle class particularly admired the figure of the aggressive gang leader, successful businessman, and hearty drinker.

When Cermak began to climb among the Czechs, there were few Czechs of ward-leadership status; rather, the political leaders of the Czechs were Czech Jews. In the train of these were the Novaks and the Cerveneys, who were creatures of these leaders. Cermak, along with several contemporaries, began to vie for the political leadership of the Czechs. Most of Cermak's rivals were, like John Cervenka, lacking the common touch. Most of them were not power seekers of the Cermak caliber; they were as much interested in business as in politics. Such men as Vopicka, Sokol, and Triner did not manifest the persevering interest in political power and office holding manifested by Cermak; they did not fight either to gain or to maintain power and offices as Cermak did. Others, like Kerner, seemed absolutely reluctant to accept political office or party responsibility; and although this type achieved a certain degree of political success, upon Cermak's death these men voluntarily left the political fray. But regardless of the intentions or potentialities of these men, Cermak, once in power, developed techniques for containing any major ambitions they may have had. Each of the aforementioned individuals, and many others of the same classification, received appointive office through Cermak sponsorship.[7] Not only did this tactic tend to neutralize would-be rivals, but Cermak could also use these appointments as evidence of his success in gaining recognition for the Czechs and of his faithfulness in rewarding the political service of these persons.

But many of Cermak's rivals of the sort mentioned above forfeited all real chances of succeeding Cermak. Most of them, upon achieving a degree of business or professional success, left Lawndale, either physically or socially. It has been pointed out that this is often the case with the sort of leaders who rise in minority groups: "In a minority group, individual members who are economically successful, or who have distinguished themselves in their professions, usually gain a higher degree of acceptance by the majority group."[8] This places them culturally on the periphery of the underprivileged group and makes them more likely to be marginal persons. They are fearful of having their good connections endangered by too close contact with the relatively underprivileged components of their ethnic group, who are not acceptable to the cultural majority. Nevertheless, because of their status and power, such persons may often gain and maintain leadership, in the absence of leaders more closely identified with the people.

Cermak offered the Chicago Czechs a real alternative to the lukewarm assimilationist type of leader, and they were eager to accept the alternative. For the Chicago Czechs, at the same time that they accepted American middle-class standards and values, insisted upon retaining their cultural individuality, preserving it in numerous institutions. . . . . Thus, a cardinal reason for Cermak's three decades of leadership of the Czechs was his willingness to remain one of them and among them. He stayed in Lawndale, in body and in spirit.

He succeeded in convincing his Czech constituency that their power and status were inextricably bound up with his. Luckily, shortly after he became leader of the Czechs, his position in the party hierarchy was influential enough to enable him to distribute sufficient patronage and secure enough places on the ballot to demonstrate his probable future success.

But just as Cermak used the Czechs in his rise to power, so the Czechs had their influence upon his political development. Although it was true that they accorded their political leaders a great deal of honor and deference, they nevertheless kept a jealous and critical watch on them. Although the Chicago Czechs as a group were ambitious and eager to win political recognition, they accepted certain American ideals of "clean" government. Beginning with the earliest days, the Czech wards were among the "most decent."[9] Studies of dishonest elections have consistently omitted the predominantly Czech wards. Moreover, Cermak's ward voted intelligently on public issues.[10] Thus, it was incumbent upon Cermak to maintain a reputation of at least minimum political cleanliness. This restraint eventually served as one of the factors making him acceptable to the "forces for good" as an alternative to Thompson.

Cermak was fortunate in rising among an ethnic group that was ready, willing, and able to accede to political power, and that had certain advantages over other urban minority groups. First of all, the Czechs set great value upon participation in the processes of government. And in spite of the exclusion from political processes that they had suffered in their history on both sides of the Atlantic, their tradition also included ancient memories of independent ethnic government, as well as more recent successful demands for recognition from a dominating foreign group—Bohemia having been by the end of the nineteenth century the most autonomous non-German, non-Hungarian entity in the Austro-Hungarian Empire. Thus, exclusion from participation in government was not sufficient to cause a feeling of group hopelessness. Moreover, the tradition of participation, plus the experience in self-government in voluntary associations, fitted the Czechs as a group for political activity. The group was also highly literate, had a high rate of naturalization, and showed great aptitude in adjusting itself to American life. At the same time, the Lawndale Czechs remained cohesive, stable, self-contained, and self-sufficient. They demanded recognition as a distinct group, and were enraged at being lumped with other Slavs and Eastern and Southern Europeans.

Since the 1890's, the Chicago Czechs had been overwhelmingly Democratic. Thus, the vehicle for group political recognition was the Democratic party, in the same way that Cermak's own party vehicle was predetermined. The Democratic party in Chicago by that time was the party of the immigrant. The chief ethnic components were the entrenched Irish, the Germans, the Jews, and the Poles. During this period the number of Italians in the party was negligible, and the total Italian population in Chicago was not significant. Among the other numerous ethnic groups in the city, the Scandinavians and the Negroes at that time were even more overwhelmingly Republican than the Czechs were Democratic.

Although the Irish, Poles, Jews, and Germans all were larger population groups than the Czechs, within the Democratic party itself the Czechs were not so greatly outnumbered. A very large part of the Germans, and perhaps 50 per cent of the Poles, were considered Republican voters at the beginning of Cermak's rise and in general up to his death. The Jews as Jews, because of internal cleavages (recently somewhat obscured by the advent of the state of Israel and the resultant efforts at solidarity), cannot be considered a homogeneous ethnic group. None of the Jewish subgroups equalled the Czechs in numbers. Further, a significant group of Jews who were members of higher economic classes tended to be Republican.

These other ethnic groups within the Democratic party labored under certain handicaps when compared to the Czechs in the race for group political preferment. In the case of the Jews, without reference to internal division, all labored under the disadvantage of anti-Semitism. Up to the time of Cermak's death few Jews rose to positions of greater power and prestige than the leadership of overwhelmingly Jewish wards. The case of Horner is really no exception, inasmuch as Horner was more a creature of Cermak's making than a reflection of the political power of the Jews as a group.

The Poles had a less favorable tradition of political prestige and participation than did the Czechs; moreover, the proportion of peasants pure and simple was much higher among the Poles than among the Czech group, which contained so many skilled workmen, artisans, and small businessmen. As a result, the group feelings of deprivation in the political sphere was much less pronounced among the Poles, and their demands as a group for recognition much less intense and heartfelt during most of Cermak's career.[11] The internal community structure of Chicago Poles was less favorable for gaining political power as a group than that of the Czechs. In contrast to the Czech community, the Polish community was hierarchically organized, with a high degree of control exercised by the church. Apparently the most important end served by church, family, and voluntary associations was the resistance to contamination of the Polish-American community by the larger culture. This end appears to have been considered far more important than group participation in the political process and the winning of political prestige. The Czechs, in contrast, although wishing to retain their cultural identification, were nevertheless able to accept American standards and ideals, perhaps because these closely approximated their own cultural standards and ideals. Among the measurable results of the Polish-American cultural rigidity was the less accelerated rate of naturalization as compared to the Czechs, and a greater reluctance to allow symbolic assimilation, such as, for example, the use of the English language. This cultural rigidity put certain inflexible boundaries in the paths of Polish political leaders in their attempts to form alliances with other groups. Because of the combination of these factors, until recent years the Polish vote has been considered, next to that of Negroes, the most "deliverable" in Chicago. All of these conditions taken together made the Poles as a group less likely than the Czechs to gain political power in the first two decades of this century.

The Germans, besides dissipating their ethnic strength by the adherence of a great many to the Republican party, were among the highest in point of assimilation of all immigrant groups not from the British Isles. This reduced their strength as a distinctive group, as did an ethnic organization relatively less cohesive than that of the Czechs. Moreover, the degree of influence exercised by the Germans in the Democratic party was sharply reduced as a result of the feelings engendered by the First World War.

Cermak was thus the beneficiary of the advantages and aptitudes of his group, of its mass feeling of discontent, and its self-conscious determination to win political recognition. He was fortunate in that no entrenched indigenous non-Jewish leadership existed among the Czechs prior to his rise. From the beginning he acted as leader—to capture his ward from German leadership; to gain recognition for the Czechs (and for himself) from the Irish in his nomination to the state legislature; and following this, to go on in similar fashion to offices of increasing importance.

Concurrently with his rise among the Czechs, Cermak began to play the role of the leader of the entire foreign-born population. His earliest vehicle for this role was his office in the United Societies (1906). It is important to note that he acceded to this office in part because of his already acquired status among the Czechs, although at that date his undisputed leadership was several years away.

The United Societies . . . . . was a huge conglomeration of constituent ethnic societies and individual members. At different times the number of member societies was well over a thousand, and the number of individual members for whom the United Societies was spokesman was well over 200,000. Obviously, at a time when Chicago's population was closer to two million than to three million, this was a sizable number of votes. Of course, it was not a bloc. Among the ethnic members there were mutual antagonisms and hostilities. Nevertheless, on two policy issues they stood as one against nativists and Americanists; these were their unanimous support of the unrestricted sale and use of liquor and their resistance to anti-foreign legislation.

Cermak's position in the United Societies was important in several ways. It brought him in contact with other ethnic leaders as well as the rank and file of self-conscious ethnic groups. As the recognized spokesman for the organized liquor industries, he had at his disposal large sums of money to use as he saw politically fit. The United Societies provided him a platform from which to publicize himself and gave him an opportunity to make a name for himself with regard to the issue that was to be conspicuous throughout his career—that of "personal liberty." This was an issue which could be relied upon for rallying the support not only of ethnic groups but also of Chicago voters in general, who were as a whole overwhelmingly Wet in sentiment. Ultimately, Cermak was able to weld already Democratic elements among the United Societies membership into a bloc within the Democratic party which was able to challenge the entrenched Irish for party leadership. Also in part owing to his United Societies connections—as well as to judicious use of patronage—he was able to convert large groups (some Germans, many Poles, some Scandinavians, some Italians) and their leaders from Republicanism to Democracy. Several of these ethnic groups had their own history of feelings of aggression against the Irish because of their virtual monopoly of the

Democratic party. Cermak's roles as leader of the foreign born and leader of the Wets were given the largest share of credit not only for his accession as Democratic leader but for his entire political career by Mayor Kelly, Mayor Harrison, and many others.[12]

Although Cermak's roles as leader of the Wets, the Czechs, and the foreign born generally were of great importance in his political rise, the institution of the political party was also indispensable. Shortly after his arrival in Chicago, we have seen that Cermak made his initial contact with the Democratic party. From that time to his death he held successively nearly every party position in the local and state party organizations. As he rose from court attaché to mayor of Chicago, he also rose from assistant precinct worker to boss of the local and state party and national committeeman from Illinois. What factors were instrumental in his success within the party?

The tremendous amount of experience in the intricacies of party organization at every level and the accumulated knowledge of the most successful kinds of manipulation at every level must be reckoned as a major factor. Closely connected with this were Cermak's long and varied experiences as an office holder. The combination of these two elements gave him an intimate and rich fund of information concerning the complicated local government structure, which was second to none among local politicians. The continuous office holding also gave Cermak a steady stream of personal patronage which was used to satisfy not only the demands of the Czechs but the expediencies of party and factional advancement. Cermak was always careful to distribute patronage methodically, fairly, and with nice attention to payment of political obligations.

His early rise in his ward was a product of his aggressive personality, his limitless willingness to work, and a higher intelligence than that of competing precinct captains. Once he was ward committeeman, his ward became and continued to remain one of the best Democratic wards. Later, when he became spokesman for all of Chicago and Cook County Czechs, his influence in the party and in the various factions thereof was immeasurably increased.

In his rise within the party his use of the existing factionalism could scarcely have been improved. When he joined the party, the Harrison faction enjoyed the allegiance of Chicago and Cook County Czechs. Thus Cermak became a Harrison man. He maintained this connection as long as it was profitable; however, even before the Harrison faction was destroyed, Cermak had made important contacts with other Democratic factions. In these contacts his role as Wet spokesman was invaluable. From the demise of the Harrison faction, Cermak became an important member of the Regular Democrats (the Regulars from 1916 on *were* the party); and he was to remain such until the end of his life. But this did not imply blind party loyalty. During this entire period Cermak mastered and practiced the fine art of bipartisan trading. In the practice of this art he played no favorites. From time to time he made alliances with every faction of the fragmentized Republican party.

For years Cermak was recognized as the chief among the Democratic ethnic bosses, as well as the custodian of the Democratic party's "liberal attitudes" and later their Wet planks. This dual source of influence— Wet and foreign born—greatly enhanced his intrafactional influence vis-à-vis the Irish leadership.

His prestige within the party was further reinforced by his widely recognized vote-getting ability. Few Democratic party functionaries could match him in this regard. Similarly, he was looked upon as one of the most able Democratic officeholders. Given the level of performance of most party hacks who were nominated for office by Chicago Democracy, the general approval won by Cermak from civic groups and newspapers, especially in the last fifteen years of his life, was a welcome boon to the local machine.

All of the preceding elements were brought together and reinforced by certain of Cermak's forceful personal qualities. His fellow politicians were in general much impressed by his political know-how; his wide knowledge of governmental affairs; his manifest physical strength; and his reputation for a willingness to indulge in personal violence—"You dasn't monkey with Tony." They were also impressed by his seemingly endless fund of energy and by his practically limitless willingness to devote himself to party affairs.

Finally, Brennan and the Irish leadership were confident of their ability to control the "Bohunk." Although by the mid-twenties Cermak's power was acknowledged to be great, Mayor Kelly stated that he was considered by the Brennan leadership as only an "errand boy."[13] This attitude was held in spite of Cermak's leadership of the foreign born, his pre-eminence as a Wet, his control after the defeat of Dever of the most powerful patronage office in the hands of a local Democrat. The attitude of the Irish showed misjudgment not only of Cermak's capacities but of the temper of the non-Irish elements of the Democratic party. Historically, Chicago Irish Democrats, although usually not completely united, were so much more united than the other ethnic elements of the party that they had succeeded in dividing and conquering.

Of Cermak's skills, aptitudes, capacities, techniques, and attitudes that were important in his political life, perhaps most vital was his mastery of the art of manipulation, what has been called group diplomacy. He was able to create favorable power balances by creating or reinforcing support and by successfully wooing or neutralizing the apathetic or the hostile.

He had considerable sensitivity to strength and direction of social and economic tendencies and their probable impact upon the well-being of political parties. Frequently he displayed acute perception of possible courses of action to meet a pending crisis and then took quick and positive measures.

He rarely made errors in his selection of personnel, either as public official or party functionary. As public official it was his habit to make some very good appointments. There is no case on record of any important Cermak-appointed subordinate who had to be removed for dereliction of duty. It is true that Cermak never allowed good appointments to occur in such numbers as to hamper his freedom of action in matters of patronage and spoils; nevertheless, such appointees made possible a minimum of effective government by the various Cermak administrations, lending the color of respectability to Cermak as public official. As party functionary Cermak selected workers largely on the basis of effectiveness, but it is noteworthy that most of the men closest to him could be described as being of mediocre talent. Cermak took no chances on building up a rival or possible successor. In a very few cases when some lieutenant showed either unusual qualifications or ambition, he was eliminated, either by a promotion to a nonlocal office or by less subtle means. As a result of his policy of personnel selection Cermak at no time in his career had to face rebellion in his own ranks; and upon his death no Cermak lieutenant was qualified to step into his shoes.

Every qualified observer interviewed by the writer emphasized Cermak's qualities as a peerless party organizer and as an administrator. Usually attention was called to the organization of the ethnic groups and the country towns, and to the great dent Cermak's efforts made in local Republican ranks. By the time of his death he had even begun to make some inroads on the solid Republican Negro vote.

Cermak could by no stretch of the imagination be described as an orator. In the latter years of his career, however, he developed into an effective impromptu haranguer. Even in the earliest years, when speaking to his own or other immigrant constituencies, or when discussing his favorite issue, he was unusually effective. Other audiences, such as women's organizations or "silk stockings," were often impressed by his forthrightness and apparent seriousness of purpose.

One of Cermak's chief techniques as officeholder was his continual use of citizens' advisory committees, invariably packed with distinguished names. Through these committees Cermak went through the motions of public consultation and power sharing. However, the committees were usually so well organized, through the appointment of a few key Cermak men plus the control of the agenda and of full-time committee experts, that recommendations to which Cermak himself was opposed seldom eventuated. The use of these committees may be reckoned as a chief weapon in Cermak's successful drive to enlist the support of "the forces for good."

Another technique of first importance was Cermak's habit of giving a minimum of effective administration in every elective office. This was especially noteworthy in the field of public welfare during his terms as president of the county board. As a result, when Cermak ran against Thompson, he was able to campaign as a master public executive. Whenever Cermak was accused of graft or inefficiency, the ubiquitous citizens' committees were summoned. They investigated and often cleared Cermak; and they made recommendations for corrective action, which Cermak immediately accepted. He was never caught twice in an embarrassing situation in the same administrative area.

Cermak was a tireless worker in every public and party position. It was partly owing to this willingness to exert himself and partly owing to his refusal to delegate to others any responsibility that he could carry himself that he gained his deserved reputation as a master of detail.

Cermak also had a reputation for scrupulous payments of political debts. It was widely admitted, even by his enemies, that his political word was good. He rarely gave off-the-cuff assent to requests for favors or jobs; but once he had made a promise, he rarely failed to abide by his pledge.

In Cermak's long career he was careful not to become wedded to many issues or policies. The few that he embraced, such as Wetness or home rule, were overwhelmingly popular. There is no case on record where Cermak was a proponent of a measure not favored by the majority. Cermak was a true conservative. His entire social, political, and economic orientation reflected the views of the dominant groups in America with the possible exception of his attitudes concerning liquor. Although he rose from a proletarian background, his thinking was entirely that of the rugged individualistic, laissez-faire entrepreneur. He was not guilty of proposing any major social innovations. This steady conservatism, however, was not inflexible. Thus, in the emergency of the depression he was one of the first local politicians to recognize not only the permissibility but the desirability of federal assistance.

In Cermak's political life, as in the lives of all men, chance and certain situational factors over which he had no control played an important part. . . . . . [He] had personal qualities and skills which were suited to his time and place. In many ways he was similar to his colleagues of both parties. His main difference lay in his more single-minded dedication to the quest for power, political position, and prestige; in his role as representative of a cohesive, fairly large, relatively capable, and highly ambitious ethnic group; in his role as official leader of the organized Wets and as spokesman for the unorganized proponents of free-flowing alcohol; and in his high level of administrative ability in party affairs and in public office.

NOTES

1. Harold P. Lasswell, *Power and Personality* (New York: W. W. Norton, 1948), pp. 21–22.

2. Ibid., p. 53.

3. Franz Alexander and T. M. French, *Studies in Psychosomatic Medicine* (New York: Ronald Press, 1948), pp. 121–22.

4. Ibid.; cf. Alexander, *Psychosomatic Medicine* (New York: W. W. Norton, 1950), p. 119; Karl Abraham, *Selected Papers* (London: Hogarth Press and Institute of Psychoanalysis, 1927), p. 376.

5. R. A. Ginsburg, "Czechs in Politics," *Czech and Slovak Leaders in Metropolitan Chicago* (Chicago: Slavonik Club of University of Chicago, 1934), pp. 262–64.

6. Statement by Joseph Houdek, personal interview.

7. John A. Cervenka, whose career ran parallel with Cermak's for many years, was very specific in describing the many devices Cermak used for achieving these ends. Cermak kept Cervenka continuously in office from 1910 on; Mr. Cervenka charges that this was among Cermak's devices for neutralizing him as a serious rival. The most extreme instance occurred during Cermak's tenure as county board president. One appointment he offered Cervenka was as superintendent of one of the county institutions, which would have required Cervenka's residence on the institutional premises, some distance from Lawndale. Personal interview.

8. Kurt Lewin, "The Problem of Minority Leadership," *Studies in Leadership*, ed. Alvin W. Gouldner (New York: Harper and Bros., 1950), p. 193.

9. Mayor Harrison, personal interview.

10. Harold Gosnell, *Machine Politics: Chicago Model* (Chicago: University of Chicago Press, 1937), pp. 138–42, especially figure 9.

11. The attitude of the Polish community in this respect has sharply altered over the past thirty years.

12. Personal interviews.

13. Statement in personal interview.

3.

Two Irish Politicians

EDWARD M. LEVINE

THE CHANGES IN SOCIAL PERSPECTIVE AND POSITION OF THE IRISH AND
Irish politicians can be traced through a biographical sketch of Mayor
Richard J. Daley, who represents the link between the "old" and the
"new" Irish politicians. His career is also compared with that of his predecessor, Mayor Martin H. Kennelly, to illustrate the differences between
a "typical" and an "atypical" Irish politician.

Daley was born in Bridgeport, just a block away from his current residence (3536 South Lowe), which is not far from the stockyards where he
worked as a boy to supplement a meager family income. He attended
Roman Catholic schools, enrolling at De LaSalle Institute when its student body was predominantly Irish (Mayors Kelly and Kennelly were also
students there), and graduated with a law degree from De Paul University in Chicago's Loop.

Mayor Daley's political career is not only a most impressive one, but
is the governmental counterpart of the once-lauded American "inner-
directed" business tradition: the young man who began his career as a
stock boy and, after wide and invaluable experience gained in the course
of working his way up the company ladder, finally won recognition by
being appointed president and chairman of the board. The offices, in the
order in which Mayor Daley has held them, are: Secretary of the Chicago
City Council (1925); Illinois State Representative (1936); Illinois State
Senate (1938); Illinois State Director of Revenue (1949); Clerk of Cook
County (1950); Chairman of the Cook County Central Committee
(1953); and Mayor of Chicago (1955). Daley was also a precinct captain

From *The Irish and Irish Politicians* by Edward M. Levine, pp. 211–216. Published 1967 by the University of Notre Dame Press, Notre Dame, Indiana, and reprinted by permission.

from 1924 until 1947, when he became committeeman of the Eleventh Ward Regular Democratic Organization, a position he continues to hold.

Daley lost only one election in his career—when he ran for the office of Sheriff of Cook County (1946), a position that is invariably a dead-end in Chicago Democratic politics. Apart from this incident, Daley sought and achieved the highest positions in both the municipal government and the party......

Daley has remained in touch with those he has known longest and best, a few of whom he consults for their opinions on issues with which he must deal, and is still most at ease when chatting with fellow politicians. His immediate assistants at City Hall are usually other Irishmen from the Eleventh Ward whose families he has known for years. His expanded political and social interests have not altered the habits of a lifetime. Daley firmly believes that a strong Democratic party and Democratic administrations are the best assurances that Chicago's future, to which he is so consummately dedicated, will be one of great accomplishment and attractive change. Above all, he hopes to bequeath his family the reputation of having been responsible for Chicago's revitalization and its entering the ranks of the foremost cities of the world.

In having become the indisputable head of the Democratic party in the city and the most influential Democratic figure in county and state politics, Daley is nonetheless involved in a paradox. His current interests and ambitions necessarily incline him to seek status gratifications that have in the past been wholly atypical of both himself and of most other Irish politicians. Evidence of the inclusion of such interests (which involve a change in political style) is found in his having been listed as one of the ten best-dressed men in the country, and having been responsible for the State Department's placing Chicago on the scheduled tours of visiting foreign dignitaries. In 1959, Mayor Daley was host to the Queen of England, a gesture prompted by his strong personal interest in achieving status for both his city and himself.

Other status considerations that have become a standard part of his political activities include his frequent appearances at civic association banquets (where he is invariably accorded a standing applause upon his entry) and the formal cocktail parties that he periodically attends and at which he remains abstemious. The Mayor also serves as honorary chairman of such cultural enterprises as the Free Concerts Foundation and makes many speeches throughout the city at testimonials recognizing efforts of community leaders and the activities of community organizations. He formally honors the universities in the Chicago area, and acknowledges the contributions of their more celebrated faculty. As a result, he has acquired a degree of academic prestige, having been invited by out-of-state universities to address their students and faculty on political affairs.

Such status activities and interests have modified Daley's political style. In recent years, for example, the Mayor rarely yields in public places or during interviews to his strong resentment of sharp criticism, justifiable or otherwise. Rather, he usually gives the impression of a calm, thoughtful, attentive, senior statesman patiently listening to the objections, and at times tawdry cavilling, of his critics and opponents.

It also appears that status considerations have absorbed Daley's time at the expense of important political matters and responsibilities. Informed persons have claimed that had Daley been as aware of party political affairs just a few years ago as he was in the past, he would have known of new power alignments within the party that would have precluded his conceding to Alderman Keane's (after Daley, the most powerful individual in the party) demand that either his brother or Seymour Simon be nominated by the party for the office of President of the Cook County Board of Commissioners. Nor does it seem likely that Daley would have misjudged the public's mood, had he been thoroughly engrossed in politics, when the six bond issues he recommended were defeated at a special referendum in 1962......

Martin H. Kennelly's entry into politics may very well be unique in the annals of Irish politics, for he had never held a party or governmental office prior to his nomination. He had not, therefore, "earned" the nomination by rising in the ranks of the party. Moreover, he did not seek the office—he was sought by the party's Central Committee, which nominated him as its "blue ribbon" candidate to replace the incumbent Democratic Mayor Edward Kelly under whose administration graft and corruption had run rampant—"everybody had his snout in the trough."

Before becoming the party's nominee for mayor, Martin Kennelly was widely known and highly respected as a civic leader and an eminently successful businessman. He had headed Red Cross fund drives four times and had been president of the Warehouseman's National Association, president of the Traffic Club of Chicago, and vice president of the Chicago Association of Commerce and Industry. Kennelly had also been a member of the Industrial Advisory Committee of the Federal Reserve Bank of Chicago, and had declined offers to serve unexpired terms as Sheriff of Cook County and State Director of Finance. As a prominent Roman Catholic layman, he had served as a trustee of De Paul University and board chairman of Holy Cross Hospital.

Kennelly's administration was chiefly noted for the following accomplishments: the expansion of civil service coverage; the establishment of an independent school board; the introduction of a general purchasing system; and the initiation of such urban renewal projects as the Lake Meadows apartment complex and the Congress Street Expressway.

Living at the Edgewater Beach Hotel, on Chicago's far northside, Kennelly was geographically, socially, and politically remote from party officials, politicians, and party workers. However, it could not have been otherwise given his background, which was responsible for his commitment to being an independent, business-minded, efficient mayor, a man who was expressly disinterested in the maintenance and control of the patronage system. What is more, Kennelly was so politically naive as to be unaware of the need to act assertively with the city council to have his policies confirmed. His failure to be an aggressive mayor enabled the city councilmen increasingly to ignore his wishes.

A number of those who knew him thought Kennelly was especially indecisive and that the party suffered from the emergence of factions which sought to fill the power vacuum he created. His inability or unwillingness to centralize power and strengthen the party led one Irish politician to say of Kennelly, "The people are entitled to more than an honest mayor." Another politician observed that "He'd rather have somebody else lead him than lead [others]."

No one could make such remarks about Daley, who has earned the respect and admiration, if not the affection, of politicians and bureaucrats. He has been instrumental in the revitalization and strengthening of the party, and is equally responsible for a relentless and forceful insistence upon administrative performance, if without equal concern for substantive considerations. Whatever his shortcomings, Daley has emerged as the strongest and most effective mayor and party chief Chicago and the Democratic party have ever known, and is, perhaps, the prototypical Irish politician.

4.

I'd Do It Again

JAMES M. CURLEY

BOSTON HAS BEEN CALLED THE MOST EXPLOSIVE POLITICAL COMMUNITY in the United States, and I, James Michael Curley, have been labeled "the most controversial political personality during the first half of the present century." . . . . .

By 1949, when I was seventy-four years old, I had, after devoting half a century of my life to public service, been Mayor of Boston for sixteen years, a Member of Congress for eight years and Governor of Massachusetts for two years, after completing a stormy and turbulent political apprenticeship at the beginning of the century. When I was elected Mayor for the first time, one of the Boston Brahmins looked down his long patrician nose and said:

"Curley never would have been elected Mayor if his ancestors hadn't been driven over by the potato famine."

I used this curious remark as the theme of a political sermon I delivered during one campaign early in my career:

"No land," I said, "was ever saved by little clubs of female faddists, old gentlemen with disordered livers, or pessimists cracking over imaginary good old days and ignoring the sunlit present. What we need in this part of the country are men and mothers of men, and not gabbing spinsters and dog-raising matrons in federation assembled."

Boston was the most class-bound city in America when I picked up my political shillelagh. Its traditionally Republican government reflected banker and big-business control. It was almost as appropriate in those snobbish days to say that Boston was a part of Beacon Hill and the Back

Bay, as it was to say later, when the Irish assumed political control, that Boston was part of South Boston, stronghold of the refugees from the widely heralded potato famines of 1847 and 1867.

You have been told of the political skulduggery of the Boston Irish, but what have you heard about the inhumane numbskulduggery of the Yankee overlords who preceded them? Even Bostonians are unaware of the maladministration of the Yankee mayors that began in 1822, when the town became a city, and John Phillips became the first Mayor of Boston. From that time forward, every Boston mayor except one until 1885 was an aristocrat who did little for the average citizen. Samuel Turrel Armstrong, who served in 1836, boasted of only one accomplishment: "the erection of an iron fence for the enclosure of three sides of the Common, and the extension of the mall through the burial grounds of Boylston Street." Incidentally, when he left office, the annual expenditure of the city was $816,000, and the debt was over $1,500,000. The tax rate was $4.75.

These Yankee mayors could by no charitable stretch of the imagination be said to be touched with the commonplace, and it was as a protest against cavalier rule that Charles Wells was elected in 1832 as a representative of the middle classes. Wells served without distinction, however, and it was not until the "down-trodden Irish majority" elected Hugh O'Brien in 1885 that the do-nothing era came to an abrupt end, and the Irish dynasty began.

Since then, there have been only two other Yankee mayors. In 1917, the moneyed interests, waving the already tattered banner of the Good Government Association, pushed a wealthy Protestant Yankee, Andrew J. Peters, into the Mayor's chair. Charles Angoff, no Celt fresh from the Emerald Isle, said about that noble "reform" experiment: "His administration turned out to be one of the most incompetent and graft-ridden in Boston's history."

When I retired from office in 1925, the interregnum Mayor was a Yankee named Malcolm E. Nichols, who had somehow persuaded President Calvin Coolidge to appoint him Collector of Internal Revenue. His closest friends admitted later that his administration was "one of complete confusion." It was said that only Charles Innes and Curley knew what was going on in City Hall. One wheeze was to the effect that Innes was "the day mayor," and Nichols was "the nightmare." Another story, well founded on fact, was that "Robert Bottomley was the morning mayor, Charlie Innes the afternoon mayor, and Ernie Goulston the night mayor."

I was Mayor during three depressions, the third being the most severe in history, yet I left office at the end of my third term with a lower tax rate than when I assumed office, and with every obligation of the city paid. All this despite the fact that welfare expenditures had increased over ten million dollars annually. In 1946, a magazine of national circulation said: "The only hospitals, schools, solariums, subways, tunnels and municipal improvements that Boston has received in the past thirty-five years, were built by Curley."

Opposed while mayor by organized wealth and influence, I was also the target of cunning political bosses and the subsidized press. I have been handed the hot end of the poker since memory runneth not to the contrary, to borrow a phrase from Daniel Webster, who was no less pilloried in his day than I was in mine. Hurling the epithet has long been a favorite Brahmin diversion. President John Adams, one of the first Brahmins, called Secretary of the Treasury Alexander Hamilton "that bastard immigrant son of a Scotch pedlar," and equally picturesque appellations have been bestowed on Curley by John's descendants. The Brahmins and their ilk whose powers of description often surpass their judgment have badgered me constantly, and today every insult conjures up fond memories, recalling the joys and rewards of stormy contention as Curley fought for a more abundant life for the underprivileged, the underpossessed and the undernourished. Politics is a rock-and-sock game in which one must become accustomed to unsolicited appraisals. Over the years I have been called "Sympathy Jim," jailbird, convict, brigand, buccaneer, spellbinder and highbinder, a ruthless monster, the Irish Mussolini, the Ambassador to South Boston, and the Kingfish of Massachusetts.

Curley has been described as an old ham actor, political Barnum, the low-brow mayor of a high-brow city and a combination of Santa Claus, Robin Hood, a Chinese warlord and the late John Barrymore. More discerning critics have labeled me "the political kingpin of Massachusetts" and "the most unpredictable and colorful politician in American history." In his book, *Inside U.S.A.*, John Gunther says of Curley: "A fantastically effective speaker, either to great crowds or alone with friends, he had—and has—a gift of gab almost unrivaled in America. I heard one man say of him, with a kind of wistful affection, a man who certainly had no reason to be fond of him, 'I suppose that fellow is the damnedest single human being I ever met.'"

The mellowing influence of age often softens the asperity of judgment, and I have observed recently, and not without a certain measure of regret, that some of my most articulate critics have had some kind things to say about Curley. It is not for me to say whether this new reappraisal of my public service, which was my business, should be ascribed to their advancing senility or to a more careful reading of the record. In any event, the insults have become less barbed and more infrequent. One reason for this, of course, is that some of the Philistines who used to curse and revile Curley (in terms that were only occasionally printable) have by this time answered roll-call at Judgment Day, a frightening Day of Atonement for many of them, I am certain. During the past few years they have been referring to Curley as "The Old Gray Mayor" and have set him down as the last of the old-time, big-city, paternalistic bosses. This charge I shall not deny, although I am sure that the readers of these only slightly expurgated memoirs (surely you do not expect me to reveal *everything* that Dan Coakley called me) will admit that Curley differed in a number of comforting respects from other big-city bosses.

A New England conscience has been described as one that doesn't prevent you from doing anything, but that prevents you from enjoying it afterwards. Many of Curley's pious-talking enemies were handicapped by such a conscience. My own conscience is clear. I would do the same things all over, had I the first portion of my life to relive. And yet I must remind my readers, before taking them behind the political curtain, that politics and holiness are not always synonymous. Successful politicians do not expect to be canonized or even achieve the state of blessedness to which persons of more polite and leisurely pursuits may aspire. There are times, as you will see presently, when, if you want to win an election, you must do unto others as they wish to do unto you, but you must do it first. It is not always sufficient to return blow for blow. "In a pinch, swing hard" is an excellent proverb for a politician.

Since I expect to live for another half-century,* it is with deep reluctance that I have finally accepted the verdict of loyal constituents who wish me a life of comfort and repose outside the political arena. "It's only you I was thinking of, Governor, when I voted for Hynes last time," one taxicab driver told me. "I don't give a damn what happens to Hynes, but I don't want you to get one of them coronaries."

I was not thoroughly convinced until I entered the Hyde Square Spa in Jamaica Plain, after being defeated in 1951 in my fifth bid for the mayoralty.

"What happened, Joe?" I asked the proprietor.

Joe Favarola was a little uneasy. "Governor," he said, "there must have been a hundred people walk in here today and tell me they voted for you the last thirty years, but they couldn't see their way clear to doing it this time. They figured it would be harmful to send you back to office at your age."

This was one of the most touching tributes I have ever received......

*He died the following year, 1958.

Over an oil portrait that hangs in the main reception hall of the Boston City Hospital is a plaque inscribed by the late David I. Walsh, who served the Commonwealth as Governor and Senator. The plaque reads:

THE HON. JAMES M. CURLEY,
MAYOR OF THE POOR

It is as the friend and defender of the poor, the alien and the persecuted that I hope to be remembered—as the "Mayor of the Poor."

5.

New York's La Guardia—Hybridism,
Power, Conscience

ARTHUR MANN

SOME MEN GO TO THE TOP IN POLITICS WHEN SOCIETY SEEMS TO BE A
going concern and the people have need of an amiable figurehead who
is content to stand still. It is usual for such a leader to avoid conflict, stress
harmony, and celebrate what is: to assure and reassure the electorate that
they've never had it so good. Government is not supposed to be an instrument for social change, but is considered an exercise in caretaking. Such
is the leadership of normalcy.

Neither by temperament nor intellect was La Guardia the sort to
administer a going concern. Unable to slow down long enough to stand
still, he was inclined to shock and mock the celebrators of the status quo
and to celebrate only the possibilities of the future. He throve on conflict,
not harmony, in situations that made reform possible. It was no accident
that the Anti-Injunction Act,* for which La Guardia and Senator George
Norris had agitated futilely during the so-called normalcy of the 1920's,
should suddenly have been passed by Congress at the beginning of the
Depression. Fiorello was the kind of leader who comes into his own when
a crisis in the old order creates opportunities for new directions.

Yet the laws of heredity and environment that produce a La Guardia
have still to be discovered. His biographer can only call attention to his

*This milestone in social legislation, which President Hoover signed on March 23,
1932, restated the right of workingmen to bargain collectively and also declared that
government had the responsibility to help them do so. Among other provisions, the
Norris-La Guardia Act forbade Federal courts to issue injunctions against a strike or
against peaceful activities to carry on a strike unless the employer could prove that he
had tried to settle the strike, been threatened, or that the strike would cause him irre-
parable harm.

most important characteristics, infer their probable source from available evidence, and relate them to the culture in which they flourished. Three characteristics of the fifty-one-year-old man who entered City Hall in 1934 deserve special mention and elaboration: his hybridism, his ambition for power and fame, and his passion to do good.

His hybridism derived from an extraordinary mobility. Born in Greenwich Village but raised on Western Army posts and growing to maturity in the Balkans, he returned to his native city at twenty-three and later spent much of his adult life in the nation's capital as a Congressman. All his life he had been learning how to live in someone else's culture and he acquired a working knowledge of half a dozen languages besides English: Italian, French, German, Yiddish, Hungarian, and Serbo-Croatian. He was a true cosmopolitan, which is to say that he was at home nearly everywhere, but without the roots that bind a true insider to the group and the place in which he was born.

His parentage foreordained that he would be what sociologists call a marginal man. Achille Luigi Carlo La Guardia and his wife Irene Coen emigrated to America in 1880 and returned to Italy with their children twenty years later. Theirs was a mixed marriage—Achille was a lapsed Catholic and Irene a lukewarm Jew—and while in the United States they raised their children as Episcopalians. When, in 1906, Fiorello returned to America, where everyone has an ethnic label or gets one, he considered himself an Italo-American. But his being a Protestant set him apart from his ethnic group, which was, of course, overwhelmingly Roman Catholic.

Observers have asked why Fiorello did not identify himself as a Jew. His inheritance is again instructive. Irene Coen La Guardia, his Trieste-born mother, thought of herself as Austrian in nationality, Italian in culture, and Jewish only in religion. There was no Jewish community in the army towns where Fiorello grew up while his father was serving in the United States Army as a bandmaster. When Fiorello met Jews in large numbers—first as a consular agent in Fiume, then as an Ellis Island interpreter, and later as a labor lawyer on Manhattan's Lower East Side—he met Jews unlike his mother. They were Eastern European, not Mediterranean, Jews. They spoke Yiddish, their ritual was Ashkenazic, and they considered themselves a nationality and a cultural group as well as a religious body. Neither by descent nor religious upbringing was Fiorello one of them.

Nor was it expedient for him to be known as Jewish when he broke into politics in the 1910's. He started out with handicaps enough against him. His aberrant appearance and unpronounceable name put him at a disadvantage to the dominant Celtic and the vanishing Anglo-Saxon types who ran the city. Nativism was rising and would shortly culminate in restrictive legislation against the new immigrants from eastern and southern Europe. It was hard enough to be an Italo-American fifty and more years ago without inviting the derisive taunt—which his enemies would hurl at him in the 1930's after his mother's origins became known —"the half-Jewish wop."

So he made little of his Jewish background in public but exploited his Italian name and built a political base in Little Italy from which to launch a career. By 1934 not even Primo Carnera or Benito Mussolini exceeded the Little Flower as a popular idol in the colony. What is more, after establishing his public image as a Latin he championed a number of Jewish causes, sometimes in Yiddish, but as an understanding and compassionate *outsider*. This was smart politics in the largest Jewish city in the world (the Jews and the Italians together constituted almost 45 per cent of New York's population in the 1920's and 1930's). It was also, and nevertheless, sincere. Free from self-hatred, La Guardia was a man of mixed loyalties.

The son of Jewish and Italian immigrants who attended services in the Cathedral of Saint John the Divine, but who was married to his first wife in the rectory of Saint Patrick's and to his second wife by a Lutheran minister, was clearly the most remarkable hybrid in the history of New York City politics. Belonging, yet not fully belonging, to nearly every important ancestral group in the city, including the British-descended community of Episcopalians, Fiorello was a balanced ticket all by himself.

His being marginal to many cultures had a deeper significance still. The mayor of New York, like the leader of any pluralist community, must be a political broker. This had been a familiar role to the hyphenated Congressman who started his career on the Lower East Side as a mediator between immigrant and native America, interpreting one to the other. A friend in court for the poor and the persecuted, he also had served as a go-between for reformers and professional politicians and a bridge connecting urban and rural progressives in Congress.* The mayoralty would enlarge the scope of previous experience. La Guardia would have to balance the demands of a variety of competing interest groups in the city, and also bargain and trade with borough, county, state, and Federal officials whose power impinged on his own as chief executive.

---

*John A. Simpson, president of the National Farmers' Union, described La Guardia to a colleague in these words: "Coming right out of the heart of the biggest city in the United States, . . . [he had] a sympathy and an understanding of farm problems that surpassed most of the Congressmen from agricultural districts." Simpson to Milo Reno, April 25, 1933, Milo Reno Mss. (privately held).

But an effective leader must not only mediate and negotiate, he also has to command, take the initiative, make policy, and break through channels when necessary to get things done. Such a leader seeks power, enlarges it, and enjoys its use. La Guardia was like that by 1934. One of the few pieces of sculpture the Mayor owned was a bust of Napoleon that he first put on his desk when he began to practice law at twenty-eight. When he bought that object is unknown, but Bonaparte may have been his model at an even earlier age.

"Ambitious for promotion"—that is how the American Consul General of Budapest, who was given to the understatement of his New England birth and education, described his Italo-American subordinate in Fiume at the turn of the century. Commissioned a consular agent at twenty-one, Fiorello's pride of ranks was inordinate. He expanded his jurisdiction whenever possible, breaking archaic rules and bringing them up to date on his own authority. The results of his innovations were often salutary, but his aggressiveness antagonized superiors. He quit in a huff after two and a half years, writing in 1906 to the State Department "that the service is not the place for a young man to work up. . . ."

During World War I, as a major in command of American aviation in Italy, La Guardia was something of a virtuoso in running around, over, across, or simply straight through the protocol of two armies and one foreign government. Not having resigned his seat in Congress, he either impressed or intimidated higher ranking officers with his political connections. And forced to improvise on America's forgotten front, he improvised brilliantly, whether in training pilots, conferring with cabinet ministers, speeding up the production of planes, or rallying Italians to their own war effort after the disaster of Caporetto. "I love him like a brother," one Italian official exclaimed.

Many voters in America felt much the same way. Between 1914 and 1934 La Guardia ran for office twelve times, and apart from a first and hopeless try, he lost only twice. His victories were particularly impressive in view of the fact that New York City was virtually a one-party (Democratic) town. Elected president of the Board of Aldermen in 1919, he was the first Republican to win a city-wide contest without Fusion backing since the creation of Greater New York by legislative act in 1897. At one time during the 1920's La Guardia was the sole Republican Congressman from Manhattan outside the silkstocking district.

His most obvious asset as a campaigner was his grasp of relevant issues and his ability to dramatize those issues, and himself as well, in colorful language and forceful terms. And once in office he was conscientious in serving his constituents. He was particularly popular with immigrants and their children, who accounted for 75 per cent of New York's population when he was rising to power. He was fighting their battle, and his, too, for recognition and against bigotry. One of the few ethnic groups that could not claim the multi-hyphenated Little Flower through blood were the Polish-American, yet *Nowy Swiat*, a Polish-language newspaper, looked up to him as "head of the family . . . father, leader, judge, authority, and educator—like in the village. . . ."

But there was a Machiavellian, even diabolical, side to La Guardia's melting-pot politics. When haranguing an audience in any of seven languages, he was not above exploiting its fears, insecurities, prejudices, and hatreds. There were ways and ways of getting out the vote. After one such a harangue to an Italo-American crowd in the campaign of 1919, he turned in pride to an associate and said: "I can outdemagogue the best of demagogues."

He justified such tactics by insisting that he had to fight the Tammany Tiger with its own weapons, and it was said of the Little Flower during his life that he was no shrinking violet. What a negative way of putting it! Fiorello was a superbly conditioned political animal who not only struck back when attacked but who really enjoyed the brutal struggle for office in the Manhattan jungle. No matter what he said in public to the contrary, La Guardia was a professional politician, bruising, cunning, tough, and with a strong stomach for the sordid methods and grubby details of election politics in his part of the world. "I invented the low blow," he boasted to an aide in the 1920's. In East Harlem, which he represented in Congress for five terms until 1932, he commanded a superb personal organization of his own and gave lessons to Tammany at election time in machine campaigning.

The Mayor knew how to get power, all right, and how to keep it, as his record for election and re-election proves. But why did he want it? There are very many gifted men, after all, for whom public responsibility is distasteful and whose main thrust is for money, leisure, travel, or women. Those had been the tastes of Mayor Jimmy Walker, who gladly let the Tammany bosses govern New York City while he relentlessly pursued pleasure on two continents.

Some of La Guardia's associates thought, and still think, that in reaching out for power he was compensating for feelings of inferiority deriving from a hypersensitivity to his size, his lack of formal education, and his origins. To reduce the complexity of Fiorello's behavior to an inferiority complex is too pat and too simple. His wife, who knew him as well as anyone, has dismissed the idea as preposterous. Yet it is a matter of historical record that the Little Flower *was* hypersensitive and, therefore, easily insulted and ferociously combative.

Who can forget the fury, for example, with which the Mayor banned organ-grinders from the streets of New York? Those foreign-looking men, with their broken English, farcical little monkeys, and panhandling canned music, called attention to one of several disreputable Italian stereotypes that the Little Flower had labored all his life to refute and overcome. And although he himself might joke about his height and that of other men, no one else was allowed to do so in his presence. Once, when an associate made the mistake of being playful about a pint-sized applicant for a municipal job, La Guardia lost control of himself and screamed: "What's the matter with a little guy? What's the matter with a little guy? What's the matter with a little guy?"

The Mayor was clearly a man of explosive resentments. They were long-standing and are a key to his personality. As a boy growing up on army posts he had resented the children of officers for lording it over the children of enlisted men. Why was he not as good as they? Later, in the Foreign Service or in the Army, on the Board of Alderman or in Congress, he would resent superiors he thought intellectually and morally inferior to himself. By what rights should they be placed over him? To measure one's self against others is normal for competitive men, but in La Guardia's case it was excessive. His resentfulness heightened his competitiveness and his competitiveness intensified his resentfulness, so that he was constantly in rivalry with nearly everyone he met and forever proving that he was number one.

"I think he put on a great deal of his brutalities to test people out," C. C. Burlingham, who knew La Guardia well, has shrewdly observed. "If they could stand up against him it was all right, but if they couldn't they were in bad luck."

That La Guardia was ambitious will surprise only those people who think that a stained-glass window of Saint Francis is really a sufficient monument to the Mayor's memory. Yet only a mistaken realism would conclude that there was nothing more to his nature, and to human nature in general, than the promotion of self. Ed Flynn, the Democratic boss from the Bronx who prided himself on being a realistic judge of men, made that kind of mistake. That is why Flynn was never able to understand and appreciate—or cope with—the *direction* of La Guardia's drive.

The direction was a liberal one. La Guardia wanted the power of public office not just to assert himself, it must be emphasized, but so that he could also be in a position to right social wrongs. Joining his resentments to a cause, he made a career for himself as a leader of the have-nots against the haves, or as he would have put it, the People against the Interests.

That was the image he had of himself—when he strove as a consul agent and interpreter to defend the humanity of immigrants against bureaucratic mindlessness and heartlessness; when he contributed his services as a lawyer and an orator to the trade unions that began to emerge in the 1910's from the squalid sweatshops of the Lower East Side; when as an over-age aviator he went off to war to make the world safe for democracy; when as president of the Board of Aldermen he defied the governor of New York State and fought against an increase of the five-cent fare on the subway (the poor man's ride) and the repeal of the direct primary (the people's defense against bossism); when as a Republican Congressman he bolted his party to join the Progressive Party of 1924 in a crusade against the credo of the day that the business of America was business, not welfare. Had La Guardia done nothing else he still would have passed the bar of American liberalism in 1934 for the anti-injunction law he co-authored two years earlier with Nebraska's Senator Norris. . . . . .

La Guardia entered City Hall with a sense of injustice that was still bottomless, with a capacity for outrage that was still boundless, with a determination to reform society that was still enormous. His social conscience was as highly developed as his instinct for the jugular in political combat. The mayor's office, toward which he had reached out three times before finally capturing it, would give him the power he had wanted so long in order to realize his humanitarian goals.

The thrust of an enormous internal drive to establish his own high place in the sum of things carried La Guardia very close to the top in American politics, and in that process he found more gratification in public fame than in the pleasures of private life.

When Fiorello returned to New York in 1906 after resigning from the consular service in Fiume ("Look here, Mother," he said in explanation, "I'm going back to America to become a lawyer and make something of myself"), he arrived without friends or family. His father had been dead for two years and his mother chose to remain in Europe with her married daughter. The next decade and a half were devoted to the struggle to gain a foothold in the city he would someday rule. Not until 1919, when he was thirty-six, back from the wars as a hero, and finally established in his career, did Congressman La Guardia take a wife, an exquisite young blonde from Trieste, Thea Almerigotti.

That marriage was, and would remain, the high point of La Guardia's private emotional experience. Setting up housekeeping in Greenwich Village, the couple enjoyed a semi-Bohemian life, one that was full of love and fun and music and good eating. La Guardia adored children, and in 1920 Thea gave birth to a daughter, who was named Fioretta after Fiorello's maternal grandmother. Yet La Guardia's personal happiness flickered for only a moment. Throughout 1921 he suffered the agony of watching his baby, and then his wife, waste away and die of tuberculosis. For the next eight years he threw himself into his work with an energy that can only be described as ferocious.

His second marriage in 1929 to Marie Fischer, his secretary since 1914, was a union of two mature persons. It was not blessed with children. The couple adopted a girl, Jean, in 1933 and a boy, Eric, the following year. At fifty-one, the Mayor was the foster father of very young children and had known married life for a total of only seven years.

In the nearly three decades he had lived in New York Fiorello acquired few personal friends, but rather many admirers, acquaintances, colleagues, allies, patrons, protégés, and advisers. He was too competitive to get along intimately with his equals. Only with children could he give himself completely. Hobbies he had none, other than a fondness for classical music. He was as mayor to surround himself with more intellectuals than any of his predecessors, but he had either no time or no taste for literature, not even for biography and history, and rarely read anything not directly relevant to his work. He had lived, and would continue to live, mostly for his career and, what is equally important, for the affectionate acclaim that his public personality generated in a vast but impersonal audience. New York had in 1934 a full-time mayor.

La Guardia brought other qualities to the mayoralty in addition to his hybridism, his ambition, and his compassion for the oppressed. There was his gusto for work and his slashing wit, his quick but retentive mind and his theatrical flair. He also brought a considerable experience, stretching back to 1901 when he received his commission as consul agent from John Hay, Secretary of State under the first Roosevelt. By 1934 La Guardia had spent all but six years of his majority in one Government job or another. Public service was a way of life for him.

He clearly qualified for the office sometimes described as second in difficulty only to the Presidency as an elective office in American government. And by the late 1930's Republicans of the stature of William Allen White were booming him for the Presidency itself. Twelve years after his death in 1947, Professor Rexford G. Tugwell saluted him as "a great man in the Republic" and, excepting only F.D.R. among his contemporaries, as "the best-known leader in our democracy. . . ." Many people today accept that estimate as valid.

PART II

Electoral Pathways to City Hall

"DEMOCRACY IS THE WORST FORM OF GOVERNMENT, SAVE ANY OTHER," said Winston Churchill. Indeed, in the readings which follow, it is difficult not to be impressed with the irrationality, the apathy, and even the demogoguery which often pervades urban electoral politics. But, at the same time, it can be argued that elections and party competition at least direct the struggle for power toward more responsible ends by bringing that struggle into the open, a viewpoint that is also supported by the readings in this section.

The first selection, "The Alienated Voter," sets the tone. Here, Murray B. Levin accounts for individual feelings of estrangement from the political system. On the basis of survey data collected after the 1959 Boston mayoralty election, he discusses how a large proportion of the voters in that city felt powerless because of their belief that the selfish few continue to control irrespective of elections and that the professional politicians invariably "sell out." The author argues that one of the sources of political alienation is unrefined popular acceptance of democratic theory in its classic form without a realistic appraisal of the necessary roles of leadership—a matter to be fully explored in the present volume. Complementing Levin's appraisal of Boston politics is M. Kent Jenning's analysis of power relations in Atlanta, "The Role of Community Influentials;" it details the substantial influence of leading business interests in the selection and election of mayors.

Charles G. Mayo's article on "The 1961 Mayoralty Election in Los Angeles" sheds light on another aspect of urban politics; namely, what happens when party competition is poorly structured. A standard theme of many political scientists is that a responsible political system must have at least two active and identifiable parties which present a clear choice to the electorate. They contend that where this is absent, as in "nonpartisan" Los Angeles, the voter cannot properly assess the implications of his vote. Mayo's case study gives the reader the opportunity to judge this for himself.

A prominent feature of big-city politics is ethnic and religious contention over programs and issues. Especially during elections, latent antagonisms of this kind come to the surface, often with the subtle assistance of the candidates themselves. The next two selections—"Manipulating the Jewish Vote" by William F. Buckley and "Ethnic and Religious Tensions During Lindsay's Campaign" by Oliver Pilat—were written by active participants in the 1965 New York City mayoralty election. Buckley was the Conservative party candidate for mayor and Pilat was a campaign aide to the Republican candidate, John V. Lindsay. Their writings, though reflecting mutual dislike, reveal the way in which social tensions can be played upon and exploited, an important consideration in any attempt to assess the workings of democracy. Another dimension has recently been added to ethnic tension with the election of Negro mayors in the cities of Cleveland and Gary. How it happened and what it portends for race relations is the subject of the last article, "The Making of the Negro Mayors, 1967."

1.

The Alienated Voter

MURRAY B. LEVIN

THE BOSTON MAYORALTY ELECTION OF 1959 WAS ONE OF THE MOST stunning upsets in the history of the city. John F. Collins, register of probate, with practically no endorsements from important public figures and a small campaign fund, defeated his opponent, John E. Powers, president of the Massachusetts State Senate, whose election was regarded as a certainty by almost everyone.

Powers had put together an organization which seemed as formidable as the machine that made James M. Curley the city's foremost politician of the twentieth century. Both Senators from Massachusetts and almost all the major political leaders of Boston endorsed his candidacy; he appeared to have large sums of money at his disposal, was much better known than his opponent at the start of the campaign, and had a decided edge in political experience. From the moment the first returns came in on the night of November 3, however, it was evident that Collins had won easily. When all 278 precincts had reported, Collins received 114,074 votes to Powers' 90,035......

When the results of the election were announced, a sample of the city's voting population was constructed. This sample was composed of 500 persons who were interviewed in their homes, within 72 hours after the polls closed. For the purpose of the sample, 50 of the city's precincts were chosen, from 12 of the 22 wards. Ten voters in each precinct were interviewed and asked several questions which they were free to answer in any manner they chose. They did not select answers from a list given to them by the interviewer......

Our analysis of this post-election survey has shown that a large proportion of the electorate feels politically powerless because it believes that the community is controlled by a small group of powerful and selfish individuals who use public office for personal gain. Many voters assume that this power elite is irresponsible and unaffected by the outcome of elections. Those who embrace this view feel that voting is meaningless because they see the candidates as undesirable and the electoral process as a sham. We suggest the term "political alienation" to refer to these attitudes. Since sufficient information is available from other American cities to indicate that feelings of political alienation are widespread, we feel justified in theorizing about the forms of political alienation, the mechanisms by which it is handled, and its implications for democratic politics.

Hegel first used the term alienation to denote man's detachment from nature and himself arising out of man's self-consciousness. Other observers have seen alienation within man, between man and his institutions, and between man and man. They have attributed the origin of feelings of alienation to machinery, mass communications, the size of modern communities, the transition from *gemeinschaft* to *gesellschaft*, original sin, mass society, lack of religion, and capitalist commodity production. Some view alienation as unique to modern society while others see it as a permanent condition.

Feelings of alienation are labeled "good" or "bad" according to whether they arise from causes or lead to results which the critic approves or disapproves. The essential characteristic of the alienated man is his belief that he is not able to fulfill what he believes is his rightful role in society. The alienated man is acutely aware of the discrepancy between who he is and what he believes he should be.

Alienation must be distinguished from two related but not identical concepts: anomie and personal disorganization. Alienation refers to a psychological state of an individual characterized by feelings of estrangement, while anomie refers to a relative normlessness of a social system. Personal disorganization refers to disordered behavior arising from internal conflict within the individual. These states may correlate with one another but they are not identical.

In this chapter we shall examine political alienation as typified in the Boston election and will trace individual feelings of estrangement from the political structure, on the basis of the data previously presented. From the Powers-Collins controversy and its outcome we shall delineate four types of political alienation, examine the causes for them, and specify several mechanisms for the handling of feelings of political alienation.

The data collected in this post-election survey indicate that voting was based on distrust and negativism rather than on positive conviction. "Collins is the lesser of two evils. He is not much better than Powers." "Neither candidate appealed to me." "Felt neither one would make a good mayor." "Voting wouldn't do any good." ". . . both no good." "I don't like the caliber of the candidates." "I think they're all the same. It doesn't matter who you vote for." "Felt they were all no good." These negative feelings reflect a widespread belief that politicians are somewhat dishonest. "I guess they're all a little crooked," "A typical Boston politician is a crook," ". . . they tie-up with racketeers—All of them do it. . . ." "I don't think he will have too many crooks around." "He probably would not steal as much." "I don't believe he has too much integrity." "I knew they were crooks, but I don't like to see it right on TV." "He gave a lot of double talk." "Talks too much, does very little."

The view that the candidates were primarily interested in furthering their selfish ends rather than the general welfare was expressed by several voters ". . . he is an opportunist—out for himself with the interest of Boston secondary." "He was against everything that might have helped Boston, was all for himself." "Collins is for Collins."

Some respondents believe that the candidates were obligated to and dominated by a small group of self-interested contributors. "Powers was being sponsored by too many business interests. I mean those people not concerned with the social welfare of the voting public." "Too much of a politician, commitments to groups." "I thought he might be looking out for those racketeers." "Tied up with racketeers." "His affiliation with other big politicians and use of the machine." "Too many prior commitments—too many political entanglements." "You can't tell me Collins didn't have one thousand people on his back." "Collins is a political appointee . . . he must have tie-ins like everybody."

The candidates and their backers were seen as a power elite which controls the city in its own interest. "He is tied up with professionals—type with cigars, part of the South Boston crowd who have the city in their pocket, and take care of themselves." "I don't like the idea that since all the big guys are for him, the little people, like us, should be for him too." "He has too many prior commitments although I don't think he is a racketeer." "Too many apron strings, hard to hold office without doing favors." "His connection with big business. He wasn't doing his own talking."

Campaign contributors are stereotyped as buyers purchasing future political favors. The extravagance of the campaign is interpreted by many as a measure of the degree to which the candidate is under obligation to pay back a profitable return. "He spent too much money campaigning.

I thought of where all those funds came from." "Powers was spending so much money and had so much political backing I began to wonder what everybody was expecting to gain from his election." "I felt he made deals with backers of the campaign." "In the Charlestown paper there was so much about Powers I got sick of him. Everyone was supporting him, it seems as though there was a fear of him." "His high-pressure tactics—too much money—too powerful."

Many voters complained that the candidates did not present a serious and meaningful discussion of issues. "He didn't have any program at all and I didn't know what to make of him other than he's done a good job to bring his family up." "He seemed to be more against Powers as an individual rather than on the issues." "In his campaign all he did was attack Powers and hardly ever talked about the issues." "Powers' failure to present a campaign—he didn't have much confidence in the intelligence of the public." "No concrete platform; too evasive." "He didn't say anything and I heard him speak for 45 minutes." ". . . both men were talking in circles about Boston's needs and how to meet them." "He had a lot of phony talk."

These feelings of the electorate go beyond resentment toward the particular candidate in this election; they indicate a widespread disgust and disillusionment with the political process and politicians in general. "Voting wouldn't do any good—both no good." This negativism fosters a belief that reform is impossible and highly unlikely, and that it makes little difference which candidate wins the election. Of those who voted for Powers 43 per cent thought he would be no better when in office than Collins, while 57 per cent of those who voted for Collins thought he would be no better than his opponent. Under these conditions, politics, as it is characterized in American political folklore, tends to lose its meaning. The average voter believes that he is not part of the political structure and that he has no influence upon it.

The attitudes described above are not universally held in Boston. There are voters who believed that their candidate is honest, has integrity, and will fight for the best interest of the community. Some individuals who voted for Collins saw him as "courageous," "honest," "a crusader," and "sincere"; others who voted for Powers pictured him as "intelligent," "experienced," and "honest." However, these views are not shared by a large segment of the electorate who disliked the candidates, distrusted politicians in general, and believed that voting makes no difference. It is this group which feels alienated.

Since feelings of political alienation were so significant in determining the outcome of this election, an analysis of the forms of political alienation is indicated. We believe that this election is sufficiently typical of American municipal elections to warrant putting these conclusons in general terms.

The Forms of Political Alienation

Political alienation is the feeling of an individual that he is not a part of the political process. The politically alienated believe that their vote makes no difference. This belief arises from the feeling that political decisions are made by a group of political insiders who are not responsive to the average citizens—the political outsiders. Political alienation may be expressed in feelings of political powerlessness, meaninglessness, estrangement from political activity, and normlessness.

Political powerlessness is the feeling of an individual that his political action has no influence in determining the course of political events. Those who feel politically powerless do not believe that their vote, or for that matter any action they might perform, can determine the broader outcome they desire. This feeling of powerlessness arises from and contributes to the belief that the community is not controlled by the voters, but rather by a small number of powerful and influential persons who remain in control regardless of the outcome of elections. This theory of social conflict between the powerful and powerless is not identical to the Marxian theory of social conflict between capitalists and proletarians. The powerful are not necessarily capitalists, they may be professional politicians, labor leaders, underworld figures, or businessmen.

Many voters believe that the powerful, who are most often identified as politicians, businessmen, and the underworld, continuously exploit the public. The politician needs campaign contributions, the businessman needs licenses, tax abatements, and city contracts, and the underworld needs police immunity. This provides the setting for the mutually satisfactory relationships among the powerful, from which the average voter is excluded. The feelings of powerlessness among the electorate are sharpened by the view that regardless of the outcome of the election, the powerful remain in control by realigning themselves with the newly elected. These voters view the political process as a secret conspiracy, the object of which is to plunder them.

Political alienation may also be experienced in the form of meaninglessness. An individual may experience feelings of meaninglessness in two ways. He may believe that the election is without meaning because there are no real differences between the candidates, or he may feel that an intelligent and rational decision is impossible because the information upon which, he thinks, such a decision must be made is lacking. The degree of meaninglessness will vary with the disparity between the amount of information considered necessary and that available. If the candidates and platforms are very similar or identical, it will be difficult to find "meaningful" information on which to base a voting decision.

In municipal politics another source of meaninglessness is likely to be present in the nature of city government. In theory, and to a large extent in practice, there are no issues in a controversial sense. Indeed, in the usual textbook version, a city government is a "bundle of services." In practice the political choices available to the administrators of a city government are severely circumscribed by economic realities and by state law. There exist only a small number of ways in which revenue can be raised and these are generally exploited to their fullest. At the same time the services which the city must maintain pre-empt almost all of the city's budget. The police force, the fire department, and the school system must maintain the standards of a going social system. Therefore the minimal facilities which a city must provide to maintain its viability tend to be not much less than the maximal facilities it can achieve with available funds. The municipal public official necessarily operates within a narrow range of alternate programs.

Municipal elections therefore tend to center around the inefficiency or dishonesty of the administration, not its program. Consequently, the "honesty" of the candidate is often the variable about which most information is demanded by voters who wish to make a "meaningful" decision. However, information concerning the honesty of the candidate is difficult to secure because corrupt and dishonest activities are carefully hidden from the public. It is precisely the absence of information on this problem which brings about feelings of meaninglessness.

Under these circumstances an individual who feels alienated in the "meaningless" sense will tend either not to vote, to believe his vote makes no difference, or to make his decision in terms of what he believes are inadequate standards. Since relevant factors are absent, many voting decisions are based on "gut reactions"—intuitive emotional responses to the candidate's physical appearance, voice, and personality. "Don't like his looks," "tough," "ugly looking," "smug—looks crooked," "something about his eyes."

Feelings of political meaninglessness give rise to a low sense of confidence among many voters that their voting decision was correct: that their candidate would be a better mayor. When relevant facts are not available, voters cannot predict the future course of political action with any sense of certainty. This also contributes to feelings of powerlessness.

Feelings of political alienation may also be experienced in the sense of the lowering of an individual's political ethics. This occurs when standards of political behavior are violated in order to achieve some goal. This is likely to occur when the political structure prevents the attainment of political objectives through institutionally prescribed means. An example of this would be an individual who believes that paying off a public official is illegitimate, yet does so. The fact that the individual may be reluctant to bribe a public official does not alter the fact that he is lowering his standards of political ethics.

When individuals believe that corrupt practices are the only ways to achieve political goals and when they feel that corruption is widespread, there will be a greater tendency to resort to it. If the corruption becomes the generally accepted method of dealing with public officials, the stigma attached to it tends to disappear and the political community becomes normless, *i.e.*, anomic.

Political estrangement refers to the inability of an individual to find direct satisfaction in political activity itself, that is, gratification from fulfilling his obligations as a responsible citizen. Both politically active and politically inactive individuals may be politically estranged. Political activists are estranged if their activity is motivated by goals of personal monetary gain rather than a sense of their obligation as citizens. Individuals who do have a sense of community responsibility are likely to find other community activities, such as support of a symphony orchestra, charities, or clubs, a more rewarding way of fulfilling this obligation than being politically active. This is political estrangement.

Social Characteristics of Political Alienation

Four aspects of political alienation—powerlessness, meaninglessness, the lowering of norms, and estrangement—have been distinguished. The extent to which a particular individual is affected by any one of these forms can be related to such variables as social class, age, and religion.

Separation of a population according to income tends to include separation according to education and occupation as well. Data on income was obtained in this survey and will be used as a gross measure of social-class difference. The majority of the Boston electorate, who are elementary or high-school graduates, employed in blue-collar or white-collar jobs, and in the lower-income group, might be expected to feel alienated primarily in the sense of powerlessness. It is this group which is in fact furthest removed from the seats of political power. They have relatively little contact with the city as compared to home owners and businessmen, and when they do have contact, they lack the economic means to participate in the "business" of politics. Collins' major campaign appeal was directed to those who feel powerless. His campaign slogan was "Stop Power Politics," and he presented himself as leading a battle against the politicians. Powers' prolific use of political endorsements did not hinder the image Collins was creating. The data collected in our survey shows that the lower-income groups switched from Powers to Collins in larger proportions than did the middle- or upper-income groups. This implies that feelings of powerlessness were greater in the lower-income groups.

In contrast to the lower-income groups, the upper-income groups, who have more economic power, might be expected to experience political alienation in the forms of meaninglessness, lowering of norms, and estrangement more than in the form of powerlessness. Upper-income groups have more education, which tends to develop more rigorous standards of clarity of information on which to base decisions. The data shows that this group had greater interest in political programs and expressed fewer "gut reactions" than did lower-income groups. With higher standards of clarity there are likely to be stronger feelings of political meaninglessness.

The upper-income groups include businessmen and property owners who necessarily have more contact with the city because they may require license of various kinds, tax abatements, and building inspection certificates. Since they have economic power, they are in a position to purchase special political consideration. Those who do this will experience political alienation in the form of lowering of political norms.

Upper-income groups include some individuals with a sense of community responsibility. Because of the disjunction of their political values and the political structure, they are likely to be active in nonpolitical civic activities such as charities or service organizations.

Age is another variable related to political alienation. Older persons, who have lived in Boston for many years and have observed the political structure over a long time, might be expected to show greater feelings of alienation. This age group had the largest proportion of individuals who thought that the man they supported would be no better than his opponent. Having observed more elections, they seem to feel more strongly that the effect of their vote makes little difference in the long run.

Religion is another sociocultural variable to be considered. Since Boston is a strongly Catholic city, it might be expected that Protestants and Jews, having less political power, would have stronger feelings of political alienation. In support of this are the facts that a smaller percentage of Protestants and Jews voted than did Catholics and that a greater proportion voted for Collins, whose campaign was largely an appeal to the politically alienated.

Mechanisms of Expression of Political Alienation

Feelings of political alienation may be expressed through rational activism, withdrawal, projection, or identification with a charismatic leader. These are conscious or unconscious mechanisms by which an individual may handle the uncomfortable feelings of political alienation. Some forms of alienation lead to specific mechanisms, for example, feelings of estrangement inevitably lead to withdrawal because gratification is found only in nonpolitical activity. Other forms may result in one or more of several mechanisms, for example, feelings of powerlessness may lead to political activism or to projection and identification with a charismatic leader.

Rational activism is political action based on a realistic evaluation of the political situation, the object of which is to promote a political structure consonant wth political values. The frustration arising from political alienation can be a spur to rational activism; feelings of powerlessness can lead to increased political activity. Feelings of meaninglessness can lead to demands for more information rather than withdrawal or "blind" voting. And guilt, resulting from normlessness, can result in activity directed toward raising political standards. Mature individuals, who are those able to tolerate frustration and to act on their beliefs, are those most likely to handle their feelings of political alienation through rational activism. This activity may occur within existing political institutions or it may be directed toward the creation of a new set of political institutions. Rational activism is more likely to be the response to feelings of political alienation when individuals believe that their activity has a reasonable chance of bringing about a change.

Political withdrawal is the removal of an individual's interest and activity from politics. This may occur as a result of a conscious rational decision based on a realistic estimate of the political situation or as an affective, unconscious response. In the latter case the anger and resentment of political alienation may be internalized within the individual rather than expressed outwardly. This mechanism is more likely to occur when the individual feels that any political effort on his part has little chance of producing an effect.

Although an individual may have withdrawn from political interests, he is not likely to escape entirely from politics. Municipal problems of education, traffic, and taxes may affect him personally, or he may note the recurrent exposure of corruption in newspapers. Consequently, additional mechanisms of expression of political alienation are likely to be used. There may be projection, identification with a charismatic leader, or rational activism.

Feelings of anger and resentment which arise from political alienation may be projected on to some other individual or group. This group is seen as participating in a hostile conspiracy. Political leaders may use this mechanism* because it establishes a sense of identity between them and the voters to whom they are appealing.

The conspiratorial theory is particularly appealing to individuals who have feelings of powerlessness and normlessness because it accounts for the absence of power and the lowering of values in a simple and easily understood fashion. The individual who projects sees himself as powerless because sinister forces have successfully conspired to destroy the traditional political rules in such a way that he is excluded from exercising his rights. Hofstadter has observed that:

> this kind of thinking frequently occurs when political and social antagonisms are sharp. Certain audiences are especially susceptible to it—particularly, those who have obtained a low level of education, whose access to information is poor, and who are so completely shut out from access to the centers of power that they feel deprived of self-defense and subjected to unlimited manipulation by those who wield power.[1]

Another mechanism for dealing with feelings of political alienation is identification with a charismatic leader. This is the attempt of an individual to feel powerful by incorporating within himself the attitudes, beliefs, and actions held by a leader whom he perceives as powerful. "Charismatic" refers to an extraordinary quality of a person regardless of whether this quality is actual, alleged, or presumed.[2] In taking over the attributes of a charismatic leader, the individual may enter into activity he would otherwise abhor. German *bourgeoisie* who identified with Hitler approved of and took part in behavior their consciences would otherwise not allow them to do.

Rational activism is behavior based on logical reasoning and an undistorted perception of political realities. Withdrawal may be a rational response in some situations and an irrational, affective response in other circumstances. The mechanisms of projection resulting in conspiratorial thinking and identification with a charismatic leader are irrational, affective responses. They are also regressive, in that they are more characteristic of a child's than of an adult's handling of a problem.

When feelings of political alienation are widespread, individuals will adopt one or more of the mechanisms we have described to handle the frustration and anxiety associated with them. The political behavior of

---

*"There are certain types of popular movements of dissent that offer special opportunities to agitators with paranoid tendencies, who are able to make a vocational asset out of their psychic disturbances. Such individuals have an opportunity to impose their style of thought upon the movements they lead—" Richard Hofstadter, *The Age of Reform* (New York: Alfred A. Knopf), p. 71. This is more likely to occur when the electorate has feelings of political alienation which may be handled through projection.

each individual will be affected by the particular mechanism or mechanisms he selects.

We have described the forms of political alienation and the mechanisms by which they may be expressed. When political alienation is widespread, it may be a major factor in determining the outcome of an election. The astute politician is aware of this; consequently his strategy takes these factors into account.

Political Strategy and Political Alienation

The election we have analyzed took place in a community where feelings of political alienation, frustration, and disillusionment with the political process are widespread. When this situation exists, the voting behavior of the electorate is less predictable than otherwise, since a decision is likely to arise from negative rather than from positive convictions and may change on the basis of minor issues, fleeting incidents, or "gut reactions."

The analysis of the statements of the individuals we interviewed shows that they hold an image of the political structure which is similar to that developed by modern political science. They perceive the hierarchical arrangements of power and influence, and they relate various power groupings to each other. They are aware of the uses and abuses of political office; and they know that their role is not the one that the grammar-school version of democratic theory taught them. They have, however, greatly exaggerated their lack of power and, perhaps, the extent of corruption. The election, after all, resulted in the downfall of the group associated with one candidate and the elevation to power of another group which probably did not believe it had a serious chance of winning. All the money that was given to the group which lost the election and all the promises that may have been made to the contributors have been to no avail, for the personnel now in power are different. The antagonisms built up during the campaign may mean that the "outs" are really out of City Hall in the near future.

The election upset was to a large extent a response to feelings of political alienation. Senator Powers followed the time-honored rules of campaigning. He spent large amounts of money on advertising which portrayed him as a devoted public servant and friend of the people, shook as many hands as possible, attended numerous house parties, recounted his experience, contributed to charities of all faiths, was photographed with prominent religious leaders, attacked his opponent, and emphasized the support of municipal, state, and national politicians; but although he had 54 per cent more votes than Collins in the primary, he failed to win. This has shaken politicians' faith in the traditional vote-getting techniques.

Although there are many reasons why Powers lost, it is clear that one of the most important was the fact that he presented himself as a powerful professional politician—a serious mistake in a community where a considerable amount of political alienation exists. The alienated are not positively disposed toward those whom they identify as powerful. Under these circumstances, the candidate must re-evaluate old methods, reformulate his strategy, and experiment with new techniques. A number of countervailing strategies are available to him.

The candidate may create a strong sense of identity with the electorate by presenting himself as the underdog in a struggle against a power elite. Whether he does this or not, he certainly should not emphasize a background of power or the massive support of other political figures who may also be associated with "the powerful." Since an elaborate campaign is viewed as collusion with "the powerful," the candidate must avoid the appearance of an opulent campaign.

Of course, a candidate may appeal to regressive mechanisms of projection and identification with a charismatic leader. Collins successfully appealed to those who tend to think in conspiratorial terms (a form of projection) via his slogan, "Stop power politics, elect a hands-free mayor," and such techniques as his essay contest on a definition of "power politics." The electorate, however, did not view him as a charismatic leader.

The professional politicians may court popular esteem by throwing the support of "the organization" behind a "clean" amateur; that is, some well-known citizen who has not had contact with the politicians and therefore does not share their stigma. The stigma which is attached to "the politician" by the alienated is not likely to rub off on such an individual, at least during the beginning of the campaign. The difficulty with this procedure, from the point of view of "the organization," is that such a candidate may be unreliable.

Democratic Theory and Political Alienation

Theories concerning the causes of alienation refer to almost every conceivable "malady" of modern civilization from the decline of religion to the effects of mass production. Students of politics who have dealt with political apathy and indifference customarily point out that the size of modern states and the technical nature of so many political questions tends to dwarf the individual voter and make him politically inept. Many scholars who have analyzed the structure and distribution of power in modern political parties indicate that the need for specialization and division of labor requires a hard core of active leaders who determine policy with the passive approval of the membership. Others point out that the remoteness of political events and the barriers to the flow of accurate political information prevent the voters from developing an accurate picture of political realities which makes it difficult for them to make what they consider to be meaningful choices. All of these factors tend to reduce, if not annihilate, the political power of the individual voter which leaves him bewildered, apathetic, and alienated.

Prominent among these explanations of the causes of political alienation is Kornhauser's theory of "mass society." Kornhauser[3] defines mass society as a

> situation in which the aggregate of individuals are related to one another only by way of their relation to a common authority, especially the state. That is, individuals are not directly related to one another in a variety of independent groups. A population in this condition is not insulated in any way from the ruling group, nor yet from elements within itself.

He argues that the absence of autonomous groups through which individuals may unite to forward their political interest by bringing pressure to bear on the elite leaves the population in an atomized situation which leads to feelings of alienation.

In such a situation the alienated are disposed "to engage in extreme behavior to escape from these tensions." When an independent group life is absent, individuals are ready for mobilization by elites for membership in mass movements which provide opportunities for expressing resentment. Kornhauser indicates that the alienated are likely to pressure elites through direct and immediate action for satisfactions which were previously supplied through membership in a plurality of independent and proximate groups. Mass action, that is, action which is not mediated through independent groups, "tends to be irrational and unrestrained, since there are few points at which it may be checked by personal experience and the experience of others." Direct mass action tends to be undemocratic because it is not restrained by institutions which are designed to insure majority rule and minority rights. Thus Kornhauser sees mass society as producing the atomized and alienated man who tends to search for new and direct modes of political action.

Although most scholars who have advanced these theories point out that democratic theory as it was developed in the seventeenth and eighteenth centuries is archaic, the elementary and secondary schools continue to teach it and the students continue to believe that it is eminently workable. The latter tend to place the blame for political apathy and frustration on the improper functioning of democratic institutions, particularly corruption. This permits them to identify political alienation as a temporary aberration which will disappear when city hall is cleaned up. The fact is that city hall is sometimes cleaned up and the average voter continues to feel that he is the political outsider. This is partly because he continues to believe in the classical theory of democracy which leads him to expect more from the political system than is possible.

Since feelings of political alienation arise from the disjunction of political values and structure we must examine both. We choose to examine liberal democratic values and structure, although an analysis of political alienation in terms of nonliberal values and structure is possible.

The Lockian version of democratic theory which dominates American political thought holds that government should be based on the rule of majority. According to this view the masses play the active role by framing and answering political questions while elected officials act as passive agents executing their will. The theory presupposes the ability of the majority to change the government through peaceful constitutional procedures, or, as a last resort, through revolution. The state in Lockian theory is a neutral agency settling disputes according to objective principles of reason and justice.

The roles which the democratic citizen should play according to this scheme are numerous. He is supposed to be interested in political affairs, have a capacity for discussion, and expose himself to, and rationally evaluate, information which may or may not be congenial to his political taste. The democratic citizen is also expected to act on the basis of principles (natural law) which are self-evident and which refer not only to his personal interest but also to the common good.

Those who accept this theory expect that they will be powerful, that is, have the power to select, influence, and remove officials. They also expect that they will have enough information to make what they consider to be a rational choice between meaningful alternatives. Finally, they expect that they will be able to do this through existing institutions without violating their standards of political ethics. Thus, democratic man assumes that he has the right to feel politically powerful, meaningful, and moral.

Democratic man not only expects that he will be able to play these roles but he also expects rational, legitimate, and honest behavior by public officials. He expects, in other words, regularity of public performance, order, and due process of law for all. In a political system where many individuals believe that corruption is widespread and political power is concentrated and abused, the expectations of the citizens with respect to order and due process of law are not met, and they come to believe that they are foreigners (aliens) in the political structure. In other words, for them the political structure, as structure, as regular performance, has ceased. This causes them to feel politically alienated.

In effect, democratic theory is one of the sources of political aliena-tion. Feelings of political alienation will arise when the political role that an individual expects to play and believes is rightfully his cannot be realized. These feelings may result from the fact that the role assignments are unrealistic, that is, they demand more than can be fulfilled or promise more than can realistically be implemented. The fact that they cannot be realized does not mean that they will not be desired. If the roles are, in fact, possible, feelings of alienation may arise from the fact that the po-litical structure prevents the playing of the roles. Thus political roles may be utopian or realistic, while political structures may lead to the fulfill-ment or denial of those roles which are possible. If the roles are utopian, no political structure can lead to their realization.

Feelings of alienation will arise in individuals who accept the classical democratic theory because it demands more of the individual citizen than he can realistically fulfill and promises more than can be delivered. Most citizens do not and cannot play an active role or display the sustained interest in politics required of them by the theory. The majority do not engage in true discussion, are not well informed or motivated, and do not vote on the basis of principles.[4] Indeed, the principles of right reason and justice, which are supposed to be self-evident and to supply a frame-work for political action, are precisely what appear to be so much in dis-pute. The theory also fails to account for the necessary roles of leadership and exaggerates the active role of the masses. Those who do lead are therefore regarded as potential usurpers of what rightfully belongs to the electorate. The theory also leads its followers to believe that the bargain-ing and compromising, which is so essential to democratic politics, is necessarily evil. In short, the roles as defined by eighteenth-century demo-cratic theory are too demanding and the political structure designed to implement them cannot be what it is supposed to be. This does not mean that democracy is impossible or that its normative value system should be abandoned as incompatible with the nature of man. It does mean that the classical theory of democracy must be revised to fit the realities of modern politics. We accept the view of Berelson that "the classical polit-ical philosophers were right in the direction of their assessment of the virtues of the citizen. But they demanded those virtues in too extreme and doctrinal a form."[5] If individuals continue to believe in the classical view, they will feel politically alienated.

This discussion of political alienation raises the question of how these feelings can be handled if we are to have a democratic society. This is the problem of political maturity.

Political Maturity and Political Alienation

Political maturity is the ability of an individual to handle feelings of political alienation through rational rather than regressive mechanisms. To achieve this, one must perceive the realities of the political structure, hold political goals which are potentially operational, and attempt to develop institutions through which these goals may be realized. Political maturity, like political alienation, refers to a quality of an individual rather than a system. A particular political system may encourage or discourage the ability of individuals to be politically mature. For example, a government which monopolizes the means of communication may hinder accurate perception of the political reality. A society whose educational system promulgates political values appropriate to the eighteenth century will encourage goals which cannot be operational. A government which forcibly prevents formation of opposition movements will make difficult the development of institutions through which political goals can be rationally achieved.

The amount and form of political alienation also have an effect on the level of political maturity. A moderate amount of alienation may stimulate rational activism since the discomfort is not great enough to prevent attention to the source. An overwhelming amount, however, is likely to lead to regressive mechanisms, since extreme feelings of powerlessness interfere with the perception of political reality and lead to projection and identification with a charismatic leader. We have already pointed out that powerlessness and normlessness tend to lead to projection and identification with a charismatic leader because these mechanisms account for the absence of power and the lowering of values in a simple manner, while meaninglessness and estrangement tend to lead to withdrawal. Those who experience political alienation in the forms of meaninglessness and estrangement are more available for politically mature behavior than those who experience powerlessness and normlessness, since the former interferes less with the accurate perception of political reality.

Since feelings of political alienation may lead to the use of regressive mechanisms, such as projection and identification with a charismatic leader, they can be a threat to democratic society. It is therefore important to minimize these feelings. This may be accomplished in part by replacing eighteenth-century democratic values with a more realistic theory of democracy. We do not pretend to have a solution to this problem. We suggest that a more realistic theory must start from the fact that the masses do not and cannot play the active role, and that elections seldom reveal the "will" of the majority. A revision of theory alone, however, will not seriously reduce feelings of alienation. A re-examination and reorganization of the political structure is also indicated.

N O T E S

1. The history of American political theory offers many examples of conspiratorial thinking. On this point see Richard Hofstadter, *The Age of Reform* (New York: Knopf), pp. 20–31.

2. From Max Weber, *Essays in Sociology*, translated, edited, and with an introduction by H. H. Gerth and C. Wright Mills (New York: Oxford University Press, 1946), p. 295.

3. William Kornhauser, *The Politics of Mass Society* (Glencoe: The Free Press, 1959), p. 32.

4. Cf. Bernard Berelson, Paul Lazarsfeld, and William McPhee, *Voting* (Chicago: University of Chicago Press, 1954), pp. 307–9.

5. Ibid., p. 322.

2.

The Role of Community Influentials

M. KENT JENNINGS

MAYOR WILLIAM HARTSFIELD HAS HAD A LONG POLITICAL CAREER IN his home town, Atlanta. Beginning in 1923, he served as alderman for six years and then as a state legislator before his first election as mayor in 1936. Since then, he had been mayor, except for one two-year period, until his retirement in 1961. After a defeat in 1940, he came back to win a special election by an overwhelming majority. Hartsfield's support emanated from four main sources: business leaders, who provided financial and strategic aid; most of the city administration and board of aldermen; the middle- and upper-class voting precincts; and, increasingly over the years, the Negro precincts.

Hartsfield was the ideal incumbent in a weak mayor system, for he had the temerity and political shrewdness to exercise leadership despite the constraints of the formal governmental structure. His very strengths, however, were also weaknesses that alienated many citizens of Atlanta. The Atlanta newspapers, for example, although they eventually gave him their electoral support, on some occasions aimed caustic shafts at him. Editor and publisher Ralph McGill said of him: "because he is of an intense and impulsive nature, he creates many unnecessary foes and often exasperates those who regard him fondly after seeming to go out of his way to make it difficult for those who wish to support him."

From *Community Influentials: The Elites of Atlanta* by M. Kent Jennings, pp. 130–140. Copyright © 1964 by The Free Press of Glencoe, a division of The Macmillan Company, and reprinted by permission. On page 19 of his book, Jennings defines the three classes of "influentials" that figure in this extract as follows: ". . . occupants of major economic posts in the community—*economic dominants*; those who hold positions formally designed to sanction and facilitate the exercise of influence in the community—*prescribed influentials*; and those who are perceived by significant others as being the most influential in community decision-making—*attributed influentials*" —Ed.

In Hartsfield's [1957] primary fight . . . . . he barely eked out a victory over his opponent, Fulton County Commissioner Archie Lindsey. Hartsfield's dependence on both the upper and lower socio-economic strata was clearly demonstrated by the financial aid and voting support he received. He had relied upon his usual campaign oratory and public addresses to carry him through. The coincidence of the omnibus bond program with the mayoralty primary campaign greatly increased the incumbent's opportunities for exposure and speechmaking. Despite the carping of the press during much of the campaign, the *Constitution* and the *Journal*—and the *Daily World* as well—endorsed him. Still, toward the end of the campaign, he realized that he was in a tough race and that he needed more money to carry out his campaign. A few days before the election, a close friend (an attributed influential) was informed that Hartsfield was in need of funds. The friend replied that he would do his best to help.

The benefactor immediately phoned a number of his own associates (a large proportion of whom were attributed influentials) who wanted a continuation of the incumbent administration and the general direction of Atlanta's development. He told them straightforwardly about the request he had received; all indicated their willingness to contribute. About one hour later, the benefactor collected the donations in person and immediately transformed them into cash. He then went directly to Hartsfield's office, laid down several thousand dollars in cash, and said, "Here's what you need Bill; it comes from some of your friends around town." Although Hartsfield may have known the general source of these funds, he did not know the specific contributors nor the amounts they had given. Specific political obligations and political demands were thus avoided.

In edging out Lindsey, Hartsfield followed a long established pattern in his elections. He carried the more prosperous precincts of the city (although voting was lighter than usual there), held his ground spottily in other areas of the city, carried the predominantly Negro districts by heavy majorities, and soundly lost in the lower middle-class and lower-class white sections of the city. Although he had never done well in these last wards, he publicly noted his astonishment at their outright rejection of him. Hartsfield's voting support thus came from both the upper and lower (assuming Negro status in the South) socio-economic extremes.

While Hartsfield expressed concern with the distribution of his vote, some of his political advisers were privately expressing more sophisticated partisan worries about the pattern. Two of them, both second-level attributed influentials, had frequently supplied the mayor with technical and political information. We shall refer to these two actors as "Alpha" and

"Beta". They analyzed the returns and recognized that the strong anti-Hartsfield vote represented a distinct threat to the acknowledged coalition that governed the community—the loose alliance between business-civic leaders, Negro leaders, and Hartsfield and his administration. It was a very real threat because, according to private surveys recently completed at that time, a substantial proportion of Atlanta's newcomers were from the rural areas of Georgia. In the primary election, more of these people had apparently voted than ever before, and they had expressed their rural attitudes and prejudices by voting against an urbane and moderate mayor. Numerically, Alpha and Beta reasoned, these immigrants could well shift the balance against the combined Negro and upper middle-class voters who had given Hartsfield the primary victory.

Ordinarily such considerations would not have constituted a problem for the mayor and his friends. The winner of the "nonpartisan" primary election is usually elected in light balloting in a general election six months later. Independent candidates can, however, qualify to run against the nominees. Hartsfield had once been so challenged by a businessman and had defeated him handily. Less than a month after Hartsfield's narrow victory in the 1957 primary, however, speculation abounded that an independent candidate would challenge the mayor, and that other nominees would also be opposed in the election. By the end of the second month after the primary, such a mayoral candidate had emerged. In his opening statement, he declared that he was running because he felt the people wanted a businessman, rather than a politician, at the city's helm. While he had had little previous political experience, other potential candidates with much more political acumen and experience also began to appear.

In the midst of these ominous warnings, Alpha and Beta and two or three of their associates (one of whom was a civic staffer) communicated to a half-dozen or so key Hartsfield supporters their concern over the primary-vote distribution and its possible meanings in the event of a serious challenge in the general election. Those key supporters included five first-level attributed influentials, three of whom had played significant roles in the bond-issue program and one of whom was among the mayor's closest friends.

On our decision-making continuum, we may call this step the initiation stage. Undoubtedly some of the events that followed would have occurred even if analysts of the primary had not brought the matter to the attention of others with greater power resources at their disposal. But this example of filter power marked the first major step to thwart any attempt to deprive Hartsfield of his seeming victory.

The next step consisted of an event apparently unprecedented in Atlanta. Under the guidance of two or three of the alerted group of attributed influentials, a conference of about twenty "top leaders" was held. Some men returned from outside the city to attend the session. Such strategy sessions are usually held among a much smaller group of people or even by phone. In this case, however, a consciously organized and planned meeting was arranged. Apparently, the threat posed by the Citizens Council's attempt to have the Urban League dropped from the United Appeal added further urgency to the need for a "summit" meeting. Both the electoral threat to Hartsfield and the Community Chest conflict stemmed from the same basic source—discontent among conservative, rural-minded citizens.

Those at the meeting (only one who was invited failed to attend) numbered about twenty. They included approximately fifteen attributed influentials, most of whom had considerable access to financial resources and some of whom themselves held elective or appointive governmental positions. The rest were all financially affluent. Virtually all attending were well known to one another.

The meeting resulted in a firm resolve among the participants that they would strongly support Hartsfield both financially and in other ways against any electoral challenge. They did, however, want some guarantee that he would promote and enact a more vigorous and constructive program for the city to replace the current rather opportunistic strategy. Subsequently, two or three members of the "junta" met with Hartsfield himself, communicating their all-out support and their suggestions for a more constructive program. Actually these suggestions came from Alpha and Beta, who had been asked by the larger group to prepare a statement of community needs for further development. In a later consultation between the mayor and Beta, it seemed clear that Hartsfield had taken the advice seriously. Hartsfield had prepared an agenda that bore remarkable resemblance to the one Alpha and Beta had submitted to the top influentials only a short time before.

On our continuum, the conference of influentials represents the priority-fixing stage in the decision-making process of the mayoralty election. The conferees agreed that Hartsfield must be re-elected in order for the city to continue its general direction of development. Although they may not have mentioned it openly, their continued high access to the mayor's office constituted another equally strong reason for their defense of the mayor. In exchange for their all-out support, they bargained for the introduction or extension of certain values in the city's development plans.

Once the commitment to Hartsfield had been made, most of those at the original meeting retired from active participation. They did, of course, raise funds and communicate with other important actors in the community, but organized planning of campaign strategy with the mayor was limited to a few individuals to whom this task had been delegated at the original meeting. These individuals included three second-level attributed influentials (including Alpha and Beta), one first-level influential who served as informal chairman, two prescribed influentials, and three others. Although Hartsfield did not accept all the recommendations and suggestions of this strategy group, his later campaign was affected in the direction of the group's proposals.

This arrangement is one aspect of utilizing resources for gaining acceptance of the chosen alternative. In addition to advising Hartsfield on strategy, the group also persuaded press executives to be more gentle and positive in their treatment of him. A survey of the two major papers reveals, in fact, that, after the initial threat to his apparent victory and recognition of the potential anti-Hartsfield vote, they did indeed change their approach to the mayor and his administration.

Meanwhile the potential opposition gathered momentum. A newly formed Atlanta Improvement Association decided to hold a nominating convention. Since the Atlanta primary had been conducted without party labels, this group argued that the winners were not official Democratic nominees. The Association planned to nominate a candidate to run against Hartsfield and did not preclude the possibility of nominating candidates for aldermen as well. Another group—closely allied with the Association—was directed by an unsuccessful candidate for city board of aldermen. This movement sought petition signatures and other forms of support for a two-time loser to Hartsfield. Lines of communication between the two groups were close.

Both Hartsfield and Margaret MacDougall, chairman of the city's executive committee in charge of elections, denounced the proposed convention and plans to place people on the ballot via the petition route as unfaithful to the purpose of the primary. The Improvement Association received another setback from Governor Marvin Griffith, who declined an invitation to address one of their meetings.

The self-styled "Democrats" of the city held their convention, attended by a handful of people. They did not nominate candidates at that convention. Subsequently, however, they sent "Democratic pledge cards" to the winners of the primary asking for their allegiance to the party. Former State Senator Everett Millican, informed of the letters and pledge cards, advised each nominee by special delivery letter that he had been "chosen as a nominee in a perfectly legal and regular primary . . . which has always been recognized as a regular Democratic Primary." He urged them not to sign the cards. His advice was followed.

As the deadline for qualification drew near, the mayor's twice-defeated opponent withdrew. But restaurateur Lester Maddox, a political neophyte, gathered sufficient signatures on petitions to qualify as an opponent. The disgruntled "Democrats" of the city failed to name a slate after two abortive public meetings. In fact, they eventually voted to support all the primary nominees. The Improvement Association was also disbanded, although Maddox undoubtedly gained support from its former membership.

In the ensuing campaign, Maddox emphasized the mayor's moderate stand on racial matters, hit at his dictatorial administration, and spoke of corruption. Hartsfield concentrated on the more positive aspects of his program and often avoided the temptation to argue the race question. The general election brought a turnout only slightly below that of the primary. Hartsfield scored a decisive two-to-one victory over Maddox. True to expectations, the victor carried the higher socio-economic precincts and the Negro precincts to achieve his margin. This election marked the legitimation phase.

We may look upon the contest as a struggle between episodic and permanent political influentials. Neither Maddox nor most of his leading supporters had played a significant part in past decision-making in Atlanta. Conversely, Hartsfield and his major supporters had not only been seriously involved in other elections but had also exercised influence in a wide range of other policy-making processes in the city. Over the years, various anti-Hartsfield elements in the city had opposed him in one way or another. In this particular election, the principal opponents offer especially good examples of sporadic participants. Although they did not achieve the ultimate goal of winning the mayor's office, they did continue the open opposition to the mayor and to those parts of the power structure associated with him. Maddox, however, later emerged as the main opponent to Ivan Allen, Jr., Hartsfield's successor, in the 1961 election. In the following year, he gained a run-off election for the office of lieutenant governor but was defeated.

The successful engineering of Hartsfield's victory may also be viewed as an example of the successful exercise of positive power. The individuals who supported the mayor (including himself) were able to achieve their goals completely. No visible concessions were granted the opposition.

We have so far stressed the most important actors in this issue. We noted that both prescribed and attributed influentials, especially the latter, played leading roles. Turning to the questionnaire data, we can outline more generally the relative participation of the status-groups in the issue. As [the table] shows, the attributed and prescribed influentials outrank the economic dominants in virtually all the more critical types of electoral participation. This preponderance is especially clear in such categories as

ACTIVITIES OF STATUS-OCCUPANTS IN THE
MAYORALTY CAMPAIGN

| Activities | ATTRIBUTED INFLUENTIALS | | PRESCRIBED INFLUENTIALS | | ECONOMIC DOMINANTS |
	First Level	Second Level	Government Officials	Civic Staff	
None	5%*	9%	21%	14%	5%
Spoke to friends	75	91	75	73	95
Urged members of organizations to vote	65	58	33	59	42
Contributed money	55	48	29	18	40
Helped devise campaign strategy	50	27	21	18	0
Helped formulate platform	35	27	21	14	5
Gave public endorsement	30	21	7	23	21
Did publicity work	35	21	17	27	5
Number	(20)	(33)	(24)	(22)	(19)

*Percentages do not total 100% because actors performed more than one of the activities.

developing campaign strategy, helping formulate the platform, and handling publicity. The attributed influentials tend to be slightly more engaged in the crucial activities than do the prescribed influentials. This engagement is partly the result of reluctance among some professional government officials, particularly those working for Fulton County, to become active in political campaigns.

That no more than 65 per cent of the first-level and 58 per cent of the second-level attributed influentials performed any of the actions listed (with the exception of speaking to friends) is strong evidence against presuming a very extensive general elite that can be defined on the basis of nomination-attribution. Attributed influentials do contribute the largest share of individuals performing critical roles. Although they compose only 47 per cent of our total sample of status-occupants, they account for 54 per cent of those engaging in publicity activities, 59 per cent of the financial contributors, 64 per cent of the platform builders, and 68 per cent of the strategy planners.

We noted at an earlier point that Hartsfield's success in holding office for an extended period of time derived in part from the financial and strategic support of leading business interests in the community. Approximately two years after the general election of 1957, it became apparent that this business leadership might withdraw its support from Hartsfield. Several factors accounted for the change of attitudes. Hartsfield was growing old, and his cantankerous behavior seemed to be increasing. He had fought a series of political contests that had gradually created considerable hostility among voters in the city. Finally, he seemed to be losing control over the aldermen's board. . . . . . Aldermen did not identify with him so strongly as they had before. Newer political figures were coming onto the scene, and many of them did not feel so indebted to him and his coalition as had others in the past.

There were at least one formal and two informal clues that Hartsfield's tenure might be ending. The first involved a first-level attributed influential, a man probably as close to the mayor as any top influential in the city, who had suffered from the mayor's waning control over the aldermen's board. He reported that, at one of his not infrequent dinners with the mayor, he had indicated that he and other of the mayor's friends thought that Hartsfield should probably not run for office again. "Then," he said, "I suggested that Hartsfield indicate his preferences for the next mayor and that we would try to go by his recommendations. The mayor is a good politician; he knows who could be elected and he knows who would make a good mayor." Unless radical events intervened, it seemed highly probable that Hartsfield would heed this advice.

A second informal move came when Hamilton Douglas resigned from the city board. Everett Millican was selected by the mayor and the board to replace him. Part of the early strategy in placing Millican on the board was the possibility of grooming him for the mayor's seat. Millican was amenable to such a move.

A more formal notice of all-out opposition to Hartsfield was the announcement of three candidacies for the mayoralty. Included among these candidates was James Aldredge from the county commission.

The final decision on whether Hartsfield would run again perhaps hinged on the advice of Robert Woodruff of Coca-Cola. It is no secret that Woodruff had supported Hartsfield in the past and that there is mutual respect between them. As one informant remarked:

> There is probably only one business interest that Hartsfield would not buck if he *really* wanted something. And that is the Coca-Cola outfit. There is a tacit understanding that if Hartsfield cannot raise enough money elsewhere then Woodruff will ultimately furnish it to him. Let me give you an exemple of how the mayor is tied to Woodruff.
>
> Not long after I first acquired my governmental position I and some of my colleagues had before us a measure which would have involved regulating some of the advertising practices of Coca-Cola. Let's call that Item A. We also had another measure which we will just call Item B. Well, one day the mayor called us into his office on the pretext of discussing Item B.
>
> When we walked in there was the mayor and three representatives from

Coca-Cola, including the major hatchetman, _____. After the introductions were concluded, _____ started talking about Item A, not Item
B. He would talk a while, then ask us if we didn't agree with him. Frankly,
most of us didn't, and we said so. Then he would go on, all the time becoming more excited.

Finally Hartsfield intervened with words something like these: "Now
boys, Coca-Cola is a friend of the city and has done a lot for the city. I'm
sure we wouldn't want to do anything to hurt them." Well, when he said
that we had no real recourse. The motion was made, seconded, and carried
that Item A be constructed so as not to hurt the company. I've seen Woodruff's hand in matters subsequent to this. The mayor responds to him.

Postscript.

As it developed, Hartsfield did decide against running for re-election in
1961, probably for many reasons. As a successor, he first seemed to favor
M. M. ("Muggsy") Smith, a state representative from Fulton County.
Smith was also the choice of the younger and more forceful Negro leaders.
Much of the big-business community, however, rallied to the support of
Ivan Allen, Jr., a well-to-do merchant from an established Atlanta family.
Banker Mills B. Lane, Jr., is said to have led the fight for Allen, and he
eventually persuaded much of the Hartsfield clique to back Allen. The
other serious candidates were Fulton County Commissioner James H.
Aldredge and Lester Maddox, the unsuccessful challenger to Hartsfield in
1957. Allen and Aldredge adopted a moderate position on the race issue.
Allen and Maddox emerged as the two top vote-getters in the primary. In
the run-off election, Allen defeated Maddox by a sizable margin. Allen
relied on much the same voting coalition as had Hartsfield: the Negro and
the higher socio-economic-class white precincts.

3.

The 1961 Mayoralty Election in Los Angeles

CHARLES G. MAYO

NONPARTISANSHIP IN MUNICIPAL POLITICS IS PREMISED ON THE assumption that city government is different from government at the state and national levels. The reformers of the first decade of the twentieth century believed that the two-party system, with its supposedly inherent vices of bossism, patronage, and spoils, would distort democracy at the local level and divert attention from the important issues of public policy. They saw government at the local level as being essentially apolitical or, at least, capable of having its political element reduced to a minimum.

That the proponents of nonpartisanship in municipal politics were successful in their efforts is evidenced by the fact that by 1913 all local government officials and judges in California were elected on nonpartisan ballots. This has continued to the present day, with all city, county, and district officials being elected "under a nonpartisan system in which party labels do not appear on the ballot nor are party-nominating primaries employed."[1]

Eugene Lee has recently reported that a survey of local officials and party leaders in 192 California cities revealed that in eighteen of the cities, parties had been active in city or school elections during the preceding four-year period. He thus has demonstrated that "political parties may play an influential role in local politics, regardless of the ballot form."[2] Lee's study is, however, centered on the nonpartisan political process in six small California cities. The purpose of this paper is to examine partisan

From "The 1961 Mayoralty Election in Los Angeles: The Political Party in a Non-partisan Election" by Charles G. Mayo, *Western Political Quarterly* 17 (June 1964), pp. 325–337. Copyright © by the University of Utah and reprinted by permission. The paper draws on the author's doctoral dissertation of the same title completed at the University of Southern California in 1962.

political activity in a mayoralty election in the state's largest city, and to focus attention upon an unusual aspect of it: the fact that the Democratic party found itself in the anomalous position of opposing the election of a Democrat who was running against a Republican in a nonpartisan contest.

I

On May 31, 1961, after two terms as mayor of Los Angeles, Norris Poulson was defeated in his bid for re-election. The victor, Samuel W. Yorty, won the election the hard way, having been opposed by all the Los Angeles daily newspapers and, unofficially, by his own political party.[3] Earlier, on April 4, Yorty had earned the right to run against Poulson in the general election by garnering more votes than any of the seven other candidates entered in the primary contest.[4] Poulson, while not an exceptionally popular mayor, had nonetheless kept his political fences so well mended that his defeat surprised even impartial observers.

A number of explanations for Yorty's victory have been advanced by political scientists, journalists, and the candidates themselves. Some persons attribute his success to the support of minority groups, particularly Negroes and Mexican-Americans, which were protesting against alleged police brutality and discrimination under the Poulson administration. Others find the cause of his victory in a heavy suburban vote which reflected dissatisfaction with the way in which the city had met the needs of the sprawling San Fernando Valley and its burgeoning population. Still others hypothesize that the basis of Yorty's victory lay in the fact that the identification of Democrats with the Democratic party was so strong that even the Democratic party was unable to divert support to a Republican.

Certain characteristics of the election have also led to speculation that alienation was a factor favoring Yorty. This hypothesis finds support among those who see an analogy between the 1961 mayoralty election in Los Angeles and the 1959 mayoralty election in Boston as described in *The Alienated Voter*.[5] Another explanation advanced is that Yorty owed his victory to his adroit use of television and to the support of community newspapers.

II

Machine politics of the kind found in some eastern cities has not been a characteristic part of the Los Angeles political landscape. The Progressive era's emphasis upon the trappings of direct democracy and the absence of partisan organization have militated against the establishment of a boss-dominated system. San Francisco experienced machine politics early in the twentieth century under Boss Reuf, and it was the corruption of his organization that brought the Progressives into power. Los Angeles, too, has had a "bossed" city hall from time to time, but periodic reform movements have succeeded in ridding city hall of its corrupt occupants.

Typically, the campaign team of a candidate for mayor is formed on an *ad hoc* basis, having no past and having no future, as an organization, beyond election day. A candidate gathers together an assortment of journalists, public relations specialists, and volunteer workers who perform the various campaign tasks—often with inadequate coordination. A candidate who possesses fairly ample campaign funds may obtain the services of a professional campaign management firm.[6] The image which the campaign strategists try to create by means of the mass media is one of nonpartisan devotion to the affairs of the city of Los Angeles.

A candidate who is a Republican and who is acceptable to "business" may obtain the backing of the downtown business interests and the Chamber of Commerce. Poulson was drafted by a group of prominent businessmen to run for mayor in 1953, and was prevailed upon by them to run for re-election in 1957 and 1961. Labor unions, on the other hand, have never played an important role in the recruitment or support of mayoralty candidates in Los Angeles.[7]

The Democratic and Republican parties have not organized the city of Los Angeles for municipal elections. The parties have been active in statewide campaigns, but even activity at that level was, prior to 1958, restricted because of the absence of effective two-party competition. With the election of Edmund G. Brown as governor, and with the subsequent abolition of cross-filing by the California legislature, nonpartisanship as a campaign technique lost a great deal of its unique utility, and the words "Democrat" and " Republican" became more meaningful labels in California politics. The Democratic party, by means of the 1960 reapportionment, has reinforced its political hold on the state, a position reflected in its four-to-three registration advantage.

Because of the weakness of official party organizations, unofficial bodies, the California Republican Assembly (CRA) and the California Democratic Council (CDC), have undertaken the function of endorsing candidates prior to the primary. This function was, of course, particularly important at the time when cross-filing was permitted. In recent years the CRA has lost much of the influence that it wielded when it was an integral part of the political organizations of Governors Earl Warren and Goodwin J. Knight. The CDC, and its constituent clubs, has come during the last ten years to overshadow its Republican counterpart.

The CDC itself has quite recently lost some of its influence, however, because of a split within the Democratic party. This split can be characterized, in general terms, as reflecting the differences between the "ins" and the "outs" in the party. The "in" group, *circa* 1962, was composed of persons never closely identified with the CDC, and included Edmund G. Brown, the governor; Jesse M. Unruh, the speaker of the California Assembly and probably the most powerful member of the state legislature; and Carmen Warschaw, chairman of the Women's Division of the Democratic State Central Committee. The "out" group, composed of persons who were active in CDC work and who represented the liberal wing of the party, included Paul Ziffren, former Democratic national committeeman; Joseph Wyatt, former state president of the CDC; and Richard Richards, state senator from Los Angeles County.

The "ins" were solidly behind John F. Kennedy and his campaign for the Democratic nomination in 1960. The CDC group, on the other hand, was closely identified with Adlai E. Stevenson in 1952 and 1956, and was disappointed when he was denied a third chance as the Democratic party's candidate. This division in the ranks of the leadership of the Democratic party was reflected in the activities of the party in the 1961 mayoralty election in Los Angeles.[8]

III

Entered in the primary election which was held on April 4 were nine candidates. Norris Poulson, the incumbent, was born in Baker, Oregon, in 1895 and came to Los Angeles in the early 1920's. He obtained his license as a certified public accountant in 1933 and was engaged in accounting work for several years. A lifelong Republican, he was elected to the Assembly of the California legislature in 1938 and was re-elected in 1940.

In 1942, Poulson was elected to Congress, was defeated in his campaign for re-election in 1944, but won again in 1946, 1948, 1950, and 1952. He resigned from Congress in 1953 in order to campaign against Fletcher Bowron for mayor of Los Angeles. Poulson made his opposition to public housing, a position espoused by Bowron, one of the principal issues in that election. Having been persuaded by his business backers to seek re-election in 1957, Poulson was returned to office by a substantial majority. His opponent was Robert A. Yeakel, a successful automobile dealer who had become known to many Los Angeles voters because of his extensive television advertising.

In May 1960 Poulson announced that he would not run for a third term, but in September 1960 he changed his mind. A *Los Angeles Times* editorial responded to Poulson's decision not to run, as follows: "Norris

Poulson . . . has announced that he will not run for a third term after he has finished his eighth year. The news is not surprising, but it is bad news . . . Poulson is the best mayor modern Los Angeles has had and it will not be easy to find a successor to measure up to him."[9] The announcement by Poulson that he would seek a third term was the occasion for the following editorial comment: "We are happy to support Mr. Poulson again. No man is indispensable but a few are irreplaceable."[10]

When asked why he decided to become a candidate in the 1961 election, Poulson indicated that he sincerely had had no desire to run when, in May 1960, he said that he would not do so. He desired, after many years of public service, to leave the political arena. He reversed his position only because prominent business and professional groups, including the *Los Angeles Times*, prevailed upon him to run, promising to underwrite all the financial aspects of the campaign. Poulson informed the persons who urged him to enter the campaign that he was not prepared to expend any of his personal funds.[11]

Poulson's 1961 campaign was dealt a serious blow when, early in the campaign, he developed a throat condition that permitted him to speak only in a hoarse whisper. This handicap persisted throughout the campaign and, although it was diagnosed by Poulson's physician as being minor, it restricted the mayor's activities and provided a "health issue" to be exploited by his opponents.

Samuel W. Yorty was born in Lincoln, Nebraska, in 1909. Moving to Los Angeles in 1927, Yorty launched his political career by winning election as a Democrat to the Assembly of the California legislature in 1938. He acquired a reputation for being a "liberal" by sponsoring legislation for slum clearance and legislation regulating the activities of loan companies, dairy interests, public utilities, and the oil industry. Furthermore, he voted for legislation to fix the work week at thirty hours, to curb strikebreaking, and to limit the use of the court injunction in labor disputes. Yorty endorsed the attempt by President Franklin D. Roosevelt to reorganize the Supreme Court. While an assemblyman, he also introduced a resolution that established the first California Un-American Activities Committee and served as its first chairman.[12]

In 1938, Yorty was eager to run against Frank Shaw for mayor of Los Angeles but was unable to obtain sufficient support. In April 1939 he ran unsuccessfully for the Los Angeles City Council in a close race. In 1940, Yorty broke with Governor Culbert L. Olson because Olson refused to act on Yorty's assertion that the Los Angeles office of the California State Relief Administration was ridden with "Communist termites."[13]

Yorty ran for the Democratic nomination for United States senator in 1940, but Hiram W. Johnson, the Republican incumbent, captured both party nominations. Yorty campaigned without the benefit of a strong organization and lost badly. He made intervention the central issue in his campaign and used billboards which read "Stop Hitler Now! Elect Sam Yorty." In 1941, Yorty started to enter the race against Mayor Bowron who was running for re-election, but withdrew when he found the field too crowded. He announced his intention to campaign for governor in 1942, but changed his mind when Earl Warren became a candidate. In 1942, Yorty won the Democratic nomination for his old Assembly seat which he had forfeited when he ran for the Senate. Once again, however, he met with defeat.[14]

After military service in World War II, Yorty ran sixth among thirteen candidates in the 1945 mayoralty election in which Bowron was re-elected. In 1949, he was successful in winning back his old seat in the Assembly at Sacramento. The following year he won the seat in Congress vacated by Helen Gahagan Douglas, who had entered the race for the United States Senate against Richard M. Nixon. During his two terms in Congress, he worked with his fellow California congressman Norris Poulson to block the Central Arizona Project which involved Colorado River water rights.

In 1954, Yorty, with the endorsement of the California Democratic Council, won the Democratic nomination for Nixon's unexpired term in the Senate, but lost in a close race to Thomas H. Kuchel. In the campaign, Yorty questioned Kuchel's war record, and, in turn, his opponent alleged that Yorty had abused his congressional franking privilege by sending copies of his speeches to California voters at a cost of $500,000 to the taxpayers.[15]

Yorty was unsuccessful in his bid for the Democratic nomination for United States senator in 1956, having failed to secure the endorsement of the CDC in a bitter session that left scars on all the participants.[16] When state Senator Richard Richards received the endorsement of that body, Yorty charged that the CDC was "wired, stacked, rigged, and packed" by a "rule or ruin clique." He also accused Democratic National Committeeman Paul Ziffren of attempting to control the California Democratic party "in the pattern of a Chicago machine."[17]

From 1956 to 1961, Yorty was engaged in the practice of law. In October 1960 he further alienated himself from the leadership of the Democratic party by announcing that he supported Vice President Nixon in his campaign against Senator John F. Kennedy for the presidency. He avowed that he had no personal quarrel with Kennedy but said: "I cannot convince myself that John F. Kennedy is ready to be President of the United States at this critical point in history." He based his support of Nixon rather than Kennedy on five arguments: (1) The Kennedy family had obtained the nomination by the expenditure of "lavish amounts of money and a calculated exploitation of his religious affiliation." (2) Kennedy had criticized United States foreign policy but as a senator had offered no concrete suggestions for changes. (3) Kennedy would utilize federal controls to a greater extent than would Nixon in dealing with domestic problems. Thus, Kennedy would attempt to solve the farm problem by putting the government in the farming business. (4) Kennedy was dissatisfied with "tight money" policies but was unable to explain how he would meet the cost of the domestic and defense projects and the high farm prices that he promised. (5) Kennedy was much more under the influence of labor leaders than Nixon.[18]

From this review of the political career of Samuel W. Yorty, it can be seen that on three occasions prior to 1961 he entertained the idea of running for mayor of Los Angeles: in 1938, 1941, and 1945. On the first two occasions he failed to enter the race because of lack of support; on the last he entered the primary but was defeated. The factors which motivated him to enter the 1961 mayoralty election are probably as complex as his political career. Yorty explains that his decision was based on the premise that Los Angeles needed a change and that he was the man to effect it.[19]

Another explanation, one which is less personal but which is compatible with the former, is that Yorty had so thoroughly antagonized the leadership of the Democratic party of California by his actions in 1956 and 1960 that the only chance for reviving his political life lay in a campaign for a nonpartisan office. Yorty denies that his entrance into the mayoralty election was dictated by the assurance of support from any particular groups. On the contrary, he maintains that his decision was determined by an intuitive feeling on his part that large numbers of Los Angeles voters wanted a change and that they would support him.[20]

Also entered as mayoralty candidates in the primary election were seven other hopefuls. Councilman Patrick D. McGee, elected to the Los Angeles City Council in 1957, while a Republican member of the Assembly of the California legislature was the only one of these who was considered by most observers to be a serious contender. A resident of Van Nuys, McGee represented the Third Council district, which encompasses the western portion of the San Fernando Valley. Prior to the election, McGee had been critical of the way in which Poulson had managed tidelands oil development of the Los Angeles harbor and of some oil leases let by the city during Poulson's administration.

The other candidates entered in the primary were, in California political terminology, "self-starters." They were William Carpenter, a transportation counselor; Oscar G. Cover, a carpenter and merchant seaman, who was a member of the Socialist Workers party; Howard M. Kessler, a real estate investor; Wallace J. Lauria, who withdrew before the primary in favor of Yorty, but whose name appeared on the ballot; Mrs. M. Garet Rogers Miller, an attorney; and Robert Carrillo Ronstadt, an industrial relations director.[21]

In addition to the candidates for mayor, there were on the primary ballot two candidates for city attorney, four candidates for city controller, a large number of candidates vying for seats on the City Council and the Board of Education, and several charter amendments and bond issues.

IV

The primary and general election campaigns were witness to sensational charges made by both Poulson and Yorty. Yorty promised, if elected, to wrest the city government out of the hands of the "machine" behind Poulson and to restore popular government to Los Angeles. Poulson countered by alleging that Yorty had associated with gamblers, had operated a rubbish dump which had been cited for violations by the county engineer's office, and had underworld connections. These charges led Yorty to file a $2,200,000 defamation suit in Superior Court against Poulson and his campaign managers.

The Baus and Ross Company, a professional campaign management firm, undertook the overall direction of the Poulson campaign. In 1953 and 1957, the firm had supervised all aspects of the mayor's campaigns. In 1961, however, the organizational structure of the Poulson campaign was complicated by the fact that a citizens' committee and Snyder-Smith Advertising, a firm to which work with the Democrats and minority groups was subcontracted, refused to subordinate their activities to the overall planning and direction that Baus and Ross sought to exercise. The Baus and Ross Company is closely identified with the business-Republican interests of the city. The firm believed that the wisest political strategy would be to ignore Yorty's charges of machine politics, not to attempt to enlist the support of Democrats through blatantly partisan appeals, and to keep Poulson from displaying his voice difficulties by avoiding public appearances. Snyder-Smith Advertising and the citizens' committee did not subscribe to these views, and at times pursued strategies directly counter to those favored by Baus and Ross.[22]

Because Yorty's campaign was not nearly as well financed as Poulson's, the Yorty "team" was less professionalized in terms of its personnel and its techniques.[23] During the primary campaign, Yorty had the backing of only a small corps of volunteer workers, headed by Eleanor Chambers. Irvin L. Edelstein provided mass media services through his advertising agency. Television was the principal vehicle by means of which Yorty communicated his case to the voters, and news commentator George Putnam was his greatest ally in the use of that medium. After the primary, the number of campaign workers increased substantially, but the Yorty campaign organization remained essentially amateurish in comparison with the Poulson organization.[24] The professionalism of the Poulson campaign was, however, dissipated by lack of coordination, and it was probably more than matched by the enthusiasm of the supporters of Yorty.

v

Norris Poulson, a lifelong Republican who had served in Congress under that party's banner for more than ten years, entered the 1961 mayoralty election with the tacit, if not expressed, blessings of the Republican business and professional groups of Los Angeles. In 1953, 1957, and 1961, Poulson was recruited as a candidate by these groups, and it was they who underwrote the financial aspects of his campaigns. During his tenure as mayor, Poulson had done little to disturb the political milieu that these interests favored. In fact, because on the threshold of the election, few persons—Republicans and Democrats alike—appeared to be unhappy with the way in which Poulson had managed the city's affairs, the Republican party probably saw no need to intervene, officially or unofficially, in the 1961 election. The mayor's campaign was to be managed by a professional campaign management firm which was closely identified with the Republican business interests and which had successfully directed his 1953 and 1957 campaigns. Also, in view of the fact that only approximately 409,000 of the city's 1,128,070 registered voters were Republicans, the Republican party no doubt considered nonpartisanship to be a political necessity. Julius A. (Jud) Leetham, chairman of the Los Angeles County Republican Central Committee, announced, on May 23, his personal endorsement of Poulson, but at the same time emphasized that it should not be construed to be an official endorsement by the Republican party.

The Democratic party in southern California unofficially intervened in the 1961 mayoralty election largely for a punitive purpose. It wished to exact revenge against Yorty because of his criticisms of the party hierarchy and his endorsement of Nixon in 1960. Particularly displeased with Yorty were Richards, Ziffren, and the CDC faction of the party. Jesse M. Unruh, speaker of the Assembly of the California legislature, and Stanley Mosk, state attorney general, shared the CDC's antipathy toward Yorty, but, because of the factional split within the party, did not feel that they could work effectively with the CDC to defeat him.[25] One consideration which probably motivated the Democrats to seek Yorty's defeat was the fear that he might support Nixon if Nixon were to decide to run for governor of California in 1962.

The Baus and Ross Company counseled that partisanship should not be made an issue in the election. While the heads of that firm saw the necessity to gain the support of as many Democrats as possible, they nevertheless feared that an appeal to Democrats to vote against a "traitorous" Democrat might boomerang.[26] For this reason, the firm worked unobtrusively through John R. MacFaden, the head of a professional campaign management firm, in the primary to reach Democratic voters and members of minority groups. After the primary, Baus and Ross, at the insistence of Poulson and Martin Pollard, chairman of the citizens' committee, replaced MacFaden with Snyder-Smith Advertising. It was Snyder-Smith that engineered the general election effort to use partisanship as a weapon against Yorty.

The split in the Democratic party between the CDC and the non-CDC elements was reflected in the way in which efforts were made to solicit the support of Democrats. Baus and Ross worked through Joseph Wyatt, former state president of the CDC, and Ziffren. Wyatt attended several strategy conferences held at the Baus and Ross campaign headquarters, and he talked with members of CDC clubs about the need to back Poulson. Ziffren discussed campaign strategy with Baus and Ross by telephone on a number of occasions. Assemblyman Unruh and Carmen H. Warschaw, chairman of the Women's Division of the Democratic State Central Committee, worked through Snyder-Smith and participated in the strategy planning of that firm.[27]

The efforts of the Snyder-Smith group to convince Democrats that they should vote for Poulson resulted in the publication of two editions of the *Los Angeles Democrat*, a newspaper created for the specific purpose of arousing antagonism toward Yorty among Democrats. The editorial board for the first edition, which was dated May 1, was composed of Rosalind Wyman, member of the Los Angeles City Council; Thelma Thomas, coordinator of the Los Angeles County Council on Political Education (COPE), AFL-CIO; Berrien Moore, state president of the Young Democrats; and Delwin Smith, partner in Snyder-Smith Advertising. The paper bore the headlines "Democrats Benefit by Progress with Poulson," and on the front page appeared a picture of President Kennedy and the Coliseum in which he accepted the Democratic nomination in 1960. Poulson was praised for his role in the negotiations that brought the 1960 Democratic National Convention to Los Angeles and for the fact that he had appointed a number of Democrats to important positions in his administration.

The following editorial, entitled "The Best Man for the Job," was printed in the first edition of the *Los Angeles Democrat*.

By the same fair and impartial standards that he has used in evaluating the best men and women to serve our city, Norris Poulson qualifies as the best man for the biggest job—Mayor of Los Angeles.

As Democrats, we can point with pride to the eight-year record of our nonpartisan mayor. In this and subsequent issues of the *Los Angeles Democrat*, we are presenting highlights of Mayor Poulson's outstanding achievements in office—achievements which have greatly benefited the Democratic Party as well as our entire city.

The partisan issue has been injected into this campaign not by Mayor Norris Poulson nor by leaders of the Democratic Party.

The partisan issue has been injected by a renegade Democrat, Samuel Yorty, who is trying to whitewash himself by hurling false accusations against Mayor Poulson—just as he has repeatedly done against the Democratic Party and its leaders.

Yorty has repudiated the Democratic Party, not once but many times. He has called conventions of Democrats "rigged, stacked, wired and packed." He has denounced State Senator Richards for "slick double-talk," and Governor Brown for "failing to meet a challenge."

Yorty has accused President Kennedy of "destroying the internal integrity of the Democratic Party" and of "a calculated exploitation of his religious affiliation."

Yorty has injected much more than the partisan issue into this campaign. He has injected dishonesty, false accusations, appeals to prejudice. He is an embittered little man who tries to explain away his own failures and short comings by crying "I was robbed!"

If, because of a lack of action on the part of honest Democrats, Yorty should win election as Mayor of Los Angeles, it would be a disgrace to the Democratic Party—and a catastrophe to our city.

We must not let this happen!

Norris Poulson has proved himself a man of principle. His appointments have been on the basis of merit, without prejudice. Minority groups, as well as both major parties, are actively represented in our City Government.

Poulson has proved himself as an able administrator, he has kept pace with the explosive growth of our city during the past eight years, and prepared for the breathtaking rate of Los Angeles' continued expansion. He has acted, to the best of his knowledge and ability, for the good of all citizens.

Mayor Poulson proved a major factor in bringing the 1960 Democratic

National Convention to Los Angeles. Under his administration, the Democratic Party has thrived in Los Angeles, Democrats have participated actively in our City Government and all have shared in the prosperity and progress of our city.

We must do our share now.

Norris Poulson has worked for us—we must work for him! For our best interests, as Democrats and as Angelenos, we must re-elect Mayor Norris Poulson.

On the four pages of the paper appeared photographs of, and/or statements from, the following Democrats: Rosalind Wyman; Paul Ziffren; state Senator Richard Richards; United States Senator Clair Engle; Congressman Chet Holifield; Assemblymen Jesse M. Unruh and Augustus F. Hawkins; Berrien Moore; B. Jack Ansley, vice-chairman of the Los Angeles County Democratic Central Committee; W. J. Bassett, secretary-treasurer of the Los Angeles County Federaiton of Labor; and Carmen H. Warschaw. In addition, photographs were printed that showed Poulson performing various civic acts which, in the opinion of the editor, illustrated the progress which had been achieved under the Poulson administration.

The second edition of the *Los Angeles Democrat* was published on May 25, and it carried the headline, "Yorty Traitor to Democrats." The editorial board remained the same as that which prepared the first edition except for the omission of the name of Rosalind Wyman. The front page bore a cartoon which pictured Yorty in the act of stabbing President Kennedy in the back. The editorial, which appeared on page two, was entitled "Protect Our City and Our Party."

Over this mayoralty election hangs a sinister threat to the clean government of our city and to the clean politics of our party.

Los Angeles has been able to keep itself free from the corruption that plagues eastern cities, where control of many city governments has fallen into the greedy hands of rubbish racketeers and gambler gangsters.

The all-out attempt of the multi-million dollar rubbish octopus to grab a stranglehold on our city—including bribery, blackmail, intimidation, even to arson and murder—was broken by Mayor Poulson during his first term in office. He had full County and State cooperation in cleaning up the private rubbish racket—including a clean-up of Sam Yorty's dump in San Pedro, with its 24 bad reports and 6 citations for violations.

Los Angeles' present municipal operation and plans, by which its citizens are in control of waste disposal, has won national acclaim as a model for keeping the city clean, in more ways than one.

Our city has also maintained a strong stand against the encroachment of gambling syndicates. Renewed, intensive pressure to break into Los Angeles can now be expected from Las Vegas gamblers, as a result of the State of Nevada's campaign to promote attractions other than gambling.

We must be more than ever on guard!

Sam Yorty has shown his true colors. Documented evidence points to his connection with private rubbish operations and outside gambling interests. He failed to comply with the law in operating his own rubbish dump, and tried to foist another one on the city at high cost.

As special assistant attorney for the gambling town of Cabazon, Yorty was to receive his payoff as commission on the sale of municipal water bonds. For "exerting his political influence" to obtain licenses for Las Vegas gamblers, Yorty received checks for $12,500.00

As Congressman in 1954—the last elective public office he held—Yorty betrayed the public trust by free-franking his own campaign literature at a cost to the taxpayers of more than $120,000.00.

We do not attempt to predict what Sam Yorty would do as Mayor of Los Angeles. No one can—he is too adept at talking out of both sides of his mouth.

But we can and do ask, whether such a man can be entrusted with the management of our city. Can we risk our public funds with a man who has shown himself irresponsible and wasteful of the people's money? Can we endanger the integrity of our city by having as mayor a man whose connections with rubbish and gambling interests are strongly established? Can we allow the threat of underworld and overworld control of our city government?

The answer must be an overwhelming "NO!" As good citizens of the City of Los Angeles, we must repudiate Sam Yorty and all he stands for by an overwhelming defeat at the polls on May 31st.

And as good Democrats, we must repudiate this renegade turncoat. Sam Yorty has denounced state and national nominees of the Democratic Party. He has termed the Democratic platform "of little importance."

By word and deed, Yorty has proved a TRAITOR TO THE DEMOCRATIC PARTY AND ITS PRINCIPLES.

We must repudiate this traitor by democracy's most effective and decisive weapon—the vote!

To protect ourselves—our families—our city—our party—we must RE-ELECT MAYOR POULSON May 31st!

As in the first edition, the second edition contained pictures of, and statements from, prominent Democrats who urged rank-and-file members of the party not to vote for Yorty. Both editions of the *Los Angeles Demo-*

crat were mailed to registered Democrats residing in Los Angeles. The mailing list was compiled through the use of precinct sheets.

Persons identified with the CDC and the non-CDC factions of the Democratic party signed a joint letter which was mailed to registered Democrats during the last week of the general election campaign. The signatures of Jesse M. Unruh; Paul Ziffren; Carmen H. Warschaw; Joseph Wyatt; Berrien Moore; B. Jack Ansley; Edith Seros, secretary of the Democratic State Central Committee; Elizabeth Snyder, former chairman of the Democratic State Central Committee; and Milton Gordon, Edward A. Hawkins, and Jack J. Spitzer, members of the Los Angeles County Democratic Central Committee, were reproduced on the mimeographed letter. In the letter, which was not dated, Democrats were reminded of the "disloyal" actions of Yorty and told that only by supporting Poulson could the good government of Los Angeles be assured and the Democratic party be protected.

On several occasions during the primary and general election campaigns, leaders of the Democratic party announced their backing of Poulson. Unruh and Ziffren were quoted most often by the metropolitan press about their strong preference for Poulson. During the last week in May, Yorty attempted, without success, to obtain the support of the Los Angeles County Democratic Central Committee, and this appears to have been the only time that he sought to inject partisanship into the campaign. To the actions of Unruh, Ziffren, and the County Central Committee, Yorty responded with the charge that the Democratic party was "bossed" like a political machine. On May 14, the *Los Angeles Times* quoted Yorty as denying that he had ever sought official Democratic party support and alleging that

... [Poulson] has deliberately sought official partisan Republican support.

I have not sought official Democratic Party support although many Democrats are supporting me right alongside many Republicans who really believe the office of mayor should be nonpartisan.

I don't think they can induce Democrats to vote for the machine candidate just because I have not allowed so-called Democratic leaders like Paul Ziffren to dictate to me or determine my course of action contrary to my independent judgment.

Poulson has no record of ever being independent enough to differ with the Republican Party bosses.

The real hypocrisy of the campaign is now emerging. Republicans are to be ordered to vote for Poulson because he is a Republican. Democrats are to be told they must be nonpartisan and must not support me because I have a record of independence.

In other words, true nonpartisanship, to which the Poulson press gives lip service is to be twisted and turned to mean nonpartisanship only for the Democrats.[28]

VI

In concluding this discussion of the role of political parties in the 1961 mayoralty election in Los Angeles, it must be emphasized that the Democratic party took no "official" part in the election. It is, however, difficult, if not impossible, to distinguish between official and unofficial actions in a campaign in which the party's leadership made such a bold appeal to partisanship. No funds were taken from the treasury of the party, because, as one party official stated, there were no funds available to be spent.[29] Nonetheless, the Democrat who received copies of the *Los Angeles Democrat* and the letter was scarcely in a position to make the subtle distinction between official and unofficial.

What questions are raised by the election? Certainly one of the most significant is the question of the extent to which the partisan activity in that election was typical of the nonpartisan election process in municipal politics in California. In other words, was the intrusion of the Democratic party merely an isolated occurrence or was it, as Lee suggests, a not uncommon example of the partisanship which frequently underlies a "nonpartisan" election contest?[30]

An answer to this question must be partial and tentative, given the incompleteness of research on nonpartisan politics. With respect to the Los Angeles political scene, it can be said that the 1961 election was atypical of the city's mayoralty elections since in no previous election had either of the two major parties felt obliged to enter a campaign, officially or unofficially. What makes the 1961 election particularly interesting is the way in which partisanship was introduced into the campaign. More case studies of the sort attempted here will be required to answer the question of how typical the election was of political party activity in nonpartisan municipal elections in California and in other areas of the United States.

Another question relates to the nonpartisan expectations of the electorate. Is it not possible that many of the Democrats who were the targets of the Democratic propaganda against Yorty were offended by the crudity of the partisan attack and, in effect, cast their votes for Yorty in protest against it? It might be hypothesized, therefore, that nonpartisanship may be so much a part of the political thinking of the electorate of Los Angeles that party identification cannot be invoked in the way that it can in partisan state and national elections. It could be argued, however, that the anti-Yorty strategists were too successful in identifying Yorty as a Democrat, renegade or otherwise, and that as a consequence they were unable to divert support to a Republican. If this had been true, the counsel of Baus and Ross that partisan appeals might backfire would have had some substance. According to this proposition, the Democrats might have succeeded if they had been able to utilize partisanship in a positive rather than a negative form.[31]

Some practitioners of the campaigner's art contend that the Democratic party would benefit if partisan municipal elections were instituted in Los Angeles. With its preponderance of registration—678,000 as opposed to a Republican registration of 409,000—it could, they say, place a "loyal" Democrat in the mayor's office and probably control the City Council. By organizing the city on a partisan basis the Democratic party would thereby acquire a valuable means of recruiting potential gubernatorial candidates and of manufacturing support for the party at the state level. Indeed, in view of the intensification of partisan alignments in Sacramento, it might be prophesied that, even in the present nonpartisan electoral system, the Democratic party may seek to introduce partisanship into the municipal politics of Los Angeles in support of Democratic mayoralty candidates. In the 1961 mayoralty election prominent leaders of the Democratic party unsuccessfully attempted to persuade Democrats to vote *against* a Democrat who was campaigning for a nonpartisan political office. This may be one step toward the party's attempting to mobilize support *for* a Democrat in such an election.

NOTES

1. Eugene C. Lee, *The Politics of Nonpartisanship* (Berkeley: University of California Press, 1960), p. 14. The legal basis for nonpartisanship in the municipal politics of Los Angeles is found in Section 326 of the city charter, which provides that "there shall be nothing on any ballot indicative of the party affiliation, source of candidacy or support of any candidate." The legal requirement of nonpartisanship in ballot preparation does not, of course, prevent campaign activity on the part of political parties. The failure of either of the two major parties to enter Los Angeles municipal politics before 1961 may partly be attributed to the belief of a majority of Californians that municipal government and politics ought to be insulated from partisan state and national elections, and to the virtual absence of effective competition at the state level before 1958.

2. Ibid., p. 98.

3. The distribution of votes between Poulson and Yorty in the general election was: Poulson, 260,381 (48.34%); Yorty, 276,106 (51.26%); scattering, 2,192 (0.40%).

4. In the primary election Poulson received 181,653 votes (39.74%) and Yorty, 123,810 (27.09%). Patrick D. McGee, Los Angeles city councilman, ran third with 116,774 votes (25.54%).

5. Murray B. Levin, *The Alienated Voter* (New York: Holt, Rinehart & Winston, 1960), excerpted in preceding article.

6. For information on professional campaign management, see Stanley Kelley, Jr., *Professional Public Relations and Political Power* (Baltimore: Johns Hopkins Press, 1956); Robert J. Pitchell, "The Influence of Professional Campaign Management Firms in Partisan Elections in California," *Western Political Quartely*, 11 (June 1958), 278–300; and Charles G. Mayo, "Professional Campaign Management Firms in California Politics" (Master's thesis, University of Southern California, 1960).

7. James Q. Wilson, *A Report on Politics in Los Angeles* (Cambridge: Joint Center for Urban Studies of the Massachusetts Institute of Technology and Harvard University, 1959).

8. For additional information concerning the CDC, see Francis Carney, *The Rise of the Democratic Clubs in California* (New York: Holt, 1958); and James Q. Wilson, *The Amateur Democrat* (Chicago: University of Chicago Press, 1962).

9. *Los Angeles Times*, May 5, 1960.

10. Ibid., September 2, 1960.

11. Interview with Norris Poulson, June 14, 1962.

12. Jack Smith, "Samuel Yorty: Often on Floor, Now on Top at City Hall," *Los Angeles Times*, June 25, 1961.

13. Ibid. See also Robert E. Burke, *Olson's New Deal for California* (Berkeley: University of California Press, 1953), pp. 129–36, 156–57, 168.

14. Smith, loc. cit.

15. Ibid.

16. A candidate who is not endorsed by the appropriate pre-primary endorsing body is disadvantaged with respect to obtaining his party's nomination. See Carney, op. cit.

17. Ibid.

18. *Los Angeles Times*, October 25, 1960.

19. Interview with Samuel W. Yorty, June 20, 1962.

20. Ibid.

21. *Valley Times Today*, April 1, 1961.

22. Interview with William B. Ross, June 26, 1962.

23. Campaign receipt and expense statements filed by the candidates and their campaign committees with the office of the county registrar of voters indicate that $345,044.81 was spent in Poulson's primary and general election campaigns and $22,176.87 in Yorty's.

24. Interview with Irvin L. Edelstein, June 22, 1962, and interview with Eleanor Chambers, June 19, 1962.

25. This information was obtained in an interview with an official of the Democratic party who asked that his name not be revealed.

26. Interview with William B. Ross, June 26, 1962.

27. Ibid.

28. *Los Angeles Times*, May 14, 1962.

29. Interview with official of Democratic party who asked that his name not be revealed.

30. Lee, op. cit., pp. 98, 102.

31. In a post-general election survey which utilized a quota sample, it was found that 48.3 per cent of the Democratic respondents cast ballots for Yorty, whereas only 11.3 per cent voted for Poulson. Among Republican respondents, 45.0 per cent voted for Poulson and 25.6 per cent voted for Yorty.

4.

Manipulating the Jewish Vote

WILLIAM F. BUCKLEY, JR.

It was a tiny studio, thirty feet by thirty, totally inadequate for the legion of photographers, reporters, staff. The broadcast was to be live, and the candidates posed for the cameras for several minutes, the rules of the debate were respecified (a theme, to be dropped by the moderator, two minutes each for the candidates to comment on it, working clockwise from Beame, to myself, to Lindsay, according to the draw); the producer ejected as many bodies as he could pry out of the room, leaving it packed, so much so that other than the principals and the moderator, most were forced to stand: and off we went.

Was this a city of fear? asked the moderator intending a discussion of the police problem. Beame rattled on about what had been done to increase the size of the police force, etc., etc., and it was my turn. I had decided to touch on the most untouchable subject in New York.

"I agree that this is a city of fear, and I believe that John Lindsay is doing everything in the world that he can do to cultivate that fear. Every newspaper in New York is talking about his neat operation of the past five or six days. And that operation is explicitly leveled at the Jewish voters of New York City. Mr. Lindsay has been trying to say to them, in his special kind of shorthand, 'Do you realize that Buckley is really in favor of concentration camps?' This single maneuver is intended to take votes away from Mr. Beame on over to himself. . . . [Thus] Mr. Lindsay . . . [characterizes] all my attempts to solve some of the pressing problems of New

From *The Unmaking of a Mayor* by William F. Buckley, Jr., pp. 157–168. Copyright © 1966 by William F. Buckley, Jr. Published by The Viking Press, New York City, and reprinted by permission. The book concerns the 1965 New York City mayoralty race in which the three candidates were William F. Buckley, Jr., Conservative; Abraham Beame, Democrat; and John V. Lindsay, Republican-Liberal—Ed.

York as [calling for] one or another form of concentration camps, summoning up all kinds of Nazi versions of horror, aimed especially at members of the Jewish race."

Lindsay was visibly stunned. His turn came next, and after a considerable pause, he reverted to the subject of the police, ignoring the challenge. On it went around again, dealing with diverse subjects, Beame, Buckley, Lindsay, Beame, Buckley, Lindsay, Beame, Buckley, Lindsay—whereupon as if finally reached by a delayed fuse, he exploded: . . . "First of all, Mr. [Moderator], I'd like to say this to Mr. Buckley, that Mr. Buckley's statement that I in defending myself against his ultra attacks and those of his people and his supporters in this campaign, that I am appealing to Jewish voters, is an offensive and irresponsible comment and I'll ask him not to make it again." *Ce n'est que la vérité qui blesse.* It came back to me; Mr. Beame, during his two minutes, stayed very well out of the way, and I remember an instant's temptation to reveal the names of the three prominent reporters—whom Lindsay could have reached over and touched without getting out of his chair—who had clinically discussed Lindsay's operation with me just a few minutes before. I resisted the temptation because I didn't want to embarrass them. My timing, I later thought, was off. I could have said, without any fear at all that Lindsay would have called me on it: "Mr. Lindsay, do you want me to give you right here and now the names of three prominent reporters from *The New York Times,* the *Tribune,* and the Washington *Post,* who were discussing your appeal to Jewish fears with me as recently as fifteen minutes ago? Perhaps you will want to forbid *them* to publish their analysis?" Lloyds of London would have given a million to one that old JVL would have changed the subject. I said, instead, angrily I fear:

Somewhere along the line, Mr. Lindsay, in the course of his self-infatuation, decided that he could give me instructions about what I might say and what I might not say. You *did* hear him [I was addressing the moderator], a moment ago, *instructing* me not to repeat a certain charge? Well, I'm *going* to repeat it. . . . I can find Mr. Lindsay five hundred references published in the press during the past two weeks to the effect that he is trying to appeal to the Jewish voters.[1] And he is trying to appeal to the Jewish voters by *scaring* them. He is trying to do to the Jewish voters what the Ku Klux Klan has been trying to do to the white people in the South, keep them scared. . . . Mr. Lindsay is saying in effect to the Jewish voters, "Vote for me—because this is, over here, an ultra-rightist, who is trying to bring bloodshed to the city, whose statements are reminiscent of, quotes, 'some of the worst moments in history.' " What do *you* think he's talking about? Everybody else knows [what he is talking about] and Mr. Lindsay can't have it both ways. . . . Now let Mr. Lindsay, having finished giving me instruction, perhaps receive one from me: Cut it out, Mr. Lindsay, and I'll cut it out. Stop this . . . business about the ultra-right and concentration camps. . . .

"BUCKLEY CHARGES LINDSAY APPEALS TO JEWISH FEARS," the *Times* headlined the next day, recounting the exchange. Followed by a background paragraph:

From the beginning of the mayoral campaign, political leaders in both parties have concluded that Mr. Lindsay would have to attract the votes of large numbers of Jews, otherwise Democratic or independents, if he was to stand any chance of defeating Mr. Beame, himself a Jew.

The Washington *Post* ran a more detailed story October 29. Again the writer, Mr. Julius Duscha, recounted the exchange; and continued:

Dressed in their basic campaign blue, the three candidates shook hands and came out fighting for 55 minutes as a moderator asked them questions while reporters, jammed into the small room, took notes.

The discussion revolved around the key Jewish vote in Tuesday's election, which, if Lindsay wins, will turn him overnight into a national Republican figure.

Jews cast a third of the vote in New York, and the most political observers here believe that the Jewish vote will spell the difference between victory and defeat for Mr. Lindsay.

When Mr. Lindsay entered the race for Mayor last spring, he counted heavily on the Jewish vote. He is popular among Jews because he reminds them of John F. Kennedy, whom they supported, and speaks of issues in the intellectual terms New York's Jewish voters like to hear.

But when Beame won the Democratic primary last September, he presented Jewish voters with a painful dilemma. New York has never had a Jewish mayor, and Jewish voters now had to choose between Lindsay and Beame, a lackluster bookkeeper from Brooklyn who is nevertheless one of their own.

Polls and other political soundings have indicated that Beame is running extremely well in Jewish areas and is cutting deeply into the margins Lindsay had expected in those areas.

To counteract this trend, Lindsay has shifted his campaign strategy to an all-out attack on Buckley as right-winger who calls up memories of "some of the worst moments in history."

The Lindsay strategy is aimed at convincing Jews that his defeat by Beame—Buckley has no chance of winning—would be interpreted as an encouragement to right-wing groups throughout the country, many of which are anti-Semitic.

. . . It is believed that the race for Mayor is extremely close with the election only a few days away, and the charges and counter-charges hurled during the debate seem to bear out the nervousness in both the Lindsay and Beame camps.[2]

The maneuver by Lindsay (and later by Beame) was a conjunction of design and opportunity. I provided the opportunity; but the plan was originally that of Dubinsky and Rose, leaders of the Liberal Party, who hotly urged on Robert Price, Lindsay's manager, and on Lindsay, from the very outset, that he conduct a campaign "against the radical right," that being a tested hobgoblin in New York, as witness the Goldwater debacle of a year earlier. Price resisted, his contention being, at that point, that Lindsay's candidacy was best served by flatly ignoring his Conservative opponent, which Lindsay proceeded assiduously to do. Price's stratagem was manifestly inconsistent with his subsequent decision that Lindsay should agree to appear with both Beame and myself in a series of scheduled debates. Lindsay, in the first debate, was badly hemmed in by the dilemma. He tried bravely to ignore my presence, by referring only to Beame during the first three-quarters of the program, and answering only Beame's genteel taunts; but, finally, he gave up—had to, the situation having become theatrically intolerable—and started to denounce the theretofore invisible candidate seated across the table. But even after that debate, and the succeeding one, I was an "unperson" in his press conferences and other than at face-to-face meetings, and it was not until the first newspaper poll was published, which gave the Conservatives an astonishing ten per cent of the vote, and until after Lindsay had faced at public meetings noisy anti-Lindsay demonstrations, that the decision was made to alter the strategy. The *Times* front-paged the decision:

LINDSAY AND BUCKLEY DUEL—ATTACK SHIFTS TO BUCKLEY

John Lindsay, the Republican-Liberal candidate for Mayor, dropped his seeming unconcern about William F. Buckley Jr. yesterday by delivering a stinging denunciation of the Conservative candidate.

Mr. Buckley answered in kind.

. . . Until now, Mr. Lindsay had concentrated almost all his political fire on the Democratic candidate, Controller Abraham D. Beame, and had tried to ignore Mr. Buckley, treating him somewhat as a noisy but essentially harmless mosquito.

But recent newspaper polls have shown Mr. Lindsay trailing Mr. Beame, with Mr. Buckley showing unexpected strength and possibly holding the balance of power.

One poll taken by the *Tribune* and still in progress, showed today that Mr. Beame was leading with 44.3 per cent of the vote, followed by Mr. Lindsay with 36.9 per cent and Mr. Buckley with 11.2. Another survey, done for the *World-Telegram* by the political analyst Samuel Lubell, indicated that Mr. Lindsay's chances were being jeopardized "by a major split in the Republican vote."

Conversations in the Lindsay camp yesterday tended to confirm the impression of many political observers that the attack on Mr. Buckley was an acknowledgment that he was a serious threat and could draw off enough votes to cost Mr. Lindsay the election.

The question inevitably arose at Lindsay headquarters: What, precisely, to do? The Dubinsky-Rose Smite-the-Right strategy was obvious, but what specifically to pin it on? Hardly my proposals on how to meet the transit crisis. And there had been no endorsement from Senator Goldwater to chew on. . . .

Lindsay seized on two openings. In my position paper on welfare, I had recommended a "pilot program to explore the feasibility of relocating chronic welfare cases outside the city limits."

Consider, [the paper said, in what were to become the most controversial paragraphs I wrote in the course of the entire campaign] for instance, the mother with three illegitimate children. She costs the city in direct welfare payments about $2,700 per year. If her children are of school age, their schooling costs the city a minimum of $2,100 per year. If she and her children live in subsidized housing, she may receive a subsidy that may cost the city as much as $1,000 per year. The cost to the city of that family's share of the police, hospital, welfare overhead, etc., is incalculable; but it is considerable.

It is indisputable that such a family needs special services, special opportunities, special protections, a special environment, special teaching. To provide it within New York is especially difficult. Housing in New York is scarce. Temptations are abundant. Demoralization is a special problem. Disadvantaged children, and incontinent mothers, might be better off—and certainly New York would be better off—in the country, with special schools, and special supervision, aimed at true rehabilitation. New York City has nothing to gain from keeping such persons within its metropolitan limits.

Let New York continue to accept the burden of their education, and board, and housing—but in another area. It is conceivable that it would greatly ease any number of New York's problems: the housing problem, the school problem, the crime problem, the narcotics problem: if welfare payments to such chronic cases were made available elsewhere, in areas established by New York City as great and humane rehabilitation centers. . . .

The free translation of this suggestion by John Lindsay and Senator Javits:

"Senator Javits . . . accused Mr. Buckley of advocating 'sending people on welfare to concentration camps.' " (*Times,* Oct. 19)

"Mr. Lindsay said his Conservative opponent . . . had advocated 'deportation camps' for welfare recipients. . . . 'The vile implications of what Buckley advocates, and Beame sees fit not to condemn,' he said, 'would destroy the last fiber of decency for every minority-group member and all citizens of New York.' " (*Tribune,* October 26)

"Senator Jacob Javits [charged that Buckley] wants to send welfare people to 'concentration camps.' " (*Times,* Oct. 29)

"John Lindsay angrily labeled this a proposal for 'concentration camps.' " (N. Y. *Post,* Oct. 31)

I managed to add fuel to the situation by advocating, in a position paper on the narcotics problem (see below) the forcible detention of narcotics addicts, it having become finally clear to me that narcotics addiction is a contagious disease: and this, of course, renewed the fever. But by this time, Abraham Beame's participation was clearly overdue. He tried to make up for the lost time by summoning the press on Friday afternoon, October 29, and reading his statement. The *Times* headlined:

BUCKLEY A CLOWN / BEAME DECLARES

Democrat Assails "Sinister"
Views of Conservatism

And reported:

Abraham D. Beame, [the article began], the Democratic candidate for Mayor, called William F. Buckley, Jr., yesterday a sinister "clown" whose campaign exploited fear, prejudice and hatred.

Mr. Beame insisted that the Buckley role as "spoiler" dedicated to the defeat of John V. Lindsay was "a sham and a fraud." Actually, Mr. Beame declared, Mr. Buckley's major effort has been directed at luring voters from the Democratic candidate.

"A vote for Buckley is not just a wasted vote—for he obviously cannot win—but it is a vote for Lindsay and national Republican philosophy, a vote to encourage the wild-eyed radicals of right extremism," Mr. Beame asserted.

"Perhaps the most dangerous facts in the New York campaign this year have gone unexposed because of the mask of humor. Comparatively few New Yorkers have taken William Buckley seriously because of an attitude of 'it can't happen here.'

"Nevertheless, behind his warped humor and twisted wit are sinister and evil philosophies. Mr. Buckley has not hesitated to conjure up repulsive images in the Machiavellian hope that a snicker would cover the deadly serious intent of his proposals.

"This Clown Prince of Politics has appealed to the base instincts of mankind. He has campaigned on a program of fear and prejudice, of hatred of neighbor for neighbor—concepts which have always been repugnant to New Yorkers. I believe his philosophy and program go beyond Goldwaterism.

"For example, Mr. Buckley's suggestion of concentration camps for drug addicts is frightening. Drug addicts today; which group would he quarantine tomorrow?" . . .

Back of the Beame broadside apparently was the realization in his camp that Representative Lindsay, the Republican-Liberal candidate, had a good thing in the theme that Mr. Buckley was a "spoiler" seeking the defeat of Mr. Lindsay and the eventual takeover of the Republican party by the radical right.

Just before Mr. Beame gave his views at a news conference at the Summit Hotel, his campaign manager, Edward N. Costikyan, conceded that in recent days many voters, frightened by warnings of an upsurge of the radical right, had swung to Mr. Lindsay. However, he contended, the trend was being reversed as voters realized that the rightist extremists had no chance of getting control of New York.

Mr. Lindsay commented last night that Mr. Beame had "belatedly discovered the ultra-reaction and the snarl of bigotry that lies behind the quip façade of William Buckley." . . .

The evening of the following day, I addressed the Conservatives' final rally of the campaign at Queens and acknowledged Beame's broadside, relating it to what had become the central theme of the campaign:

. . . Poor Mr. Beame. I am told I have neglected him. Perhaps I have. So, perhaps, will the voters of New York. Mr. Beame thought himself up a frenzy yesterday. In doing so, he appeared to be secretly jealous of Mr. Lindsay, because it was Mr. Lindsay who first discovered that anyone who is in favor of neighborhood schools; who opposes the politicalization of justice through a civilian review board; who scoffs in disbelief at the suggestion that the federal government is going to finance New York City's mania for spending tax dollars; who favors taking positive action to relieve New York City of the curse of drug addiction—it was Mr. Lindsay who first discovered that these ideas are best summed up in the haunting evocation of "concentration camps." So Mr. Beame lathers himself up and informs the city that "Mr. Buckley's suggestion of concentration camps for drug addicts is frightening. Drug addicts today; which group would he quarantine tomorrow?" (My answer is: lepers.)

Mr. Beame, you will have noticed, spent the first four weeks of the campaign resenting Mr. Lindsay's unfairness. Didn't Mr. Lindsay say that Mr. Beame was responsible for making New York City the heroin capital of the world? Mr. Beame's voice quivers with rage and resentment, a rage and resentment which I took to be a true reflection of his feelings. Mr. Beame was defended by gentlemen of the left and of the right, against so unfair an insinuation.

He even imported Franklin Roosevelt, Jr., to defend him against Mr. Lindsay's subsequent charge that Mr. Beame had prayed for an early death for Mrs. Roosevelt and Mr. Lehman, which indeed if it was the case, surely suggests that Mr. Beame's prayers are hardly efficacious, since Mrs. Roosevelt and Mr. Lehman took their own time in passing on to a better world. So Mr. Roosevelt, Jr., came to New York to denounce Mr. Lindsay—quite rightly, I believe, since Mr. Beame over the years clearly and consistently identified himself with the policies of Mrs. Roosevelt and Mr. Lehman— and to shrive Mr. Beame of any perfidious activities.

So we all felt sorry for Mr. Beame. That, it seems to me, is a little harder to do at this point. It has become a little bit like feeling sorry, as a result of all the insults hurled at him, for Drew Pearson. Now I repeat, Mr. Beame is, I feel quite sure, a very nice man, but I am no longer very sure that he is an honorable man, at least if one supposes that honor has any role to play in politics. If he does not know the difference between a quarantined hospital for sick people, and a concentration camp, I suggest that he ask someone who has been in a concentration camp what that difference is. If he feels that anyone who wants to quarantine drug addicts, because modern research clearly establishes that it is addicts themselves who spread the poison, is the kind of person who would want to quarantine other people just for the sake of it, then he must harbor deep suspicions of all doctors, and health inspectors, and statesmen who through the ages have believed that it is indeed the responsibility of society to protect itself from infectious diseases. By Mr. Beame's standard, Florence Nightingale was at heart a fascist. (As a matter of fact, Lytton Strachey was the first to make that discovery; but Mr. Strachey never asked the people of London to make him their Lord Mayor.)

The answer, of course, is that Mr. Beame believes no such thing, but that someone around him persuaded him yesterday or the day before yesterday, that he was losing the contest to hobgoblinize the conservative population of New York City. I can see it. "Abe," someone says, "Lindsay is getting a lot of publicity on the concentration camp bit. Why don't you upstage him, and suggest that the Conservative Party plans concentration camps for *everyone* in New York City?" Come on, Abe, show the voters that *you too* can be a demagogue. Mr. Beame replies, "I owe a great debt to New York City. I grew up in New York City. New York City sent me to college. I have worked for the city for thirty-five years. . . . I am the experienced candidate. . . ."[3] Yes, yes, Abe, just here. . . .

I expect that is how it went. And thus Mr. Beame showed himself fully qualified to earn the trust and respect of the voters *The New York Times* approves of. . . .

The next morning, at noon, the candidates assembled together with the two Marxist candidates for an hour's television show sponsored by the League of Women Voters—a wild show, it turned out to be, in part because literally all the mayoralty candidates were foregathered, for the first and only time, including the Socialist Worker and the Socialist Labor. I took my place between Mr. Lindsay—and Mr. Beame. He turned to me and whispered: "Bill, I was really sorry about that business Friday. I mean, about that *word*. When I read the statement to the press, I actually left it out." (Shades of Mr. Truman!) "Goddamnit, Mr. Beame," I whispered back, "What kind of good could that do—the press release went out with 'the word' in it—all the papers and radio and TV ran it—'concentration camps'—and I gave you hell for it last night at Queens." "I know," he said sadly, and went back to his notes.

I never before, or since, felt more keenly the benumbing cynicism of politics, and its devastating effect on people. My rage wasn't at Abe Beame, who so clearly had yielded to a committee document, which he dumbly endorsed; but at what it had done to him to sign it, since he now felt constrained, because of an irrepressible decency, to whisper his apologies to his antagonist. I was wild with impotent indignation and only remember pledging that some day I would record, for those who care, that the transparent cynicism of all that concentration-camp talk was not called by a single one of the egregious metropolitan moralizers who were busy identifying the advent of John Lindsay with a better day, a cleaner day, for New York politics, stressing his moral and spiritual superiority over the little bookkeeper whose conscience was the only one that stirred during those final bitter days.

There was a final surprise, two months after the election. It was at a large party, and the birds and beasts were there. The city editor of a major metropolitan newspaper, whom I have known slightly and pleasurably over the years, approached me amiably.

I thought, he said (in declining to quote him directly, in the absence of a transcript, I observe his own newspaper's high ethics)—I thought, he said, that you were a bright guy, but you sure fooled me. That last speech —that one phrase—cost you a hundred thousand votes.

I literally had no idea of what he was talking about.

You know—the business of the "vision of a new order." It lost you one hundred thousand votes.

I professed an astonished ignorance, and I do believe that he thought I was being coy. I wrenched it out of him. A "vision of a new order" is associated in the mind of every Jewish voter over thirty-five years old (he maintained) with Anne Morrow Lindbergh's book *The Wave of the Future, A Confession of Faith* (1940) hailing (his word) the forthcoming fascist order; and it was the opinion of this sophisticate that the use of those five words had sharply estranged, on Election Eve, 100,000 Jewish votes that would otherwise have come to me. He would not believe me when I told him that in the sixty days since the election I had not heard another soul mention the apparent indiscretion. (My exact words had been, in the wind-up talk televised on Election Eve: ". . . if the Conservatives roll up a substantial vote, it is the beginning of a new dawn for New York. I am not asking you to vote for me, but for a vision of a new order.") Now it was actually being suggested, by one of the most urbane and influential journalists in New York, that this had been a red flag flourished (however inadvertently—therein, he said, I had been merely "stupid") in the face of the Jewish community.

I disbelieve his analysis, let me note.[4] But I remain in awe that he should have thought as he did, which must mean that there are others who thought the same thoughts. CBS reported—I have no way of knowing whether it is so, but no reason to believe CBS would report other than the truth as its own researchers saw it—that I got only 3 per cent of New York's Jewish vote.

The afterthoughts. Let us not moralize, merely inquire. The usefulness for political purposes of the other fellow's racial or religious slurs, real or alleged, is tediously well known. The best known example in American political history is, of course, the Catholics' resentment of the "Rum, Romanism, and Rebellion" crack, the failure to disavow which is said to have cost James Blaine the Presidency. In contemporary history, La Guardia accused his opponent of anti-Semitism in 1933. Herbert Lehman accused John Foster Dulles of anti-Semitism in 1949. Samuel Stratton, seeking the Democratic gubernatorial nomination in 1962, was accused. Roughly everybody accused Barry Goldwater of (objective) anti-Negroism in 1964. Paul Rao of the Beame Team accused Moynihan of the Screvane Train of anti-Italianism. "The students at Benton," Randall

Jarrell wrote in his novel,[5] "yearned for the discovery of life on the moon, so that they could prove that *they* weren't prejudiced against moon-men." It is probable that for so long as groups of voters exist who are religiously or ethnically identifiable, political technicians will seek means by which to move them *qua* members of their creed, or race, and that the day after the day after tomorrow, a Saron will be calling a Swift, whether with or without the permission of his Kramarsky, to suggest means by which ethnic or religious or nationality group A can be brought to transfer its allegiance to B. And, that being the way with human beings, it is likelier that such movements can be stimulated by causing the group to be angered by A, than to be attracted by B: because—it is reluctantly conceded by most democratic theorists—voters tend to register their protests, rather than their affirmations: which, one pauses to observe, is not a bad convention.

The dilemma is part of the long shadow of the politics of the universal franchise. Once committed to the notion that anyone with (say) a sixth-grade education can vote—more, that anyone who can vote, should vote—it becomes necessary to accommodate to the fact that prejudice and passion and narrow self-interest are the proximate movers on Election Day for a heavy percentage of the voters. John Stuart Mill, so often thought of as the theoretical patron of the idea of the universal franchise, is not widely recognized as the author of the startling reservation, that of course he assumed that everyone who *did* vote, would vote with reference to the best interests of the community as he saw it, rather than merely his own. Mill, as Professor Harry Jaffa has so dramatically demonstrated ("On the Nature of Civil and Religious Liberty," *The Conservative Papers* [New York: Doubleday, 1963]), would have been disappointed in the workings of his axiomatic democracy at various times and places in the twentieth century. He would have been shocked at the extent to which the accommodation to the narrowest and most irrational concerns of the voters had gone—not by those modern politicians who are commonly accepted as demagogues but by those who are commonly accepted as not being such. *"Drug addicts today; which group would he quarantine tomorrow?"* The question is whether an attempt should be made to jam the dialogue between the demagogue and the masses: by the society's *ex officio* censors, the columnists, the editorial writers, the ministers, the preachers, the professors—again, the lords spiritual. "I once thought it would be amusing," Albert Jay Nock wrote, "to attempt an essay on how to go about discovering that one is living in a dark age." Surely one might begin by opening the newspapers and observing whether anybody is there, active and impartial, interfering with the flow of demagogy. I do indeed dream, wistfully, of a vision of a new order. But I also recognize that this may be a form of rationalist utopianism, and that rationalists have as much business in politics as—to use the most absurd example that comes to mind—I do.

N O T E S

1. Well, a dozen. Sample: "To win in November, Lindsay must strengthen his appeal with these wavering Jewish voters . . ." (Samuel Lubell, October 11, 1965). "In trumpeting the charge that 'A vote for Buckley is a vote for Goldwater,' the Lindsay camp seems to be appealing to . . . Jewish Democrats who are likely to be alarmed by nothing so much as a threat from the right wing" (Richard Witkin, *The New York Times*, October 26, 1965). See also: New York *Post*, October 21, 1965; *National Observer*, October 25, 1965; Samuel Lubell, New York *World-Telegram*, October 13, 1965 and October 26, 1965; *The New York Times*, October 28, 1965; etc., etc.

2. The article finished: "Only Buckley seemed to be enjoying himself in the radio studio." (I wasn't enjoying myself; I sensed that, in fact, Lindsay had got the better of the situation, that though he had forced me to say what was in fact true, I had nevertheless hurt myself rather than Lindsay. By merely affirming that some Jewish votes were deployable, I wounded more feelings than the candidate who had tried to deploy them.) ". . . after Beame, who holds a degree in accountancy, accused Buckley of initating 'a vicious conspiracy,' Buckley airily said: 'it seems I'm involved in so many conspiracies that it takes an accountant to keep track of them.' "

3. These were the lines with which Mr. Beame usually opened, and closed, his public appearances, *i.e.*, his public signature.

4. Shortly before this manuscript was finished, I received a letter, the only letter on the subject I ever received, from a gentleman who used the stationery of the 92nd Street Young Men's and Young Women's Hebrew Association: "Bill baby," it began; ". . . It is common knowledge that the Nazis used the term 'New Order' to describe the Third Reich. I cannot accept as pure coincidence your utterance . . . to the effect that: 'a vision of a new order' was in sight. Just what were you trying to say Bill, baby? No one chooses those terms without a knowledge of their former meaning and significance. Not even you. Especially not you."

5. Randall Jarrell, *Pictures from an Institution* (New York: Knopf, 1955).

5.

Religious Tensions During Lindsay's Campaign

OLIVER PILAT

Friday, October 15

THE PERSISTENT TENSION AND SHRILLNESS OF THE CAMPAIGN NOWADAYS are nerve-wracking at close range. I wonder how much of what is actually happening percolates through the excitement and the noise to the public. If an election can be considered a man-to-man struggle, then Lindsay is carrying the fight to Buckley after forcing Beame temporarily to step aside. Last night Lindsay appeared before an almost totally hostile audience of 800 at a Parents and Taxpayers Association meeting in Queens. According to PAT officials, Beame accepted an invitation to address this group but he did not appear and when asked by reporters about it over the telephone he asserted blandly that the invitation never reached him.

As Lindsay and a half dozen others of us moved into the Richmond Hill High School auditorium, keeping close together in instinctive self-protection, the heat could be felt immediately. "Here's the gang that supports John JUDAS Lindsay," roared one fellow wearing an orange Buckley button who readily gave his name and address to reporters. The whole audience seemed to be wearing orange buttons. When Lindsay began to speak his words could scarcely be heard over the heckling. "If you'll stop being rude," he said at one point, in his faintly English manner, "we'll get to it."

Lindsay had the nerve to broach his plan for a civilian review board in the police department. Booing began immediately. "I'll tell you this: it will do more to reduce tension in this city than anything else." More booing. "It will help the police." The booing became so loud and continuous that his remarks were blanketed for a while. The metamorphosis of audience into mob was occurring before our eyes. "Down with Lindsay —shoot him in the back" shouted one fat man as we started to leave the auditorium.

A question popped into my mind which I could not answer then or now: Was Lindsay being inflammatory accidentally, instinctively, or deliberately, to reveal the rabid quality of the Buckley opposition? From two advance men left behind to report by radio-telephone we learned that Buckley entered the school auditorium to hysterical applause with a personal escort of six policemen headed by Captain John Peterson of the 102d precinct. The pandemonium did not subside as Buckley deftly plucked at alarmist strings in his harpsichord. Unlike the members of his own all Irish-Catholic slate, he said without any particular emphasis, Lindsay is a "white Protestant." Lindsay and Beame do not dare to attack Powell, he added, because Powell is a Negro. So it went.

Today our headquarters released a 22-page booklet on the restoration of fiscal stability in New York. Lindsay tried to expand on this at his morning news conference but the reporters were bent on headier things. They wanted comment on Buckley's white-Protestant and Negro references and they were determined to get it, one way or another. Lindsay responded with a comparison between Barry Goldwater and Buckley.

"I was never quite sure Senator Goldwater knew the consequences of his acts," he said. "Buckley does. That makes him doubly dangerous. In the streets, the Buckley campaign becomes a racist campaign, but let me emphasize that I am not saying Buckley is personnally a racist. This kind of campaign plays on public apprehension. The next mayor will have to face the fear which now grips the city. Fear, as you know, can be as dangerous and epidemic as any disease."

Under persistent questioning, he gave them what they wanted. "The city," he said, "is a powder keg, and Buckley is doing his best to light the fuse."

Saturday–Sunday, October 16–17

One way of exploiting religious prejudice in a campaign is to accuse the opposition of raising the issue. This is particularly effective if it is true. Getting outsiders to make the accusation has obvious tactical advantages. Accordingly, a citywide group of four Rabbis and five Protestant ministers, most of whose names are quite familiar at headquarters, have protested the "incident" at Richmond Hill High School. Their statement, prepared by a minister very favorable to Lindsay, was issued outside headquarters on unidentifiable sheets of paper.

"As clergymen," they said, "we deeply regret that Mr. Buckley resorted to racial and religious slurs. Elections are to increase the vigor and efficiency of community administration—not to create divisions and rasp past frictions. The incident is especially shocking inasmuch as eyewitnesses suggest that Mr. Buckley was 'playing' to already unruly bigots in the audience. Mr. Buckley should, we believe, apologize for his unruly remarks."

Somewhat later and perhaps more spontaneously the Flatbush Ministers Council, representing fifteen churches in that central area of Brooklyn, called Buckley "cheap and underhanded" for citing Lindsay's WASPishness at the PAT meeting. The leader of this group cited Buckley's expressed hope of exercising "a form of cultural leadership in a nation of moral imagination," and added: "We suggest to the candidate that his unethical attitude on Mr. Lindsay's religious affiliation makes him a poor choice for such leadership."

Buckley had hardly finished explaining that nothing was farther from his intention than bias of any kind when Costello* attacked him on religious grounds. Costello's remarks were not cleared in advance at headquarters. They were not expected. The effect of them was to reverse our favorable position in the religious controversy at the worst possible time.

Costello's deeply engrained liberal Catholicism was one of his qualifications for inclusion on the fusion slate. He may have blundered in this instance but I do not intend to join in the susurrus of unfriendly comment at headquarters among the GOP stalwarts who are always ready to criticise the Liberal party. I am sure Professor Costello spoke carefully after considerable thought.

What he said was sweeping enough: that Buckley's "negative, divisive preachings are a threat to peace on earth, progress in the nation, the uplifting of our city, and the propagation of social doctrine of the Catholic Church."

In a Fordham University talk during which he mentioned favorably the names of the late Cardinal Hayes, Cardinal Spellman, Monsignor Harry Byrne, Father Henry Brown, Father Ahearn, Father Fitzpatrick, the Dominican Sisters, the Nursing Sisters of the Sick Poor (whom he serves as a consultant), the Carmelites, and various others, ranging from Mother Seton to Mother Cabrini, Costello added: "All of us, as New Yorkers, as Americans, and as Catholics, were inspired by Pope Paul's peace mission to the United Nations, yet the radical right, including spokesmen like Bill Buckley, can only mock that world organization for peace.

*Dr. Timothy Costello was Lindsay's running-mate for the position of City Council President—Ed.

"Our Church is no new combatant in the war on poverty, injustice, and man's inhumanity to man and in the war against war itself, yet Mr. Buckley could smirk at the magnificent encyclical of the beloved Pope John, 'Pacem in Terris,' as a mere 'venture in triviality.'

"And on Pope John's other great encyclical, Mr. Buckley could only parrot: 'Mater, si, Magister, no.' This is no longer corrosive wit. This is corrosion. . . ."

Costikyan, the Protestant campaign manager of a Jewish candidate for mayor, issued a statement begging the two Catholic candidates to halt their "reckless and headlong flight into the gutter." He indicated his preference between them by characterizing Costello's attack on Buckley as "the lowest tactic of the campaign."

"When you speak of convictions," replied Costello, "you have to let such matters as tactics take care of themselves."

He soon discovered how primitive the reaction to a religious issue can be at the street level. During a walking tour Saturday afternoon in the Astoria and Sunnyside sections of Queens he was jeered in unruly unison by the Birchite pickets who normally hounded Lindsay. One shopkeeper called him a Communist while a nearby woman shopper praised him for "guts." Some passersby scowled and walked away from him, others shook his hand with unusual warmth.

In response to a panicky phone call in the late afternoon, Costello and his entourage hurried to Queens Liberal party headquarters in Jamaica While everybody was out taking part in the walking tours the place had been entered, apparently by means of a skeleton key. Vandals had smashed desks and chairs, pulled telephones from the wall, overturned filing cabinets, torn up files, and spread a layer of garbage over the debris.

Buckley himself took a sophisticated approach to the controversy. "If I am a bad Catholic," he said in one of a series of Sunday TV appearances, "I shall be punished by Someone I fear far more than the New York Catholic voters. To whom I say this: I don't want your vote for me because I am a Catholic. I want your vote for me because of the positions I take."

Having made this claim, Buckley went on to defend his right to take positions. He would always "listen respectfully" to the views of Pope Paul or Pope John on the UN, civil rights, or other matters, he said, but he was not required to share their views. "A Pope can direct me to love Mr. Khrushchev in the abstract but he cannot direct me to love the United Nations or the World's Fair. To imply that I am anti-Catholic is as convincing as to imply that Mr. Beame is anti-Semitic which, at this rate, Mr. Lindsay will be doing next week."

6.

The Making of the Negro Mayors, 1967

JEFFREY K. HADDEN

LOUIS H. MASOTTI

VICTOR THIESSEN

THROUGHOUT MOST OF 1967, BLACK POWER AND VIETNAM KEPT THIS nation in an almost continual state of crisis. The summer months were the longest and hottest in modern U.S. history—many political analysts even felt that the nation was entering its most serious domestic conflict since the Civil War. Over a hundred cities were rocked with violence.

As the summer gave way to autumn, the interest of the nation shifted a little from the summer's riots to the elections on the first Tuesday of November. An unprecedented number of Negroes were running for office, but public attention focused on three elections. In Cleveland, Carl B. Stokes, a lawyer who in 1962 had become the first Democratic Negro legislator in Ohio, was now seeking to become the first Negro mayor of a large American city. In Gary, Indiana, a young Negro lawyer, Richard D. Hatcher, was battling the Republican Party's candidate—as well as his own Democratic Party—to become the first Negro mayor of a "medium-sized" city. And in Boston, Louise Day Hicks, a symbol of white backlash, was conducting a "You know where I stand" campaign to capture the mayoralty.

Normally, the nation couldn't care less about who would become the next mayors of Cleveland, Gary, and Boston, but the tenseness of the summer months gave these elections enormous significance. If Stokes and Hatcher lost and Hicks won, could Negroes be persuaded to use the power of the ballot box rather than the power of fire bombs?

Fortunately, November 7 proved to be a triumphant day for racial peace. Stokes and Hatcher won squeaker victories, both by margins of only about 1,500 votes; in Boston, Kevin H. White defeated Mrs. Hicks by a 12,000 plurality. Labor leader George Meany was exultant—"American voters have rejected racism as a political issue." Negroes in the three cities were also jubilant. In Gary, the most tense of the cities, Richard Hatcher urged the mostly Negro crowd at his headquarters to "cool it." "I urge that the outcome of this election be unmarred by any incident of any kind. . . . If we spoil this victory with any kind of occurrence here tonight, or anywhere in the city, it will be a hollow victory." The evening *was* cool: joyous Negroes danced and sang in the streets.

But beyond the exultation of victory remain many hard questions. Now that Cleveland and Gary have Negro mayors, just how much difference will it make in solving the many grave problems that these cities face? Will these victories cool militancy in urban ghettos or will the momentum of frustration prove too great to put on the brakes? A careful analysis of how these candidates won office may help provide the answers.

The focus of this report is on Cleveland because as residents of Cleveland, we are more familiar with the campaign and the election, and . . . . . because, in 1965, [Cleveland] had a special census. By matching voting wards with census tracts, we can draw a clearer picture of voting behavior than we could in the other cities, where rapid neighborhood transitions have made 1960 census data quite unreliable in assessing voting patterns. Having examined Cleveland in some detail, we will draw some comparisons with the Gary and Boston elections, then speculate about their significance and implications.

Cleveland—City in Decline

Cleveland has something less than 2,000,000 residents. Among metropolitan areas in America, it ranks eleventh in size. Like many other American cities, the central city of Cleveland is experiencing an absolute decline in population—residents are fleeing from the decaying core to the surrounding suburbs. The city certainly ranks high both in absolute and proportional decline in the central-city population.

Between 1950 and 1960, the population of the central city declined from 914,808 to 876,050, a loss of almost 39,000. By 1965 the population had sunk to 810,858, an additional loss of 65,000. But these figures are only a partial reflection of the changing composition of the population, since new Negro residents coming into the central city helped offset the white exodus. *Between 1950 and 1960, nearly 142,000 white residents left the central city, and an additional 94,000 left between 1960 and 1965 —nearly a quarter of a million in just fifteen years.*

During the same period the number of Negro residents of Cleveland rose from 147,847 to 279,352—an increase from 16.1 per cent to 34.4 per cent of the city's population. There is no evidence that this dramatic population redistribution has changed since the special 1965 census. Some suburbanization of Negroes is beginning on the east and southeast side of the city, but the pace is not nearly so dramatic as for whites. In 1960, approximately 97 per cent of the Negroes in the metropolitan area lived in the central city. This percentage has probably declined somewhat since then—16,000 Negro residents have moved to East Cleveland. But the basic pattern of segregation in the metropolitan area remains. The development in East Cleveland is little more than an eastward extension of the ghetto, and the older, decaying residential units the Negroes have moved to are hardly "suburban" in character.

While the population composition of Cleveland is changing rapidly, whites are still a significant majority—about 62 per cent. Again like many other central cities, a significant percentage of the white population comprises nationality groups that live in segregated sections, with a strong sense of ethnic identity and a deep fear of Negro encroachment. (In 1964, the bussing of Negro students into Murray Hill, an Italian neighborhood, resulted in rioting.)

In 1960, the census classified 43 per cent of the central city's white residents as "foreign stock." In that year, five groups—Germans, Poles, Czechs, Hungarians, and Italians—had populations of 25,000 or greater; at least twenty other nationality groups were large enough to be contended with in the political arena. But today these ethnic groups—although unwilling to admit it—have become less than the controlling majority they constituted before 1960.

The Cuyahoga River divides Cleveland, physically as well as socially. When Negroes first began to move into the city, during World War I, they occupied the decaying section to the south and east of the central business district. As their numbers grew, they continued pushing in this direction and now occupy the larger part of the eastside (except for some ethnic strongholds). There are no stable, integrated neighborhoods in the central city—only areas in transition from white to black. To the west, the Cuyahoga River constitutes a barrier to Negro penetration.

Ever since 1941, when Frank Lausche was elected, Cleveland has had a succession of basically honest but unimaginative Democratic mayors. These mayors have kept their hold on City Hall by means of a relatively weak coalition of nationality groups. At no point in this twenty-six-year dynasty did a mayor gather enough power to seriously confront the long-range needs and problems of the city.

By early 1967, the city had seemingly hit rock bottom. A long procession of reporters began arriving to write about its many problems. The racial unrest of the past several years had, during the summer of 1966, culminated in the worst rioting in Cleveland's history. This unrest was continuing to grow as several militant groups were organizing. Urban renewal was a dismal failure; in January, the Department of Housing and Urban Development even cut off the city's urban-renewal funds, the first such action by the Federal Government. The exodus of whites, along with business, shoved the city to the brink of financial disaster. In February, the Moody Bond Survey reduced the city's credit rating. In May, the Federal Government cut off several million dollars of construction funds —because the construction industry had failed to assure equal job opportunities for minority groups. In short, the city was, and remains, in deep trouble. While most ethnic groups probably continued to believe that Cleveland was the "Best Location in the Nation," the Negro community—and a growing number of whites—were beginning to feel that Cleveland was the "Mistake on the Lake," and that it was time for a change.

Carl Stokes's campaign for mayor was his second try. In 1965, while serving in the state House of Representatives, he came within 2100 votes of defeating Mayor Ralph S. Locher. Stokes had taken advantage of a city-charter provision that lets a candidate file as an independent, and bypass the partisan primaries. Ralph McAllister, then president of the Cleveland School Board, did the same. For his hard line on *de facto* school segregation, however, McAllister had earned the enmity of the Negro community. The Republican candidate was Ralph Perk, the first Republican elected to a county-wide position (auditor) in many years. A second generation Czech-Bohemian, Perk hoped to win by combining his ethnic appeal with his program for the city (Perk's Plan). He had no opposition for his party's nomination. The fourth candidate was Mayor Locher, who had defeated Mark McElroy, county recorder and perennial candidate for something, in the Democratic primary.

It was in the 1965 Democratic primary that the first signs of a "black bloc" vote emerged. The Negroes, who had previously supported incumbent Democratic mayoral candidates, if not enthusiastically at least consistently, made a concerted effort to dump Locher in favor of McElroy. There were two reasons. 1. Locher had supported his police chief after the latter had made some tactless remarks about Negroes. Incensed Negro leaders demanded an audience with the mayor, and when he refused, his office was the scene of demonstrations, sit-ins, and arrests. At that point, as one of the local reporters put it, "Ralph Locher became a dirty name in the ghetto." 2. Stokes, as an independent, and his supporters hoped that the Democratic primary would eliminate the stronger candidate, Locher. For then a black bloc would have a good chance of deciding the general election because of an even split in the white vote.

Despite the Negro community's efforts, Locher won the primary and went on to narrowly defeat Stokes. Locher received 37 per cent of the vote, Stokes 36 per cent, Perk 17 per cent, and McAllister 9 per cent. Some observers reported that a last-minute whispering campaign in Republican precincts—to the effect that "A vote for Perk is a vote for Stokes"—may have given Locher enough Republican votes to win. The evidence: The popular Perk received only a 17 per cent vote in a city where a Republican could count on something closer to 25 per cent. Had Perk gotten anything close to 25 per cent, Stokes would have probably been elected two years earlier.

Although he made a strong showing in defeat, Carl Stokes' political future looked bleak. No one expected the Democratic leaders to give Stokes another opportunity to win by means of a split vote. Nor were there other desirable elected offices Stokes could seek. Cleveland has no Negro Congressman—largely because the heavy Negro concentration in the city has been "conveniently" gerrymandered. The only district where Stokes might have had a chance has been represented by Charles Vanik, a popular and liberal white, and as long as Vanik remained in Congress Stokes was locked out. Stokes's state Senate district was predominantly white; and a county or state office seemed politically unrealistic because of his race. So, in 1966, Stokes sought re-election to the state House unopposed.

Between 1965 and 1967, Cleveland went from bad to worse, physically, socially, and financially. With no other immediate possibilities, Stokes began to think about running for mayor again. The big question was whether to risk taking on Locher in the primary—or to file as an independent again.

The Primary Race

In effect, Stokes's decision was made for him. Seth Taft, slated to be the Republican candidate, told Stokes he would withdraw from the election entirely if Stokes filed as an independent in order to gain the advantage of a three-man general election. Taft had concluded that his best strategy was to face a Negro, alone, or a faltering incumbent, alone, in the general election, but not both. In a three-man race with Locher and Stokes, Taft correctly assumed that he would be the man in the middle with no chance for victory. (Taft would have preferred to run as an independent—to gain Democratic votes—but the county Republican leader threatened to file another Republican candidate unless Taft ran as a Republican.)

Meanwhile, Locher committed blunder after blunder—and Democratic party leaders began to question whether he could actually win another election. In the weeks before filing for the primary, Democratic leaders even pressured Locher to accept a Federal judgeship and clear the way for the president of the city council to run. But the Democratic leaders in Cleveland are not noted for their strength or effectiveness, as is evidenced by the fact that none of the Democratic mayors since 1941 were endorsed by the party when they were first elected. When Locher refused to withdraw, the party reluctantly rallied behind him.

Another Democratic candidate was Frank P. Celeste, former mayor of the Republican westside suburb of Lakewood. Celeste established residency in the city, announced his candidacy early, and—despite pressure from the Democratic Party—remained in the primary race.

There was always the possibility that Celeste would withdraw from the primary, which would leave Stokes facing Locher alone. But the threat of Taft's withdrawal from the general election left Stokes with little choice but to face Locher head-on in the primary. A primary race against Locher and a strong Democrat was more appealing than a general election against Locher and a weak Republican.

Now, in 1965 Stokes had received only about 6,000 white votes in the city in a 239,000 voter turnout. To win in the primary, he had to enlarge and consolidate the Negro vote—and increase his white support on the westside and in the eastside ethnic wards.

The first part of his strategy was a massive voter-registration drive in the Negro wards—to reinstate the potential Stokes voters dropped from the rolls for failing to vote since the 1964 Presidential election. The Stokes organization—aided by Martin Luther King Jr. and the Southern Christian Leadership Conference, as well as by a grant (in part earmarked for voter registration) from the Ford Foundation to the Cleveland chapter of CORE—did succeed in registering many Negroes. But there was a similar drive mounted by the Democratic Party on behalf of Locher. (Registration figures are not available by race.)

The second part of the Stokes strategy took him across the polluted Cuyahoga River into the white wards that had given him a mere 3 per cent of the vote in 1965. He spoke wherever he would be received—to small groups in private homes, in churches, and in public and private halls. While he was not always received enthusiastically, he did not confront many hostile crowds. He faced the race issues squarely and encouraged his audience to judge him on his ability.

Stokes's campaign received a big boost when the *Plain Dealer*, the largest daily in Ohio, endorsed him. Next, the *Cleveland Press* called for a change in City Hall, but declined to endorse either Stokes or Celeste. But since the polls indicated that Celeste was doing very badly, this amounted to an endorsement of Stokes.

More people voted in this primary than in any other in Cleveland's

TABLE I

	City Totals			Negro Wards		
	1965 General	1967 Primary	1967 General	1965 General	1967 Primary	1967 General
Registered Voters	337,803	326,003	326,003	103,123	99,885	99,885
Turnout	239,479	210,926	257,157	74,396	73,360	79,591
% Turnout	70.9	64.7	78.9	72.1	73.4	79.7
Stokes Votes	85,716	110,769	129,829	63,550	70,575	75,586
% Stokes Votes	35.8	52.5	50.5	85.4	96.2	95.0

	White Wards			Mixed Wards		
	1965 General	1967 Primary	1967 General	1965 General	1967 Primary	1967 General
Registered Voters	159,419	152,737	152,737	75,261	73,421	73,421
Turnout	111,129	88,525	119,883	53,962	49,105	57,113
% Turnout	69.7	58.0	78.5	71.7	66.9	77.8
Stokes Votes	3,300	13,495	23,158	18,866	26,699	30,872
% Stokes Votes	3.0	15.2	19.3	35.0	54.4	54.1

history. When the ballots were counted, Stokes had 52.5 per cent of the votes—he had defeated Locher by a plurality of 18,000 votes. Celeste was the man in the middle, getting only 4 per cent of the votes, the lowest of any mayoral candidate in recent Cleveland history.

What produced Stokes's clear victory? Table I reveals the answer. The decisive factor was the size of the Negro turnout. While Negroes constituted only about 40 per cent of the voters, 73.4 per cent of them turned out, compared with only 58.4 per cent of the whites. Predominantly Negro wards cast 96.2 per cent of their votes for Stokes. (Actually this figure underrepresents the Negro vote for Stokes, since some of the non-Stokes votes in these wards were cast by whites. Similarly, the 15.4 per cent vote for Stokes in the predominantly white wards slightly overestimates the white vote because of the Negro minority.)

Newspaper and magazine reports of the primary election proclaimed that Stokes could not have won without the white vote. Our own estimate—based on matching wards with census tracts, and allowing for only slight shifts in racial composition in some wards since the 1965 special census—is that Stokes received 16,000 white votes. His margin of victory was 18,000. How would the voting have gone if the third man, Celeste, had not been in the race? Many white voters, feeling that Stokes could not win in a two-man race, might not have bothered to vote at all, so perhaps Stokes would have won by an even larger margin. Thus Stokes's inroad into the white vote was not the decisive factor in his primary victory, although it was important.

Stokes emerged from the primary as the odds-on favorite to win five weeks later in the general election. In the first few days of the campaign, it seemed that Stokes had everything going for him. [He] was bright, handsome, and articulate. His opponent, Seth Taft, while bright, had never won an election, and his family name, associated with the Taft-Hartley Act, could hardly be an advantage among union members. In addition, he was shy and seemingly uncomfortable in a crowd. Both the *Plain Dealer* and the *Cleveland Press* endorsed Stokes in the general election. The wounds of the primary were quickly (if perhaps superficially) healed, and the Democratic candidate was endorsed by both the Democratic Party and Mayor Locher. Labor—both the A.F.L.-C.I.O. and the Teamsters—also endorsed Stokes, [who also] had a partisan advantage. Of the 326,003 registered voters, only 34,000 (10 per cent) were Republican. The closest any Republican mayoral candidate had come to winning was in 1951, when—in a small turnout—William J. McDermott received 45 per cent of the vote. Stokes had 90,000 or more Negro votes virtually assured, with little possibility that Taft would make more than slight inroads. Perhaps most important, voting-behavior studies over the years have demonstrated that voters who are confronted by a dilemma react by staying home from the polls. Large numbers of life-long Democrats, faced with voting for a Negro or a Republican by the name of Taft, were likely to stay home.

Had this been a normal election, Democrat Carl Stokes would have won handily. But this was not destined to be a normal election. During the final days of the campaign, Stokes knew he was in a fight for his political life. Those who predicted that the cross pressures would keep many voters away from the polls forgot that the variable "Negro" had never been involved in an election of this importance.

On Election Day, an estimated 90 per cent of those who voted for Locher or Celeste in the Democratic primary shifted to Taft—many pulling a Republican lever for the first time in their life. Was this clearly an unequivocally bigoted backlash? To be sure, bigotry did play a major role in the election. But to dismiss the campaign and the election as pure overt bigotry is to miss the significance of what happened in Cleveland and the emerging subtle nature of prejudice in American society.

The Non-Issue of Race

A closer look at the personal characteristics and campaign strategy of Seth Taft, the Republican candidate, reveals the complexity and subtlety of the race issue.

In the final days of the Democratic primary campaign, Taft repeatedly told reporters that he would rather run against Locher and his record than against Carl Stokes. On the evening of the primary, Taft appeared at Stokes's headquarters to congratulate him. As far as he was concerned, Taft said, the campaign issue was, Who could present the most constructive program for change in Cleveland? Further, he said he didn't want people voting for him simply because he was white. A few days later, Taft even presented a strongly-worded statement to his campaign workers:

"The Cuyahoga Democratic party has issued a number of vicious statements concerning the candidacy of Carl Stokes, and others have conducted whisper campaigns. We cannot tolerate injection of race into this campaign. . . . Many people will vote for Carl Stokes because he is a Negro. Many people will vote for me because I am white. I regret this fact. I will work hard to convince people they should not vote on a racial basis."

Seth Taft's programs to solve racial tensions may have been paternalistic, not really perceptive of emerging moods of the ghetto. But one thing is clear—he was not a bigot. Every indication is that he remained uncomfortable about being in a race in which his chances to win depended, in large part, upon a backlash vote.

Whether Taft's attempt to silence the race issue was a deliberate strategy or a reflection of deep personal feelings, it probably enhanced his chances of winning. He knew that he had the hard-core bigot vote. His task was to convince those in the middle that they could vote for him and not be bigots.

Stokes, on the other hand, had another kind of problem. While he had to draw more white votes, he also had to retain and, if possible, increase the 73 per cent Negro turnout that had delivered him 96 per cent of the Negro votes in the primary. Stokes's campaign leaders feared a fall-off in the voter turnout from Negro wards—with good reason. The entire primary campaign had pushed the October 3 date so hard that some Negroes could not understand why Carl Stokes was not mayor on October 4. Full-page newspaper ads paid for by CORE had stated, "If you don't vote Oct. 3rd, forget it. The man who wins will be the next mayor of Cleveland!" So Stokes felt he had to remobilize the Negro vote.

The moment came during the question-and-answer period of the second of four debates with Taft in the all-white westside. Stokes said: "The personal analysis of Seth Taft—and the analysis of many competent political analysts—is that Seth Taft may win the November 7 election, but for only one reason. That reason is that his skin happens to be white." The predominantly white crowd booed loudly and angrily for several minutes, and throughout the rest of the evening repeatedly interrupted him. Later, Stokes's campaign manager revealed that his candidate's remark was a calculated risk to arouse Negro interest. Stokes probably succeeded, but he also gave Taft supporters an excuse to bring the race issue into the open. And they could claim that it was Stokes, not Taft, who was trying to exploit the race issue.

To be sure, both candidates exploited the race issue. But, for the most part, it was done rather subtly. Stokes's campaign posters stated, "Let's do Cleveland Proud"—another way of saying, "Let's show the world that Cleveland is capable of rising above racial bigotry." A full-page ad for Stokes stated in bold print, "Vote for Seth Taft. It Would Be Easy, Wouldn't It?" After the debate, Taft was free to accuse Stokes of using the race issue—itself a subtle way of exploiting the issue. Then there was the letter, signed by the leaders of twenty-two nationality clubs, that was mailed to 40,000 members in the city. It didn't mention race, but comments such as "protecting our way of life," "safeguard our liberty," and "false charges of police brutality" were blatant in their implications. Taft sidestepped comment on the letter.

No matter how much the candidates may have wanted to keep race out of the picture, race turned out to be the most important issue. Both Taft and Stokes could benefit from the issue if they played it right, and both did use it. And although the Stokes's remark at the second debate gave white voters an excuse to vote for Taft without feeling that they were bigots, many whites probably would have found another excuse.

Taft as a Strategist

The fact is that Taft, for all his lackluster qualities, emerged as a strong candidate. He was able to turn many of his liabilities into assets. He was able to insulate himself against his Republican identity. He successfully dissociated himself from his uncle's position on labor by pointing to his own active role, as a student, against "right to work" laws. At the same time, he hit hard at Stokes' record as an off again–on again Democrat. This strategy neutralized, at least in part, Taft's first political disadvantage —running as a Republican in a Democratic city.

A second liability was that he came from a wealthy family. Taft was an Ivy League intellectual, cast in the role of a "do-gooder." He lived in an exclusive suburb, Pepper Pike, and had bought a modest home in Cleveland only a few weeks before declaring his candidacy. How, it was frequently asked, could such a man understand the problems of the inner-city and of the poor? Almost invariably the answer was: "Did John F. Kennedy, Franklin D. Roosevelt, and Nelson Rockefeller have to be poor in order to understand and respond to the problems of the poor?" Taft's campaign posters were a side profile that bore a striking resemblance to President Kennedy. Whether he was consciously exploiting the Kennedy image is an open question. But there can be little doubt that when Taft

TABLE II

PERCENT STOKES VOTE BY WARD

WHITE WARDS	% Negro	1965 General	1967 Primary	1967 General
1	.6	3.2	17.2	20.5
2	.3	1.9	12.8	17.4
3	.9	2.5	13.6	22.1
4	.3	3.0	18.2	20.9
5	.6	1.7	11.8	17.8
6	.8	2.3	15.1	16.7
7	.6	3.4	16.5	23.7
8	3.0	6.1	24.7	29.3
9	.2	1.9	12.4	16.4
14	1.4	1.1	12.7	13.0
15	1.4	1.2	9.2	14.1
22	5.7	8.1	22.5	26.3
26	1.1	2.8	16.3	19.9
32	2.4	2.9	10.0	15.3
33	.3	2.5	17.7	21.4
Average		3.0	15.2	19.3
NEGRO WARDS				
10	91.3	88.7	97.3	96.7
11	91.8	86.3	95.9	96.0
12	82.7	76.9	90.4	90.5
13	75.2	75.8	90.7	88.4
17	99.0	86.6	98.1	97.9
18	89.3	84.0	96.0	95.7
20	91.0	83.0	95.0	92.8
24	92.6	90.6	98.1	98.1
25	90.9	91.3	98.4	98.2
27	85.7	85.2	95.6	94.0
Average		85.4	96.2	95.0
MIXED WARDS				
16	56.6	50.7	69.9	70.1
19	25.3	29.2	48.0	39.9
21	61.1	55.2	66.3	68.9
23	20.3	9.8	18.2	23.2
28	28.5	26.5	54.8	57.3
29	24.4	26.8	43.2	42.3
30	51.7	51.5	75.3	71.4
31	21.8	16.9	31.8	39.0
Average		35.0	54.4	54.1

mentioned his Republican heritage, he tried to project an image of the new breed of Republican—John Lindsay and Charles Percy. This image didn't come across very well at first, but as he became a seasoned campaigner it became clearer.

Another liability was that Taft had never held an elected office. His opponent tried to exploit this—unsuccessfully. Taft could point to twenty years of active civic service, including the fact that he was one of the authors of the Ohio fair-housing law. Then too, the charge gave Taft an opportunity to point out that Stokes had the worst absentee record of anyone in the state legislature. Stokes never successfully answered this charge until the last of their four debates, when he produced a pre-campaign letter from Taft commending him on his legislative service. But this came moments after the TV cameras had gone off.

Still another liability emerged during the campaign. Taft's strategy of discussing programs, not personalities, was seemingly getting him nowhere. He presented specific proposals; Stokes, a skilled debater, succeeded in picking them apart. Stokes himself discussed programs only at a general level and contended that he was best-qualified to "cut the red tape" in Washington. His frequent trips to Washington to confer with top Government officials, before and during the campaign, indicated that he had the inside track. Taft, realizing at this point that his campaign was not gaining much momentum, suddenly switched gears and began attacking Stokes' record (not Stokes personally). Stokes had claimed he would crack down on slumlords. Taft discovered that Stokes owned a piece of rental property with several code violations—and that it had not been repaired despite an order from the city. He hit hard at Stokes's absenteeism and his record as a "good" Democrat. He put a "bird-dog" on Stokes and, if Stokes told one group one thing and another group something else, the public heard about it.

The upshot was that in the final days of the campaign Taft captured the momentum. Stokes was easily the more flashy debater and projected a superior image; but Taft emerged as the better strategist.

Should Taft Have Withdrawn?

One may ask whether all of this discussion is really relevant, since the final vote was sharply divided along racial lines. In one sense it is irrelevant, since it is possible that a weaker candidate than Taft might have run just as well. It is also possible that a white racist might actually have won. Still, this discussion has buttressed two important points. [1.] Taft was not all black, and Stokes was not all white. Taft proved a strong candidate, and—had he been running against Locher instead of Stokes—he might have amassed strong support from Negroes and defeated Locher. [2.] By being a strong candidate, Taft made it much easier for many white Democrats, who might otherwise have been cross-pressured into staying home, to come out and vote for him.

Some people felt that Taft should have withdrawn and let Stokes run uncontested. But many of the same people also decried white liberals who, at recent conferences to form coalitions between black-power advocates and the New Left, let black militants castrate them. It is not traditional in American politics that candidates enter a race to lose. Taft was in to win, and he fought a hard and relatively clean campaign—as high a compliment as can be paid to any candidate.

Yet all of this doesn't change the basic nature of the voting. This is clear from the evidence in Table II. Stokes won by holding his black bloc, and increasing his white vote from 15 per cent in the primary to almost 20 per cent in the general. An enormous amount of the white vote was, whether covert or overt, anti-Negro. It is hard to believe that Catholics, ethnic groups, and laborers who never voted for anyone but a Democrat should suddenly decide to evaluate candidates on their qualifications and programs, and—in overwhelming numbers—decide that the Republican candidate was better qualified. The implication is that they were prejudiced. But to assume that such people perceive themselves as bigots is to oversimplify the nature of prejudice. And to call such people bigots is to make their responses even more rigid—as Carl Stokes discovered after his remark in the second debate with Taft.

This, then, is perhaps an important lesson of the Cleveland election: bigotry cannot be defeated directly, by telling bigots that they are bigoted. For the most part Stokes learned this lesson well, accumulating as many as 30,000 white votes, nearly five times the number he received in 1965. But another slip like the one in the second debate might have cost him the election.

A few words on the voting for Stokes ward by ward, as shown in the table. Wards 9, 14, and 15—which gave Stokes a comparatively low vote —have the highest concentration of ethnic groups in the city. Not only is there the historical element of prejudice in these areas, but there is the ever-present fear among the residents that Negroes will invade their neighborhoods. (This fear is less a factor in ward 9, which is across the river.)

Wards 26 and 32 also gave Stokes a low percentage of votes, and these wards are also the ones most likely to have Negro migration. They are just to the north of East Cleveland, which is currently undergoing heavy transition, and to the east of ward 27, which in the past few years has changed from white to black. In these two wards, then, high ethnic composition and a fear of Negro migration would seem to account for Stokes's 19.9 and 15.3 percentages.

The highest percentage *for* Stokes in predominantly white areas was in wards 8 and 22. Ward 8 has a growing concentration of Puerto Ricans, and—according to newspaper polls—they voted heavily for Stokes. Ward 22 has a very large automobile-assembly plant that employs many Negroes. Now, in 1965 the ward was 5.7 per cent Negro—a large increase from 1960. Since 1965, this percentage has probably grown another 2 or 3 per cent. Therefore, if one subtracts the Negro vote that Stokes received in this ward, the size of the white vote is about the same as in other wards.

'Imminent Danger' in Gary

The race for mayor in Gary, Ind., was not overtly racist. Still, the racial issue was much less subtle than it was in Cleveland. When Democratic chairman John G. Krupa refused to support Richard D. Hatcher, the Democratic candidate, it was clear that the reason was race. When the Gary newspaper failed to give similar coverage to both candidates and sometimes failed to print news releases from Hatcher headquarters (ostensibly because press deadlines had not been met), it was clear that race was a factor.

Even though race was rarely mentioned openly, the city polarized. While Stokes had the support of the white-owned newspapers and many white campaign workers, many of Hatcher's white supporters preferred to remain in the background—in part, at least, because they feared reprisals from white racists. Hatcher didn't use the black-power slogan, but to the community the election was a contest between black and white. And when the Justice Department supported Hatcher's claim that the election board had illegally removed some 5,000 Negro voters from the registration lists and added nonexistent whites, the tension in the city became so great that the Governor, feeling that there was "imminent danger" of violence on election night, called up 4,000 National Guardsmen.

Negroes constitute an estimated 55 per cent of Gary's 180,000 residents, but white voter registration outnumbers Negroes by 2,000 or 3,000. Like Stokes, Hatcher—in order to win—had to pull some white votes, or have a significantly higher Negro turnout.

The voter turnout and voting patterns in Cleveland and Gary were very similar. In both cities, almost 80 per cent of the registered voters turned out at the polls. In the Glen Park and Miller areas, predominantly white neighborhoods, Joseph B. Radigan—Hatcher's opponent—received more than 90 per cent of the votes. In the predominantly Negro areas, Hatcher received an estimated 93 per cent of the votes. In all, Hatcher received about 4,000 white votes, while losing probably 1,000 Negro votes, at most, to Radigan. This relatively small white vote was enough to give him victory. If Stoke's miscalculation in bringing race into the Cleveland campaign gave prejudiced whites an excuse to vote for Taft, the glaring way the Democratic Party in Gary tried to defeat Hatcher probably tipped the scales and gave Hatcher some white votes he wouldn't have received otherwise.

The School Issue in Boston

The Boston election, unlike the Cleveland and Gary elections, didn't pose a Negro against a white, but a lackluster candidate—Kevin White —against a 48-year-old grandmother who had gained national attention over the past several years for her stand against school integration. On the surface, Mrs. Hicks seems to be an obvious racial bigot. But she herself has repeatedly denied charges that she is a racist, and many who have followed her closely claim that this description is too simple.

Mrs. Hicks, perhaps more than any other public figure to emerge in recent years, reflects the complex and subtle nature of prejudice in America. Her public denial of bigotry is, in all probability, an honest expression of her self-image. But she is basically unaware of, and unwilling to become informed about, the way her views maintain the barriers of segregation and discrimination in American society. In 1963, when the NAACP asked the Boston School Committee to acknowledge the *de facto* segregation in the schools, she refused to review the evidence. Meeting with the NAACP, she abruptly ended the discussion by proclaiming: "There is no *de facto* segregation in Boston's schools. Kindly proceed to educational matters." Later, when the State Board of Education presented a 132-page report on racial imbalance in Massachusetts schools, she lashed out at the report's recommendations without bothering to read it.

Mrs. Hicks, like millions of Americans, holds views on race that are born out of and perpetuated by ignorance. John Spiegel, director of Brandeis University's Lemberg Center for the Study of Violence, has summed up the preliminary report of its study of six cities:

"... the attitude of whites seems to be based on ignorance of or indifference to the factual basis of Negro resentment and bitterness. ... If white populations generally had a fuller appreciation of the just grievances and overwhelming problems of Negroes in the ghetto, they would give stronger support to their city governments to promote change and to correct the circumstances which give rise to strong feelings of resentment now characteristic of ghetto populations."

Prejudice is born not only out of ignorance, but also out of fear. There is much about the Negro ghettos of poverty that causes whites, lacking objective knowledge, to be afraid, and their fear in turn reinforces their prejudice and their inability to hear out and understand the plight of the Negro in America.

In Boston, the voter turnout was heavy (71 per cent) but below the turnouts in Cleveland and Gary. White accumulated 53 per cent of the vote and a 12,000 plurality. Compared with Stokes and Hatcher, he had an easy victory. But considering Mrs. Hicks's lack of qualifications and the racial overtones of her campaign, Boston also experienced a massive backlash vote. Had it not been for the final days of the campaign—when she pledged, unrealistically, to raise police and firemen's salaries to $10,000 without raising taxes, and came back from Washington with "positive assurance" that nonexistent Federal monies would cover the raises—she might even have won. But throughout the campaign Mrs. Hicks repeatedly revealed her ignorance of fiscal and political matters. Mrs. Hicks had another handicap: She is a woman. The incredible fact that she ran a close race demonstrated again the hard core of prejudice and ignorance in American society.

The Meaning of the Elections

Now let us consider the broader implications these elections will have on the racial crisis in America. To be sure, the immediate implications are quite different from what they would have been if Stokes and Hatcher had lost and Mrs. Hicks had won. . . . . . As Thomas Pettigrew of Harvard put it a few days before the election, "If Stokes and Hatcher lose and Mrs. Hicks wins, then I just wonder how a white man in this country could ever look a Negro in the eye and say, 'Why don't you make it the way we did, through the political system, rather than burning us down?' "

But do these victories really alter the basic nature of the racial crisis? There is, true, some reason for hope. But to assume that anything has been fundamentally altered would be disastrous. First of all, it is by no means clear that these elections will pacify militant Negroes—including those in Cleveland, Gary, and Boston. In Boston, some militants were even encouraging people to vote for Mrs. Hicks—because they felt that her victory would help unify the Negro community against a well-defined foe. In Cleveland, most militants remained less than enthusiastic about the possibility of a Stokes victory. Of the militant groups, only CORE worked hard for him. In Gary alone did the candidate have the solid support of militants—probably because Hatcher refused to explicitly rebuke Stokely Carmichael and H. Rap Brown, and because his opponents repeatedly claimed that Hatcher was a black-power advocate.

If the Stokes and Hatcher victories are to represent a turning point in the racial crisis, they must deliver results. Unfortunately, Hatcher faces an unsympathetic Democratic Party and city council. Stokes has gone a long way toward healing the wounds of the bitter primary, but it remains to be seen whether he will receive eager support for his programs. Some councilmen from ethnic wards will almost certainly buck his programs for fear of alienating their constituencies.

Stokes and Hatcher themselves face a difficult and delicate situation. Their margins of victory were so narrow that they, like Kennedy in 1960, must proceed with great caution. Enthusiasm and promises of change are not the same as the power to implement change. The two mayors must share power with whites, and they must demonstrate to Negroes that their presence in City Hall has made a difference. But if their programs seem too preferential toward Negroes, they run the risk of massive white resistance.

This delicate situation was clearly seen in the early days of the Stokes administration. Of his first ten appointments, only two were Negroes. Although relations with the police have been one of the most sensitive issues in the Negro ghetto, Stokes' choice for a new police chief was Michael Blackwell, a 67-year-old "hardliner." This appointment was intended to ease anxieties in the ethnic neighborhoods, but it was not popular in the Negro ghetto. Blackwell, in his first public address after being sworn in, lashed out at the Supreme Court, state laws, and "publicity-seeking clergy and beatniks" for "crippling law enforcement." Cleveland's Negroes are already beginning to wonder whether a Negro in City Hall is going to make any difference.

Some observers believe that Stokes is basically quite conservative, and point to his sponsorship of anti-riot legislation. To be sure, Stokes' position on many issues remains uncertain, but what does seem fairly clear from his early days in office is that his effort to gain support in white communities is going to lead to disaffection among Negroes. How much and how quickly is a difficult question.

Race relations are only one of many problems that these two new mayors must face. Stokes has inherited all of the problems that brought national attention to Cleveland last spring—poverty, urban renewal, finance, transportation, air and water pollution, and so on. Hatcher faces similar problems in Gary, and must also cope with one of the nation's strongholds of organized crime. If they fail, the responsibility will fall heavier on them than had a white man failed. Some whites will generalize the failures to all Negro politicians, and some Negroes will generalize the failures to the "bankruptcy" of the American political system.

Almost certainly, Washington will be a key factor in determining if these two men succeed. The national Democratic Party has a strong interest in making Stokes and Hatcher look good . . . . . but how much can the party deliver? The war in Vietnam is draining enormous national resources and Congress is threatening to slash poverty programs. Even if Federal monies were no problem, there is the question whether *any* of Washington's existing programs are directed at the roots of ghetto unrest. Many informed administrators, scientists, and political analysts feel they are not. And the chances for creative Federal programs seem, at this moment, fairly dim.

Another clear implication of these elections is that white resistance to change remains large and widespread. More than 90 per cent of the Democrats in Cleveland who voted for a Democrat in the primary switched, in the general election, to the Republican candidate. Now, not many American cities are currently composed of as many as 35 per cent Negroes; the possibility of coalitions to elect other Negro candidates appears, except in a handful of cities, remote. Additional Negro mayoral candidates are almost certain to arise, and many will go down to bitter defeat.

Stokes and Hatcher won because black-voter power coalesced with a relatively small minority of liberal whites. It was not a victory of acceptance or even tolerance of Negroes, but a numerical failure of the powers of discrimination, a failure that resulted in large part because of the massive exodus of whites from the central city. The election of Stokes and Hatcher may break down white resistance to voting for a Negro, but this is, at best, problematical. Also problematical is how bigoted whites will react to the election of a Negro mayor. Their organized efforts to resist change may intensify. As we have already indicated, the pace of white exodus from the central city of Cleveland is already alarming. And an acceleration of this pace could push the city into financial bankruptcy.

In short, while the implications of the November 1967 elections are ambiguous, it does seem that the victories of Stokes and Hatcher, and the defeat of Mrs. Hicks, kept the door open on the growing racial crisis. America, at best, bought a little time.

On the other hand, we do not find much cause for optimism in those elections—unlike George Meany, and unlike the *New York Times*, which, five days after the election, published a glowing editorial about "the willingness of most voters today to choose men solely on personal quality and impersonal issues." To us, it would seem that the elections have only accelerated the pace of ever-rising expectations among Negroes. If results don't follow, and rather rapidly, then we believe that the Negro community's frustration with the American political system will almost certainly heighten.

PART III

The Mayor As Chief Executive

I N HIS ROLE AS CHIEF EXECUTIVE, THE MAYOR IS MORE THAN THE SUPERVISOR of administrative agencies; invariably, he must assume responsibility for all that happens in the city whether it be the growing crime rate, a teacher's strike, traffic congestion or a flu epidemic. Duane Lockard expounds on this in "The Mayor As Chief Executive." The style, vigor, imagination and skill with which they bear their duties is the basis of the author's fourfold classification of mayors—the reformer, the program-politician, the evader and the stooge.

Of particular importance here, almost irrespective of the man in office, is the effect of formal governmental structure on the mayoralty. Elaborating upon the dispersion of authority in Los Angeles ("Formal Structure Limits Leadership"), Winston W. Crouch and Beatrice Dinerman show just how limited the mayor's influence over the administrative agencies can be. But even where the city charter is more deferential to the executive, as in New York City, problems of control abound. Nat Hentoff's interview of Mayor John V. Lindsay convincingly illustrates the difficulty of activating and guiding the organized bureaucracies in a giant metropolis ("A Mayor Speaks on the Bureaucracy").

Crucial to the mayor's effectiveness as chief executive are the various means of direction and control at his disposal. With regard to this, both the power of appointment and the budget require special consideration. In describing the intricacies of "The Appointment Process" in New York City, Wallace Sayre and Herbert Kaufman present an analytical model valid for almost all big cities. The reader should note that the mayor's stakes are substantial here, for appointments are a major form of currency for bargaining with political party leaders, interest groups, bureaucratic organizations, and others. Henry W. Maier (the present Mayor of Milwaukee), in his discussion of "The Tactics of the Executive Budget Message," shows that the budget is the key to almost all that the city might wish to achieve, socially and economically. A mayor who does not understand this or who is naive about the requisite budgetary strategies is likely to be an unsuccessful mayor.

The final selection by Allan R. Talbot, "Tacky's Job," demonstrates how one mayor, Richard Lee of New Haven, managed to conquer the bureaucracy, a feat that few others in this august office can claim; under him, New Haven has come to be regarded as the pioneer city in successful urban redevelopment.

1.

The Mayor As Chief Executive

DUANE LOCKARD

IT IS SOMETIMES SAID THAT THE DIFFERENCE BETWEEN MAYOR-COUNCIL and manager-council government is that the former retains the traditional American principle of separation of powers and that the latter system has legislative supremacy. The reasoning is that the mayor stands in somewhat the same theoretical position as does a governor or the President, both of whom deal with a separate legislative body in a government where both branches have independent authority and neither is subordinate to the other. In manager-council government, however, the manager is seen as an expert administrator who is analogous to a prime minister in a parliamentary system, at least in the sense that he is subordinate to the legislative body.

The distinction is more apparent than real. On the one hand, specialization of governmental tasks has produced in the British government a sharp separation of actual power between the executive and the legislative elements of government, the classic interpretation of the British constitution notwithstanding. By the same token, it is nonsense to talk of American government at the national or state level as if the executive and legislative branches were islands apart. As Richard Neustadt has wisely said of the federal government: "The constitutional convention of 1787 is supposed to have created a government of 'separated powers.' It did nothing of the sort. Rather it created a government of separated institutions *sharing* powers."[1] Exactly the same thing can be said of mayor-council relationships. True, they are apart in a sense, indeed often in violent conflict (although some of this is sound and fury only), but they are harnessed to the same load and must share power not only between themselves but with other governmental elements and with nongovernmental elements as they all bargain, deploy, and maneuver in the making of public policy. So, too, with managers and their councils. Managers have their separate bailiwicks to defend against council interference, and the council has its provinces and prerogatives. Cooperation, conflict, maneuver, and pressuring are as characteristic of manager-council relationships as they are of other executive-legislative relationships. The theory of absolute subordination of the manager to the council is not even good theory, for it presupposes an executive who is supine and without any notions of his own which, if it were in fact to prevail, would surely spell the defeat of the system in the long run—perhaps not a very long run, either.

Far more promising as an analytical approach to the two forms of government is an evaluation of the fact that the mayor is subject to popular election, the manager is not. Direct election involves a major source of power; yet, paradoxically, it also harbors potential weakness. Popularity is itself a reservoir of power, and a popular mayor can make much of his public endorsement. Opponents perforce respect popularity, for it can be translated into votes and into pressure for compliance with the mayor's desires. Moreover, the ethos of American democracy makes it morally right and inwardly satisfying to go along with a popular leader; complementally, a mayor who has won by a good margin and who feels he has substantial support may feel morally as well as politically justified in pressing his demands because he has been sanctified by the ballot. Under certain circumstances this can produce strong and resourceful leadership—true whether the objectives of the leadership are ignoble or grand—a debauchery of public service, or a noble program of community improvement.

It does not, however, follow that leadership necessarily inheres in the system of direct election. The system opens the way to resourceful leadership—no doubt more so than any other kind of local governmental structure yet tried in this country. But it does just open the way—it does not assure that it will be forthcoming, for in many communities the rule becomes "Risk Not, Lose Not." If the vox populi can inspire leadership, it can also encourage evasion. If those who stick their political necks out for policies that are unpopular seem invariably to get them chopped off, and those who avoid contentious issues are rewarded with reelection, the lesson for the ambitious is quickly apparent: endorse popular issues to keep in the public eye, but never promote a controversial issue. It appears that communities go through cycles of evading and avoiding until some crisis arises or until difficulties are so pressing that the need for action finally steels the nerve of some political entrepreneur who then risks bold proposals and actions. Then the cycle repeats itself. This phenomenon is by no means limited to the city with the mayor-council system of government, of course, but the difficulties of hideaway leaders do seem to stand as a countervailing possibility to the leadership potential of popular election.

Direct elections cannot help being at least in part popularity contests. If a candidate is affable, has joined the right lodges, has been a regular communicant at his church, these are assets on election day. That such seemingly irrelevant qualifications are criteria for judging mayor candidates distresses many observers of local government, for it seems a most inept way of choosing a man to administer a multimillion-dollar operation. And it is undeniably true that sometimes popular election does bring to office men who lack either administrative ability or essential honesty, if not both. Of course, the infallible method of selecting executives in business, government or elsewhere has yet to be devised, but if one assumes that the essence of the mayor's task is to be an administrative overseer it seems that more propitious methods of choice could be found. In fact, the method of choosing city managers is unquestionably more orderly and more likely to produce trained administrators than is the elective process.

But does it follow that the appropriate criterion is the question of administrative expertise? It is obvious that other criteria are used. For the mayor no less than the governor is commonly conceived to be a representative. He is chosen in part because voters believe he shares their values, their aspirations, and their attitudes. They wish him to be responsive to their preferences; accordingly, candidates compete in pledging to do just that. The components of voter motivation in making choices among potential candidates are enormously complicated, and one is well advised to be chary when generalizing about them, but it does seem justified to say that voters usually do not much concern themselves with the relative managerial talents of candidates. Indeed most voters would probably be ill-equipped to do more than judge between the grossest extremes of excellence and ineptitude in managerial capacities. What therefore may seem irrelevant criteria to one who assumes administrative ability to be the crux of mayoral qualifications may be quite relevant to the person seeking a mayor to represent him and act more or less consistently with his (the voter's) preferences. Thus the question of criteria is a question of values.

In this connection it is important to recall that the larger the city, the less likely it is that a mayor will in fact involve himself in the minutiae of administrative detail. This does not mean that he has no concern with management problems—inevitably he will often be involved in administrative matters—but he will be more concerned with the broader problems of the government than with operating details. He will be attempting to convince others of the rightness of programs, promoting school-bond campaigns or urban renewal programs, seeking to get the governor's support for a state highway bypass to relieve downtown traffic, mediating between real estate developers and the city planning board about a new project, etc. These are the kinds of political problem the mayor works on, and as a result he has neither much time nor much need to involve himself in the workings of the police department or the treasurer's office. As Sayre and Kaufman sum up the problems of the New York Mayor: "It is political help (in the broadest sense of the word 'political') rather than managerial assistance that the Mayor most needs."[2] In short, mayors at least in the larger cities are, like governors, far more concerned with being policy formulators than being administrative managers.

This does not mean that ability and a reputation for intelligence and decisiveness are unimportant attributes for a candidate. The urban community of today is no longer the city of a half-century ago, when ethnic minorities were herded to the polls by political bosses to vote in blind obedience. A new era has come to urban politics. The day of the prototype of the ethnic politician who could identify with the ethnics and could do little more is gone. James Michael Curley's formula of a touch of brogue, some recognition, a little gravy, and a patronage job no longer works—indeed, it had ceased to work for Curley himself and forced him to retire long before he wanted to. It is likely that a candidate for mayor of Boston who seemed invincible in view of his fitting the standard patterns of the Boston politician and the formidable backing he had, lost the election of 1959 because he

> . . . fitted too well the image of the Irish politician that the Irish electorate found embarrassing and wanted to repudiate. . . . It appears . . . that the nationality-minded voter prefers a candidate who has the attributes of his group but has them in association with those of the admired Anglo-Saxon model. The perfect candidate is of Irish, Polish, or Jewish extraction, but has the speech, dress, and manner and also the public virtues (honesty, impartiality, devotion to the public good) that belong in the public mind to the upper class Anglo-Saxon.[3]

It is appropriate to emphasize differences among mayors in operation, not only because there are enormous differences among them but because this offers a convenient way of analyzing the office. Although mayors might be classified in many ways the following categories will serve to illustrate the major variatons—the reformer, the program-politician, the evader, and (inelegantly) the stooge.

1. THE REFORMER TYPE

Invariably dramatic and often demagogic, always courageous but inclined to moralistic tilting with windmills, the reform mayor is surely one of the more colorful breeds of American politician. The flaming political success of some reformers has led lesser imitations to talk the language of the reformer, confusing spectators about the genuine and the bogus reformer types. But the prototype of the reform mayor is unmistakable and genuine—he rides to power against sin, promising to clean the Augean stables promptly and dramatically. Flamboyance aside, the successful reformer is a competent politician; his success depends upon his ability to weld together a following—both a wide following in the community and a narrower set of devotees who carry out the operations of the reform administration.

The conditions of urban politics at the turn of the century offered more than ample grounds for the reformer's art. All across the nation reform movements—both lasting and fleeting—sprang up and challenged entrenched political machines. The number one requisite for these movements was a colorful and resourceful leader as the focus for attention, someone to provide leadership and to take office as mayor once the dragon was slain. Thus "Golden Rule" Jones of Toledo, Ohio, and his friend Tom Johnson of Cleveland were dramatic and successful leaders who inspired devoted followings and passionate opposition as well, but their popularity made them unbeatable at the polls. Jones acquired his nickname from his simple belief in the New Testament principle; his sympathy and love for the downtrodden immigrants and his relentless efforts to improve their lot made him unchallengeable politically. Johnson, a wealthy owner of transit franchises, gave up his monopolistic operations to go into politics after being converted to Henry George's single-tax ideas. Lincoln Steffens, while making his muckraking tour of American cities, called Johnson the best mayor in the United States. Brand Whitlock, a disciple of Jones and close friend of Johnson, succeeded Jones as the mayor of Toledo and continued to win public support with reformist ideas. Significantly, none of these reformers was a doctrinaire supporter of nostrums for "solution" of municipal problems.[4]

No other reformer—past, present, or even, one is tempted to say, in the probable future can quite match Fiorello La Guardia of New York.

Flamboyant egoist, demagogue, driving political master, and chief flagellant of the party leaders of New York City, La Guardia stands alone.

> It must be admitted that in exploiting racial and religious prejudices La Guardia could run circles around the bosses he despised and derided. When it came to raking ashes of Old World hates, warming ancient grudges, waving the bloody shirt, tuning the ear to ancestral voices, he could easily outdemagogue the demagogues. And for what purpose? To redress old wrongs abroad? To combat foreign levy or malice domestic? . . . Not on your tintype. Fiorello La Guardia knew better. He knew that the aim of the rabble rousers is simply to shoo into office for entirely extraneous, illogical and even silly reasons the municipal officials who clean city streets, teach in schools, protect, house and keep healthy, strong and happy millions of people crowded together here.[5]

La Guardia attracted not only a popular following among voters (he was Mayor from 1934 to 1945) but devoted and unusually able lieutenants. Rexford Tugwell points out, La Guardia had to depend upon these people who in many respects knew more about the government of the city than he did—but none of them could be elected mayor. It took the personal qualities that this man possessed to make a personal organization and a personal movement to hold power and to do things for the city. As Tugwell also says:

> It is hard to estimate even roughly how many words La Guardia devoted to telling New Yorkers about their city and its operations. There must have been millions about the budget alone, and anyone who thinks it easy to talk about finances and hold the attention of voters is innocent indeed. And especially if budgets are not your own best subject.[6]

There are other reform mayors, of course, some of them currently operating or only recently departed for other activities. Richardson Dilworth in Philadelphia carried on the reform mayor role that Joseph Clark relinquished when he went to the United States Senate. Neither Clark nor Dilworth has the flamboyant qualities of a La Guardia, but both came to and held power because of their crusade against a corrupt Republican organization that had long dominated Philadelphia politics. Both demonstrated that an upper-class Yankee Protestant is not disqualified from political leadership in the large cities of the East.[7] DeLesseps Morrison, until recently a reform mayor of New Orleans, demonstrates that ability and upper-class status are no disqualification even in the rough and demagogic politics of Louisiana's largest city. The decline of the old fashioned machine has reduced the reformer's opportunities to ride the white charger against bona fide bosses, for an essential precondition to effective reform mayor operations is a sufficiently deteriorated political climate to make the public receptive to the reformer's charms.

It is not quite accurate, perhaps, to say there is a stereotype of incompetence associated with the mayoralty, but something close to that seems to prevail in many minds. The maledictions pronounced on urban government in its truly unholy past still cling and are applied today as if no change had occurred in the intervening years. Thus, Robert S. Allen in the introduction to his book *Our Fair City*, asserts that there had been no essential change in American local government in the forty-three years since Lincoln Steffens had pronounced the American city "corrupt and content." "There is not a major city in the country," said Allen, "that does not possess . . . a dismal record. Nauseous misrule, fleeting, and often inept, reform, and then back to old garbage cans. Still 'corrupt and content' is distinctly the underlying motif of municipal rule in our country."[8]

Writing off contemporary urban government as misrule and mayors as incompetents is not justified, however. Admittedly there are many American cities run by less than Periclean standards, but the picture of universal misrule is inaccurate. Seymour Freedgood, writing in *Fortune* in 1957, expressed a view remarkably unlike Allen's. Observing that the large cities (those over half a million population) are hard pressed by suburbanization, financial problems, state limitations and so on, Freegood says they need "top notch leadership," and adds:

> They have it. Since the 1930's, and at an accelerating rate after the second world war, the electorate in city after city has put into office as competent, hard-driving, and skillful a chief executive as ever sat in the high-backed chair behind the broad mahogany desk. At the same time they have strengthened the power of the office.
>
> This has not been a victory for "good government." To most people, good government is primarily honest and efficient administration, and they believe that the sure way for the city to get it is to tighten civil service, eliminate patronage, and accept all the other artifacts of "scientific" government, including the council-city-manager plan. But today's big city mayor is not a good government man, at least in these terms, and if he ever was, he got over it a long time ago. He is a tough-minded, soft-spoken politician who often outrages good-government people, or, as the politicians have called them, the Goo-Goos.[9]

The tough-minded, soft-spoken, hard-driving politician has turned up, not only in the big city, but in not a few smaller communities in the last decade. The office of mayor seems to have intrinsic challenge and is as well an inviting stepping stone to higher political rewards. Candidates accordingly have included some able aspirants. Program-oriented in order to attract support, ready to work with a political organization and to use patronage and other traditional tools to get and hold office but unready to depend upon these alone, the program-politician type of mayor is a leader and a promoter. Freedgood describes tellingly the characteristic traits of the breed:

> The profile of today's big-city mayor—with one difference—is quite similar to that of the chief executive of a large corporation. Typically, the mayor is a college graduate, usually with a legal or business background and is now in his late fifties. He puts in hard, grinding hours at his desk, sometimes six or seven days a week, and his wife suffers as much as his golf game. The difference is in salary: he usually makes $20,000 to $25,000. . . .
>
> "Public relations" take a big chunk of his time. He is aggressively press-conscious, holds frequent news conferences, often appears on TV-radio with his "Report to the People"; and from his office flows a flood of releases on civic improvements. About five nights a week there are civic receptions, banquets, policy meetings, and visits with neighborhood civic groups. In between he may serve as a labor negotiator, or a member of the Civil Defense Board. . . .
>
> Despite the fact that His Honor is likely to be a Democrat, he gets along well with the businessmen, though he is apt to feel that they have a lot to learn about political decision-making. . . .
>
> Above all the mayor is a politician. True, he may have risen to the office on the back of a reform movement. But he is not, as happened too often in the past, a "non-political" civic leader who rallies the do-gooders, drives the rascals out of City Hall, serves for an undistinguished term or two, and then withdraws—or gets driven out—leaving the city to another cycle of corruption. Instead, he fits the qualifications of the mayors whom Lincoln Steffens called on the public to elect: "politicians working for the reform of the city with the methods of politics." His main interest is in government, not abstract virtue, and he knows that the art of government is politics.[10]

It would be easy to cite a long list of competent program-politician type mayors. Mayor William B. Hartsfield, twenty-four years the mayor of Atlanta, is a good example; he led Atlanta into the ranks of the metropolitan cities, giving it improved management and budgeting procedures, providing leadership for urban renewal, recreational, cultural, highway and other projects. "An unabashed ham," wrote a *New York Times* reporter on the occasion of Hartsfield's announcement of his retirement,

"He often put [that quality] to use when it seemed in the city's interest."[11]

A comparable mixture of ham, determination, hard work, and resourceful leadership make Richard C. Lee of New Haven, Connecticut, one of the more remarkable mayors of recent years. Urban renewal has been the cornerstone of Lee's political career, and so successful has he been in promoting renewal in New Haven that he has acquired for the city more federal aid per capita than any other city in the land and he has also parlayed the remaking of the downtown core of the city into a political bonanza. Hard-headed bankers and businessmen, not usually accustomed to giving campaign backing to liberal Democrats, have backed him financially and otherwise in his four successive re-election campaigns between 1955 and 1961. (He first won the office in 1953, having lost twice in earlier bids—once by a heartbreaking two votes.) Predecessors had been satisfied to muddle along, allowing a slow deterioration of city assets, offering little leadership. Lee reversed this process, asserting strong leadership and beginning to reconstruct the city—doing so, moreover, without raising tax rates.[12]

One could cite others: Mayor Raymond Tucker of St. Louis, an erstwhile professor of engineering; Murray Seasongood and Charles Taft, the only outstanding mayors that come to mind who served in manager cities; or Frank P. Zeidler or Daniel Webster Hoan of Milwaukee. Even though it was apparently not expected by many observers, the current mayor of Chicago [Richard J. Daley] has turned out to be an effective executive leader. As Freedgood has said, "When he was elected, many people believed he would sell City Hall to Cicero [meaning the gangsters] without a qualm. Instead, Daley went along to a remarkable extent in putting into effect reform legislation that tightened and improved the structure of Chicago's city government.[13] He may not be elegant in speech (he is reported to have said at a "town-and-gown" dinner at the University of Chicago, that "We will go on to a new high platitude of success"), but his control over the political organization of the city and his determination to achieve improvements in the city appear to be getting results.

There are others, leaders distinguished by the common drive to move the city ahead, or at least in some direction that it was not going in before. In this sense they might be labeled liberal or progressive in outlook and program. But the driving, tough leadership mantle does not belong solely to the progressive. Mayor J. Bracken Lee of Salt Lake City, for instance, is a professed and active conservative. As strong and resourceful a mayor as any of the progressive types, he won the office over a liberal Democrat in 1959, having campaigned against heavy spending in government, a goal he has vigorously pursued ever since. In his first budget he cut a quarter of a million from the requests, and got into a row with a popular chief of police and fired him over the prospective budget cuts in the police department. This and some other maneuvers have stirred up hornets' nests of opposition, but has won him support at the same time.[14]

3. THE EVADER TYPE

It is difficult to compose a list of well-known evader types; their careers do not commend them to national audiences. Indeed, it is the capacity to *not* attract notoriety or excessive publicity as pushers of anything notable that is their major stock in trade. To assure their tenure they avoid commitments, seek zealously to placate disputes, and follow the lead set by councilmen or other actors. Of course, all mayors use the evader routine on some issues; the conditions of political competition demand it occasionally. But there is a difference between being evasive occasionally and being evasive permanently.

The evasive stance is most common in smaller communities that are not growing or that have not developed serious problems of slums, finances, traffic bottlenecks, transit failures, or the like. But the larger cities have nurtured the type also, however serious their problems. New York City has had such mayors. Vincent R. Impellitteri, who ran in 1950 as an Independent against candidates from the divided and discredited Democratic organization and a Republican, won the election. He seemed not to know what to do with his prize. He "retreated into his self-described role as presiding officer of the Board of Estimate, sharing initiative and responsibility generously with any who would ease his burdens of accountability.[15]

The weak mayor system seems at times to discourage mayors from even attempting leadership, since their resources for backing up their initiatives are limited, but weak mayor system or strong there is also involved a matter of basic attitude and a calculation of the probable consequences of risking leadership resources. It is claimed that P. Kenneth Petersen, until recently mayor of Minneapolis, one of the few large cities with what approximates a classic form of weak mayor government, zealously avoided commitment on issues. Alan Altshuler in a study of Minneapolis politics attributes the following strategy to Petersen:

> He does not actively sponsor anything. He waits for private groups to agree on a project. If he likes it, he endorses it. Since he has no formal power with which to pressure the Council himself, he feels that the private groups must take the responsibility for getting their plan accepted. He never attempts to coerce aldermen. Instead, he calls them into his office to reason with them. . . . The Mayor has let citizens' groups use the facilities of his office to work out solutions to certain pressing and highly controver-

sial problems. Such solutions are often then seized upon by him and by the Council and adopted without amendment.[16]

Others claim that Petersen did not even employ the resources at hand such as press conferences to embarrass the council when it was vulnerable.

Some mayors ride into office as reformers but end up as evasive, long-term tenants at city hall. Such was the long career of Jasper McLevy of Bridgeport, Connecticut. Running as a Socialist candidate in 1933, he won the office because he was neither a Democrat nor a Republican in a city where a corrupt dual machine had discredited both major parties. He held the office for the next twenty-four years. Notwithstanding his Socialist label, his tenure was marked by penuriousness that would have done credit to the arch-conservative J. Bracken Lee, by the creation of a well-oiled local organization to support his biennial candidacy, and by a gradual decline of conditions in the city until another reformer displaced the reformer-turned-evader.

One final example may serve to illustrate another variation in the pattern. Mayors of Chicago, according to Meyerson and Banfield in their study of a Chicago public housing controversy, were traditionally eager to make the most of public housing projects: "Back in 1915 Mayor William Hale [Big Bill, the Builder] Thompson had demonstrated a formula for winning elections which had proved itself time and again; it called for (among other things) assiduous cultivation of the Negro vote and an energetic appeal to the booster spirit which gloried in vast public works. Politicians of both parties had not forgotten this time-tested formula, and public housing seemingly fitted the formula perfectly since it was presumed to appeal both to Negroes and to boosters.[17] But Mayor Martin H. Kennelly fooled those who predicted he would behave as his predecessors had. In time the promoters of public housing realized he was not going to be mayor in the same sense that his predecessors had been, "or, indeed, in any sense at all. Until 1948 it was reasonable for them to suppose that the Mayor was the person with whom a general understanding would have to be reached. But when it became evident that the city government was to be run by the 'Big Boys' of the Council, it would not have been easy for the heads of the [Housing] Authority, even if they had tried, to reach an understanding with them."[18] Bereft of the focused leadership of the mayor's office, the program drifted, and in good measure so did the city itself.

4. THE STOOGE TYPE

Happily, contemporary politics affords few examples of this species. It took the old-fashioned machine to pull off the election of a pliant, controlled candidate to the office of mayor. Once chosen, the proxy mayor would be careful to do the bidding of the boss who called the signals from the background. The old Philadelphia organization and that of Edward Crump in Memphis, Tennessee, handpicked minions for the front office to respond puppet-like to the bidding of the real political power source. Not only party organizations and factional groups managed to get pliant mayors to do their bidding—it has often been claimed with considerable truth that business groups achieved the same sort of dominance over "their" mayors, and apparently the underworld on rare occasions achieved similar control.

No doubt the practical relationships of the "subordinated" mayor with his masters were not entirely one-sided; the possession of the formal authority of office counted for something, at least, and there was always the possibility of a break with the masters and an attempt to strike out independently. Many mayors tried to get out from under such domination—some were successful for brief periods, but the odds were against it. The reason is simple: if the political conditions of a community are such that an organization has strong enough control over access to office to choose a compliant stooge, then it is likely that the power can be used to squash a rebel.

How widespread this phenomenon is today, it is difficult to say. Probably there are communities where in essence this does prevail, although it is difficult to believe that any political organization today can muster the quasi-totalitarian sweep of powers that sustained the old fashioned proxy mayor and backstage boss relationship. Doubtless the relationship where it exists today is a modified one, best described perhaps as a cooperative relationship with dominance of the mayor on most but not all questions.

N O T E S

1. Richard E. Neustadt, *Presidential Power: The Politics of Leadership* (New York: John Wiley & Sons, 1960), p. 33. Italics in original.

2. Sayre and Kaufman, *Governing New York City*, p. 668. See page 166 in this section, "The Appointment Process."

3. Edward C. Banfield, "The Political Implications of Metropolitan Growth," 90 *Daedalus* 61, 72 (1960). See Murray B. Levin, *The Alienated Voter* (New York: Holt, Rinehart and Winston, Inc., 1960), excerpted on page 62, for a view of the 1959 election that in part confirms and in part denies Banfield's interpretation.

4. Whitlock's fascinating autobiography stands beside Steffens' as required reading for those who want a view of the conditions of municipal

government and politics fifty years ago: *Forty Years of It* (New York: Apple-ton-Century-Crofts, Inc., 1914). Whitlock's discussion of Jones (pp. 112–50) and of Johnson (pp. 151–75) are particularly recommended; on his own mayoralty see, pp. 180ff. He says at one point: "I shall not attempt in these pages a treatise on municipal government. . . . Nonpartisanship in municipal elections, municipal ownership, home rule for cities—who is interested in these? . . . One cannot discover a panacea, some sort of sociological patent medicine to be administered to the community, like Socialism, or Prohibition, or absolute law enforcement, or the commission form of government" (p. 215).

5. Robert Moses, *La Guardia: A Salute and a Memoir* (New York: Simon & Schuster, 1957), pp. 37–38.

6. *The Art of Politics, As Practiced by Three Great Americans: Franklin Delano Roosevelt, Luis Muñoz Marin, and Fiorello H. La Guardia* (Garden City, N.Y.: Doubleday & Company, 1958), p. 131. See Arthur Mann's psychological analysis of La Guardia in Part I of this volume.

7. On Clark and Dilworth, see James Reichley, *The Art of Government: Reform and Organization Politics in Philadelphia* (New York: Fund for the Republic, 1959).

8. *Our Fair City* (New York: Vanguard Press, 1947), p. 15. If Allen would not still in the 1960's defend such a position, there are others who would.

9. "New Strength in City Hall," 56 *Fortune* 156 (November, 1957), and reprinted in *The Exploding Metropolis* (Garden City, N.Y.: Doubleday & Company, 1958), p. 63. Quoted by courtesy of *Fortune* Magazine. © 1957, Time, Inc. All rights reserved.

10. Ibid., pp. 67–68. Quoted by courtesy of *Fortune* Magazine. © 1957, Time, Inc. All rights reserved.

11. *The New York Times*, June 11, 1961.

12. See the profiles by Joe Alex Morris, "He is Saving a 'Dead' City," 230 *Saturday Evening Post* 31 (April 19, 1958), and Jeanne R. Lowe, "Lee of New Haven and His Political Jackpot," 215 *Harper's Magazine* 36 (October, 1957). See also the forthcoming work (from Yale University Press) by Raymond Wolfinger, *The Politics of Progress*.

13. Seymour Freegood, "New Strength in City Hall," *The Exploding Metropolis* (Garden City: Doubleday), 1958, p. 74.

14. See the typically *Time*titled article, "Nettled Nickle-Nipper," 75 *Time*, 14–15 (April 4, 1960), on Lee's successes and problems.

15. Sayre and Kaufman, op. cit., p. 697.

16. A *Report on Politics in Minneapolis* (Cambridge, Mass.: Joint Center for Urban Studies of M.I.T. and Harvard University, 1959), pp. II, 14–15, (mimeographed).

17. Martin Meyerson and Edward C. Banfield, *Politics, Planning and the Public Interest* (New York: The Free Press of Glencoe, Inc., 1955), p. 61. See excerpt on page 209 of this volume.

18. Ibid., p. 258.

2.

Formal Structure Limits Leadership

WINSTON W. CROUCH *and*
BEATRICE DINERMAN

THE STRUCTURE OF CITY GOVERNMENT IN LOS ANGELES HAS PRODUCED several results that affect the city's role as a contender for metropolitan leadership. The first effort to modernize and strengthen the formal government was made in 1903. From then until 1924 the city charter was amended numerous times to permit new departments to be added and to set policies. In the midst of the city's great expansion period a board of freeholders was selected to write a new charter, because it was believed that the growing city needed a more carefully designed governmental structure.

Under the previous charter, the mayor was elected for the relatively short period of two years. There was no formal limitation upon eligibility for re-election, however. The mayor appointed the Chief of Police, Fire Chief, Health Commissioner, and members of several commissions, the latter with the approval of the City Council. Commission members held office for four year terms, staggered in such a manner that no two positions on a commission became vacant normally in the same year. The mayor was given unusual responsibility with respect to police and fire administration, being designated chairman of the commissions heading those departments. The balance of membership of both commissions consisted of two citizens appointed by the mayor, with the approval of the Council. Most other commissions, including those for harbor, public service, and public works, had authority to appoint their chief administrators. The mayor's formal powers with respect to the city administration were limited, both by reason of the restraints upon his power of appointment and his relatively short term of office.

From *Southern California Metropolis* by Winston W. Crouch and Beatrice Dinerman, pp. 169–175. Published by the University of California Press, 1963, and reprinted by permission of The Regents of the University of California.

155

The City Council was elected at large. All nine members were elected at the same time and for the same length of term as the mayor. Being elected on an at-large basis, each council member could take a citywide view in considering policy problems. None was obligated to obtain public works or factors for any particular area or to please a place-oriented constituency. They were concerned, however, with publicity media that were citywide in coverage and influence, and were respectful of those sources of campaign funds having a major interest in municipal affairs. Generally, the successful candidates for council offices were residents of the older portions of the city.

The changes produced in city government structure by the new charter emphasized checks upon the executive power. Although the mayor's term was doubled, from two to four years, the chief executive was expected to coördinate the various administrative departments by indirect rather than direct means. Additional commissions were created, and older commissions were increased in membership, to give the mayor more opportunities to appoint citizens whom he wished to associate with the city's administration. All these appointments were subject to council approval, however. Each commission was authorized to appoint the administrative head of the department and to supervise departmental operations. Because commissioners' terms were staggered, a newly elected mayor could not obtain control of any commission until the third year of his term, or normally appoint a complete commission unless he were reëlected for a second term. In substance, the charter placed the supervision and direction of the city's administration upon the part-time lay commissioners, who were relatively independent of the mayor and inclined to be preoccupied with a single program.

An elective city controller was to have responsibilities for post-auditing city expenditures. The city attorney, also an elected officer, advised the mayor, council, and other municipal officers on legal matters.

A new concept of budget preparation and control was introduced by the 1924 charter. A central administrative unit, the Bureau of Budget and Efficiency, was created to provide staff assistance to the mayor and council. However, it was placed in a position of dual responsibility that compelled it to be moderate and cautious. The director was to be chosen by the mayor, with the approval of the council, and the council was given equal authority with the mayor to direct the bureau to provide information and make studies.

Council membership was increased from nine to fifteen, and the at-large method of election was replaced by a single-member district plan. Each council member became the spokesman for a geographic district and a set of local constituents. Each proved to be greatly concerned with public works construction and maintenance in his district and with the activities of the service departments. The charter required the council to meet in session five days per week and gave it authority to pass upon many routine administrative matters. The post of council member thereby became a full-time responsibility. Initially, the council majority came from districts located in the older sections of the city, because the bulk of population was concentrated there. Council members elected from districts that included the harbor, West Los Angeles, Hollywood, and the San Fernando Valley represented constituencies that required street improvements and public works to meet the needs of developing areas. As population increased more rapidly in the outlying districts than in the older sections, the struggle to realign district boundaries became intense.

The mayor, as the city's chief executive with a citywide constituency, had to reckon constantly with the council's interest in local parts of the city. Furthermore, as indicated previously, the mayor had limited power to impose his program views upon the departments. His efforts to initiate, to coördinate, and to plan were subject to checks at every turn by powerful forces.

The first really significant effort to coördinate the city administration was begun in 1951, when the charter was amended to create the position of City Administrative Officer. This position was superimposed upon the Bureau of Budget and Efficiency, which became the nucleus of the Administrative Officer's staff. The CAO, appointed by the mayor with the approval of the City Council, became a pillar of strength for the mayor in regard to administrative matters, but he was not exclusively the mayor's aide. He was assigned extensive responsibilities for budget preparation and budget execution and for studies relating to improvement of organization and procedures. Within the framework defined for him, the City Administrative Officer was able to establish a role displaying some strength. In the area of administrative management, the CAO established a niche in which he and his staff were respected and given considerable influence. Among the accomplishments was a performance budget method by which the process of central review and evaluation of departmental spending was strengthened.

The impact made upon the city government by the City Administrative Officer was due to several factors, including the management skill of the first incumbent, an uninterrupted tenure of ten years in service, and an experienced technical staff of civil servants available upon taking office. Mr. Samuel Leask was first appointed by Mayor Bowron in 1951 and remained to serve for the eight years of Mayor Poulson's administration. Throughout this ten-year period, the City Administrative Officer held the confidence of the mayors and the City Council alike, but also possessed strength independent of both sets of officers. Upon Leask's resignation in 1961, to join the state administration, the incoming mayor (Yorty) appointed Mr. George Terhune, who had been Chief Assistant CAO and a career man in the city's budget office. In January, 1962, Terhune gave way to Mr. Edwin Piper, a former career administrator in the federal government.

Amendments to the 1924 charter have changed the status of departmental general managers and strengthened departmental management. Department heads have been given greater security of tenure by placing them in the classified civil service, and their powers, with respect to the management of departmental operations, have been clarified. They continue to be appointed by the commissions, but their removal is limited by civil service procedures. Commission responsibilities are less administrative than formerly and relate more to policy making. The managers are responsible for directing the work of the departments, within the framework of commission policy. Changes in the position of the departmental managers tended to produce greater continuity in the city's management and resulted in developing a group of professional administrators. This result greatly strengthened city program administration, although it did little to improve coördination between departments.

Civil service control over selection, classification, and promotion of a large percentage of city employees provided a permanent corps of administrative personnel. By charter amendment, adopted in 1903, Los Angeles became one of the first cities in the country to have a formal civil service program (see table). A considerable number of positions are exempt, although, except for a relatively small number allocated to the mayor's staff, most of the exempt positions are not subject to direct appointment by the mayor. Departments such as water and power, library, parks and recreation, airport, and harbor have substantial control over their personnel programs, other than for examinations and promotions.

The mayor has relatively little formal responsibility for personnel policies. Similarly, mayoral control of departmental programs and policies, to the extent it exists, has been accomplished by informal methods, outside the limits of the 1924 charter. For example, when Mayor Bowron took office, following the recall of Mayor Shaw in 1938, he took advantage of the situation to demand the resignation of all commissioners. Ultimately, he reappointed a considerable number, but he also reconstituted the police, fire, and civil service commissions. From that point, all commissioners were Bowron appointees. Although this action did not result in a continual involvement of the office of Mayor in departmental affairs, it did strengthen the idea that the mayor should have cognizance over departmental policies. This was continued, when Congressman Poulson defeated Mayor Bowron, by the incoming executive again requesting

TABLE

Employees in Classified and Exempt Services
City of Los Angeles

Services	1903	1907	1912	1916	1920	1924	1928	1932	1936
Classified	563	2,017	9,589	4,234	4,566	9,705	13,872	13,464	15,803
Exempt	560	87	8,057	1,936	2,123	3,828	3,627	3,793	3,962
Total	1,123	2,104	17,646	6,170	6,689	13,533	17,499	17,257	19,765

Services	1940	1944	1948	1952	1956	1961
Classified	a	15,565	25,547	28,063	30,918	34,027
Exempt	a	515	1,167	1,919	2,462	3,000
Total	20,761	16,080	26,714	29,982	33,380	37,027

Source: Unpublished data supplied by Los Angeles City Civil Service Department.
aFigures not available.

the resignation of all commissioners. Poulson, too, reappointed many who had served previously, but his action emphasized the prerogatives of the mayor. When Mayor Poulson, in turn, was defeated by former Congressman Samuel Yorty in 1961, the new mayor followed the precedents set by his two predecessors. Mayor Yorty, however, reappointed relatively few commissioners; instead, he reconstituted most commissions and espoused a policy of strong executive participation in public works, police, health, planning, harbor, and airport programs. The mayor's prerogatives were further strengthened when two commissioners who refused to resign because they clung to the view that commissions were responsible for their department's programs were superseded by City Council action approving the mayor's nominations of replacements.

The 1924 charter undoubtedly produced a system of city government that depends upon maintaining a delicate balance between the mayor, the council, and the commissions. The mayor appoints commissioners, proposes a budget that includes support for most departments other than the so-called proprietary departments of harbor, water and power, and airport, and may veto appropriations and ordinances approved by the council. The council adopts, modifies, or rejects the mayor's proposals for ordinances and appropriations, and exercises a check upon his appointing powers. The commissions have responsibilities specifically assigned them by the charter, and in performing those responsibilities, they find it necessary to have continuing relations with both the mayor and the council. After the City Administrative Officer was injected into the structure, a fourth force was involved in the bargaining process that produces the city's policies and programs. Largely through his influence on the budgetary process, the CAO makes a considerable impact upon the whole system. Yet, it cannot be said that the system of city government created by the charter provides strong executive leadership, in the sense that the term has generally been used in American government and administration.

Proposals to further rewrite the Los Angeles city charter in order to strengthen the mayor's position, or to make the city a stronger contender for metropolitan leadership, have often stirred the opposition of groups that were loath to see changes made that might attract suburban areas to seek annexation, expanding the city's boundaries still farther. It was reasoned that a city preëminently successful in managing its affairs might well attract suburban communities to join it, as many had done in the 1920's.

Charter changes that would permit decentralization, by means of a borough plan, were regarded by these groups as devices to make the city more attractive to suburban communities. A number of those who spoke glowingly of the general concept of the borough plan felt that if the plan worked successfully, suburban communities would undoubtedly be attracted to apply for annexation, and would seek to protect their community status by organizing as boroughs. Others, such as Councilman Ernest E. Debs, advocated that "The only possible answer to the problem [metropolitan government] is the consolidation of all cities and areas into one county government under a borough system."[1] Either use of the borough plan, if it produced expansion of the Los Angeles City area in any appreciable degree, would have upset the modus vivendi with respect to service territories that had been established between the city Water and Power Department and the privately owned utility. Upsetting that balance would have meant reopening the political struggles of the 1920's among the utility groups, and a number of influential leaders at city hall were loath to see that occur.

A more remote and less specifically stated fear was expressed against altering the balance of power in the city's formal governmental structure. It was concerned less with the potentialities of a strong mayor than with the unpredictable consequences that might arise from a complete rewriting of the city charter. Groups that were accustomed to working with the various units of city government had adjusted themselves to its manner of doing business and to the key persons who were involved in making decisions. These groups felt that if a complete rewriting of the charter were to be undertaken in order to clarify the role of the mayor, there would be no opportunity to prevent other changes from taking place. The status quo appeared to be much more satisfactory than an unpredictable future of continuing change.

1. Los Angeles *Daily News*, Nov. 12, 1947.

3.

A Mayor Speaks on The Bureaucracy

NAT HENTOFF *interviews* JOHN V. LINDSAY

"FOR THE FIRST TIME, I THINK THERE'S AN AWAKENING AMONG SOME OF
the labor leaders to their responsibility to be more flexible. That's a big
step—a very big step. We've still got problems with the municipal unions,
though, particularly with regard to our right to move men around, which
is an essential right. Take the Fire Department. I was struck with luck in
appointing Bob Lowery as Fire Commissioner. He turned out to be a brilliant administrator. Furthermore, he knows when to roll with a punch and
when not to. And he's very senitive to what the pros call the high-hazard
areas for fires. However, over the years fire companies have put down
deep roots in certain neighborhods. For a long time, the men were given
limited privileges to moonlight in neighborhoods where they were sta-
tioned, and those part-time jobs have made for even deeper roots. Until
Bob, no Fire Commissioner had moved them, even when more men were
needed in the high-hazard areas. Since he is doing that, he's anathema
to the heads of their unions. When Bob took men who weren't needed
after dark in lower Manhattan and put them in Bedford-Stuyvesant,
where there are twelve fires a night, Gerald Ryan, the president of the
Uniformed Firemen's Association, was appalled. I said to him, 'Gerry,
isn't it logical we do this shifting around?' 'Well, no, not exactly,' he said.
'These people are part of that neighborhood. They have their cars there.
They have to get those cars washed at a certain hour—that kind of thing.'
It hasn't been easy, and Lowery, while skillful, is a Negro dealing with
a largely white organization. So sometimes he needs reassurance, and that's

why I spend a good deal of time with him. I told him, 'If it gets to that point, crack Ryan over the head publicly, and I'll support you.' "

With some relish, as if at the prospect of more head-cracking to come, the Mayor continued, "This business of trying to get the separate parts of the administration working at maximum efficiency leads to all kinds of resistance. For example, in the Human Resources Administration, under our reorganization plan, there'll be a major division advising me on public-education policy. The Board of Education resisted the idea, but we told them it wouldn't kill them. I've finally got the Police Department responsive to the Mayor, and now the Board of Education and its empire cannot continue to travel in its own orbit. Education has to be made an integral part of community development, and therefore it has to be subject to a good deal of guidance from City Hall. No matter how many asbestos walls are put between me and the Board of Education, at the end I get the blame if there's trouble, and so I bloody well ought to have something to say about what's going on.

"God, they're slow in that empire! You remember when Freeport, on Long Island, refused a federal program based on teaching machines? The government was going to supply not only the money but bodies to go with it. You couldn't get a better package. We read about it in the paper, and I asked the Board for an immediate decision on whether we should take it over. No, they said, they needed a month to decide. Bernard Donovan, the Superintendent of Schools, was in Europe, and someone else was away. I told them they had twelve hours. You never saw such a crisis and so many telephone calls, but they came to a decision within those twelve hours, and we got the program.

"Then, there was the time the people filming 'Up the Down Staircase' wanted the use of a school building. The Board said it would take months to come to a decision, and that, besides, the picture might present a poor image of our school system. The filming was to take place during the summer, mind you. The schools were empty. So what if they showed a brick going through a window? At least, that would indicate a little activity. Anyway, I called Moe Iushewitz, a labor official who's on the Board. 'Do you realize that you're losing a million dollars in jobs by taking this stuffy attitude?' I asked him. 'How would you like to see that in the paper, Moe?' I signed him up and he delivered the rest of the Board."

Lindsay broke into laughter. "I've got a new slogan—'Wasp Power!' Thought of it the other day. Someone was teasing me about the number of Jews in the administration, and I said 'We Wasps may have only eleven percent of the vote in this city, but someday we're going to rise.' "

A phone call was put through. The Mayor, striking his desk with a pencil, listened for a while, and then he said "Well, do what you have to do, I'll back you up." He hung up and turned back to me. "The things you have to deal with!" he said. "We had a very interesting one a few weeks ago. We got word that the Ku Klux Klan in Baltimore planned to march through Harlem. Howard Leary, the Police Commissioner, sent a couple of smart guys to talk to them—to tell them they were damn fools and they'd get their skulls split open. I thought they'd been convinced, but two weeks later Leary got a telegram signed by the big Grand Wizard saying they were coming by way of the George Washington Bridge in full regalia, and since it was to be a peaceful march they demanded police protection. Leary called me 'Well, chief, what do I do now?' he said. 'What are the rights and liberties on this one?' Lee Rankin of the Corporation Counsel was in transit somewhere and couldn't be reached. But I happened to be talking to Bruce Bromley. He's a former Court of Appeals judge who's now a partner in Cravath, Swaine & Moore. He volunteered to research this one himself. The next day, he called me up in triumph. He'd found an old statute that goes back about a thousand years. 'Does Rankin know?' he said, 'that it's illegal to walk through New York City with something on your head other than a hat?' Well, we didn't actually use that statute. Leary sent the Wizard a telegram that said, 'You are coming to New York only to incite racial disturbance. Don't come. If you do, we'll lock you up.' That settled it. And here I'd had visions of a great scene on the George Washington Bridge. Before we were sure they wouldn't come, by the way, Leary asked me what to do if they did come. 'Surround them with Negro cops,' I told him, 'and you and I will go up to the roof of a tenement and throw bottles at them.'" Lindsay roared with laughter......

I had been in the Mayor's office for nearly an hour, and, as in February (an earlier visit) I had been feeling the pressure rise—on him, and on me as an obstacle to the furthering of city affairs. The lights on the Mayor's phone had been flashing almost continually, and frequently the door would open and a head would pop in, look at me—reprovingly, I thought—and pop out. But I did want to find out in the time I had left how much progress, if any, there had been in making certain that new policies, once adopted by the Mayor, were actually being carried through on the lower levels of the administration.

When I asked about this, the Mayor sighed. "Sometimes I feel I'm pushing my shoulder against a mountain," he said. "My feet are churning away and the mountain won't budge. But I'm determined to blast things through. Every week, I tell the commissioners at the cabinet meeting to get out of their offices into the streets and find out what their departments are doing with people. I'm always on them to act, and to follow through on the action. I'd rather they made three errors out of ten decisions, as long as they made decisions and got them into operation. I know it's tough, and sometimes the bottlenecks have nothing to do with the people in the lower echelons. I've walked by those rattrap buildings in East New York—the ones with rubble and beer cans inside, and, at night, a few guys mainlining it. They've been abandoned by owners we can't find. All the city can do is board them up. Three days later, the boards are down. The logical thing to do would be to tear down those buildings, blacktop the area, and put a basketball or handball court there. Or a place to get cars off the street. But by law you can't pull the mess down without going to court over the damn thing. But I did see one terrible block in East New York and I told the Buildings Commissioner to just pull down the buildings. Sometimes that's the way you have to operate. I learned that in the Navy during the war. Before I became gunnery officer on my destroyer, I was in charge of damage control. I was the housekeeper. My job was to get the necessary repairs done, get the guns we needed, get the ship painted, and get out to sea. You stole from the next guy, you borrowed from somebody else, but you got it done. Cumshawing, we called it. If you'd waited for the paperwork to get to you from this agency and that agency in Washington, you would never have got out to sea again." Lindsay suddenly looked glum. "Of course, you had a great advantage in the Navy. You could shove off. Nobody could do anything to you once you were in the middle of the Pacific." His spirits seemed to rise again. "But the thing is to keep moving and to keep others moving," he said. "We'll break through. And that's one of the reasons I go out into the streets as often as I can—to show movement, to show concern."

"What if you're just raising hopes in the ghettos when you're out in the streets—hopes that will turn into even deeper frustration if movement doesn't lead to visible change?" I asked.

The Mayor frowned. "I've done a lot of thinking about that, but I honestly believe people are reasonable. They don't expect miracles. They do expect some understanding and knowledge of their troubles. And when I'm around they do see some signs of visible change on some level. I was in a Bronx neighborhood where a kid got killed because there was no traffic light. When I left there, I called Henry Barnes, the Traffic Commissioner, and made sure it wouldn't take the usual four months to get a light where the people wanted it. I will not walk out of a situation like that without being able to assure the people in the neighborhood that there'll be immediate action." Lindsay grinned. "Sometimes there's even action before I get there. The Sanitation Department, for instance, has a real information system. If they find out I'm going to be in a certain neighborhood, they'll clean it up before I come. That's what they've always done with Mayors. But I don't always tell them where I'll be. Sometimes I don't tell anyone where I'm going. And then, when I get there and see they haven't been moving their butts, I yell and scream to get the trucks into that neighborhood. And I go back, or I send someone back, to see if they've followed through. Also, going out on those streets is of immense value to me. It's the one way I can really find out what people are sweating about, what they care about. I wouldn't have had those houses in East New York torn down if seeing them hadn't hit me in the guts. You see so much grief on those streets."

4.

The Appointment Process

WALLACE S. SAYRE *and*
HERBERT KAUFMAN

MORE OFFICIALS ARE APPOINTED TO OFFICE [IN NEW YORK CITY]—
some of them by elected officials, some by other higher-ranking appointed
officials—than are elected. All those positions occupied by the people
usually described as "employees" of the governments in the city are also
filled by appointment. Thus the process of appointment to public office
or to public employment pervades the politics and government of the
city.

The appointing officers see the offices and positions which they are
dispensing from one angle of vision; the groups seeking to influence the
appointing process see the offices and positions from a quite different perspective; and the individual who seeks the office or position for himself has
still another view. For the appointing officer, the office or position for
which he must choose an incumbent is an asset to be expended to meet
past commitments (perhaps acquired during his own efforts to secure
nomination, election, or appointment to his present position), or to
strengthen the hand of the appointing officer in carrying out his present
responsibilities, or to improve the appointing officer's own future career
prospects. To the extent that the appointment may involve him in
the risks of greatly displeasing some groups while pleasing others, the appointing officer may also regard it as a painful choice between his several
opportunities and competing costs and perhaps as more of a liability than
an advantage. To the parties and other groups seeking to influence the
appointing officer, the office or position is seen as an opportunity to
secure preferred access to the official or the employee when future deci-

From *Governing New York City: Politics in the Metropolis* by Wallace S. Sayre
and Herbert Kaufman, pp. 212–231. Published by the Russell Sage Foundation, 1960,
and reprinted by permission.

sions of importance to the group are to be made, or to prevent the appointment of an unfriendly candidate, or to reward friends and allies and supporters, or to enhance the general prestige of the group by a display of influence in the appointment process. To those who are themselves candidates for the office or position, the appointment is significant in terms of salary and tenure, its usefulness as a rung in the career ladder, its prestige and utility.

The appointing officers make their choices of the appointees under pressures from the full range of the participants in the city's political process. Some choices are more hotly contested than others. Some are the object of attention from a great number of participants; others are the concern of only a few, while others may be the focus of a single almost monopolistic influence. Still other appointments are closely hedged in by formal rules, devised to narrow the discretion of the appointing officer. Only in rare instances is the appointing officer allowed to regard an appointment as an act of his own uninhibited judgment. In almost all instances an appointment is the result of bargaining between the appointing officer and other strategically placed participants, a bargaining which takes place under rules or practices which confer differing advantages upon the participants.

APPOINTING OFFICERS AND APPOINTIVE POSITIONS

CONSTITUTIONAL AND STATUTORY APPOINTING POWERS are widely distributed among and within the governments of the city. There are numerous appointing officers, and the rules under which they exercise the appointing power vary greatly. This multiplicity and variety increase the number of participants in the process (since each appointing officer and set of rules is surrounded by a distinct constellation of forces) as well as the range of their methods of exerting influence on appointments.

The Mayor as Appointing Officer

The Mayor [of New York City] is the most important single appointing officer in the city government. He appoints, with but few exceptions, the heads of all departments, the members of all city boards and commissions, and (as the charter puts it) "all other [city] officers not elected by the people, except as otherwise provided by law," including, of course, the assistants and other members of the staff in the Office of the Mayor. The Mayor also appoints the City Magistrates, Special Sessions justices, justices of the Domestic Relations Court, and has the power to appoint judges, who serve until the next election, when vacancies occur in the Municipal Court. In addition, the Mayor has the power, which is frequently exercised, to appoint advisory or *ad hoc* committees composed of officials, citizens, or both.

In the exercise of these appointing powers, the Mayor's formal act of appointment is final; the formal approval of no other body is required. Unlike most important appointments by the Governor or the President, which must be approved by the upper houses of the state legislature and Congress, respectively, the Mayor is not required to seek the formal approval of either the Council or the Board of Estimate for his appointments.

The Mayor is also able, by virtue of his position as the city's chief executive, to supervise and control in considerable degree the appointments made by certain other appointing officers. He ordinarily requires department heads to discuss with him in advance, and secure his approval of, their nominees (or to accept his nominees) for appointment to such positions as deputy commissioner and departmental secretary, and, less frequently, for other positions "exempt" from civil service selection procedures, positions being filled by "provisional" appointees (pending establishment of a civil service eligible list), and even for such key "competitive" positions as bureau chief.

Other City Appointing Officers

The Comptroller, Borough Presidents, and the President of the Council severally exercise the appointing power within their own departments and staffs. They are under no formal obligation to discuss these appointments with the Mayor. Jointly, as the Board of Estimate, they appoint the chiefs of the Board's four bureaus (Secretary, Franchises, Engineering, Retirement and Pensions), the bureau staffs, and, from time to time, special consultants and experts.

The City Council appoints the City Clerk and Clerk of the Council, the Staff of the City Clerk, and the "attachés" of the Council (Chief Clerk, committee clerks, legislative clerks, and sergeant-at-arms). The Council also appoints the four Commissioners of Elections upon the recommendations of the two major political party organizations in New York and Kings counties.

Each of the five District Attorneys elected within the city appoints his own staff.

Both the elected and appointed judges have authority to appoint their own law assistants and law secretaries. The various courts appoint their staffs and attendants. The Country Clerks are appointed by the Appellate Division. The Public Administrators are appointed by the Surrogates, who also appoint guardians, and executors and administrators of estates under certain circumstances. A Commissioner of Records is appointed by the Chief Justice of the City Court. Several of the courts appoint referees.

Heads of administrative agencies, including department heads and the members of boards and commissions and special authorities, though themselves appointees, are appointing officers for their own staffs. Collectively, the appointments which they make outnumber by far the appointments of all other appointing officers. But their importance in the appointing process is reduced by three factors: (1) each of them acts separately in the appointment process; (2) the Mayor can and usually does closely supervise their exercise of the appointment powers for the higher positions in many of these agencies; and (3) civil service statutes and rules sharply limit their discretion in most other appointments.

The Governor and Other State Officials

The Governor, the state Comptroller, the Attorney General, and the heads of state departments and agencies are important participants in the appointment process, who in various ways affect the city's politics and government. The Governor, for example, makes interim appointments when vacancies occur in certain offices and judgeships in the city. Even more importantly, the Governor and his state government colleagues make many appointments to state government positions located within the city, and appoint many city residents to state government positions located in Albany or elsewhere in the state. All these appointments tend to affect, and some to be intimately involved with, the appointment process of the city government. Sometimes a state position represents a step up the career ladder for a city official; sometimes a city position is an advancement for a state official. Both state and city positions are therefore frequently included in some of the intricate bargaining among party organizations, public officials, and nongovernmental groups.

The President and Other Federal Officials

The President, United States Senators and Representatives, and federal agency heads as appointing officers also have significant influence in the city's politics and government. The President nominates and appoints, with the advice and consent of the Senate, a considerable number of officials to positions of importance to the city's government and politics. United States District judgeships, United States District attorneyships, city postmasterships, and other federal positions located in the city, as well as federal positions outside the city filled by city residents are presidential appointments. Since, under the federal government's appointment practices, the President delegates considerable initiative to Senators and Representatives of his party, those from New York are in essence *de facto* appointing officers for many federal government positions in New York City.

THE APPOINTING OFFICER is almost invariably the object of attention and advice from one or more other officials when he makes an appointment. The Mayor exercises greater or less "supervision" over department heads in their choice of subordinates, and the department heads, in turn, are likely to watch their subordinates' choice of their subordinates. But participation by other officials in the decisions of appointing officers is a still broader practice. Some officials, especially elected officials, have their own "following" or protegés, and for these they tend to seek appointments whenever feasible from any appointing officer to whom they have access. Other officials have jurisdictional interests which impel them toward participation in the choices of appointing officers, as when a District Attorney advises the Mayor on the selection of a Police Commissioner or of a Chief Magistrate, or when the Traffic Commissioner offers advice to the Police Commissioner on the choice of the Police Inspector to be in charge of the Police Traffic Division. Still other officials see in the appointment process an opportunity or a necessity for bargaining and trading in which a series of appointments, perhaps involving several appointing officers, are linked together, as when the recognition of one ethnic, racial, religious, geographical, or factional group in one appointment must be "balanced" by the recognition of another or several competing groups in the actions of other appointing officers. Most appointing officers thus become accustomed to the intervention of other officials in some number and degree whenever an appointment is pending.

Party Organization Leaders

Influencing the choices of appointing officers is one of the historic functions of party organization leaders. In the era of uninhibited patronage practices, the party leaders were alleged to have a virtual monopoly on such influence. They are still perhaps the most systematic participants in the business of influencing the appointment process, and their attention to appointing officers is more extensive in its range than is that of any other participant. All other interveners are more specialized in their attention than are the party leaders, whose interest and scrutiny include federal, state, and local positions, whether executive, legislative, or judicial, and at all levels of salary and status.

But the zealous and systematic interest of party leaders in influencing the choices of appointing officers does not make the party invariably the most influential participants in the appointing process. In fact, their competitors have steadily narrowed the areas in which the party leaders have the strongest voice. Civil service rules and procedures have made the appointments of more than three fourths of the city's employees (as distinct from its officials) relatively immune to the influence of party leaders, and a comparable evolution has taken place in similar state and federal positions in which the city's party leaders once had an ascendant appointing role. In addition, the party leaders have gradually been forced to yield ground to other participants in particular appointment areas: to the organized bureaucracies, for example, in the Police, Fire, Sanitation, and Education departments; to professional associations in the Health, Welfare, and Traffic departments; and to labor leaders in some other agencies. Symptomatic of these trends has been the increasing disinclination of Mayors to permit party leaders to nominate themselves for high appointive office, a trend given sharp emphasis by Mayor Wagner's declaration following his election in 1953 that District and County Leaders were not eligible for appointment as heads of departments or agencies.

There are some areas, however, in which party leaders have preferred access in influencing appointments. First in importance in this respect are the appointments made by the judges and the courts. For these positions . . . . . the party leaders have not only the most effective opportunities for "nomination" of eligible appointees, but it is to these positions that party leaders are most successful in securing appointments for them-selves. Some of these positions in the courts (especially in the Surrogates' Courts) are highly prized by the party leaders, whether held by them-selves or by their nominees. A second favorable area for party leaders comprises certain appointments made by the Mayor, especially to the positions of deputy commissioner, departmental secretary, and city Magistrate, but the success of party leaders in influencing these appointments varies from administration to administration and, in the case of the first two categories, from department to department. Another area of favorable opportunity for party leaders is the staff appointments made by the five District Attorneys in the city (although for twenty years Dewey and Hogan in the New York County office have turned to bar associations, law firms, and law schools more often than to party leaders for staff suggestions). Borough Presidents and Comptrollers are also generally favorably disposed, as is the Council, to party leaders' nominations.

Among department heads, boards and commissions, and special authorities, the party leaders find greatly varying reactions to their nominees for appointment to subordinate posts, reactions ranging from cold hostility through aloofness to cordiality. But in almost all these appointments, the party leaders can usually count upon strong competition from other participants in the appointing process. When city party leaders turn to gubernatorial and other state government appointments, they encounter comparable obstacles and trends, similar areas of advantage, and similar growth of competition.

The influence of party leaders depends on whether the officials upon whom they exert their leverage are of their own party or at least of an allied party. Within each party, party leaders also compete with each other. The County Leaders within the city contend with each other to influence all those appointing officers who have more than a countywide jurisdiction, and, within the county organizations, Assembly District Leaders vie with each other for both quality and quantity in appointive positions "allocated" to them. This intraparty rivalry tends to increase the chances for other participants in the appointing process to exercise influence on the choice of officials and employees.

In the sixty years of the Greater City,* the influence of party leaders in the appointing process has slowly, but for the most part steadily, declined. Many forces have contributed to this, but not least has been the rise of other competitors in the appointing process, transforming it from its earliest characteristics of close bargaining between appointing officers and party leaders to more extensive competition among many participants, a competition varying from appointment to appointment.

Nongovernmental Interest Groups

These numerous groups play a varied but influential role in appointments. If it tends to be either sporadic or specialized in contrast to the systematic and comprehensive role of the party leaders, it is nevertheless a significant factor in the decisions of appointing officers. And if nongovernmental groups tend to give other goals than appointments a higher emphasis in their formal and publicized group objectives, they nevertheless do not fail to give persistent and frequently effective attention to the particular positions they regard as important to their interests. Quite often the nongovernmental interest groups will assert that they do not nominate or endorse specified individuals for appointment, but that they stress instead the kind of qualifications and the kinds of policies which should be represented in the appointees. This posture, however, will not ordinarily deter the group from presenting to an appointing officer, especially if requested

---

*The present boundaries of New York City were established in 1897 when Brooklyn, Queens, and Staten Island were added. Before 1874, when the west Bronx was annexed (the rest of the Bronx was annexed in 1895), New York City was confined to Manhattan Island—Ed.

to do so, a list of prototypes or eligibles for his guidance. This point of protocol enables the interest groups to maintain their claim to being nonpolitical, but does not noticeably reduce their influence in the appointing process.

Most nongovernmental groups . . . . . limit their participation in politics to special sectors of the government. Their interest in appointments specifically is similarly restricted. Thus, for example, the Citizens Committee for Children will focus its attention upon those appointments in the several agencies which are charged with carrying out programs affecting children; the Citizens Housing and Planning Council upon appointments to positions in housing and planning agencies; the county medical societies upon appointments in the health and hospital agencies; the bar associations upon appointments to the Corporation Counsel's staff, to the courts, and to District Attorney's staffs; the labor unions upon appointments to agencies dealing prominently with labor questions; the religious organizations upon appointments in the welfare and educational systems; tax-conscious groups upon appointments to managerial and fiscal positions; and real estate groups upon appointments in building inspection, licensing, and enforcement agencies. No group will necessarily confine its participation in the appointment process exclusively to such specialized areas, but the attention of most groups will be most heavily concentrated upon appointments in selected agencies or functions.

A smaller number of groups seek broader participation in the appointment process. Some civic organizations (for example, the Citizens Union, or the League of Women Voters) are concerned with the "improvement" of the appointment process in general. These groups frequently urge appointing officers to use procedures which would make their choices among alternative candidates more visible and open, by announcing tentative choices in advance of appointment and allowing time for "public" comment on their qualifications before formal appointment, or by holding public hearings on the qualifications of proposed appointees. These are in essence proposals to broaden the number of participants in the appointing process and are seemingly designed to reduce the influence of "insiders" in the process by making it more open and competitive, serving also—and not just incidentally—to enhance the influence of the civic groups themselves. Still other groups, particularly ethnic and racial associations, concentrate more upon general claims for "recognition" and "balanced representation" in appointments than in influencing appointments to particular positions, although once such recognition is obtained in a particular office the ethnic or racial group is likely to regard it as a permanent acquisition of the group. These ethnic and racial groups also seem more inclined than most other nongovernmental groups to use the party leaders as intermediaries in seeking to influence appointing officers, although some other groups (for example, labor unions, real estate groups, religious groups) also find the party-leader channel at times useful and appropriate.

No single category of nongovernmental interest groups (professional, business, labor, ethnic, racial, religious, or civic) can realistically regard itself as having greater influence upon appointments than the party leaders as a group, except in the interest group's own area of special concentration. But the exception is of great significance, for cumulatively the interest groups span the whole range of appointing officers and thus some of them compete with the party leaders almost everywhere on approximately equal terms, and often on quite favorable terms. If they often refrain from naming a specific appointee, they at least draw the profile of qualifications in such specific terms that the appointing officer's range of choice is quite narrow and in effect confined to the list of prototypes or eligibles presented by the interest group or groups.

The Organized Bureaucracies

The organized bureaucracies are even more specialized in their participation in the appointment process than are the nongovernmental groups, but they are nonetheless potent participants. Most of the organized bureaucracies confine their attention to the appointments made in the agency in which their membership is concentrated. Their basic aspiration in the appointment process is, it would seem, to confine all such appointments to their own members, invoking for that purpose the values of "career service," "promotion from within," "nonpolitical appointments," and other doctrinal formulae for controlling the discretion of appointing officers and limiting the intervention of other competing participants in the appointment process. To these appeals is frequently added an emphasis upon the risks and costs of appointing an outsider whom the staffs will allegedly resist.

Like nongovernmental groups, bureaucratic groups characteristically refrain from urging the appointment of a particular person but emphasize instead the source from which the appointee should be chosen (that is, from the eligible membership of the permanent staff of the agency). The Police bureaucracy has been among the most successful participants in the appointment process, its accomplishments being demonstrated by the steady trend, almost uninterrupted over more than a generation, toward the appointment of Police Commissioners and deputy commissioners "from the ranks." The Fire Department bureaucracy, the Corrections bureaucracy, the Sanitation bureaucracy, the Welfare bureaucracy, and the teachers' bureaucracies have not been much less successful as participants in the appointment process in their several agencies. The Transit bureaucracy has had less time and less success, but it has not been denied an increasingly influential role. In departments and agencies where professional staffs predominate, the influence of these bureaucracies upon appointing officers is likely to be substantial, as is also the role of other cohesive bureaucracies in other departments, agencies, and bureaus. If they cannot always be influential in the appointment of department and agency heads, these groups can usually play a significant part in appointments to such subordinate positions as deputy commissioner, division director, or bureau chief.

The city bureaucracies find their optimum opportunities for influence on appointing officers in the departments and agencies under the Mayor. They have fewer opportunities and lesser influence on judges and courts as appointing officers, and on District Attorneys, Borough Presidents, or legislators. The state government and federal government bureaucracies also exercise influence mainly on the appointing officers in the executive branch agencies, playing no consistently significant part in the choices made by other state and federal appointing officers.

The Press and Other Communication Media

The communication media have a distinctive function in the appointing process. The newspapers especially, by their reports on the negotiotions and bargaining surrounding appointments as well as on the qualifications of the appointees, serve to make the appointing process more visible than it would otherwise be. This visibility tends both to increase the number of participants in the appointment process and to aid some participants while inhibiting others. In its reports and comments upon the appointment process, the press also assists—often deliberately, occasionally inadvertently—one participant or candidate as against others, and so becomes itself a participant in the process. The communication media thus may enter the appointment process as reporters, commentators, monitors, censors, or as participants.

The attention of the media of mass communication, as far as appointments are concerned, is ordinarily centered primarily upon the most prominent city offices—members of the Mayor's staff, department heads, Magistrates—and upon major appointments in and from the city by the Governor and the President. But no category of appointments entirely escapes attention. A scandal or irregularity in an agency may engender close scrutiny for a time of even minor appointments. A newspaper may itself conduct an "investigation" which will lead to its subsequent active participation in the appointment process. This participation takes varied forms, ranging from especially full reporting of the roles played by the several participants, through expressions of approval or disapproval of some of these participants, to the explicit endorsement of a type of candidate or even a particular candidate. In their usual participation in the appointment process, the communication media tend to reveal several consistent attitudes: implicit hostility (often made explicit) toward party leaders as participants; friendliness toward civic, professional, and business groups as participants; aloofness toward labor union, ethnic, racial, and religious groups as participants; and susceptibility to the claims of the bureaucracies for "career" appointments.

METHODS OF INFLUENCING APPOINTING OFFICERS

THE STRATEGIES OF THE PARTICIPANTS in the appointing process consist of narrowing the discretion of appointing officers, in most cases to a restricted category of eligibles, less frequently to specific individuals.

Restricting the Size of the Field of Choice

One extensively employed and effective method for controlling the choices to be made by appointing officers, reducing the influence of some participants while increasing the influence of others, is to establish the rules under which the appointment is to be made. The participant in the appointing process who can write these rules, or who can adapt them to his purposes, is at a great advantage. Such rules, which are numerous in the city's appointment processes, are of two major types: some of the rules specify the *qualifications* which the appointee must have; other rules prescribe the *procedure* by which the appointment must be made.

The most familiar and comprehensive of these requirements are to be found in the civil service laws and rules, regulating the appointments to the great bulk of city, state, and federal positions. These laws and rules prescribe the examinations, the construction of lists of eligibles, the certification of eligibles to appointing officers, and the ways in which appointing officers may make appointments from among the certified eligibles. These rules have their earliest origins in the efforts of certain participants (the civil service reform groups and their allies, including the communication media) to reduce—and preferably, from the reformers' perspective, to eliminate—the influence of party leaders on appointing officers. The extension and elaboration of these rules in recent decades may be attributed in large degree to the bureaucracies. The effects of these rules upon the appointing process have been several: the influence of party leaders upon many appointments has been sharply, but gradually, reduced; the officials charged with administration of the rules (the Civil Service Commissions and personnel officers) have acquired great influence over appointing officers; the bureaucracies have been able to limit the influence of other participants while increasing their own; and the nongovernmental groups, while generally benefiting, have also been compelled to divide their attention among those who make the rules, those who administer them, and those who make appointments under them.

But civil service laws and rules are not the only type of requirement which affects the appointment process. Qualifications and other requirements are frequently used to limit the discretion of appointing officers and to provide advantages or disadvantages to particular participants. Thus, for example, the charter prescribes that the Mayor may appoint as Health Commissioner only a person who is "a doctor of medicine or the holder of a degree in public health received from a college or university after at least two years of graduate study, and [who] shall have had at least eight years' experience either in public health administration or in college or university public health teaching or in both"; and that the Commissioner of Investigation must be "a member of the bar of the state of New York in good standing." Similar prescriptions specify the qualifications for a number of deputy commissioners. Other types of requirements prescribe city residence or borough residence for appointees, while still others require the appointing officer to make bipartisan appointments to certain boards and commissions. The effect of these several types of requirements is to narrow the field of choice from which appointing officers may recruit, and to confer advantage upon those participants who are the most influential in that narrower field. In general, party leaders are limited beneficiaries under those rules, while nongovernmental interest groups secure somewhat greater advantage.

These formal rules of charter and other statutory requirements are supplemented by informal rules and traditions which have substantial effects upon the appointment process. Such rules and traditions—more precisely, the expectations on the part of claimant groups and the anticipation of such claims on the part of appointing officers—usually rest on the capacity of the claimants to embarrass or hinder unresponsive appointing officers by withholding cooperation, generating unfavorable publicity, punishing the officers involved or their superiors at the polls, or similar weapons. At any rate, whatever the sources of the practices, they have developed vigorously and are scrupulously observed.

The creation of a "job image," for instance, is one of the familiar strategies of those participants in the appointment process who wish to limit the field of choice as a way of increasing their influence over an appointing officer. This partially explains the traditions or presumptions that the Police Commissioner should be a "career man," the Public Works Commissioner an engineer, the Personnel Director "a professional personnelist," the Hospitals Commissioner a doctor of medicine, the Welfare Commissioner a social worker, the Treasurer a banker or businessman, and so on. Each of these informal requirements or traditions increases the opportunities of some participants to influence the appointment process for the specific job, while it also decreases the opportunities of other participants.

Another such important restriction on the range of choice of appointing officers is the "allocation" of particular positions to a special sphere of influence. By this strategy appointing officers are persuaded that certain positions "belong" to one or another group, and the choice by the appointing officer is thus confined to appointees nominated by, or acceptable to, the "owner" of the positions. A classic illustration of this technique is the established tradition that the Mayor, in appointing the nine members of the Board of Education, shall allocate three members to each of the three main religious groups: three Catholics, three Jews, three Protestants. Another illustration is provided by the informal allocation, in effect for almost four decades, of one of the three positions on the municipal Civil Service Commission to a Negro. Other informal allocations are represented by habitual claims made by Borough Presidents and borough party leaders that particular positions "belong" to Queens, or Brooklyn, or The Bronx. These geographical allocations may in fact be claimed within counties and boroughs even by an Assembly District party leader, inclined to regard a triumph in one appointment as a permanent "grant" of the position to his district. Still other "allocations" are claimed by ethnic groups, by labor groups (as, for example, positions in the city Department of Labor), by professional groups (as, for example, the medical societies view the professional positions on the Board of Health and the Board of Hospitals), and by bureaucratic groups.

Yet another way of restricting the field is to acquire informal "veto rights," that is, the power to prevent the selection of a particular candidate for an appointment. The exercise of a veto by a group does more than block a particular individual; it also serves to indicate concretely the tolerances of the interested group, to establish criteria of acceptability, and thus to delineate the boundaries of the reservoir of eligibles. Reinforced by a kind of "courtesy" toward participants by appointing officers that makes the veto power ordinarily conclusive, it is one of the most effective and economical weapons possessed by the various participants in the appointment process. Attempts at such vetoes may, of course, range from the mild to the uncompromising, and even a vigorous effort by a marginal participant may not prevail over the will of strong supporters or a determined appointing officer. But in the main, an explicit veto by a participant of recognized status will turn the appointing officer toward another choice.

All participants find some occasions to use their veto rights in the appointment process. Party leaders use it to limit the growth of faction and insurgency; labor unions find it useful as a substitute for nominations of their own; bar associations use it in their role as monitors over appointments to the courts; and other interest groups, as well as the bureaucracies and the communication media, find the veto a sharp weapon for preventing what they regard in a particular instance as an intolerable or undesirable solution to a contest in which they have failed to achieve their own preferred goal.

Lacking sufficient power to exercise veto rights in particular cases, certain participants aspire less to exert direct measurable influence upon the choice made by the appointing officer than merely to be consulted or informed. These participants see their requirements or obligations as being substantially met if they are "in the know" in advance of the formal appointment, so that they may, if they choose, themselves inform their constituencies, their unsuccessful nominees, or even their competitors. Party leaders, for example, often urge this procedure for appointments to positions over which they recognize they have no control, thus conserving at least the appearance of omniscience. Other disadvantaged participants in particular appointment contests seek a similar preservation of their claims to influence, or at least their continued status as practitioners in good standing. The appointing officers often oblige.

All these modes of influencing appointments tend to limit appointing authorities to classes of possible appointees. The claimants do not actually name the appointees; the appointing officials still have some freedom of choice within each category. Occasionally, however, some participants feel strong enough to specify particular names; they "nominate" the candidate for elevation to public office or appointment.

Nominating Candidates for Appointment

Of all the groups engaged in efforts to influence appointments, party leaders and public officials are the ones that characteristically urge the appointment of a specific individual, only now and then suggesting more than one name. Other participants are more inclined to assume a posture of interest in "job performance" rather than in "candidates," and therefore to emphasize the *type* of appointee, the desired qualifications and other characteristics, the source of recruitment, and to present the names of prototypes or of a number of "prospects." By these means, however, such groups frequently arrange to elicit from the appointing officers "requests" for firm and specific nominations and to fulfill these requests. Sometimes the situation is sufficiently open to permit "self-nomination"; this is not typical, however, and a "self-nominator," after taking the initiative, normally seeks group support. Still more rarely, an appointee is "drafted"—but usually not without sponsorship by some influential participant or by an appointing officer determined to break a stalemate among other competing participants or to avoid an unattractive alternative appointment. Appointing officers are not infrequently confronted with the task of choosing from among a number of specific candidates, each nominated by some group he may not casually ignore, with any choice bearing costs as well as benefits.

When one of the participants in the appointment process has nominated a candidate for a position, the nominator then usually proceeds to secure endorsements from as many other participants as the nominator regards as necessary or useful; the candidate will often join actively in this search for endorsements. Some participants find it desirable to be "endorsers" more often than nominators, regarding the risks of endorsement as less than those of nomination and the benefits as equivalent. Others, especially party leaders, ordinarily prefer the role of nomination.

Trading and Bargaining

The contestants for the stakes of politics have not been slow to seize the opportunities to use the appointing process for bargaining purposes. Influence over this process has been added to the other media of political exchange, so that public policies, governmental decisions, campaign contributions, nominations to elective positions, and other forms of recognition or advantage are affected by hopes and expectations of appointment, and appointments are governed in part by concessions in these other areas. All the experienced, major participants acquire skills and aspirations for the accomplishment of simple or complex "parlays" in which risk and speculation add zest to the process. Thus officials, party leaders, interest groups, and bureaucracies sometimes work out intricate accommodations and exchanges with each other, involving perhaps a series of appointive jobs, elective positions, innovations in policies, specific governmental decisions, and other considerations. One fascination of this practice is that all the participants emerge with the feelings of winners, although no one can calculate the exact net gains.

The appointment process, then, is not a simple one. To the great variety of appointments to be made by a great number of appointing officers there must be added the interplay of numerous competitive participants using a complex set of strategies and techniques of influence. There are at least two main consequences: first, most participants in the appointment process must seek alliances and accommodations with other participants; second, most appointing officers must make their ultimate choices of appointees after weighing the claims of the competing participants as well as considering what the appointing officer perceives to be the "objective" merits of each of the candidates......

HOW MAYORS APPOINT DEPARTMENT HEADS

WHEN MAYORS APPOINT DEPARTMENT HEADS, they engage in an appointment process which has "high visibility." The communication media give these appointments prominent attention, engaging in much advance speculation about the Mayor's intentions, the rival prospects and their sponsors, and the strategies of influence being directed at the Mayor. The party leaders of the Mayor's party are alert to the impending appointments, sensitive to the fact that department heads are themselves both appointing officers and decision-makers whose future appointments and decisions the party leaders will wish to influence. Among the nongovernmental interest groups and the bureaucracies, each appointment of a department head attracts its own distinctive cluster of groups and pressures. And each such appointment is a magnet for candidates who see in the office a desirable form of public, political, or professional recognition, an opportunity for the higher exercise of personal skills or the realization of policy goals, or an upward step in a public or private career. Some offices draw more attention and competition than others, but no department head appointment is left to the wholly unassisted initiative and discretion of the Mayor himself. Invariably, there are some participants looking over his shoulder, and usually there are several attempting to direct his eyes toward a favored candidate.

A Mayor arrives at his choice for most department head positions conscious that his act is under wide observation, that many seek to influence it, and that he will be fortunate if his selection evokes more applause than criticism. The support he loses in one choice he must somehow seek to recover in another. When he completes the roster of appointments of department heads, he must hope that other officials, party leaders, interest groups, bureaucracies, and the communication media will each find sufficient satisfaction in the whole range of his department head appointments so that effective praise will exceed effective blame. He may, of course, make further concessions to disappointed participants when other types of appointments are made, as when he appoints Magistrates or when department heads appoint their deputies, but the skill and judgment with which he resolves the competition for the department head positions will be decisive for the course of his administration.

Mayors have developed several standard methods for limiting their recognized hazards in choosing department heads. The Mayor may move quickly, making the appointment before the pressures have had an opportunity to form. He may delay, hoping that undesirable nominees will lose support. He may test the strength of candidates and their sponsors by encouraging rumors that this or that prospect is being considered. He may resort to "high prestige" candidates, selected on his own initiative, to avoid appointing candidates of lesser public standing urged upon him by influential participants. Or he may change the traditional qualifications for a particular post, specifying new standards of selection which throw the customary participants off balance, forcing them to seek new types of candidates more to the Mayor's liking.

There is a discernible pattern in the appointment of department heads by New York City Mayors, a pattern in which is found a mixture of mayoral initiative and of accommodation to the claims of other participants. The pattern is blurred in some degree by the fact that many appointees owe their appointments to more than one factor or influence. Some choices may be described as "personal" appointments by the Mayor (for example, Corporation Counsels Windels by La Guardia and Burke by Wagner; Police Commissioner Warren by Walker; Investigations Commissioner Tenney by Wagner). Others are appointments reflecting the influence of professional associations and societies as participants in the appointing process (the Health, Hospitals, and Welfare Commissioners in the La Guardia, O'Dwyer, Impellitteri, and Wagner administrations). Some represent concessions to the bureaucracies as sources of recruitment (Police, Fire, and Sanitation Commissioners in recent decades). Still others reveal the personal capacity of incumbents to retain office (Park Commissioner Moses since 1934; Public Works Commissioner Zurmuhlen since 1947). The department head who receives his appointment primarily through sponsorship by party leaders has become increasingly difficult to identify during the past twenty-five years.

The considerations which influence Mayors in their choice of department heads stand in interesting contrast to the conditions which surround several other categories of "low-visibility" appointments made by the Mayor. In two of these categories the Mayor has more freedom of action than he has in choosing department heads; in two other categories he has less freedom of action. In choosing his own staff (the Deputy Mayor, the City Administrator, the several "assistants to the Mayor"), he has few insistent claimants outside his own circle of intimates. Thus he may more fully recognize here the claims of his own preferences, his own past commitments, his present need of help, and his future aspirations for himself and for his protegés. Similarly, in his virtually unlimited power to appoint citizen committees for the purpose of advice, study, or "problem-solving," the Mayor may act primarily upon his own initiative and discretion. He may be guided by strategic considerations in his selections (seeking support in some instances, delay or protection in another, delegating substantial power in others), but the strategy is mainly of his own choosing and, the selections being numerous, he may indulge his own judgment freely.

Very different are the influences affecting his choices when he appoints the members of multimembered boards and commissions. Here the claims of borough representation, of ethnic, racial, and religious group "recognition" and "balance," of party obligation, of interest group and bureaucratic demands, move in upon him in varying patterns but with insistent force. And when he turns to still another category, the appointment of Magistrates and other judges, he is beset by the urgent and persistent pressures of the party leaders with their traditional prerogatives for these positions. A Fusion Mayor may profit from the factional competition within his coalition, and thus use these appointments to suit other purposes, but a Democratic Mayor will regard himself as fortunate if he can find opportunities here to bargain with party leaders at all—usually by conceding to them on judgeships in return for his own greater freedom in making other types of appointments.

In the textbooks on municipal government, New York City's Mayor is identified as "strong" partly because of his broad appointing power unhindered by any formal requirements of advice and confirmation by other governmental organs. There is no doubt that this power has substantially improved his bargaining position in relation to other contestants for the stakes of politics. Yet it would clearly be a gross error to conclude that his appointing authority is in all respects unfettered. Because it is broad, it must be employed cautiously, for the Mayor cannot plead constitutional mandates or inability as an excuse for rejecting demands and recommendations. In some respects, the Mayor is hardly able to preserve any more freedom to name his own department heads than those officials enjoy in choosing their subordinates. The system imposes its constraints on all appointing officers from the highest to the lowest.

5.

The Tactics of the Executive Budget Message

HENRY W. MAIER

ONE OF THE MOST EFFECTIVE TOOLS AVAILABLE FOR ADVANCING A strategy of development and devising the tactics to implement it is the city budget. Here is the city's work program for the year with a dollar sign. If the municipal executive can influence the direction of the budget, he can, in large measure, advance his own broad goals of municipal development.

In Milwaukee, the mayor does not prepare an executive budget as is done in cities of the "strong mayor" type. Instead, a number of cooks are involved in the making of the budget pie. The Budget Department goes over requests with individual department heads, usually paring their requests sharply. The formal budget is prepared at hearings conducted by the Budget Examining Committee of the Board of Estimates, on which the mayor serves as chairman, together with the council's Finance Committee, the Comptroller, and the Budget Supervisor as secretary. Here is the main arena of the battle of the budget. Departmental heads can appeal the budget as prepared by the budget director, aldermen can gain a floor for their particular ward interests, citizens can gain an audience for any number of private pleas. The sessions grind on for weeks, and at the end a final budget is submitted to the Common Council as a whole— where, once again, there can be controversy.

Feeling that a strategy of public leadership required some executive direction of the city's budget-making process, early in my administration I started the practice of sending an executive budget message to the Budget Examining Committee. What is a mayor's thinking behind such

From *Challenge to the Cities: An Approach to a Theory of Urban Leadership* by Henry W. Maier, pp. 114–129. Copyright © 1966 by Random House, Inc., and reprinted by permission. Mr. Maier has been Mayor of Milwaukee since 1960—Ed.

a message? How does he attempt to advance his strategy in it? What tactics are involved?

The following section is one illustration. Excerpts from the 1963 executive budget message sent to the Budget Examining Committee before it began its hearings are followed by a commentary on the rationale involved.

The Message

During the past three budget sessions, while dealing with short-run problems, we have also, more importantly, concentrated upon meeting our responsibilities to Milwaukee's future.

This year we must consider the budget, not only in terms of holding down the municipal tax rate, but also with the courage to complete the development programs already underway.

Step by step during the last three budget periods, we have allocated our resources to establish priorities for coordinated action on broad economic, physical, and social fronts.

Just as we have budgeted in the past to strengthen our development planning, our economic growth programs, our redevelopment priorities, our future housing conservation programs, our code enforcement to upgrade our neighborhoods, so now we must budget for the new agency which holds great hope for our social development—for our aged, our troubled youth, the disadvantaged. This agency is the Community Social Development Commission. It was formed to coordinate the allocation of our metropolitan resources to attack the social problems of the Greater Milwaukee Community.

This commission has now reached a point where budgeting is of importance—after the many undramatic months spent in bringing together the various governmental and private units necessary for its existence.

It is absolutely necessary that all the component units of the commission meet their responsibilities in providing a budget for the commission. I earnestly hope that the city government of Milwaukee will be the first to contribute to the budgetary strength of the commission. This should be our top priority since the city government of Milwaukee took the lead in bringing together the various agencies to form this landmark commission.

Another area in which I urge budgetary action is in connection with the Commission on Community Relations. As I did last year, I again urge the strengthening of our programming in this field.

This bi-racial commission is one of the most long-standing in the United States. Following the suggestion of its executive committee in 1960, and closely following the commission's prescription for membership, I personally made every attempt to give it as broad a representation as possible.

The effort to fulfill this prescription commanded more time and care than any other appointive task of this administration. I am convinced that the members of this commission are citizens sincerely devoted to eliminaton of all forms of bias in the Milwaukee community.

However, the members of the commission are all volunteers with busy lives of their own. They need staff personnel to perform the research and the planning for programs to serve not only today's needs but also to prepare the way for tomorrow.

Last year I urged that a staff technician, designated as a program director, be added to the staff. I repeat this plea this year.

Beyond that, I feel that our primary goal should be to hold down the municipal tax rate as far as possible. In the long run, however, we cannot do this unless we concentrate on financial planning and smack harder than ever at the inequalities in the state-shared revenue structure.

Commentary

One of the primary goals of the preceding passage is to point out important municipal goals that can be furthered by the upcoming budget, just as advances have been made by steps taken in the past budget.

The message begins on the high plateau of budgetary thinking on which I wanted the Budget Examining Committee to act. But the message has a public audience apart from the members of the committee and the other aldermen, so I can also employ it as a forum for public education. For instance, there is a reference to a "step-by-step" process, which I happen to believe is a necessity in decision making in a democratic government. The phrase is inserted here mainly because I had pointed out previously that this is a process necessary in civil rights programming, and my political foes had set up a howl. Although some may quarrel with the repeated emphasis on a "step-by-step" process, I believe that people must be educated to the fact that there are no miracles in a government in which many must be persuaded before an inch of progress can be made.

Later paragraphs set forth my first choice of priority in the coming budget scheme. We have in prior years budgeted to bolster our physical development programs. This year I feel that it is important to provide the initial financing for the Social Development Commission of Greater Milwaukee. The commission, after long months of organization, has reached a point where it is ready for budgeting; now I hope to provide it with the staff to do the job of initiating and placing in focus the fundamental priorities for social progress in the community.

In dealing with programming in the field of human relations, I reaffirm my approach of the previous budget session, long before civil rights became an explosive issue. Once again I am carrying out my approach to decision making by improving my centers for initiation of choice. The purpose of the program director for the Commission on Community Relations is to search out ways to change the attitudes of those prejudiced against various minority groups; at present the agency is spending most of its staff energy "putting out fires."

The last paragraph is my political recognition of the citizenry's desire for official attention to economy. It is also my bridge to the next section, which takes up one of the most hidden, but most critical, issues of the city's future.

The Message

The Effect of State Action on City Property Taxes

Few of our citizens understand that our local level of taxation in large measure reflects our treatment by the state in regard to state-shared taxes.

The City of Milwaukee must move to settle some basic issues which too long have been befogged by demagoguery, or swept under the rug by outsiders who demand service of us without reckoning with our ability to pay. It is noteworthy that the state government seems to view us as the fat goose that lays the golden egg. Others view us as a gigantic service machine for the metropolitan area, but one that is self-sufficient when it comes to paying the costs of running the machine. Others view us as an island for the poor and the underprivileged, at least partially surrounded by a sea of wealthy escapees from the city and its basic problems.

Since we are so many things to so many people, certain questions arise:

Is a disproportionate amount of our land going into tax-free institutions and public lands to service the entire metropolitan area? These institutions are good and necessary, but does a basc inequity exist to the city in this area because of disproportionate absorption by the city?

How does our per capita income and our per capita return from the state compare with other communities? in the metropolitan area? in the state as a whole?

What new state aids should we fight for, if any, to rectify inequities that exist in the relationship of the central city and its problems to the state?

Present state-shared tax formulas sharpen the differences between "have" and "have-not" municipalities within the state. The "haves" get the larger slice, while those subsisting on half a loaf are handed crumbs.

This has resulted in disproportionate property tax rates.

The city too long has been entrapped in a maze of conflicting opinions about its limited resources. The question is whether our resources should be used for the betterment of the "have-nots" of the state when we may be among the "have-nots" ourselves. Certainly, there are "haves" which should be carrying a larger share of the cost of state and local government.

The broad assumption that bigness is richness must be factually challenged. To challenge this assumption, a comprehensive analysis is imperative. I, therefore, recommend:

1. That our Citizens' Committee on Revenue Distribution be supplied the funds to carry out the analysis. This committee has already demonstrated its ability in the past.

2. That the committee be enlarged to utilize the many talents of and give full representation to our metropolitan area.

3. That at a later date a full-time legislative representative be selected to present the analysis and such recommendations that the common council and the mayor may approve to those who will join our efforts for equitable tax distribution.

Commentary

A fundamental decision is reflected in this section. I feel that now is the time to open my attack on the state's revenue distribution setup. I know that this is a long-range fight; I also know that the fight has never before been made in the manner in which I intend to wage it. I have decided, after much consideration of alternative vehicles (such as the Comptroller's Office or the Bureau of the Budget), that the Citizens' Revenue Distribution Committee, a small body that has been almost anonymous, is ideally constituted to carry on the battle. I would beef up that committee after the analysis mentioned here is made. I would find out who our allies in the state might be—the "have-nots" as opposed to the "haves"—and would then, for the first time, seek to get the personnel to carry out an organized program of attack upon state revenue problems. As a beginning, I propose a "full-time legislative representative."

Notice that in the choice of language ("the fat goose that lays the golden egg," "surrounded by a sea of wealthy escapees from the city"), there is no attack on the state or the wealthy suburbs directly. I do not want a direct fight at this point.

The presentation moves on to consider the local economy in the next section.

The Message

The City's Economic Outlook

One area in which we lack precise knowledge is that of our own economy. All of our plans, in the long run, are at the mercy of that economy. All of our plans, in the long run, should be aimed at improving that economy.

One difficulty is that very meager information is available in the Milwaukee city economy, as distinguished from the metropolitan, regional, state, national, and even world economies. Yet our own economy is the ultimate measure of the taxes we will have available for vital government services and programs to promote progress.

This does not mean that we can take a provincial view of our economy and regard it as absolutely distinct from the other economies. All are linked and must be viewed in relation to one another. However, we can do little, if anything, about those other economies, and we can do something about our own. The health of the other economies does not necessarily guarantee continued health for ours. If we do not continually exercise care, we can become a pocket of poverty inside a booming metropolitan, regional, and national economy.

This is why I have urged an intensive and completely realistic economic base analysis of Milwaukee. We must pinpoint the real state of our economy, understand how it came to be, and identify the forces of change now at work. We cannot continue to operate in the dark in a day when rapid change demands quick and exact response from government. We must have a solid foundation of knowledge on which to base the very considerable improvements we have made not only in the budgetary process but in many other areas of government. I, therefore, recommend that we make a token initial appropriation for "seed money" to finance such an analysis which will provide an indication of the city's willingness to participate in this project.

As for the economic conditions which face us in this current budgeting period, we seem to be in a period of relative stability. Locally, we have the irony of probably the greatest building boom in the history of the city coupled with the loss of taxable property to the expressway program and other public works as well as diminishing values in some areas because of the withering hand of blight.

We think that our gains will continue to exceed our losses, and that is better than many communities have been able to manage. The situation, however, points up the grave need for more and more economic development activity and every penny spent constructively in this field will be worthwhile.

Commentary

In the original draft, this section was almost a throw-away near the end of the message. In deciding the final points of emphasis, I gave the section a higher priority, even though I realized that it dealt with an intermediate-range proposition and was not likely to produce tangible results during the coming year. It did, however, point up the necessity for continued development of another center of civic strategy—an economic development program.

Looking over the budget situation, I envision the flight of industry to the suburbs and the loss of middle- and upper-income groups, which under the Wisconsin tax structure weakens our base for shared income taxes. There is the nightmarish question: How long can we cope with the rising costs of the service demands on the city without an enrichment of the city's revenue base? The ultimate answer can no longer be sought in a higher property tax rate, but must come either through new or renewed economic areas adding to the assessed value of the tax base or producing more income that can come back to the city in the form of shared taxes.

In addition, without a clear notion of the local economy, the city can do no substantial financial planning. Little or no thinking has been done in the past on the economic underpinning of the city's future; decisions have been made largely on the basis of political expediency rather than on the rational basis of economic logic.

Here again, I am endeavoring to reinforce my center of future decision making. I have already organized a Division of Economic Development; now I am calling for the methodology—the economic base analysis— that will lay the groundwork for more scientific economic planning at the municipal level and provide a benchmark against which to test financial decisions.

One of the important areas for financial decisions is in the capital improvements budget, which is taken up in the next section of the message.

The Message

Capital Improvements Financing

Our city government is making additional progress in capital improvements financing. Because we planned well and last year switched some of our continually recurring capital improvements programs to a cash basis, substantial savings are falling our way. This year—for the first time in many years—we will be able to cut the net cost of principal and interest on our outstanding debt.

I favor continuation of this program, and I recommend that a portion of the sewer construction financing now be switched to a cash basis.

I realize that additional borrowing may be necessary to complete the civic center or to finance other projects delayed from previous years. These are proper uses of borrowing and must be expected in the march of civic progress. However, our program of cash financing for recurring capital improvements should be expanded regardless of special one-time borrowing needs.

I also hope that we will continue our policy of advance planning of capital improvements. It is not only good planning, but it puts the city in a position to take advantage of grants in aid offered by the federal government as part of anti-recession legislation now passed by Congress and operating on a limited scale.

The capital improvements program is not only a means of providing necessary municipal facilities for our citizens. It also can be an effective weapon in fighting recessions if our planning is sufficiently far advanced to enable rapid translation of plans into jobs and work opportunities.

Commentary

There had crept into the Milwaukee municipal financing picture a false notion that it was good policy to finance regularly occurring items on a bonded basis. In previous years, I had successfully urged a partial reversal of this policy, and street programs were switched to a cash financing basis. Now I am carrying the process a step further, asking that the sewer program go on a cash basis. The goal is to try to reduce debt over the long run and to keep borrowing allocated to the "big hump" civic expenses.

The reference to capital improvements planning in connection with the federal government is simply a "look ahead" reminder that we always face the possibility of recession and that the city must be prepared to receive federal help and accelerate its own program.

In the next section attention is focused on one of the thorniest items in any budget session.

The Message

Our city employes have shown, and I am confident will continue to show, a high level of efficiency, enthusiasm and competence. The city has found through long experience, just as private industry has found, that the greatest economy in the wage area is a fair wage. It should, therefore, be our goal to continue to provide city employes with fair treatment and a wage and fringe benefit level which is comparable to the prevailing level in the community.

One consideration is always with us. And that is the difficulty we have in filling certain positions. Here, increases in wages over and above the average granted to other employes may be required to assure adequate municipal services. In this, the economics of the marketplace may have a louder voice than any other.

In these matters, as in others, we must keep one eye on the over-all tax rate and the impact of the Legislature's tax limits for operating purposes.

As you know, we asked the current Legislature to raise our operating tax limit to a more realistic level, not only because of the demands of growth and change, but because of the fluctuating nature of many revenues which must be considered in determining the final operating tax rate.

The Legislature raised the limit slightly, but then promptly wiped out almost half of the increase by "skimming off" part of the municipal share of income tax receipts. The Legislature also capriciously enacted an amendment apparently requiring the common council to adopt the operating budget by a two-thirds vote.

Actually, the amendment is so vague that I have requested the City Attorney to give us an opinion.

Regardless, the net result of legislative action has been almost no improvement in our operating budget limit. This is crucial for two reasons. One is that we must contend with automatic wage increments, new services or positions already granted, rising costs of some supplies, materials and services, increased fire protection charges, two additional elections, and increased workmen's compensation costs. Secondly, we expect only a small increase in the property values on which we base our taxes.

Accordingly, we have no choice but to ask those who demand major new or additional services or proposed higher spending to tell us where we can get new sources of revenue.

Commentary

This passage might well be subtitled: "The mayor walks a tightrope." I am seeking to give encouragement to the wage negotiation representatives —the finance committee—without giving any basis for a complaint that I am interfering with the negotiations. In other years, the members of the committee had felt that my predecessor had weakened their position in bargaining; I want the committee to feel secure, but at the same time want it understood that the city is bargaining in good faith. I believe in bargaining in good faith, but I also believe that the welfare of the taxpayers must be kept in mind.

I praise city employes out of appreciation for their contribution to a high level of municipal performance. At the same time, I stress the need for wage equity. Again I bring up the subject of the legislature to show the strictures it places on city spending, this time to impress the negotiating committee and the department heads with the fact that there is a legal barrier to uncontrolled tax increases.

In the last paragraph, I call on those advocating new "major" expenditures to recommend new sources of revenue. By implication, I do not include in "major" expenditures my previous new spending recommendations, which are minor in terms of dollars, although their social effects could be enormous.

It should be noted at this point that legislators seem to be reluctant by nature to move in the social areas, no matter how small the sum involved. A multimillion dollar sum for a physical improvement will be approved more easily, it seems, than an authorization for a pamphlet dealing with sociological problems. If, in this budget message, I were recommending many new items of expenditure, the legislative body would balk at the sociological areas. But I have the optimum time for my presentation. This is due in part to the atmosphere created by the civil rights demonstrations. Here I have the happy circumstance of a choice coupled with events that support the choice.

The Message

Improvements in Budget Procedure

This year we are expanding the performance budget concept to include additional bureaus within the Department of Public Works. The actual performance reporting and accounting necessary to make the figures more meaningful in terms of services is underway in three important pilot areas.

As yet, of course, comparable figures for a series of years are not developed. However, progress is being made and when this program is fully developed it will present to the Budget Examining Committee, our citizens, and the department heads themselves, a better view of municipal operations—a detailed picture that should show areas for both large and small economies.

The performance budget will, in the coming year, be applied to the Bureaus of Forestry, Street Sanitation, Garbage Collection and Disposal, and Plumbing Inspection. Together with the Health Department, the Bureau of Traffic Engineering, and the Central Board of Purchases, these seven agencies will place a major segment of the municipal budget under the performance budget format. This program will, I hope, continue to be extended wherever practical to other areas of city operations in years to come.

This year for the first time the Budget Examining Committee will have available another fiscal instrument I previously recommended to assist our review. This will show in individual columns on budget worksheets the amounts requested to (a) adjust for a workload change, (b) improve the level of service, (c) provide new services, and (d) meet special one-time costs. This should provide a useful tool in analyzing budget increases and in achieving major economies.

In considering capital improvement requests, the Budget Examining Committee would do well to seek the answers to the following questions I proposed last year in connection with each project:

1. What is the relationship of the proposed project to the welfare and progress of the entire city?

2. How many citizens will be helped by it and how many citizens will be harmed or inconvenienced if the project is not constructed?

3. Will it replace a presently outworn service or structure, or is it a new venture?

4. Will its construction add to the city's operation and maintenance budget, or will the property be largely self-supporting?

5. Will it add to the value of the area and thereby upgrade city property?

6. Is its estimated cost within the city's ability to pay?

The city's budget is only sound when it is based on sound information. We have made important progress toward developing more detailed and useful information than ever before. We must maintain our momentum.

Commentary

In previous years I have stressed the need to transfer the city's budget from an object-of-expenditure basis to a performance or program basis. Since it takes several years to make the transfer complete, I am again pointing up the worthiness of the operation and the need for patience. The procedural achievement will realign the entire emphasis of spending and will enable the budget makers of the future to evaluate the city's operations with more adequate information.

The questions concerning the capital budget represent in Milwaukee a new standard for testing the evaluations of the capital improvements committee. They follow a recommendation of the Municipal Finance Officers' Association.

The message was communicated in excerpts through the radio, television, and newspaper media. Then it was read to the budget examining committee, where three of the five aldermanic members applauded it—a rare reception for such a document. On the Saturday evening following the reading before the committee, I took a revised copy of the message before the people in a television broadcast, largely because I wanted broad public understanding of my choices in order to gain, if I needed it, some public support in the days ahead when the Common Council would decide whether or not to concur with the "end of the beginning" of my strategy of development.

6.

Tacky's Job

ALLAN R. TALBOT

LEE'S FIRST TWO YEARS IN OFFICE WERE DEVOTED LARGELY TO RESHAPING and controlling the city bureaucracy so that it could support large-scale municipal reconstruction. A hint of the problems he encountered is given in an incident, which has now become a legend, about a friend of his named Tacky Dwyer who worked in the Public Works Department. One of the laborers Tacky supervised wanted desperately to get promoted, and regularly hounded Tacky to see what strings he could pull. When Tacky's friend, Lee, became Mayor, Tacky immediately began putting pressure on him to see what could be done. Lee finally relented and told the laborer to come to the Mayor's office. After sharing gossip for a few minutes, Lee finally asked the man what sort of promotion he wanted, to which the laborer quickly replied, "I want Tacky's job." As Lee soon discovered, there were many in city government who wanted Tacky's job.

The conquest of the bureaucracy broke down into three basic challenges: establishing the Mayor's authority; reorganizing; and staffing agencies with competent people. The first challenge was a natural one for Lee. He likes to be on top of things and he knew enough about the personalities and peculiarities of city government to scramble to the top. The bureaucratic situation he inherited on January 1, 1954, approached anarchy. City agencies functioned like a confederation of tribes. There was no central control exercised by the legislative branch, the thirty-three-member Board of Aldermen, because it was too large and because many of the members were not up to the effort. Those factors, plus the part-

From *The Mayor's Game: Richard Lee of New Haven and the Politics of Change* by Allan R. Talbot, pp. 29–45. Copyright © 1967 by Allan R. Talbot and reprinted by permission of Harper & Row, publishers.

time nature of aldermanic duty (they meet in regular session once a month), made the legislature a weak opponent when it came to dealing with the bureaucracy, although some aldermen exerted considerable individual influence in departments to which they were assigned as board members.

In the workings of this bureaucracy the traditional role of mayor was also weak. Citizen boards, which are common to New England local government, sat at the top of most major departments and set policy. A New Haven mayor, therefore, had no direct control over his operating agencies, and although he appointed the board members, a new mayor found that he had to deal with the appointees of his predecessor, since the terms are overlapping. Another reason for the perennial weakness of the mayor's role was that most mayors held other jobs while in office. Lee's predecessor, Mayor Celentano, for instance, was an undertaker, and maintained his business interest while in office. One of Lee's campaign pledges in all three elections had been to become a full-time mayor.

Thus the combination of an ineffectual legislative branch and a weak mayor had enabled city departments to operate according to the wishes of their executive staffs and citizen boards. The only real outside interference came from the city's powerful Board of Finance, which controlled the city's annual budget. The key to unlocking these prevailing bureaucratic practices and establishing his personal authority was clear to Lee: he had to make his presence known to the isolated departments, and he had to assume control of the city budget.

His first departmental encounter was with the Police Board, a seven-member group of which he automatically became a member under the city charter. The Police Commissioners convened on January 4, 1954, to meet their new member and to ratify a private and not entirely apolitical decision, the appointment of a new Assistant Police Chief. During the closed-door caucus before the official meeting, Lee promptly challenged their choice, announced his own candidate, and gave two warnings: if the Commissioners did not go along with his candidate, he would throw the public meeting into an uproar, and he would keep their votes in mind when it came time for reappointments. This surprise maneuver, although infuriating to the Commissioners, had the desired impact. This is how one observer described the public meeting which followed:

"They were very subdued, even solemn. Dick's candidate was nominated, seconded, and approved. Then Dick suddenly started paying a glowing tribute to the guy the Commissioners wanted for Assistant Police Chief. Then he proposed two motions—one establishing a new position of Assistant Police Chief for Plainclothesmen, the other nominating the Commissioners' man to fill it. Well, the heads had been bowed, you know, but suddenly they looked up in surprise, I guess, and quickly seconded and approved Dick's motions."

The Commissioners got the message. Lee had established himself by getting his man appointed, and then offered the other man an important appointment as a reward for good behavior. An interesting footnote to this encounter is that after the Commissioners' candidate left the force, the position of Assistant Police Chief for Plainclothesmen has been left unfilled.

Lee got away with similar tactics of bravado and surprise the next day during his first meeting with the Fire Commissioners. At their last meeting in the twilight hours of the Celentano administration, the Fire Commissioners had raged a bit out of control. They had elevated seven men to the position of lieutenant, retired the Fire Chief at 90 per cent of his salary (proposing at one point to give him the city-owned Cadillac he was driving), appointed a new Fire Chief, and, with this last-minute package, exceeded their annual budget by around $20,000. It was their intention during this first meeting under the Lee administration to look over the new Mayor and then clean up some odds and ends they had no time for in December—including the promotion of the retired Chief's clerk to the position of Battalion Chief. Lee took over the meeting. He announced at the start that the clerk would not become a Battalion Chief, that he, the Mayor, was going to review thoroughly the executive pension policies of the Fire Department, that he intended to put a freeze on all new hiring, and that if anyone did not like it he would keep that in mind when their appointments came up. He then opened the meeting to some startling new business. He proposed that the new Fire Chief be given $1,000 a year raise. This, he explained, would put the new man on the same level as the Police Chief. This surprise proposal had the multiple effect of embarrassing the new Chief, winning his friendship, and shocking the Commissioners—yet flattering them, too, because the new Chief was their appointee. The new Mayor's first signal was loud and clear. He was for the Fire Department. He wanted it to share equal status with the Police Department, but on his terms.

During a third meeting in his hectic first week Lee met with the Board of Finance to begin a slow, careful process of taking it over. The only dramatic move during this session was Lee's insistence that the city's Personnel Director, who was a regular, albeit ex-officio, participant in the Board's meetings and who had influenced some of its decisions, get out and stay out. "I wanted to be alone with my Board of Finance," Lee explains today. The reason he wanted to be alone is explained by Edward Logue:

"Dick is probably the only Mayor in New Haven's history to do what it says he should do in the Charter, be chairman of the Board of Finance. Before Dick, mayors negotiated with the Board of Finance. The way he controlled them was through his superb understanding of the budget process and his readiness to do his homework before the meetings began."

Lee gave full priority to budget matters during his first year in office. He worked at it himself, and he organized his staff to keep him one step ahead of his fellow Board members. As Logue remembers it, the city budget was his prime assignment that first year. In addition to Logue, Lee hired Fred A. Schuckman, Research Director of the Connecticut Public Expenditures Council, as his fiscal aide. He also appropriated the Controller's Office staff. The two top staff men of that department were quick to appreciate the stronger role of the Mayor and willingly helped him by performing such thoughtful services as clearing Board of Finance agenda with him before the other members saw them. No New Haven mayor in recent history was this well armed in dealing with the Board of Finance, and when fiscal expertise and solid staff support were not enough for Lee to get his way with the Board, he was not bashful about pointing out his control over their appointments, too.

By the spring of 1954, Lee was fully in charge of Board of Finance meetings, and his personal staff—mainly Logue—was preparing the Board's budget recommendation for the following year. The control of budget preparation was tantamount to control of the bureaucracy, because the budget recommended by the Board of Finance generally becomes the official city budget. The Board of Aldermen has no practical role in this process; under the New Haven Charter it usually approves the Board of Finance recommendation without authority to increase the total amount. As Logue made his budget rounds in the summer of 1954 ("like some huge bear poking for food" is how one ex-department head described him), it was becoming clear to city department heads that the Mayor's Office was in charge. There were other pointed reminders of the trend, including an executive order which prohibited any staff hiring without the Mayor's approval, the removal of all department phone numbers and the establishment of a central switchboard, the centralization of purchasing, the elimination of fifty-two jobs from the Public Works Department, the closing of neighborhood police precincts, regular cabinet meetings called by the Mayor "to promote the team spirit," and even the transfer of one outspoken critic of Lee's to the Health Department, where he was assigned as an inspector of all the barns in Connecticut which supplied milk to New Haven. Thus Lee had taken the first step in shaping the bureaucracy: he had established his control.

The next step, reorganization of municipal functions around renewal, was more difficult. Lee was not sure of how much reorganization was necessary or possible. Logue recalls that Lee became fully aware of the chaotic relations between departments during a meeting held with the Highway Department in the spring of 1954. On the city side of the table were traffic planners, city planners, representatives from Rotival's office,* members of the Redevelopment Agency, and several executives from other city departments to serve as window dressing. The meeting was called on the alignment of the downtown connector,† and every participant offered a different version of where the connector should go. Finally the perplexed Highway Commissioner, G. Albert Hill, asked Lee, "Precisely what does New Haven want?" Lee promised a specific answer for a future meeting, and after everyone left he flew into a rage, vowing that such a meeting would never happen again.

Of course the unruly highway meeting was merely a reflection of a deeper organizational disorder, which affected all areas of physical programming. Because of the previous state of bureaucratic anarchy, some city agencies were barely aware of what was happening in others, and all were unused to working together. Part of the problem was a series of personal and professional frictions. For instance, the New Haven Housing Authority was cool toward the newly established Redevelopment Agency. The reason was basically that the Housing Authority had been in the slum-clearance business since the early nineteen-forties and understandably regarded the Agency as an upstart. Relations between the Redevelopment Agency and the City Plan Commission were also poor. The directors of the two agencies did not get along. There was also poor communication among those agencies responsible for enforcing the various building, health, and fire codes. The Building Inspector, for instance, would sometimes clear construction plans without checking to see if the Fire Department had looked them over, too; and there was no coordination to speak of in enforcing code requirements for existing buildings.

In 1954, as Lee and Logue concerned themselves increasingly with purely renewal matters, they also discovered they had major problems at the very heart of the redevelopment bureaucracy. The Redevelopment Agency, which had been set up by Mayor Celentano to receive federal grants, acquire and clear land, and sell it to developers, was bogged down. It was still several months away from receiving federal approval for its first redevelopment project, Oak Street, for which planning money had been received in August 1953. The Agency Director, Samuel Spielvogel, had a number of serious problems, including an impatient Mayor who

---

*Maurice Rotival was consultant to the Redevelopment Agency Director. See page following—Ed.

†An interchange necessary to connect a new thruway on the outskirts of New Haven with a new highway complex cutting through the city proper—Ed.

kept pounding his desk for action. Spielvogel's job was made difficult by the complicated, often confusing, and untried process of putting a project together. His poor relations with the City Plan Commission Director made things harder. And as if all this were not enough, Lee had usurped Spielvogel's planning consultant, Maurice Rotival, whose staff, incidentally, included Nicholas deB. Katzenbach, whom Logue had asked to take some time from the Yale Law School to oversee Rotival's New Haven office. The end result of these intrigues was that Rotival was serving the Mayor rather than Spielvogel.* A less deliberate and cautious Agency director might have bowed to Lee's pressure and slapped a project together. Instead, Spielvogel kept on pointing out the problems and dangers of a pioneering renewal program, and put himself directly in the path of Lee and Logue, who, spurred by their sense of urgency, were more concerned with action than risks. A collision took place, and in December 1954, Spielvogel met privately with Lee to hand in his resignation, which took effect on January 21, 1955. Logue became Acting Director of the Agency. Under his direction and Lee's continual demands the madness of twenty-four-hour workdays hit the once-quiet Agency. By March 1955, the Agency staff had ground out the final Oak Street Project Report, which was funded by the Urban Renewal Administration in the summer of 1955.

Concurrent with his probing of the Redevelopment Agency and eventually appointing Logue its Acting Director, Lee was still plagued with the broader problem of reorganization. His embarrassing encounter with the Highway Department had impressed upon him the need for a quick solution. Logue was pushing for a charter revision as the most thorough solution: to create a new post of development czar—i.e., Logue —who, working directly under the Mayor, would head a new development department that would be an amalgam of the redevelopment, planning, traffic and parking, and some code enforcement functions which were then separate. Such a charter change would also include a four-year term for the mayor.

"I've always supported charter reform," Lee says today. "Our city government is obsolete. People expect a mayor to deal with twentieth-

---

*Lee's use of department consultants to take over departments was a recurring device. The prototype maneuver, of course, was his clever use of the Controller's Office staff in his domination of the Board of Finance. The consultant device was a variation. The procedure was for Lee to negotiate privately with a department consultant so that the consultant would recommend a proposal which Lee wanted. For instance, Rotival's office later recommended that Logue take over the Redevelopment Agency. It also proposed that he assume a new post of Development Coordinator. Certain changes which Lee wanted in the Police Department and his desire to establish a special traffic department were accomplished in the same manner.

century problems using nineteenth-century equipment. It's like playing quarterback for the Giants wearing nothing but knickers and a T-shirt." While supporting charter reform today and being intrigued with the idea back in 1954, Lee has been leery of it, too. In three previous unsuccessful charter reform movements, he had learned that for most voters the issues were easier to reject than to understand. Charter reform with its hearings and referendums meant open combat with an uncertain outcome and Lee avoids both whenever possible, preferring to persuade individual adversaries to his way of thinking. But there was a deeper reason for his uneasiness with the issue. A man of revolutionary objectives, but also of moderation, Lee wanted quietly to tear his city apart and put it back together again. There was no room in his plan for such side skirmishes as changing the social order, taking on major power groups, or even raising the tax rate. Charter reform, with its promise of extensive change of the standing bureaucratic order, was a potential noisemaker.

Yet despite these attitudes, in June 1954, Lee appointed a Charter Revision Commission, demonstrating another of his qualities. "Consistency," he often says, "is the virtue of fools." No one recalls precisely why Lee finally decided to expose the issue. He would suggest that he was prompted by the basic wisdom of the idea, which may be true, but judging by his more recent actions, it is also likely that he was riding to work one day and read in the paper something a department head had said that bothered him, so he exclaimed to his driver, "I've had enough of these bastards! Get me Logue on the phone when we get to the office." Unfortunately, this attempt to charter revision, like the others, eventually ended in crushing defeat and gave Lee his first public failure.

Perhaps in anticipation of the outcome, but more as an interim measure to get things moving, Lee began reorganizing the city before the Charter Commission even finished its hearings. The device he used, the executive order, was in keeping with his personal style. The legal basis for an executive order is contained in some broad powers conferred on Connecticut mayors by state legislation and in references to state laws within the New Haven Charter. These laws suggest that a mayor can issue orders to make city operations more efficient. The only practical limit on a mayor's use of the executive order is the possibility that someone may challenge it. Since no one ever has, executive orders proliferated in New Haven. One created a new post called Director of Administration. Lee ordered that the Director of Administration—Heman Averill, an ex-city manager—would work for him coordinating traditional services such as police, fire, health, and public works. The original purpose of Averill's job was to solidify Lee's early gains in controlling the city bureaucracy, and to relieve him and Logue so that they could begin reorganizing.

A second executive order, the most important issued by Lee, was a singularly autocratic document which, stripped of its pretentious legalese, simply told department heads that Ed Logue was in charge of all city functions affecting the redevelopment program. The idea of a development boss had been borrowed from Philadelphia, where Mayor Joseph Clark had helped set up a Housing Coordinator for that city's housing programs. Such a job was intriguing to Logue, although he did not like the Philadelphia title:

"*Housing* was too restricted as a term. It did not cover all that we wanted to cover in New Haven. *Coordinator* was a flat, wishy-washy term. Everyone's for coordination, but who really does it unless they're made to? So Dick and I settled on Development Administrator. That had some sex in it."

The executive order creating the post of Development Administrator and appointing Logue to fill it was issued in February 1955, but only after some preliminaries. One was a fight between Lee and Logue. Lee felt that Logue could be just as effective running development functions behind the scenes without the title. Logue wanted the trappings. That fight was successfully mediated, and their attention then focused on how the creation of the post could appear to be the recommendation of others.

One recurring phrase during Lee's administratin was "Let's do it right," and in this case doing it right meant building a suitable legal record for the decision, developing a memorandum for inside political use to justify the decision, and, of course, making it appear that it was someone else's decision. On February 1, 1955, a detailed report was sent to Lee by Rotival's office urging the creation of a Development Administrator, along with the name of Logue, as the only sensible answer to the problem of renewal administration. A few weeks later a four-page confidential memorandum was prepared by another consultant who criticized previous redevelopment efforts ("New Haven should write off its redevelopment past and start with a clean slate") and urged the Logue appointment as a way to ". . . revitalize the New Haven Redevelopment Program." At the end of the month a special committee chaired by a member of the Board of Finance followed suit and recommended the Logue appointment. Lee "bowed" to this pressure, and issued his executive order which gave Logue the authority to coordinate the activities of the Housing Authority, the City Plan Department, the Building Inspector, Traffic and Parking, and the Health Department around the renewal program being executed by the Redevelopment Agency.

During the spring of 1955, Logue, wearing his two hats as Development Administrator and Acting Director of the Redevelopment Agency, began giving day-to-day direction to the redevelopment bureaucracy. He called regular Wednesday meetings during which he outlined administration plans to execute the Rotival plan, and then set down the exact roles of each department. The job of traffic engineering was taken out of the Police Department and traffic planning out of the Parking Authority and placed in a new agency under Logue's supervision. Much later a Code Enforcement Committee was organized with Logue as Chairman, during which procedures were established for coordinated code enforcement. There was some resistance to these efforts, but Logue cut through them because the Mayor was behind him and because he went to these sessions knowing precisely what he wanted. He met the opposition with logic, forcefulness, and, when necessary, anger. Logue also paid a personal price in these battles. His critics—and there are still many in New Haven—and even those who considered themselves allies felt that during these struggles he became increasingly insensitive to those with whom he worked. A close friend at the time explained him this way:

"Sure he was tough; he had to be to get things moving and to overcome lethargy. For Ed, rebuilding the city was an emergency issue, a wartime situation which meant that anyone who delayed programs was aiding the enemy. Privately he is one of the most decent men I have ever known. But when it came to his work, the program came first, not personal considerations."

A critic, who happens to be a department head and who remembers the sessions with Logue, had this to say:

"There's a difference between telling a man he's done something wrong and humiliating him in front of his colleagues for doing it. Humiliation was a standard Logue device, and by using it he unnecessarily offended and hurt people. I think his approach to people actually slowed the program down rather than moved it."

One important factor in, although no explanation for, the Logue conduct at the time was the crushing work load he carried. He was acting director of one agency, and he was supervising most of the others. He was often seen rushing from one meeting to another reading memorandums and urban renewal regulations en route. He was working sixteen-hour days six days a week. Lee was never sympathetic to the Logue job burdens, for he had his own, including a re-election campaign that fall of 1955. In fact, Lee delighted in harassing Logue so as to challenge him to do even more. Witness these taunting memos of the period:

Dear Ed:

Now who's slipping??

The enclosed memo is the same as the one I received from you earlier today. You are getting old, boy—either that, or you have nothing to do.

Dick

Dear Ed:

What have you done about getting [their] programs launched? Precisely what are [they] doing? We might as well go all the way. Precisely what are you doing these days?

Dick

Despite the tone of these memos, it was clear to both men that the renewal program was going nowhere unless they got more staff. The immediate need was for a man to run the Redevelopment Agency full time. The program needed a professional thoroughly versed in federal regulations and able to put projects together. In June 1955, they found H. Ralph Taylor, currently an Assistant Secretary in the Department of Housing and Urban Development, and at that time director of the Somerville, Massachusetts, redevelopment program. In explaining why he chose to come to New Haven, Taylor today also offers insight into the early years of the Lee administration:

"Ed took me around the city on a Saturday afternoon and showed me the wide areas in downtown and in the neighborhoods that were slated for clearance on the maps he had locked up in his office. As he talked, he wasn't talking about something that might happen some day, but as though he could actually see the shapes of new uses that would spring up tomorrow. I was impressed, but I still felt uneasy about how a mayor would feel about this kind of program. I soon found out that Ed wasn't pushing Dick into accepting these plans. If anything, Dick was actually pushing Ed into doing more. There wasn't anything quite like it in the country. In fact, I don't really think there is today."

Taylor assumed full charge of preparing renewal projects and clearing them with the "Feds," and worked with Logue in negotiating with private developers. Much of the credit for the aggressive way New Haven has pursued federal urban renewal money goes to him. At the time of this writing New Haven had received more grant money per capita population than any other city in the United States.

As grant money came pouring into the Agency's accounts to start projects and plan new ones (the money did not go to the city's General Fund, where it would have been controlled by the Board of Finance), it became possible to hire other staff members. There was no shortage of applicants. Apart from the political job seekers, whom Lee regularly referred to Logue for hiring and whom Logue regularly referred back to Lee for other disposal, the spirit of the program as well as the national publicity it was beginning to receive attracted a number of young college graduates or recent graduates anxious to spend all or part of their lives in public service. New Haven presented an interesting opportunity. Those were the Eisenhower years, and federal service seemed stodgy and unexciting. Certainly there were no state governments offering the innovative spirit that such states as New Jersey and North Carolina have seen in recent years. Yet in New Haven, the most unlikely of places, there were two men—a strong, liberal Mayor and a tough, intelligent administrator—who were pioneering a new domestic program called urban renewal. The applications came pouring in.

The screening process was long and personal, much more like being looked over for a fraternity than being interviewed for a job. The criteria for selection were simple and straightforward: intelligence, readiness to work seven days a week, ability to withstand pressure and abuse, willingness to learn, and a high metabolic rate.

The result of the process was an unusual group of high-strung, brilliant, humorous, often naïve, arrogant but friendly, ambitious hard workers. The old-line city executives called them the "young Turks"; the New Haven *Register* labeled them "the whiz kids"; Logue referred to them in fatherly tones as "my boys"; and Lee smilingly called the building that housed them "the Kremlin."

Lee and Logue developed their recruits into a good staff in two basic ways. The first was their stampede approach to administration. Problems were often thrown out to a number of persons at the same time. The man coming up with the best answer got the prize of following through under the direct supervision of the boss. In that manner problems were not merely solved; they were crushed to death. A second method was the use of raw humiliation. If a young staff member carried out a task sloppily or proposed an action that appeared foolish, he would not be chastised privately but would receive a severe tongue-lashing in front of the others. This treatment made the newcomers a highly competitive group. Lee has admitted that he purposely kept the redevelopment staff competing among themselves, as well as with other city agencies. "It kept them on their toes; men often do their best work under pressure." Lee also knew that by encouraging intra-staff competition he could keep the group under control. Someone else might have viewed "the Kremlin" as a personal threat, but Lee knew he had the respect of its members, and his use of divisive techniques was designed mainly to keep them from getting him into trouble, which, because of their youth and inexperience they were quite capable of doing. For example, one staffer began pushing a proposal to build a nuclear reactor in the center of the city. Another casually dropped off an abbreviated draft bill at the state legislature which, according to its preliminary language, gave the Mayor full authority to do anything he wished with the structure of city government. Another wrote a speech for Lee which urged Negroes to block city traffic as part of a protest demonstration.

Everyone intimately connected with the program can also remember with fondness and some lingering trepidation Logue's staff meetings. At the large ones Logue was a no-nonsense boss, for he knew, as did Lee, that the challenge with this staff was not to arouse enthusiasm but to control it. "You do this, why didn't you do that, stop doing this," were the orders he barked to individuals around a conference table. Whenever he left the conference to receive a phone call, the petrified silence he had established would erupt into wild shouting, then subside again into silence as soon as he returned. Then there were the smaller "inner club" staff meetings, which were more informal and during which Logue would get back some of his abuse. Some of the select of the staff would have the privilege of joining Logue in his meetings with Lee, and were at first surprised as Logue would offer a serious proposal with the broadest of smiles; Lee would receive it with an equally broad smile, and when Logue concluded, Lee would break into a booming "To hell with you, Eddie, boy," at which point both men would break into laughter.

It was only through these private meetings that one could fully appreciate how close the two men were in their thinking and how their discussion of city business often took on the air of two brothers talking of family affairs, even of family pranks, with Lee usually taking the position of the older boy who would be held responsible for whatever trouble they might get into. Once a staff member got used to their style and lived up to their demands, working for Logue and Lee could be stimulating and fun. Organizational lines and titles meant nothing to those two, and they delegated important responsibilities and provided wide program experience to the young staff.

The establishment of a small band of energetic, loyal, and unusually bright staff members provided the manpower needed to grind out project reports, to negotiate and move the program. They also became the shock troops to make all city departments participate. Functions or programs such as capital budgeting, airport development, zoning, city code revision, school rebuilding, the planning of new streets and sewers, and eventually the development of the city's anti-poverty program were quietly performed by the young staff of the Redevelopment Agency, working under the guidance and supervision of the Mayor and his Development Administrator. Equally important, "the Kremlin" offered Lee the chance to get special staff help, and it eventually proved to be the training ground for new leaders once the old leaders such as Logue and Taylor departed.

By 1956 the city bureaucracy also reflected Lee's style of operation through his appointments to various citizen boards and his staffing of key positions. Two of his appointees were on the Board of Education, a new Police Chief had been installed, the Democratic Town Chairman was Public Works Director, and Lee had also found a place for Carl Lohmann, his friendly counselor at Yale, on the Park Board. On boards of agencies involved in the renewal program, Lee inclined toward men with professional rather than political credentials, although if the two could be combined in one man, so much the better. Christopher Tunnard, of the Yale Planning School; Louis H. Pollak, now Dean of the Yale Law School; Reuben A. Holden, Secretary of Yale; Herbert Kaufman, of Yale's Political Science Department; Gibson Danes, former Dean of Art and Architecture at Yale; and Maynard Mack were some of his choices from the University, not to mention some outstanding local appointees who had never been directly involved in New Haven city government before Lee. By 1960 Lee's position as an accepted leader was strong enough to allow a reversal of the process he started in 1954. He began loosening his control of the departments and promoting more departmental autonomy, but never the anarchy he inherited when he became mayor.

Lee's struggle with, and eventually conquest of, the bureaucracy went largely unrecorded in the local press, which is fortunate. The slaying of the paper monster was a matter of indifference to the general public, except of course when the blows were broadcast during a formal effort at charter reform.

PART IV

The Mayor as Chief Legislator

Contradictory as it may seem, the mayor must be able to seize the initiative in the legislature as well as in the executive branch if he is to lead the city effectively. Where the mayor cannot or will not do so, he may be a political liability to his own administration. This is especially true now, when so much depends on programs that have to be approved by the city and state legislatures.

As an illustration, the selection by Martin Meyerson and Edward C. Banfield ("The Mayor and the 'Big Boys' ") deals with a Chicago mayor whose preference for an "independent" council not only led to a problem of council factionalism but jeopardized the city's low-rent public housing program as well. Elsewhere, however, the mayor's leadership may be resisted by the council when it is offered. This has been the case in Los Angeles, where, as described by James Phelan in "Trouble in Happyland," "war" has been declared between the two branches of government. Though such a raging conflict has its ludicrous aspects, stalemate in city government can have dire consequences.

In the last article, *New York Times* correspondent Richard Reeves reports on the political impotence of Mayor John V. Lindsay, a big city Republican, before the state legislature of New York. Most urban lawmakers are Democrats who lack sympathy for a member of the opposition; and most Republicans are from upstate districts where antipathy to the metropolis is traditional. At the same time, Mr. Reeves shows how dependent the city leadership is on state government for the fulfillment of basic community needs—a lesson on the subject of "home rule."

1.

The Mayor and the "Big Boys"

MARTIN MEYERSON *and*
EDWARD C. BANFIELD

DURING HIS FOURTEEN YEARS AS MAYOR, EDWARD J. KELLY HAD BEEN
the undisputed boss of the Democratic Party in Chicago and in Cook
County. Through an alliance with Patrick A. Nash, chairman of the
County Central Committee, Kelly controlled all patronage and thus the
whole machine. As an admiring alderman once remarked, "Kelly walked
around with 9,000 jobs stuck in his back pocket."

As Mayor and as boss of the machine, Kelly was in full control of the
Council. He saw to it that his men had all of the important committee
posts and if a Democratic alderman dared to oppose one of his measures
he would call the man's committeeman to demand that he be made to
conform.

In 1947, faced with a hard campaign—public opinion was aroused by
corruption in the school system—Kelly retired. Jacob Arvey, a West Side
lawyer who had been his chief lieutenant and who succeeded him as
chairman of the County Central Committee, maneuvered successfully
to have the party nominate as Kelly's successor a candidate who would
stand for reform and who would not disturb the balance of power among
the factions then struggling to inherit Kelly's power.

Martin H. Kennelly had the qualifications that were wanted. He was
of Irish extraction and a Catholic, he was a successful businessman (he
had been in the trucking and warehouse business all his life), he had never
been prominent in politics although he had been active in one wing of

From *Politics, Planning, and the Public Interest* by Martin Meyerson and Edward
C. Banfield, pp. 79–88. Copyright © 1955 by The Free Press, a Corporation. Reprinted by permission of The Macmillan Company. The "Big Boys" of the title is a
reference to the most powerful Democratic aldermen in the Chicago City Council—
Ed.

the Democratic Party and a generous contributor to it, and he was favorably known as the head of the city Red Cross drive. All of this, of course, made him a good reform candidate. But from the standpoint of the factional leaders who were fighting for control of the party, it was perhaps an even greater advantage that he was not allied to any of them and that he clearly had no inclination to participate in the struggle for control of the machine. Indeed, Kennelly is supposed to have accepted the nomination on the explicit understanding that he would not be expected to act as a machine leader or to take directions in policy matters from the machine.

Kennelly made a campaign pledge that he would respect the independence of the City Council and after his election, when the leaders of the Council met to choose the committee heads, he made a point of being on vacation in North Carolina. Kelly had always attended meetings of the important committees of the Council; Kennelly did not even attend meetings of the Finance Committee. Moreover, Kennelly in effect declined to take a place on the County Central Committee and he seldom attended party conferences.[1] He even extended the merit system to cover a large number of minor jobs in the city government. Whether from expediency, prejudice, or principle, the new Mayor apparently believed that the aldermen should run the city with as little direction from him as possible.

Without the Mayor's help, Arvey, the chairman of the County Central Committee, could not hold the remnants of the Kelly organization together. Thomas D. Nash, committeeman for the 19th ward, formed a coalition of several South Side Democratic and Republican ward bosses to take control of the Council away from the Kelly-Arvey forces, and shortly after Kennelly's election, the alderman of Nash's ward, John J. Duffy, was elected chairman of the powerful Finance Committee over the Kelly-Arvey candidate.

For many years Duffy had had to defer to Kelly. "Kelly was a good mayor," he once told an interviewer, "but he became too powerful—the same thing happened to him that ruined Hitler and Mussolini. Kelly said, 'If you don't run the organization and its members, they'll run you.' He argued that you have to be the boss to be successful. Kennelly is a different type. He says it's the responsibility of the Council to make decisions. We get together and we throw out our views—exchange them— and we learn a lot from listening to each other."

Some of the aldermen who did not, like Duffy, gain power thereby were not so sure that it was an advantage to have a weak mayor. "What he (Kennelly) is trying to do," one of them said, "is introduce a new philosophy into Chicago government of letting the legislative branch take care of itself. The trouble with that is we have been so used to being led around that we haven't gotten used to working out our own problems. Take when Mayor Kelly was in; when I needed something I could say, 'We have to have this,' and in twenty-four hours we would have it. Today, it takes a lot longer to get something. Maybe his position is right, but it will take a lot longer to catch on."[2]

Critics of the Kennelly administration, including the liberals, most of whom had voted for him, were often exasperated by the Mayor's way of doing things. They criticized him for acting like a discussion leader instead of a politician. "Kennelly's idea of a beautiful world," one of the public housing leaders once said, "is to sit around a table and have the opposing parties come to an agreement for which he would take the credit without ever having opened his mouth."

The way the Council worked under Kennelly at the time of the public housing site selection struggle was described by Thomas Drennan, a seasoned observer of City Hall who was the *Sun-Times'* political columnist:

"As finance committee boss in control of over $200,000,000 a year for city expenditures" Drennan wrote, "Duffy has been able to set up some order among the rambunctious lads in the council.

"But this is limited mainly to deciding who gets to the jam pot first— and how much he gets. This also stops the overly-playful ones from setting fire to the aldermanic house.

"A select number of the 'big boys' are entrusted with enforcing Duffy's policies. They include Alds. Francis Hogan; Clarence Wagner; Harry Sain; William J. Lancaster and P. J. Cullerton. Important, too, because of their seniority are Alds. George D. Kells and Dorsey Crowe.

"When Edward J. Kelly was mayor and aldermanic brats were punished by the baseball-bat-in-the-woodshed system, those in this group used to dine daily in the Bismarck Inn, across from the LaSalle street entrance to the City Hall. The place featured a 75-cent lunch.

"But things have changed. Since Kennelly got in, the group may be found in the same hotel's Walnut Room where the a-la-carte lunch items run into three figures.

"These aldermen, good Democrats all, are the 'works' in operating the city's business. Through their control of key subcommittees created by Duffy, they pass on every vital measure—especially those involving spending of public money on contracts.

"So far Duffy has been able to use these lieutenants to 'deliver' the City Council for legislation wanted by Kennelly. Some liberal measures had to be crammed down their throats on the grounds of expediency. But despite long delay—the building code revision, for instance—they eventually went along.

"The rest of the aldermen, with about six exceptions, usually fall in line because of Duffy's influence with key department heads, one of whom, Lloyd M. Johnson, is superintendent of streets and electricity. He decides which streets should be repaired and maintained and how often the garbage will be collected in the wards—important decisions to an alderman.[3]

Most of these aldermanic leaders represented, it should be noted, lower middle-class wards on the South Side—wards which were mainly in conservation areas. Duffy himself came from a South Side ward where there was much vacant land and a small colony of upper-class Negroes. Wagner, his close friend and chief lieutenant, probably could expect to win only one or two more elections, so rapidly was the Negro population increasing in his ward. Horan's situation was similar. Lancaster did not come from the South Side, but his ward was a conservation area and his allegiance had been shifting from Arvey's West Side Bloc. The aldermen from these South Side wards and allied areas were a minority but possessed most of the power that was exercised in the Council, for they were its leaders.

By 1949 the Authority* had awarded many millions of dollars worth of contracts, rented thousands of units of housing, and given thousands of jobs. This was the raw material from which a mighty political machine could have been built in a city so favor-minded as Chicago. But the Authority had never been political. It had done favors, but it had done them seldom and only in trivial matters. (Curiously, no very important favors seem ever to have been asked of it.) . . . . .

In its first few years of existence the Authority, fearing party spoilsmen and jealous of its independence, had as little as possible to do with City Hall. Many people supposed that CHA was a Federal agency run principally from Washington. Some aldermen, including ones who favored slum clearance, were antagonized by its aloofness. Mayor Kelly usually ignored it, although now and then he intimated that his intentions were friendly.

By 1941, however, Kelly not only took an active interest in the Authority but made himself its sponsor and protector. CHA and the Plan Commission, he made clear, were to be "clean" agencies in his otherwise motley establishment. When Kelly talked to liberal groups—Negroes, labor, church people, and so on—he would point with pride to the Authority.

*The Chicago Housing Authority which was responsible for Chicago's low-rent public housing program.

When he talked to the real estate men and the downtown business community he would point with pride to the Plan Commission. . . . . .

As they prepared the ambitious new six-year program in 1949, [however] the heads of the Authority anticipated a difficult time with the politicians. Under Kelly it had never been necessary to get the Council's approval of specific sites; the change in the state law which gave the aldermen a veto power over sites was made after Kelly's retirement and it was an unmistakable sign that the Council meant to put an end to the Authority's independence.

By 1949 it was clear, too, that Mayor Kennelly would not give the Authority effective support. Whatever his views on public housing might be, Kennelly was pledged to let the Council run things in its own way. . . . . .

The aldermen who came from the outlying white neighborhoods—the conservation areas in the South Side—had reason for hostility. If the Authority was to build on vacant land, it would have to build in their wards since there was no suitable vacant land elsewhere. And if it built, it would inevitably bring Negroes and other "undesirable people" into neighborhoods where people had been endeavoring for years to keep them out and thus presumably to protect property values. (Of course, even if it built within the congested Negro slum areas, the Authority would inevitably displace some Negroes who would probably find their way into the outlying white neighborhoods. This possibility, however, was not widely recognized and therefore not so much feared.)

Many of the aldermen came from conservation areas. Moreover, as we have mentioned, a South Side bloc of ward bosses had challenged the remains of the Kelly-Arvey organization and had gained control of the Council. Alderman Duffy and Wagner, the two most powerful men in the Council, were both South Side leaders. In 1949, it can be seen in retrospect, they were gaining and consolidating power at the expense of the Kelly-Arvey faction.

In 1949 the principal leader of the Kelly-Arvey faction was William J. Lancaster, chairman of the Rules Committee and of the Housing Committee of the City Council, but he was shifting to the South Side bloc. Two years before, when the Kelly-Arvey faction was still dominant, Lancaster had been an effective supporter of the Authority. Now he had cooled. "I am not essentially a public houser," he remarked in the summer of 1949 when the Authority put its proposal before the Council. "I believe that any family which through no fault of its own cannot live in decent housing has the right to live there. It is our duty to give them decent housing, the public housing should stop there."[4]

Lancaster's coolness was a sign of the new distribution of power within the party and the council. . . . . .

NOTES

1. William R. Gable. "The Chicago City Council: A Study of Urban Politics and Legislation." Unpublished dissertation, Department of Political Science, University of Chicago, Chicago, 1953, p. 13.

2. Gable, p. 121.

3. *Chicago Sun-Times*, April 4, 1950.

4. *Southtown Economist*, July 24, 1949.

2.

Trouble in Happyland

JAMES PHELAN

ON THE MORNING OF MARCH 2 THE HOUSEWIVES OF LOS ANGELES opened their newspapers, blinked and went into a mass tizzy. By unanimous vote of the City Council any housewife who tossed an empty sardine can into her trash barrel would be subject to a possible six-month jail term, a $500 fine or both. To appreciate the severity of this penalty one needs to note the going rate for another kind of wrongdoing in the City of Angels. A woman convicted of prostitution is normally let off with a $50 fine.

The council's action, establishing in effect that the commingling of tin cans and rubbish is 10 times more heinous than illicitly commingling the sexes, touched off a fearsome reaction. "In my entire public life," City Council President Harold Henry commented, "I have never heard so much resentment expressed by the people." Outraged ladies rushed to their telephones, dialed their councilmen and said unpleasant things. Others sat down and wrote furious letters, one of which led off, "Dear Idiot." Capri-clad Joans of Arc unfurled banners of revolt, vowing to defy the council and suffer martyrdom in the city clink. One bold rebel summoned television newsmen. While the cameras whirred, she grimly dumped a half dozen empty dog-food cans into her rubbish barrel.

Faced with mass civil disobedience, the council scrambled back into session and unanimously junked the rubbish penalty it had imposed only five days earlier.

To an uninformed stranger, such shenanigans must have seemed incomprehensible. To the citizens of Los Angeles it was just another day in L.A.'s wacky War of City Hall.

The City of Angels . . . . . has a new [problem] these days. Along with its smog (on bad days the city vanishes), its massive freeway jams (250 autos can crunch together in a single chain-reaction collision), its canyon brush fires and the unending influx of new residents (40,000 a year), Los Angeles now has a mayor and a City Council that seem out to exterminate each other.

The Draconian penalty for lobbing a tin can into a trash barrel was not so much an act of legislation as it was a military assault by the council on its arch-enemy, Mayor Samuel William Yorty. Yorty, a handsome, highly articulate, 53-year-old political maverick, has been battling with the council about tin cans ever since he took office in 1961. Underlying this tempest in a trash barrel is a contract voted by the council, whereby L.A.'s tin cans are sold to a salvage firm called Los Angeles By-Products Co. Housewives are supposed to keep cans separate from old dog bones, newspapers and garbage.

Yorty opposes tin-can segregation and wants to integrate all rubbish. Estimating that the sale of tin cans nets the city only two cents a month per household, Yorty accuses the council of degrading housewives to "coolie labor for a salvage firm." The mayor's ability to reduce an issue to a graphic political slur and impugn his opponents' motives, all in a few vivid words, drives the City Council into a frenzy. Accordingly, when Yorty told housewives they could integrate tin cans with impunity, the council fired back wildly with the fine and jail term. "They were so sore at Sam," says one of his aides, "that they shelled their own constituents."

The tin-can conflict is not an isolated controversy. "We have Custer's Last Stand almost every week, with the mayor and the council taking turns playing Indian," reports Ridgely Cummings, veteran City Hall newsman. A U.C.L.A. political-science professor concurs. "Los Angeles is the only city in the nation," he says, "that is trying to govern itself by unrestricted warfare."

The battle that began over rubbish has widened until it rages over a long list of issues. The air resounds with accusations, recriminations, personal insults, demands for grand-jury investigations and threats of impeachment. The nonstop donnybrook has been deplored in newspaper editorials, joked about by nightclub comedians, proposed as a subject for state legislative investigation and viewed with alarm by the Governor, who warned that it is threatening the future of California's largest city.

"The third-largest U.S. city is derided around the nation for its apparent inability to make the legislative-executive functions of government work," declared the Los Angeles *Times*. "The silly season surely must end. The boys have had their fun. Now it's time for the men to take over." This outspoken disapproval from the governor and the state's largest newspaper has had no discernible effect. Shortly afterward the mayor addressed the council and wound up swapping insults with Councilman Karl Rundberg. The dialogue in council chambers ended on this brisk exchange:

MAYOR: "You, sir, are representing the Los Angeles By-Products Company. I am representing the people."

RUNDBERG: "You, sir, are a liar."

"That hall between the mayor's suite and the council chamber is no-man's-land," one of the mayor's staff reports grimly. "When you cross it, you're in enemy territory."

"We suspect our telephones may be tapped," says Councilman Rundberg. "Some of us made up an imaginary meeting in a restaurant on Sunset Boulevard and talked about it on the phone. None of us showed up, but one of the mayor's men did. Figure that out!"

Like many happenings in sun-basted Los Angeles, where yogis hold forth in stucco temples and self-certified healers recommend colonic irrigation for epilepsy and dandruff, L.A.'s uncivil War has an unreal air about it. Disputes between the executive and legislative branches of government, whether national, state, or city, are common in the United States. But L.A.'s war has a strong flavor of Gilbert and Sullivan, in that it is waged by unlikely combatants with bizarre tactics over improbable issues.

Next to the rubbish rumpus, the bitterest controversy between the mayor and the council has centered on an offshore oil lease. The lease was granted by the council without competitive bidding before Yorty took office. Yorty has denounced the lease as a "multi-million-dollar giveaway" of city resources "to a paper corporation" consisting of "a favored few." The company with the lease, Los Angeles Harbor Oil Development Co., included several figures close to the regime of Mayor Norris Poulson, whom Yorty defeated in 1961. The only assets of the firm at the start were $1,250 in capital and some filing cabinets, and it had never before drilled even a posthole. The councilmen who awarded the lease insist that the area—far offshore in deep water—is a "wildcat" venture and that no established oil firm would drill it. Today, after six years of litigation, millions of words of acrimony and three exploratory core holes, the lease has not yielded enough oil to lubricate a door hinge.

This has not deterred the mayor and council from battling over it as if it were another Kuwait or Teapot Dome. Not long ago the City Planning Commission, appointed by Yorty, zoned a large portion of these ocean depths for residential use only. Since oil drilling is forbidden in residential areas, this action restricted exploration to a small patch of the 6,400 leased acres. Stung by this move, the council countered in kind. It recommended that the waters of Santa Monica Bay, where one of the mayor's commissions was contemplating other offshore oil leases, be zoned for single residences. In both areas the Pacific is so deep that it is habitable only by fish, the hardiest of skin divers and a peculiar kind of West Coast lobster that has no claws.

The comic-opera flavor of L.A.'s war is heightened by the ferocious name-calling between the combatants. Within the council chambers the mayor has been described as "ruthless," "power-mad," "unscrupulous," "a fringe paranoid" and a "would-be dictator." "Without question," says one city father, "that man is the most arrogant egomaniac I have ever met in my life."

These violent words lead a stranger to expect a loud-voiced Boss Tweed with a coiled bullwhip within easy reach. In the flesh, Sam Yorty is a soft-spoken fellow with a ready smile and a deceptively easygoing air. A lawyer, he has spent a large part of his adult years in political office, first as an assemblyman at Sacramento, then as a California representative in Congress. He has a charming blond wife named Betty, one son and a comfortable home (with the standard California swimming pool), that once belonged to Mickey Rooney. He attributes his interest in politics to his childhood in Lincoln, Nebraska, where his father was an ardent Democrat and a friend of William Jennings Bryan.

Whatever his inclinations, Sam Yorty politically is poorly equipped to become the "ruthless dictator" that his council enemies say he aspires to be. As mayor, he has almost no patronage to dispense, other than the 125 commission memberships that pay $10 per meeting. Both the mayor and council in Los Angeles—unlike those in New York and Chicago—run without party labels. Although Yorty is a lifelong registered Democrat, he swings little weight in California's potent Democratic Party because of his maverick tendencies. In the 1960 Presidential race, he supported Richard Nixon with a signed brochure entitled "I Can't Take Kennedy," thus earning the enduring hostility of state Democratic leaders. Not long ago State Senator Hugh Burns, a powerful Democratic sachem in Sacramento, was asked, "What do you think Yorty will run for next?" Burns replied, "I hope he runs for the Mexican border."

Yorty in turn characterizes the fifteen City Council members as a Machiavellian band of "would-be ward bosses" who seek to frustrate "the will of the voters" because they are "subservient to powerful, selfish interests."

Over on the council's side of no-man's-land one finds an oddly assorted group of fourteen councilmen and one councilwoman who seem bound together by little more than their obsessive dislike of the mayor. The council includes a former newspaperman, several retired Midwestern businessmen, a fireman, the owner of a hardware store, and the former arranger for Kay Kyser's Kollege of Musical Knowledge. The feminine member is Rosalind Wiener Wyman, who won her council seat 10 years ago as a dewy-eyed U.C.L.A. graduate and was promptly dubbed "the cutest councilman in the world."

Roz Wyman is an active Democrat and the wife of State Democratic Chairman Eugene Wyman. Her dislike for Yorty is surpassed only by her affection for the Los Angeles Dodgers. Her office is decorated in what is perhaps best described as Early Walter O'Mally, with Dodger cartoons, autographed pictures, baseballs and bats pinch-hitting for the conventional watercolors and chintz. When not drawing a bead on Sam Yorty, Roz Wyman likes to have her picture taken wearing a Dodger baseball cap.

Yorty tends to characterize this lady baseball fan and her fourteen colleagues as a monolithic Alliance Against Progress. By its very nature the Los Angeles council is an assortment of disparate spokesmen for separate geographic duchies that stretch from the remote reaches of San Fernando Valley far down to the sea at distant San Pedro. Until Yorty came upon the scene the council, in the words of the Los Angeles *Times*, "could rarely agree upon the time of day." L.A. councilmen are elected by district rather than by city-wide vote. Hence they are responsible only to their own patches of constituents and then tend to take a provincial view of issues affecting the other 14/15ths of the city. A councilman representing swank Toluca Lake, with such constituents as Bob Hope, moves in a different world from the city father representing the Negro ghettos of southcentral Los Angeles or the grimy, unpainted warrens of Boyle Heights.

"I'll give Sam Yorty credit for one thing," says Rosalind Wyman. "He solidly united the council." This unity, however, consists almost entirely of voting against the mayor's proposals. The council even rejected a Federal grant of $2,500,000 for a modern data-processing system that would collect and analyze myriad facts on land use, property values, population movements and housing deterioration, as well as other data essential to effective city planning. In these days of strained budgets and competition for the tax dollar, the council's action brought some yelps of pain. Pointing out that L.A. residents had contributed the cash originally in the form of taxes, the *Valley Times* commented:

"The council (has) said in effect that Los Angeles must not take back any of the dollars we have given to the Federal government. . . . Better, the logic seems to be, we should let our share of the fund go to other cities, such as San Francisco . . . to help them set up their programs so they can compete more effectively with Los Angeles!"

An issue of this sort at least conveys to the voters the notion that City Hall is contending over matters of scope and moment. Most of the time, however, Angelenos have been onlookers at a series of Lilliputian Armageddons. The mayor and council have battled over which would send a lobbyist to Sacramento, over the mayor's use of a city helicopter, over the propriety of Yorty's serving cocktails at official luncheons—and who paid for the liquor. One council member even complained bitterly because the mayor had two parking spaces reserved for himself in the garage under City Hall. When the mayor initiated a weekly radio program entitled "Ask Your Mayor," the council demanded—and got—equal time for its own program entitled "Ask Your Councilman."

"All this might be funny if you could forget what these people are supposed to be doing," says a prominent Los Angeles lawyer. "They were elected to run a city that contains more people than twenty-five of the states in this country."

One of the reasons for the councilmen's bilious reaction to Sam Yorty undoubtedly is that they have not yet digested the impalatable fact of his election. His defeat of Poulson, an affable, conservative accountant who was seeking his third term, was one of the most remarkable political upsets since Harry Truman turned back Thomas Dewey at the threshold of the White House in 1948. Yorty's victory even caught California's most astute politician, Democrat Jesse (Big Daddy) Unruh, with his analysis down. "The *last* man I counted out of politics," Unruh says ruefully, "is now mayor of Los Angeles."

Not a single member of the council publicly supported Yorty for mayor. Neither did any of the other recognized sources of power in Los Angeles. Poulson, on the other hand, had the backing of the major metropolitan newspapers, the A.F.L.–C.I.O., the downtown merchants, the major real-estate interests and most of the contractors doing business with the city. Poulson, a staunch Republican, had the unofficial support of the G.O.P., while Yorty had the professional Democrats openly whetting their knives for him because of his defection to Nixon. On top of all these handicaps, Yorty had been out of political office for eight years and had been soundly whipped in his last two races, when he had sought the U.S. senatorship......

Unabashed by the narrowness of his victory—he won the support of only twenty-four per cent of the city's 1,128,070 registered voters—Yorty announced that he intended to be "a strong mayor." He started boldly, sweeping the city commissions clean of Poulson appointees and bringing in a bunch of "Young Turks" for his personal staff, mainly newspapermen. He announced that he would "run the government out in the open, in a fishbowl." He instituted a weekly press conference and has maintained a warm relationship with the TV news corps.

"These press sessions are the part of this job I like best," Yorty says.

"I can take my case directly to the people. Before I came into office the source of power in Los Angeles lay outside City Hall. Poulson was passive; the council was largely a vacuum. There was a small outside coterie running the city. I cut all the existing lines of influence and power."

To date none of the disasters predicted by his enemies has befallen the City of Angels. His administration has not yet had a major scandal. His commission appointments have been praised by none other than Poulson's campaign managers. Yorty retained the able and respected William Parker, "toughest cop in the country," as chief of police, and Los Angeles still is free of organized gambling and vice.

But what has happened to Los Angeles is a more subtle and destructive malaise. While the city has not gone to hell in a hand-basket, major citywide projects have hardly moved in any direction at all. With the mayor and the council entwined like Laocoön and the serpents, any city progress requiring their cooperation has been squeezed to death between them.

The council blames Yorty, of course. "The mayor just won't believe that you can have an honest difference in opinion," says Rosalind Wyman. "If you disagree with him, he questions your motives. There's no presumption of good faith." "When we disagree, Yorty takes the attitude that everyone is a liar except Yorty," complains Councilman Lemoine Blanchard. "He's attacked us with insinuations and has never proved one of his charges," says Councilman Rundberg. "He's smart, slick, and intellectually dishonest." "Yorty is irresponsible," charges Councilman James Brown.

Most of these complaints grow out of a long, loud brawl over a proposal by Yorty for a new hotel at the giant International Airport. When the council chorused its customary "Nay," the mayor charged that motel operators had raised "a $20,000 slush fund to influence the council." He took the issue to the grand jury, which summoned the council members, interrogated them and then threw out Yorty's charges. Yorty turned his fire on the grand jury, accused it of a "whitewash" and ignored the council's demand for an apology. "He had us hauled in like a bunch of gangsters on a charge that had no foundation," says one councilman. "I'll hold that against him as long as he lives."

Sam Yorty blames the civic imbroglio on the structure of Los Angeles's government. The charter of Los Angeles, an antiquated document that has been amended 194 times, is ambiguous as to who runs the city. It designates the council "the governing body" but designates the mayor the chief executive officer and instructs him to exercise "careful supervision" over all city affairs and "constant supervision over the acts and conduct of all officers and employees." Having given him this broad responsibility, the charter gives him no authority to carry out the job.

"The mayor is elected by all the people," Yorty says, "but each councilman is responsible only to his district. I spelled out a city-wide program in my campaign, and the voters approved it by electing me. Then the council sits over there and knocks it into the ashcan. Every mayor before me ran into this problem. You can either fight it or you can give up and become the council's dummy. I'm going to fight it. Sooner or later Los Angeles has to decide whether it is going to function as a city or as fifteen separate provinces."

There have been repeated attempts in the past to give the mayor greater authority and restrict the council to policy-making. When these proposals reach the council, the city fathers simply shunt them into a one-way file. Governmental bodies traditionally do not legislate a reduction in their own power and prestige, and the council is more likely to annex Los Angeles to San Francisco than to increase the mayor's power.

A new study of charter reform is nearing completion* under the auspices of Town Hall, a respected civic group. One path around the council roadblock would be to submit a charter revision to the voters. Supporters of charter reform nervously try to keep the project out of range of the current bloodletting at City Hall. Almost to a man the council opposes any change in the present split in power. "Sam Yorty wants one-man rule," says one city father. "And before I'll give it to him the Los Angeles River will freeze over forty feet deep." . . . . .

A current controversy in California revolves around the question of abolishing boxing. Yorty declined to take a stand, commenting, "If you abolish fights, what are the City Council and I going to do?"

Not long ago Councilman Blanchard came forth with a desperate proposal to end the war. He called for a "Peace Corps" to try and mediate the marathon war of the Angels. Fifteen members of the Peace Corps would be named by the council, fifteen by the mayor and fifteen by the Los Angeles Bar Association.

"Forty-five peacemakers," mused a member of the City Hall press corps. "That's five times the size of the United States Supreme Court. If I remember my history, it didn't take that many people to draft the United States Constitution." Just then his "squawk box," which pipes in the deliberations of the City Council to the pressroom, emitted a roar of angry voices as the council began its daily denunciation of the mayor.

"Forty-five," said the newsman. "It won't be enough."

*The study was completed in 1964 but the charter has not been changed. Discussion of the matter continues—Ed.

3.

Few Hits and Many Balks on Albany Legislation

RICHARD REEVES

MAYOR LINDSAY LOOKED TOWARD THE CEILING OF HIS GRACIE MANSION office during an interview about his relations with the Legislature and Governor Rockefeller and said: "They have much too much power over the city. Sometimes it makes me want to crawl up the walls."

The cause for this frustration, the Mayor's aides and friendly legislators agree, is that the Mayor has far too little power over Albany.

"Lindsay has no clout in the Capitol. Nothing," said one of the men primarily responsible for the city's dealings with the state. "The Patrolmen's Benevolent Association can line up dozens of legislators; the Mayor of New York controls four or five votes. Look at what's happened this year!"

What has happened in 1968 is that the Legislature and Governor have combined to cut back state aid to the city by more than $100-million, most of that in Medicaid payment reductions. At the same time, the Lindsay legislative program has been largely rejected or, perhaps worse, ignored. The Mayor often has trouble finding supporters among the 57 Senators and 148 Assemblymen who are willing to introduce his bills in both houses.

"We've got no place to go for sponsors," said Anthony P. Savarese, a former Queens Assemblyman who is the city's chief legislative representative. "We just reach around for someone to grab."

Before the Legislature began an Easter recess that ends today (April 29, 1968) 224 city bills had been introduced. Only seventeen have passed both houses, and five have been signed into law by the Governor.

The bills that have become law were relatively minor—one of them permits a fireman who is not the driver of a firetruck to turn on the siren. The bills that have gone nowhere—at least so far—include Mr. Lindsay's top-priority items: his Urbanaid program to channel a portion of the state income tax directly to municipalities; legislation to implement a plan to decentralize the city school system and bills establishing a public authority to build city hospitals.

Mr. Lindsay's Albany scorecard, which has certainly been affected by two years of sporadic friction with the Legislature and his abrasive personal relationship with the Governor, looks especially bad when compared with former Mayor Robert F. Wagner's record in his last year in office. In 1965 the city introduced 202 bills, 159 passed both houses, and more than 100 were signed by Mr. Rockefeller.

The comparison between 1965 and 1968, however, is far from exact for several reasons, particularly the Legislature's tradition of delaying action on important bills until the last days of a session.

The leaders of that Democratic-controlled session three years ago—Assembly Speaker Anthony J. Travia and Senate Majority Leader Joseph Zaretzki—were close political allies of the Democratic Mayor who were elected with Mr. Wagner's support after a six-week intraparty fight.

Mr. Lindsay has said he is hopeful that the 1968 Legislature will take a new look at his major programs in the closing days of this session. Two reasons for his optimism are his secret negotiations with state officials on a compromise school decentralization plan and . . . . . the Governor's announcement on Saturday that he would ask legislative leaders to at least consider Urbanaid or other methods of increasing aid to cities.

But the Mayor has given up on his school decentralization plan and will support a more modest plan that he has privately negotiated with the State Board of Regents.

The Republican Mayor readily concedes, however, that the divided, economy-minded 1968 Legislature—Republicans control the Senate, 31 to 26, and Democrats control the Assembly, 78 to 70—is not going to give him as much as Mr. Wagner won in 1965. (Mr. Wagner also had some very bad years before he dealt with his own leaders and formed a working political alliance with Mr. Rockefeller.)

In fact, party lines don't hold for Mr. Lindsay, who has never had strong ties to his own party and was elected Mayor by avoiding the G.O.P. label. Moreover, most of the Republican legislators represent rural or suburban voters who generally resent sending money or help south of Yonkers.

There are 79 Democrats and 15 Republicans in the city delegation, and most of them are sympathetic toward the Mayor's problems, if not toward the Mayor himself.

"I want to help the city," said one Democrat, "but I don't want to make Lindsay President."

Only a handful of legislators are considered solidly pro-Lindsay, according to other legislators. The names usually mentioned are the three Republicans from the Mayor's old 17th Congressional District—Senator Whitney North Seymour Jr. and Assemblymen S. William Green and John M. Burns—and two Reform Democrats from the Upper West Side —Jerome Kretchmar and Albert H. Blumenthal.

The Mayor's power base is not only small, it is also shaky, because his handful of votes cannot be delivered or traded. Mr. Seymour and the others vote the kind of very independent liberal line that Mr. Lindsay followed when he was in Congress. So the Mayor, in the words of Mr. Savarese, "tries to substitute personal appeal, his popularity with people and the press," for the political alliances that Mr. Wagner had in his later years in office.

Mr. Lindsay has tried to combine public pressure—speeches and statements stressing that "Albany must not shortchange the cities in this time of crisis"—with private persuasion, such as weekly telephone calls to legislative leaders; a trip to the opening night of Gore Vidal's *Weekend* with Senate Majority Leader Earl W. Brydges; quiet Albany trips by his personable deputy mayor, Robert W. Sweet; and "Dear Augie" notes to Orest V. Maresca, the Manhattan Democrat who is chairman of the Assembly's City of New York Committee.

Public pressure helped Mr. Lindsay score one legislative victory this year. After being bombarded by pro-Lindsay editorials and letters from home during the city's garbage strike, the Legislature refused to act on the Governor's plan for a temporary state take-over of the city's Sanitation Department.

"We're making some progress," the Mayor said. "The leadership understands our problems better than ever. But they're presiding over a lot of troops who couldn't care less."

What the Legislature seems to care about this election year is cutting back such expensive programs as Medicaid to hold off the need for new taxes. Even Mr. Rockefeller—"the great persuader," as he is sometimes called in the halls of the Capitol—has had trouble getting some of his favorite and expensive programs through the Legislature.

But Mr. Lindsay's problems go far deeper. His big bills are locked in committee. His vocal opposition did not stop the Medicaid cutbacks or the creation of the Urban Development Corporation, the Rockefeller slum-rebuilding program that the mayor said was a violation of the principle of home rule.

Some of the Mayor's lower priority items are summarily dismissed as soon as they reach Albany. His legislation to abolish the city marshal system, which was introduced after detailed disclosures of alleged abuses by marshals, was greeted with an "it'll never get out of my committee" statement by Max E. Turshen, a Brooklyn Democrat who is chairman of the Assembly Judiciary Committee. Mr. Turshen is a long-time defender of the marshal system, which civic groups have attacked as a Democratic patronage source, and the bill is still in committee.

A Lindsay bill to free the city from a state regulation requiring that the same number of policemen be assigned to each eight-hour working shift received even rougher treatment. The Mayor's argument that more police were needed at night was ignored as the Assembly passed a P.B.A.-backed bill that not only perpetuated the regulation but also mandated the exact hours each policeman had to work.

"Just another shattered lance," Mr. Lindsay said, noting that most of his predecessors have had less legislative influence than bipartisan special interest lobbies, such as the police establishment, power companies and the banking and insurance industries.

The police hours bill demonstrates the power that the State Constitution gives the Legislature over the day-to-day operations of municipalities. The state's basic law was largely shaped by upstate Republicans who assumed powers over the Democratic city to—in the language of Article 8—"prevent abuses in taxation and assessments and in contracting indebtedness by them."

"The control Albany has over the city is ridiculous," the Mayor said. "It's asinine that we have to go to them for new legislation before we can order 800 sanitation men to ticket illegally parked cars."

Mr. Lindsay, like other mayors before him, has particularly objected to frequent state legislation increasing the pension benefits of city employes represented by politically effective unions.

"Mandated pension costs," he said, "are one of the reasons we need more state aid to close our budget gap."

Although he has a good personal relationship with Mr. Brydges and Mr. Travia, the Mayor is still haunted by the bad feeling he generated in 1966 when he tried to balance the budget by asking the Legislature for permission to collect $520-million in new city taxes. When the legislators balked, Mr. Lindsay accused them of "cowardice" and threatened to campaign against anyone who opposed his tax program.

The threats did not work, and the Mayor finally went to the Capitol for a compromise—a $236-million package that included a city income and commuter tax. But Mr. Lindsay escalated the feud by continuing to threaten Albany leaders during the secret sessions that led to the compromise.

After Mr. Lindsay had left one meeting with the Governor and legislative leaders, David Ross, the majority leader of the Democrats on the City Council, who had accompanied the Mayor, said: "John, if you talked to me the way you just talked to them, I'd punch you in the nose."

The new administration's relations with the state were not helped by the Mayor's choice for his first legislative representative—Richard M. Rosen, a 30-year-old campaign worker whose chief governmental experience had been as an assistant to State Attorney General Louis J. Lefkowitz.

"You'd be surprised how many people resented that," a former State Senator said. "Lindsay was sending up a storefront kid to handle the rubes."

After one session, Mr. Rosen was recalled to handle cultural affairs at City Hall. He was replaced by a former Republican Assemblyman from Manhattan, Paul J. Curran, in 1966, and this year by Mr. Savarese, who served fifteen years in the Assembly and who is widely credited with improving City Hall's rapport with the Capitol.

When the Legislature is in session, Mr. Savarese and his five assistants fan out from a modern office in the Mechanics Exchange Savings Bank Building a block from the Capitol.

Their job, as described by Mr. Savarese, is a "mechanical" memo-sending analysis of the 11,000 bills introduced annually in Albany and back-slapping lobbying for smaller city bills.

Mr. Lindsay and his top assistants lobby personally for important legislation and Mr. Sweet is chairman of the city's Legislative Review Committee, which meets in his City Hall office each Friday morning to set policy on all bills of interest to the city.

The other members of the review committee are Mr. Savarese, Fiorvante Perotta, the Mayor's executive assistant; Assistant Corporation Counsel Norman Redlich, who is in charge of drafting city bills; John McInnis, the Budget Bureau's research director and Robert M. Blum, the mayoral assistant responsible for liaison with the Democrat-controlled City Council.

"The council is my chief ally in dealing with Albany," the Mayor said. "We have an equal stake in getting production from the Legislature, and they are always enormously helpful in dealing with Democrats in Albany."

Mr. Rockefeller has also been helpful to the city, particularly in vetoing legislation—pension increases, for example—opposed by Mr. Lindsay but passed by both houses. But, while state and city officials describe the legislative relations between the Mayor and Governor as "very good" and "professional," there is still evidence of the tension that has always existed between the two Republicans.

Mr. Lindsay was not consulted about Mr. Rockefeller's most ambitious urban program—the Urban Development Corporation, which would have the power to ignore local laws in rebuilding city slums. The Mayor, who has continually attacked the corporation, vaguely blames the lack of communication on "staff problems."

In fact, staff members—especially Mr. Sweet and Alton G. Marshall, the Governor's secretary—conduct most of the business that a Governor and Mayor might be expected to handle personally. "Somebody has to do it," said a Lindsay aide. "John and Nelson just can't seem to sit down together without getting into a fight."

But, even after years of friction and months of frustration, Mr. Lindsay said yesterday that he was still optimistic about 1968. "As long as the Legislature is in session," he said, "hope is not lost."

N O T E

Hope was not lost, but 1968 left it badly damaged. Lindsay's Urbanaid program and his bill to establish a public authority to build hospitals were killed in legislative committees. The Rockefeller proposal for an Urban Development Corporation, which Lindsay opposed, was passed. Though insufficient from the Mayor's viewpoint, $220 million in new state aid for the city was appropriated. One victory for Lindsay: a law which provided a modified plan for some decentralization of the city school system—Ed.

PART V

The Mayor As Chief of Party

AMONG SOME ELEMENTS IN AMERICAN SOCIETY, PARTICULARLY THE UPPER-strata patricians, there has been a profound skepticism of "politics" and "politicians" dating back to the days of Washington and Adams. Toward the close of the nineteenth century, such feelings became more pervasive as major scandals were revealed by muckrakers like Lincoln Steffens. This has been especially true of urban communities, where tirades against the party machines have long been a standard tactic for good government groups. Furthermore, the advocates of reform have traditionally contended that the best kind of mayor is one who stands aloof from party.

An important question in the readings which follow is the applicability of the reform thesis in the light of the realities of urban government. Most contemporary political observers seem to agree that, at best, such reasoning causes more confusion than enlightenment. The first selection, "Who Speaks for Political Purity," was written by Edward N. Costikyan, a reformer who later became leader, in the early 1960's, of New York's notorious Tammany Hall. His principal theme: politics is the essence of governing and even Mayor La Guardia, the darling of reformers everywhere, was a most astute politician. James Reichley elaborates the point in his critical assessment of the Philadelphia reform regimes headed by Richardson Dilworth and Joseph S. Clark ("Reform Party Leadership"), in which he maintains that these two mayors had only a minimal impact on the life of the city because they lacked the know-how of governing, and, having been anti-organization, they left nothing that could maintain continuity of whatever it was that they stood for.

Finally, "The Delicate Balance" by Edward C. Banfield shows just how intricate are the workings of party leadership in a formally decentralized structure of government. The mayor who is discussed here is Richard J. Daley of Chicago, a noted expert in the strategies of machine politics. Of particular interest in this selection is the way the city head must placate the good government groups while at the same time feeding gravy to the ward bosses—a difficult balancing act indeed. The overall result, however, is to weaken the party organization; and where the party has become debilitated, as it has in most other cities today, an important means of political leverage is thereby lost to the mayor.

1.

Who Speaks for Political Purity?

EDWARD COSTIKYAN

WHEN JAMES BRYCE VISITED THE UNITED STATES IN THE 1880's, HE noted that while our federal and state governments had demonstrated great competence in managing their affairs, generally our cities were badly governed.

Growing, sprawling, teeming with new arrivals mostly from Europe, far larger than the established European cities which had long been able to manage their own affairs, American city governments seemed grotesquely unsuited to their tasks.

The most obvious symptoms of this mismanagement were apparent in the activities of political leaders in New York City—Boss Tweed, Honest John Kelly, Richard Croker, not to mention Fernando Wood, mayor of the city, who, with the forty-man Board of Aldermen, soon became known as "Ali Baba and the forty thieves."

The political leaders took advantage of the incompetence of city government without restraint. Government privileges were bought and sold. New courthouses cost ten times their value. Alliances between the underworld and political leaders were common knowledge.

Soon the symptom of poor city government became the target of good-government forces. Good government and political-party government were antagonists. A political leader was, by definition, a lower form of human being—untrustworthy, likely to be mysteriously wealthy, probably allied with underworld characters, and certainly not to be emulated.

How the political parties—especially Tammany Hall—survived generations of public criticism and public exposure to be returned to power again and again is an exceedingly complex tale. In part, the longevity is attributable to the extent of alienation of new citizens from the old Americans who dominated good government movements; in part to the loyalties earned from these new citizens by the political bosses; and in part to the reforms that good-government forces occasionally forced through—civil service, public bidding, independent school boards—which limited the opportunity for political leaders to get into trouble.

But the machines survived until the New Deal, immigration legislation, good-government reforms, and a host of other factors, including population mobility, economic mobility, and World War II, destroyed the bases upon which the old machines existed.

During this long period, the good-government tradition and heritage in our cities became almost entirely an anti-machine, anti-political-leader one. "Reformer" was a term of opprobrium within the machine, and reformers looked elsewhere for political success and governmental progress.

They looked to the occasional creation of an ad hoc political force which would sporadically "throw the rascals out" and enjoy four years or so of steadily deteriorating governmental power, until the machine returned to power.

In New York, this tradition became known as "fusion." Three times in this century it succeded—in 1901 when Seth Low, president of Columbia University, became a one-term mayor, in 1913 when John Purroy Mitchel became a one-term mayor, and in 1933 when Fiorello La Guardia became a three-term mayor.*

Each time the coalition behind the successful candidate was an unstable one, each time it magically deteriorated. On one occasion a new alignment was created within the fusion movement, assigning different power positions to different groups within the coalition. This was in the case of La Guardia in 1937 and 1941, when the American Labor Party, La Guardia's own newly created party, replaced the Republican Party as the dominant force within the coalition.

In the other two successful fusion movements, 1901 and 1913, the coalition died within one term—two and four years respectively.

One reason was the absence of any political skills in the managers of the coalition. Being anti-political in orientation, and being convinced that the symptom of bad government—venal political leaders—was its cause, the fusionists disdained the political arts. Efficiency and nonpo-

---

*For reasons stated later, the Lindsay victory in 1965 was not an example of a genuine fusion victory.

litical administration would produce good government. The introduction of political skills would produce bad government.

And so each of the leaders of fusion—until La Guardia—destroyed his own coalition—out of principle. Lincoln Steffens described the phenomenon magnificently in *The Shame of the Cities:*

> . . . Certainly Mayor Low is pecuniarily honest. He is more; he is conscientious and experienced and personally efficient. . . . Is there a demand for Mr. Low? No. When I made my inquiries—before the lying had begun—the Fusion leaders of the anti-Tammany forces, who nominated Mr. Low, said they might renominate him. "Who else was there?" they asked. . . . Mr. Low's is not a lovable character. But what of that? Why should his colleagues love him? Why should anybody like him? Why should he seek to charm, win affection, and make friends? He was elected to attend to the business of his office and to appoint subordinates who should attend to the business of their offices, not to make "political strength" and win elections. . . . Mr. Low is the ideal product of the New York theory that municipal government is business, not politics, and that a business man who would manage the city as he would a business corporation, would solve for us all our troubles.

Because of this anti-political attitude, each reform-fusion movement carried within it the seeds of its own destruction. Each became a temporary protest movement, and each ran its course—until La Guardia.

La Guardia was the first fusion mayor who was principally a politician. He was anti-machine in orientation—even his own party's machine, which he had frequently opposed and which had frequently opposed him. In Congress he had aligned himself with the Midwest Progressives—La Follette and Norris—and he had within his volatile makeup a good deal of the Midwestern Progressives' animosity toward any form of power—whether of political machines or political leaders or businessmen.

Initially, La Guardia was a shaky leader of the 1933 fusion coalition (others like Judge Samuel Seabury and C. C. Burlingham were far more powerful). But La Guardia gradually assumed control, reshaped the coalition, created his own political party—the American Labor Party, which consisted largely of nationally oriented Democrats dissatisfied with the local Democratic machine—and, using his broad patronage powers, built a personal machine, loyal to him and able to support him effectively each time he ran.

It was only when he lost the support of his personal machine towards the end of World War II that he decided to abandon an attempt to be re-elected and he announced his retirement in 1945. By then, the original fusion movement which had elected him in 1933 against a divided Democratic Party was long since dead. Efforts in 1945 and 1949 to revive "fusion" behind different candidates were total failures, and the Fusion Party in 1957 and 1961, by then little more than a letterhead and a negotiable instrument, endorsed the Democratic incumbent, Robert F. Wagner.

And yet La Guardia fortified the anti-political-leader bias of the good-government tradition. His tirades against "tin-horn gamblers" and "two-bit politicians" deepened the public association between politicians and evildoers. In retrospect, his administration became a myth—a myth which equated good government with the absence of political leaders in government. But it was a myth in both respects.

The government in question was simply not that good. For example, the failure of the La Guardia administration in the field of education—the tremendous lag in school construction and the steadily decreasing quality of education in underprivileged areas—laid the groundwork for the explosive educational, employment, and civil rights problems which have beset the city ever since.

There was an equation of "honest government" with "good government" during the La Guardia years—an equation of doubtful validity. Dishonest government is bad government, but honesty in government in and of itself does not insure good government.

The second fallacy in the appraisal of the La Guardia years was the notion that La Guardia government represented government conducted in the absence of political leaders. For La Guardia was himself one of the most astute politicians ever developed in New York. A fantastic vote-getter, a shrewd utilizer of manpower, a careful dispenser of patronage, La Guardia carefully kept the political parties alive, but barely so—sufficiently strong to help win re-election for La Guardia but insufficiently strong to dominate those elected.

In this, La Guardia became the prototype for Mayor Robert F. Wagner of New York, Richard Daley of Chicago, and David Lawrence of Pittsburgh—the public-officeholder who was also the political leader.

Despite all this, La Guardia left the good-government tradition and theory where he found it—firmly oriented against political leaders, political machines, and political parties. While he privately incorporated the function of the political leader, the political party, and the political machine into his own administration and made them extensions of his own personality, he publicly railed at the politicians.

And so the spokesmen for good government remained anti-political in orientation and in utterance. The Citizens Union, the City Club, and various other custodians of the good-government tradition maintained their aloofness from the political machinery. They patiently awaited the day when the dominant Democrats, who had recaptured control of the mayoralty in 1945, would again so decline in public esteem, so fragment themselves in internal disputes, and so misgovern, that another upsurge of anti-political-leader reform would create a new fusion movement to restore good government to New York City.

As we shall see, however, during the twenty years from 1945 to 1965 the good-government tradition, in younger hands, began to seek a more permanent and more meaningful existence. With a slight but significant amendment of the good-government philosophy, it sought expression within the dominant Democratic Party. This deviant good-government tradition asserted the following propositions:

1. Political leaders were not bad per se—only bad political leaders were.

2. The principal fault with prior political leadership had been excessive autocratic control by too few men of the political machinery.

3. Prior "good-government" efforts had failed because they were sporadic, impermanent, and outside the established political machinery. These efforts, to be permanently effective, should be directed at internal party reform—to replace the rascals with honest men, not to attempt to eliminate the role of the political leader entirely.

And so for the next twenty years the good-government tradition metamorphosed. The spokesmen for political purity were no longer solely political mavericks, attacking the political machinery, but more often than not holders of political office attacking other political-officeholders.

"The Reform Movement," dedicated to party control, became the official good-government spokesman, and acquired the kind of sanctity the editorial writers had previously accorded only to anti-political-party fusionists.

From time to time editorial writers vainly called upon the reformers to abandon their Democratic Party orientation and to strike a blow for good government by "joining" a fusion movement. ("Creating" would have been far more apt, since without the Reform Democrats there was no fusion movement to join.) In 1961, these editorial pressures reached their zenith, but after some hesitation, the reformers stuck to their theory and remained within the Democratic Party and supported Robert F. Wagner for re-election.

The major cause of this new good-government movement was Adlai E. Stevenson, the Democratic candidate for President in 1952 and 1956. Stevenson was essentially a good-government man. An intellectual, a gentleman, an idealist, he set out to prove, and he did prove, that an honest man could remain honest within the context of the obligations created by wholehearted devotion to a political party.

His excellence, although occasionally dimmed, endured despite the accommodations which a political existence occasionally required. And his defeats led many of his admirers to believe there was something wrong with a political party which could not produce a majority vote for such a magnificent, honest, intellectual, articulate, witty—almost perfect—human being.

These followers decided to follow his example: to plunge into the political maelstrom, to replace the hacks who had failed, to school themselves and their followers in the techniques of political action. As he was loyal to the institution of the Democratic Party, so were they. As he had demonstrated the possibility of the good-government tradition functioning in the context of an organized political party, so would they. As he had engaged in the political drudgery of campaigning in primaries and general election, so would they. As he had engaged in political maneuvering without destroying his integrity, so, by God, would they.

By the time of Governor Stevenson's death, many of his followers had installed themselves in significant party offices throughout the country. New York's reform movement was staffed, almost to a man, with Stevenson supporters. And the people of the country at large had come to an increasing awareness of the compatibility of political activity with integrity.

One curious aspect of the phenomenon was the extent to which the Stevensonians far exceeded their mentor in practical political awareness, tactical understanding, and skill by the time Stevenson died. He had come to political activity for the first time in 1948—at the age of forty-eight. He plunged in, cold. From the good-government tradition which he represented, he tended to view politicians as enemies, as a bit outside the pale, as objects of suspicion. Indeed, because I was active in politics, there were occasions when we seemed to be talking a different language, although I was one of those stimulated by Stevenson's example, and although I was one of his law partners.

I came to feel, moreover, the same frustration with him which an older generation of politicians had been reputed to feel. This was especially true in 1964 when Stevenson was sometimes a possible candidate for U.S. senator from New York—and sometimes not. Only at the last moment, when it was too late, did he become convinced he ought to accept the nomination—but by then it was not possible to get it for him. The absence of political skill in a man who came to politics at the age of forty-eight was clear to me, then thirty-nine, who had come to politics at the age of twenty-six because of Stevenson's example. I believed (and believe) that if only he had been more comfortable in the political environment, we could have put him over.

But even though his followers may have surpassed him in their understanding of political activity and grasp of political techniques, he remained an inspiration to those who sought to translate the good-government antipolitical tradition into an internal political program.

The end result in 1965, the year of Stevenson's death, was a deep division in the New York good-government tradition. Part of it was committed to the new Stevenson tradition of good government via the political structure. Part of it—usually older voters who grew up on the La Guardia brand of good government—remained uncommitted to the new tradition, although not unfriendly to it, but basically anti-party in orientation.

And yet 1965 was an ideal year for a resurgence of the old fusion tradition:

... the Democratic Party was deeply divided, its wreckage strewn all over town;

... the city's problems seemed even more overwhelming than usual, with a profound budget deficit already in existence and an even more difficult series of deficits to be faced;

... the Republican Party had produced an extremely attractive vote-getter—John Lindsay—who had managed to put together a tri-party slate (Republican, Liberal, and Democrat) which gave at least the traditional appearance of a fusion slate.

On the other side of the coin:

... the Fusion Party, the organizational heir of the good-government tradition, announced its support of Paul Screvane, one of the Democratic aspirants;

... the Reform Democrats, while split between two candidates, William Fitts Ryan and Paul Screvane, remained committed to the Democratic Party, and the Democrat who joined the Lindsay slate, Milton Mollen, was not part of this reform movement in any way.

Nevertheless, after a twenty-year hiatus, an effort was being made to ascertain whether enough of the old good-government tradition had survived to produce a majority for a personable candidate, running with a tri-party slate against a badly divided Democratic Party.

The end result was an inconclusive draw. The Republican-Liberal "fusion" candidate for mayor, John Lindsay, was elected by a narrow margin. But along with him the people elected, by far more conclusive margins,

Democrats Frank O'Connor and Mario Procaccino to the Number-2 and -3 spots in the city government, and an overwhelmingly Democratic City Council.

The good-government tradition thus remained half-committed to each approach—the old and the new—but fully committed to neither.

This inconclusive result fairly reflected the twenty years of metamorphosis in the Democratic Party and the good-government tradition which preceded the election; and it accurately mirrored the confusion of the electorate as it sought a path to better city government.

2.

Reform Party Leadership

JAMES REICHLEY

REFORM, IT HAS BEEN SAID, IS WHAT WE HAVE IN AMERICA IN PLACE OF ideology. Political participation by those not professionally involved in politics is built around periodic attacks on the alleged corruption in government. Unfortunately, these attacks in most areas turn out to be few and far between, and the reform doctrine does not supply the kind of motivation that would keep the greater part of the population politically activated during the long dry spells between uprisings. What is the reason for this failure of "reform" to produce permanent interest in politics, and is there any possibility that it will in the future perform a function of social integration as well as eliminate the abuses at which it is primarily aimed? To answer these questions it will first be necessary to examine the nature of the reform idea.

Let us begin by turning back to the years immediately following the end of the Second World War when reform politics in Philadelphia was chiefly an exciting brew being passed from lip to lip among a little band of idealists in the city's gentleman's clubs and intellectual associations. A part of the nature of this mixture we have already suggested: Dislocated aristocrats were turning to politics as a means of winning back their own from the managerial class that was displacing them in practical life.

How was this strictly upper-class motivation, and the genuine social idealism that undoubtedly accompanied it, translated into a battle-cry that activated citizens of Philadelphia by the thousands to enlist in the army of reform? In the first place, of course, the reform spirit received its mass base by allying itself with the downtrodden city Democratic orga-

From *The Art of Government* by James Reichley, pp. 107–115, 122–125. Published 1959 by The Fund for the Republic, New York City, and reprinted by permission.

nization which had been waiting through almost half of the twentieth century for the logic of urban politics finally to sweep the local offices into the grasp of the party of the working man. But what was the aspect of the reform spirit that the Democratic politicians at last accepted, and how was it that this aspect was for a time not only acceptable but actually popular with the henchmen of the minority party organization? A clue to the answer to this question may be found in the story of the actual binding of the Democratic and reform causes.

Early in 1947, Michael Bradley, who was then chairman of the Democratic city committee and a leading proponent of alliance between his party and the reformers, gave consideration to four possible reform candidates for mayor: Walter Phillips, a leisured member of the upper class who had led the city planning crusade; Joseph S. Clark, a dabbler in Democratic politics over the years and anxious to be "rung in on things" since his return from the wars; Richardson Dilworth, a flamboyant war hero hovering on the outskirts of the city's old society; and Lewis Stevens, a starchy Philadelphia lawyer and leading lay figure in the Presbyterian Church of Pennsylvania.* Phillips had gained attention through his association with city planning, Clark through advocacy of civil-service reform, Stevens through his religious activities, and Dilworth through his publicly expressed intention to "throw the crooks out of City Hall." With little hesitation, the Democratic city chairman chose Dilworth. Emotional moralizing over the alleged corruption of the opposition, it seems clear, was the element of the reform program that most appealed to the organization Democrats. Had they not for years been threatening to "throw the rascals out"?

Dilworth's campaign in 1947 and virtually every campaign he has waged since that time have been built around the image of himself as prosecutor of the "crooks" whom he has sought to represent as the leaders of the GOP. (A young lawyer, a typical "clean-cut" Republican member of the legal fraternity with no trace of underworld connections, tells of having asked Dilworth in the early Fifties a rather difficult but fair question at one of his street-corner rallies, to which the reformer replied in rasping tones, "Young man, may I ask what numbers bank you represent?") This strategy paid off at the polls, not so much in 1947 as Michael Bradley had hoped it might, but particularly in 1949 and 1951 after the newspapers had exposed the fact that there was indeed a good deal of corruption in the Republican administration of City Hall.

More recently, such an approach has been somewhat undermined by

---

*Two of them did serve as Mayor—Clark (1951–1955) and Dilworth (1955–1962)—Ed.

the fact that it has become Dilworth's own Democratic party that controls the city administration, but the reform leader, seeking to maintain his stance as champion of the only aspect of the reform movement that has seemed much to interest him, has pretty broadly suggested . . . . . that even under Democratic rule the City Hall still has its share of crooks and that these would be likely to run riot were it not for the vigilant efforts of Richardson Dilworth. "I seem," he says, "to see the same faces in the corridors here that I saw eight years ago."

Unfortunately, the image of crook-catcher has been a little dimmed by the circumstances that Dilworth has in point of fact caught rather few crooks (the numbers racket, for instance, his special target, seems to thrive as much as ever throughout the city), and that his sometimes very courageous stands against the Democratic organization have usually been followed by back-sliding attempts to get back into the good graces of its leaders. The present mayor, it would seem, has been demoralizingly trapped between a desire to avoid Clark's outright defiance of the organization and a wish to be at the same time regarded in the public mind as the organization's reforming nemesis.

The spirit of Clark and of Walter Phillips, which dominated the first reform administration elected in 1951, may be said, in the long run, to have channeled the reform impulse in Philadelphia more successfully than Dilworth's moral preachments against the rascals in City Hall. This spirit, expressing the typical American mid-twentieth century philosophy of "good government," is less moral than institutional and economic. When Clark moved into the mayor's office in 1951, he directed, with the assistance of Phillips and the three governmental technicians who composed his cabinet, a thorough overhaul of the city's financial structure, its system of record, the operation of almost all its departments, and the entire decision-making process within the municipal hierarchy. At the same time, the new administration devoted serious attention to long-range problems like urban renewal and traffic control which had been almost completely neglected by its hand-to-mouth predecessors. Electronic machines appeared in City Hall to perform efficiently the tasks of recording that generations of ward-heelers had carried out with doubtful competence; trained economists brought fiscal sophistication to a budget that previously had been planned on the level of inky-ledgered arithmetic; employees hired under civil service replaced a large number of the party workers who formerly had given irregular service at their nominal jobs; great housing and commercial developments began to spring up in all parts of the city.

So complete were the changes made at this time that it is most unlikely that the return of any conceivable Democratic or Republican machine administration could alter many of the most important of them. It is probably true, as Lennox Moak, who served as first director of finance under Clark and now is director of the Pennsylvania Economy League in Philadelphia, says: "The reforms that will stick are the reforms that we made in the city's institutions. I cannot believe that any organization would wilfully put bad policies in place of good policies in areas where its patronage and so forth are not affected. The normal organization, once it gets into power, does things 'as they have always been done.' They will most probably in nine cases out of ten follow the precedents that we laid down for them." The city of Philadelphia will never return to the condition in which Joe Clark found it. With the single vital exception of civil service (ironically, Clark's special concern) the reforms that he and his collaborators made can almost certainly not be undone. And yet, in at least one respect, the Clark-Phillips school of institutional reform has been even less successful than the "throw-the-rascals-out" approach practiced by Richardson Dilworth.

"The problem that we have never solved is the problem of continuity," admitted Joe Clark in the summer of 1958. It is perfectly true that neither he nor Dilworth has constructed the kind of city-wide organization that could give any sort of permanence to the spirit as distinguished from the institutions of reform in city politics. Beyond a handful of activists in City Hall and the ADA, the reform movement appears to have lost all cohesiveness in the city; the Democratic organization, almost universally regarded as a "bunch of political bums," is universally rolling into power. This is due partly to certain biases within the spirit of reform. Before turning to these, however, it will be well to attempt to determine how much of the failure is due to the personalities of the two reform leaders themselves.

Despite their shared upper-class background and their common interest in reform, Richardson Dilworth and Joseph S. Clark are about as unlike as two men in public life can be. Dilworth is the warm, all-too-human, relatively simple extrovert in politics; Clark, in contrast, is reserved, reflective, some say cunning, complex, the thinker as politician. Dilworth seems to require heavy doses of admiration if not adulation from his sizable entourage; Clark, a loner by temperament, is sometimes accused of being difficult to work with. The current mayor [Dilworth], despite his retinue of supporters, runs what is in the last analysis a one-man show; all persons who deal with the city government are used to receiving phone calls from him in which pending problems are often settled in a few minutes of personal negotiation. The former mayor [Clark] was a man of the staff who operated through his subordinates whenever he could;

many of the people who now are consulted by Dilworth several times a month never had a personal conversation with Clark during his four years in office.

Dilworth rather resembles one of those heroes of F. Scott Fitzgerald, who came out of the Middle-Western gentry to be educated and make a name in the patrician East: Like them, he is charming, generous, unstable, not remarkably scrupulous, brave, ambitious, fond of high living, eager to make a splash, and fundamentally innocent. Dilworth, one feels, is forever playing out a role that he has only half understood, concentrating on the show while frequently growing bored with the substance. Like them, too, he seems to be motivated by an odd and not entirely ignoble idealism— the restless yearning to realize "the Platonic ideal of himself." It is harder to find a literary parallel for Clark. He is more tough-minded than the heroes of John Marquand whose background he shares, and he is more ambitious than the philosophic upstate squires created by James Cozzens (the Arthur Winner of Philadelphia is, in some ways, Walter Phillips). The truth is that he is the product of an upper class more deeply rooted in time than those which American novelists have usually got around to describing. To find his model one must probably turn to such European writers as Conrad, Stendhal, or Tolstoy; perhaps, even, it is in that crafty creator of a commonwealth, Shakespeare's King Henry IV, that one discerns his features most clearly.

In attitudes toward government Dilworth seems at first the more conservative, but on further thought one realizes that he is merely the more conventional (T.R. riding forth for another loud and fairly ineffectual crack at the forces of political unrighteousness). Senator Clark, who is frequently accused of being a radical, may on the other hand be "the most conservative leader in American public life today," as a friend of his calls him, but, if so, it is the calculated conservatism of Disraeli rather than the visceral conservatism of Burke. The Senator has given ample evidence for his attachment to such non-radical concepts as class, authority, and tradition, but he appears to believe that these concepts can be preserved in the modern world only with the assent of the mass of ordinary human beings. He has thus become the aristocratic leader of the commons against the "oligarchs" who seek to diminish the formal government so that their wills may be informally absolute in their private baronies.

Were (or are) either or both of these two most fascinating individuals capable of building an organization that might carry on the good-government ideal after they themselves have passed out of public life or at least out of intimate connection with city politics? Certainly they would have had great difficulties—Dilworth perhaps because he is too much the prima donna anxious to win victories and big headlines rather than to attempt any fundamental restoration of civic life, Clark perhaps because the very ruthlessness and cold intelligence that have made him personally strong tend to alienate him from the camaraderie and fellow-feeling that form the indispensable mortar to any enduring political organization. All the same, both possess great natural talents—an unfeigned fondness for humanity in the case of Dilworth, a lucid understanding of human nature in the case of Clark—which might well have suited them for the gigantic task of creating a permanent reform movement in the city. That both have so signally failed to do so (and with them the somewhat more earnest reformers like Phillips, not to mention the Republican public-relations reformers like Longstreth and Pomeroy) is, I think, partly due to the good-government philosophy itself which all have in one way or another represented.

This philosophy, in both its moral and its economic forms, seems to be oriented toward particular projects rather than toward any broad social image. It promises to perform certain worthwhile tasks of government, whether throwing the crooks out of City Hall or providing a more efficient means of circulating downtown traffic, instead of seeking to understand and to satisfy the fundamental needs of human beings. It takes the needs of human beings as given, and sets out to eliminate obstacles to the relief of these needs which it detects in the framework of society (like crooks) or which have been created by society's own rapid expansion (like street congestion). These objectives, even the moral ones, seem finally to be reducible to an economic view of the nature of man: Crooks are bad because they steal the taxpayers' money; traffic congestion is bad because it is strangling the economic life of the city; city planning is good because it provides an orderly means for the development of metropolitan commerce (though with city planning of the Bacon-Phillips kind, it must be admitted, a humanistic note is often struck)......

The economic view, coupled with a prevailing individualism which insists that government must limit itself to removing the obstacles to fulfillment of the economic needs of the population rather than undertake to fulfill them itself, makes difficult if not impossible any sustained, large-scale political effort dedicated to the objective of "reform." The declared purpose of reform is the soluton of this or that economic problem; when the problem is solved or when it has turned into a bore, the whole reason for the effort has collapsed. The possibility of "continuity" in the reform movement therefore becomes slim, and before very long it is "the same faces" of the organization politicians or ones very much like them that again begin to appear in the halls of government......

Most Americans do *not* actively participate in politics. The fact is that most Americans, except for occasional bursts of reform spirit, have been willing to permit their governments to be operated in a slovenly and irrational fashion which they would not dream of tolerating in any field in which they considered themselves to be personally concerned. The reason for this, I suspect, is that the case for good government has as a rule been presented in terms too simply economic: If elected, the reformer has generally seemed to be saying, I will save you money and I will rationalize our government so that our city will be a place in which you can make a good living. Well and good, the voter has seemed to think, and has cast his ballot for a Dick Dilworth or a Joe Clark.

But if the motive for political participation is strictly an economic one, then it must take its place within the hierarchy of similar economic motives and concerns. Inevitably, the place that it enjoys there cannot be a very high one. It must rank behind the job which is the direct source of personal income; it must rank behind the nominally social activities that are really instruments for personal advancement; it must rank behind the numerous exercises for self-improvement which can be turned back into the direct economic struggle. Since man does not live by bread alone, it will also probably rank behind the explicitly non-economic activities of leisure time. Unable to gain a high priority among economic motives, it is removed by its economic taint from competition with the activities that are labeled "pleasure." If political activity is really primarily motivated by economic concerns, as many reform politicians have seemed to assume, there is little hope that the greater portion of the population can ever be drawn for long stretches of time into active politics. Luckily, this does not seem to be the case.

Let us look again at the sense of moral frustration that has overcome the reform movement in Philadelphia and that, we have suggested, is a common characteristic of reform campaigns in this country. At first sight the frustration seems somewhat unreasonable. Since the amount of corruption carried on under the Republicans was not really so very great, and since the amount of corruption being carried on now is very likely even less, and since the institutional changes that have been made have been of a worthwhile and permanent nature, the reformers seem to have little cause for the sense of moral dismay that they clearly feel. At the same time, however, we have noted that the reform movement in Philadelphia has suffered one real failure: It has failed to change in any fundamental way the practice of politics in the city.

Let us now suggest that the sense of frustration and the real failure in fact belong together: that the reformers and the voters are frustrated today not so much because a few crooks still loiter about in the corridors of

City Hall but because they have failed in extending the opportunity for active political participation to the larger number of ordinary citizens. But why should these citizens feel frustrated over being denied the opportunity for political participation when, as we have argued, the economic motive for political activity is not a very intense one?

This returns us to the question of what the "boys" really mean when they say they "love politics." We have admitted that the quest for status is involved in this motivation, as no doubt it is with the urge that the ordinary citizen may feel toward the political realm. But we have also suggested that status hunger alone cannot explain the satisfaction the "boys" seem to gain from their work, just as it does not explain the clear emotional return experienced by a Joe Clark or a Richardson Dilworth. Let us look more closely at the concept, "love politics." What, after all, is politics? Politics, we are told, is who gets what, when, and how. Viewed in one light, no doubt. But if that is politics, then what is economics? Is not economics also who gets what, when, and how? Are politics and economics then identical? Hardly, since there are clearly economic activities —like selling automobiles and buying cucumbers—that are not political activities. Is politics, then, a division within the general class of economics? One thinks not. The feeling of frustration associated with reform, for instance, seems to have little economic basis, and neither does the feeling of camaraderie that is so valued by the "boys." Is not politics more truly defined, all things considered, as the expression of the will of the individual within the society of his fellows, or, more completely, the participation of human beings in the activities of conserving, distributing, and improving the values that are created by a civilized community? In short, is not politics the "art of government"? And if this is true, is not the question of why human beings should "love politics" similar to the question of why men should love women? Is not the answer to both, that is, that it is the nature of the beast? Is it not true, then, that political activity is a normal manifestation of human nature, and the real question is: Why should there be men who do *not* love politics?

With this question in mind, let us return for another look at the Protestant group whose mores have set the dominant pattern in the United States, and whose general lack of political interest has been used as an argument in favor of the theory that politics, insofar as it is not economic, is a "status-conferring" function. Let us suggest now that the general lack of political activity among members of the Protestant middle class is due not so much to the fact that they may be in a secure status position as to the effect of any unduly individualistic philosophy which over-emphasizes the private will at the expense of the social context in which it seeks to operate.

3.

The Delicate Balance

EDWARD C. BANFIELD

THE INFLUENCE OF THE MAYOR OF CHICAGO DEPENDS UPON HIS BEING
"boss" of the party in the county and this in turn depends upon his
ability to maintain the inner city machine while attracting support from
the "good government" forces in the outlying wards and suburbs. In
short, the mayor must bring the machine and the independents into a
working alliance.

To become the county boss, one need only have the backing of the
principal ward bosses of the inner city. There are eighty members of the
county committee, fifty from the central city and thirty from the "country towns," and their votes are weighed according to the number of Democratic votes cast in each district in the previous general election. The
inner city wards are therefore in a decided majority. These are grouped
into ethnic blocs each of which has its own boss: there is a bloc of Negro
wards under the control of Congressman William L. Dawson, a bloc of
Italian wards under an Italian leader, a bloc of Polish wards under a Polish
leader, and certain mixed wards under Irish leaders. Four or five of the
most powerful bloc leaders, together with the president of the County
Board, can, by agreeing among themselves, choose the county chairman.

Left to themselves, the bloc bosses would doubtless prefer someone
who would not trouble them with reform. They realize, however, that the
voters in the outlying areas will not leave them to themselves and that,
unless the machine's reputation is improved, it will be swept out of existence altogether. They accept, therefore—although, no doubt, as a
necessary evil and probably without fully realizing the extent of the evil

From *Political Influence: A New Theory of Urban Politics* by Edward C. Banfield, pp. 248ff. Copyright © 1961 by The Free Press, a Corporation. Reprinted by
permission of The Macmillan Company, New York City.

—the need of a leader who will make such reforms as will maintain the organization.

In choosing a leader, the bloc bosses look for someone whose identifications are with the inner city wards (he has to be a Catholic, of course, and one whom ward politicians will feel is "their kind"), whose "nationality" will not disturb the balance between the Italians and the Poles (this virtually means that he must be Irish), who knows the workings of the organization from long experience in it and who is felt to have "earned" his promotion, who has backers with money to put up for campaign expenses (for it will be assumed that the county chairman will have himself nominated for office), who is perfectly "clean" and has a creditable record of public service, and who has demonstrated sufficient vigor, force, and shrewdness to maintain the organization and lead it to victory at the polls.

Once he has taken charge of the machine, a new leader need pay very little attention to the ward bosses who selected him. If he can win elections, he is indispensable to them. Moreover, possession of office—of the county chairmanship and the mayoralty—gives him legal powers (patronage, slate-making, and control of city services, including police) which make the ward bosses dependent upon him. Without them to hold the ladder, he could not climb to his position. But once he is in it, they cannot compel him to throw something down to them.

He is likely, therefore, to prove a disappointment to them and a pleasant surprise to the friends of good government. The bloc bosses need him more than he needs them. They want "gravy" to pass out to their henchmen. But he is a county, state, and national leader, and as such his task is to limit or surpress the abuses upon which they fatten. To win the respect and confidence of the independent voters in the outlying wards and the suburbs, he must do the things that will hurt the bosses most.

The requirements of his role as a leader who must win the support of the independent voters are enough to account for his zeal to show himself honest and public-spirited. But it is likely that another circumstance will be working in the same direction. Ethnic pride may swell strongly in him and make him want to show the skeptics and the snobs that a man from the wrong side of the tracks can be as much a statesman as anyone from an "old family" or an Ivy League college.[1]

The political head is not likely to take a lively interest in the content of policy or to be specially gifted in the development of ideas or in their exposition. If ideas and the content of policy interested him much, or if he were ideologically-minded, he would not have made his career in the machine, for the machine is entirely without interest in such matters.

Similarly, he is not likely to be a vivid public personality, to be eloquent, or to have a flair for the direct manipulation of masses. The qualities that make a popular or charismatic leader would tend to prevent a man from rising within the organization. The kind of leader produced by it is likely to be, above all, an executive.

Any mayor of Chicago must "do big things" in order to be counted a success. It is not enough merely to administer honestly and efficiently the routine services of local government—street cleaning, garbage collection, and the like. An administration that did only these would be counted a failure, however well it did them. As a businessman member of the Chicago Plan Commission explained to an interviewer:

> The Mayor—no public official—is worth his salt if he isn't ambitious. That's true of you and everyone else. Now, what's a political person's stock in trade? It's government, of course. For a public official to just sit back and see that the police enforce the laws is not dynamic enough. I don't know that he would reason it out this way, but you have to get something with a little sex in it to get votes. In the old days, there were ward-heelers with a fistful of dollar bills. But that, even in Chicago, is passé.
>
> What makes a guy have civic pride? A factory worker, a cabby? He gets a sense of pride in taking part in an active community. The Mayor's smart enough to realize it. Today the tendency all over the country is for the public officials to take the lead more than they did a few years ago. . . .

Wanting to do "big things" and not caring very much which ones, the political head will be open to suggestions. (When Mayor Daley took office, he immediately wrote to three or four of the city's most prominent businessmen asking them to list the things they thought most needed doing.) He will be receptive, particularly, to proposals from people who are in a position to guarantee that successful action will win a "seal of approval" from some of the "good government" groups. He may be impressed by the intrinsic merit of a proposal—the performance budget, for example—but he will be even more impressed at the prospect of being well regarded by the highly respectable people whose proposal it is. Taking suggestions from the right kind of people will help him get the support he needs in order to win the votes of independents in the outlying wards and suburbs.

For this reason, he will not create a strong staff of policy advisers or a strong planning agency. The preparation of policies and plans will be done mainly within those private organizations having some special stake in the matters involved and by the civic associations. Quite possibly, the political head might, if he wished, assemble a technical staff of first-rate ability and, working closely with it, produce a plan far superior to anything that might be done by the private organizations and the civic associations. But a plan made in this way would have one fatal defect: its makers could not supply the "seal of approval" which is, from the political head's standpoint, its chief reason for being. On the other hand, a plan made by the big business organizations, the civic associations and the newspapers, is sure to be acclaimed. From the political head's standpoint it is sure-fire, for the people who make it and the people who will pass judgment upon it are the same.

Under these circumstances, the city planning department will have two main functions: (a) to advise the mayor on the technical aspects of the various alternatives put before him by private groups, and (b) to assemble data justifying and supporting the privately-made proposals that the mayor decides to "merchandise," and to prepare maps, charts, perspective drawings, and brochures with which to "sell" the plans to the public......

There are often fundamental differences of opinion among those whose approval the political head wants. Chicago is too big a place, and the interests in it too diverse, for agreement to occur very often. When there is disagreement within the "good government" forces, the rational strategy for the political head usually is to do nothing. Watchful waiting offends no one, and to be negative when one does not have to be is . . . . . bad politics. The political head is therefore inclined to let a civic controversy develop in its own way without interference from him, in the expectation that "public opinion" (the opinion of "civic leaders" and the newspapers) will "crystallize." Controversies serve the function of forming and preparing opinion; they are the process by which an initial diversity of views and interests is reduced to the point where a political head feels that the "community" is "behind" the project.

The political head, therefore, neither fights for a program of his own making nor endeavors to find a "solution" to the conflicts that are brought before him. Instead, he waits for the community to agree upon a project. When agreement is reached, or when the process of controversy has gone as far as it can, he ratifies the agreement and carries it into effect......

The influence structure that has been described is not stable. Although it has existed for many years without change, it is now moving rapidly toward a new and very different state.[2]

The principal dynamic factor is the tension between the demands for "good government" from the outlying areas and the maintenance requirements of the inner city machine. The outlying areas, as explained above, are constantly becoming more important to the success of the Democratic party in the metropolitan area. But all of the measures that will conciliate and attract the voters in these areas are in some way at the expense of the machine. In order to maintain itself in the outlying areas, the party must weaken the machine in its inner city heartland. Before long, it will have liquidated it altogether.

Even such a seemingly innocuous reform as the establishment of an information bureau in City Hall has weakened the machine. Helping a constituent find his way through the maze of local governmental organizations was one of the few favors the ward committeeman had left to give. When constituents found that they could get better service by calling the mayor's information bureau, another tie to the machine was cut. If a new tie took its place, it was to the mayor himself or to the City Hall bureaucracy.

The most serious blows to the machine have been the widescale extension of the merit system and the partial suppression of graft and corruption. There are still plenty of incentives for people at the top of the party hierarchy to give their time and effort: if the taste for "glory," "power," and being on the "inside" is not enough, there is still much "honest graft" to be had from the sale of legal service and insurance. At the lower levels of the hierarchy the case is very different. With few patronage jobs, and with those few much depreciated in value by the high level of general employment, there are not many incentives for ward and precinct workers. It is not surprising, then, that bribes and payoffs tend to supplement the value of patronage. If putting an old uncle on the street-cleaning force is not a sufficient incentive to make the precinct worker work nowadays, then letting his brother, a policeman, take bribes from burglars may be necessary. This is an effect of inflation.

If it is to survive, the machine must tolerate a certain amount of corruption at least until such time as competent precinct captains can be induced to work from other motives than personal gain. At present, in the working-class districts at least, the other motives do not exist. Therefore the boss must—if he is to keep his organization from falling to pieces —"look the other way" to avoid seeing the inevitable corruption. If he saw it he would have to put a stop to it, and if he put a stop to it he would weaken both his personal political position and the whole structure of governmental power.

No matter whether he looks the other way or not, some corruption is inevitable in a city like Chicago. The inevitability of corruption—and therefore the inevitability of occasional exposures of corruption—is another element in the dynamics of the situation. An occasional scandal will keep the machine in ill-repute no matter what its achievements may be, and a large scandal occurring at a particularly inopportune time may possibly destroy it forever.[3]

The inner city machine, then, is being dismantled bit by bit in order to improve the position of the party in the outlying areas.

N O T E S

1. According to Robert Moses, "Smith and LaGuardia had quite a lot in common. First and foremost, they shared the same fierce determination to demonstrate to skeptics and bigots that boys from the sidewalks of lower Manhattan could run great governments honestly, intelligently, progressively and, to an astonishing degree, without degrading politics, and thus wring reluctant admiration from the sticks, the crossroads, the Southern Tier and Park Avenue. One had the curious sense in observing Governor Smith that he was living up to a model or an example he had established for himself and that the executive was something apart from and superior to the man. It was the same with LaGuardia." (*New York Times Magazine*, September 8, 1957).

2. The argument that follows develops some points made in Meyerson and Banfield, *Politics, Planning, and the Public Interest* (Glencoe, Ill.: Free Press, 1955), Chapter 11.

3. In 1959 and 1960, scandals in the traffic court, the assessor's office, and the police department put the Chicago machine in a very bad light. Mayor Daley was not personally involved; there was no question regarding his integrity. Nevertheless, the scandals prohibited him from running for governor at that time (he might not have run anyway, of course). If he had been up for re-election just then against a strong candidate, he might possibly have been beaten.

PART VI

The Mayor and the Public—
His Ceremonial Role

More than anyone else, the mayor is the symbol of the city. When the mayor speaks, in a sense the city speaks. Whatever the chief executive does in a public way, he invariably reflects something of the life and spirit of the community which elected him. Thus it can be suggested that Jimmy Walker, New York's mayor in the early 1930's, was essentially what the city wanted him to be—a source of entertainment, even a distraction during a period of economic duress. The fact that Jimmy was indulging in shenanigans with the public treasury didn't seem to matter very much until he was caught. In "Master of Ceremonies," Gene Fowler illustrates the mayor's appeal in a city which was, and still is, the entertainment capital of the world.

The second reading by Erwin C. Hargrove ("Dramatizing Reform") highlights the mayor's need to provide drama even in the humdrum aspects of governing; for the public must be made aware of what the mayor is trying to achieve if he is to get its support at all. As described here, La Guardia was a master at this, playing each event for all its histrionic worth. Yet when carried too far, the mass media can easily turn a person's renown to notoriety—La Guardia's Achilles' heel. Another style of public salesmanship is epitomized by Mayor Lee of New Haven. His strategic attempts to influence the city's two conservative newspapers and shape public opinion in behalf of his programs are treated by Allan R. Talbot in "Retailing Development."

Finally, we glance at a different aspect of the ceremonial role. In "The Mayor Tours the Ghetto," Nat Hentoff depicts the street talents of New York City's Lindsay during times of racial and ethnic tension—in the short run, at least, a seemingly effective palliative.

1.

Master of Ceremonies

GENE FOWLER

The Board of Estimate room was not the only theatre for Mayor Walker. He gave almost three hundred open-air performances on the portico platform outside the Hall, awarding the keys of the city, scrolls, and medals to honored guests. His speeches of welcome were extemporaneous, and the crowds greatly enjoyed the ceremonies, especially the Walker asides.

Upon one occasion a five-hundred-pound cheese arrived at City Hall accompanied by a delegation of Swiss admirers. Jim thanked his visitors for bringing the huge cheese, then said, "Will someone please run out and get me a cracker?"

To Guglielmo Marconi, the Italian physicist, Walker said, "It is gratifying to realize that you did not send a wireless, but came in person. Here we do not know much about transmission, but we have some mighty fine receptions."

When Commander Richard E. Byrd appeared for a third time at City Hall, Walker said, "Dick, this has got to stop; it's getting to be a habit."

The Honorable Grover A. Whalen served as Walker's impresario at these public functions. He had succeeded his friend Rodman Wanamaker as the head of a committee of three hundred and ninety citizens to welcome distinguished visitors to New York. Members of this committee had a somewhat tubby vessel, the *Macom* (a contraction of "Mayor's Committee"), at their disposal whenever a prominent person arrived aboard an ocean liner......

From *Beau James: The Life and Times of Jimmy Walker* by Gene Fowler, pp. 185–188. Copyright © 1949 by Gene Fowler. Published by the Viking Press, New York City, and reprinted by permission.

The first large-scale reception for a distinguished guest during the Walker administration was that for Captain George Fried and the crew of the *S.S. President Roosevelt*. These mariners had rescued the master and the men aboard the British steamer *Antinoe*. There was a military parade from the Battery to City Hall. The Mayor's herald and factotum, Hector Fuller, presented a hand-illuminated scroll to the Captain.

Fuller, an advertising man, had the bearing and voice of an alumnus of the Richard Mansfield, or "smokehouse," school of acting. The Mayor's Committee entrusted him with the designing, the writing, and the presentation of the official scrolls of welcome. Hector conducted rehearsals for these showy affairs at City Hall. As described by columnist Louis Sobol, the officials practiced their parts with the fervor of extras in a forthcoming play or of bridesmaids before a wedding. Hector sometimes made verbal blunders during his introductions, as at the reception of Ramsay MacDonald, whom Fuller announced as "Prime Minister of the United States."

Queen Marie of Romania was the first "crowned head" greeted by Walker. Whether or not Her Majesty was charmed by Walker's speech of welcome or by two incidents which happened more or less off the record, the still beautiful Queen did not say. One of these occurred while Jim was attempting to pin a medal upon her coat. The lady from the Balkans owned a splendid, although somewhat buxom figure, and the place where the medal properly belonged high up, and a bit to the left— suggested, among other things, a delicate target for a carelessly directed pin.

"Your Majesty," Jim said, "I've never stuck a queen, and I hesitate to do so now."

"Proceed, Your Honor," replied the Queen. "The risk is mine."

"And such a beautiful risk it is, Your Majesty," Jim said in a low voice.

The Queen and her royal party left New York for Washington at the conclusion of the City Hall ceremonies. Although it was a raw October day, Marie was seated in an open-top automobile so that citizens along the way from City Hall to Pennsylvania Station might look upon a reigning monarch.

Jim sat at Her Majesty's left in the touring car. As the royal automobile was passing a newly begun skyscraper on Seventh Avenue, her lap robe slipped from her knees. Walker leaned over to adjust the robe. At this, one of the riveters perched on a girder of the partly completed steel framework of the building cupped his hands and called out, "Hey, Jimmy! Have you made her yet?"

Just how much slang Queen Marie understood I am not prepared to say. She turned an inquiring glance upon her host and said sweetly, "You Americans are quite droll, don't you think?"

"When you travel across our great country," Jim hedged, "you will come upon many interesting evidences of our democracy."

"Everyone seems to know you in this great city," she observed.

"Yes, Madam," Walker replied, "and some of them know me very well indeed."

2.

Dramatizing Reform

ERWIN C. HARGROVE

THERE WAS OF COURSE A GREAT DEAL OF PERSONAL EXHIBITIONISM, IN which [La Guardia] evidently indulged for the sheer fun of it: racing to fires, riding in a police car, conducting the band in Central Park, entering a fat man's race at a picnic, reading the comics over the radio to the children during the newspaper strike, and much more. His public personality was made to order for the popular New York tabloid newspapers, and their readers were constantly entertained by the antics of the Little Flower.

But there was much more than this. He was a political artist who painted pictures of reform as it developed. He carried the people with him in his fights and he prepared them for fights ahead. He did this primarily through his dramatizations. He knew that the best way to dramatize an issue was to make it colorful and alive by some characteristic act. He personified city government by giving the impression that he had every part of it at his fingertips, and at times this was not inaccurate. In his first few weeks as Mayor, his surprise invasions of city offices became famous. Suddenly he would swoop down upon unsuspecting employees in search of loafing, inefficiency, and corruption. In one west side relief station he took charge as if it were an army command post by standing on a chair and issuing instructions to thoroughly frightened employees. He invaded the Bronx Terminal Market at dawn and summoned concessionaires by the blare of police bugles. Then, reading off a proclamation that was written in "hear ye" fashion he banned the sale of artichokes in the public markets and announced his intention to drive the racketeers

From *Political Leadership in American Government* by James D. Barber, pp. 103–112. Copyright © 1964 by Little, Brown and Company, Inc., and reprinted by permission.

out of the artichoke industry. On frequent occasions he sat as a com-
mitting magistrate when the case was one of general interest, e.g. the
confiscation of slot machines and the war on gamblers. He supervised
the smashing of slot machines for the movie cameras and personally
wielded the sledge hammer. The opening of every subway and trolley line
found Fiorello, in motorman's cap, at the controls. He continually toured
the city institutions, taking along reporters. One typical tour saw him
visiting in one afternoon the new East River Drive, the Department of
Sanitation training school, several city markets, a ferry house, several
crosstown busses, and two police stations. He cross-examined city employees at these places and arranged to see some of them later at City Hall
to hear certain complaints. He let reporters into meetings in which he
and thirty examiners and forty clerks worked up the city budget. One
newspaper story described his acting:

> La Guardia pored over sheafs of papers and columns of figures. "What's
> this," he snapped from time to time.
> "Can't this wait?" he demanded as item after item foretold a mounting
> cost for the city to bear.[1]

He gave New Yorkers the feeling that their city government was
honest and concerned for their welfare. By intervening publicly and
dramatically at many points of decision he made himself the symbol of
reform.

Relations with His Commissioners

One concomitant of this dramatizing strategy was his deliberate up-
staging of his own commissioners. Joseph McGoldrick, City Comptroller
under La Guardia and a close political associate, remembered that the
Mayor did not like his commissioners talking to reporters. To get too
much publicity was to get in trouble with La Guardia.[2] If commissioners
did have to talk in public the Mayor wanted them to talk about him. In
his first month in office he directed all commissioners to speak about
general achievements of the administration rather than their own departments if they were the sole administration representative at meetings
and banquets.[3]

He did not hesitate to ridicule his commissioners in public, or push
blame off on them, or take credit for himself that they deserved. It was all
part of his political strategy. One public tiff between the Mayor and his
Commissioner of Welfare was described in the press as follows:

> In curt and unvarnished language Mayor La Guardia yesterday bluntly
> rescinded 121 salary increases in the Department of Public Welfare and

hinted Commissioner William Hodson's department may face a shakeup . . .

"You will revoke all salary increases where the pay is over $45 a week" La Guardia declared in an amazingly brusque message to Hodson.

"You will submit at once a table of organization of the Home Relief Bureau and the Works Division showing duties of each office and pay. I want this immediately . . . "

But the Mayor was not content with this one jab at his own appointee. He declared that the entire Home Relief Bureau must be revamped, if it is true as testified at aldermanic hearing that 15 per cent of those on relief are chiselers and not worthy of aid.[4]

The Mayor had himself given this memo to reporters, evidently in order to push criticism of the relief program off onto Hodson and away from himself. This was an instance of his grand acting scheme in which he took all the credit, and others the blame. A comment by Rex Tugwell, one of his commissioners, suggests that La Guardia's bullying of his associates had deeper roots in his personality than simple political strategy. Tugwell remembered that La Guardia was "more incapable of friendship than almost anyone I ever knew." Admitting that political leaders must often sacrifice loyalty to associates to more general goals, Tugwell felt that the Mayor carried this to an extreme:

> It showed itself in many ways of which anyone trying to stay close to him and to be helpful had to be aware. There was never a real sharing of confidence; there was always suspicion, more or less acute; there were always rough manners, and sometimes there was downright ingratitude.[5]

"Them"

As in his congressional days he kept up a rapid drumfire against "Them." When New York milk companies raised their prices one cent a quart, he publicly accused them of "chiseling" both the farmers and the public. He fought the increase by buying milk at lower prices from independent producers and distributing it to city baby health and welfare stations. For a little extra drama he ordered ten Health Department trucks to cruise the streets selling milk to the public at the old prices. Eventually, he won his fight when the Borden Company rescinded the increase.

He helped the hotel restaurant workers win a strike against the hotels by sending city health inspectors to inspect scab waiters during the height of the dinner hour. If this had not worked, he was prepared to send out the fire and safety inspectors.

He forced the taxicab companies to share the division of an illegally collected tax with their drivers in a fifty-fifty ratio by ordering city police to stop the drivers and ask them their number of children, their income, the number of hours they worked, etc.

He verbally lashed the private utilities for "Insullism" and when they retorted that his plan for a publicly owned power plant was "socialism," he responded by condemning their "Private rascalism."

When the elevated railway, the Manhattan Railway Company, announced that it was going to raise the funds to liquidate a back tax lien held by the city, La Guardia wrote them a caustic open letter in which he supplied the address of the City Treasurer's office, since "it is such a long time since Manhattan has paid taxes that perhaps you have forgotten the address."

Fighting Tactics

His color, combativeness and quick sense of timing were the chief components of his political skill. As soon as he took the oath of office in 1934 he plunged into a fight with Governor Lehman and the State Legislature. He requested authority to upset the budget planned for 1934 by the previous Tammany administration in order to cut payrolls and reduce his deficit. As a dramatic ploy he raised the spectre of an increase in the five cent subway fare if his request was not granted. He also dashed off to Washington and got a promise of millions in PWA funds contingent on a balanced budget in New York City. He hurled all of this at Albany daring them to block him, and face the consequences. He then went on the radio and attacked Tammany Hall as having padded city payrolls with political hacks whom he wanted to bounce. Better to "save a home than save a politician" he cried. He finally got modified approval from the State to write his own budget. He had succeeded only because of his use of all the resources of influence at his command.

He used the same approach on the Democratic-nominated City Council more than once. In 1938 he asked for new restaurant, liquor and cigarette taxes. In the same motion he cut relief taxes and told reporters that the reductions could be restored only if the Council approved his tax requests. At a crucial moment in Council debate he rescinded the relief cuts but warned the Council that they would be responsible for permanent relief cuts unless they went along with him. They did and he won.

The conclusion that must be drawn from this survey of La Guardia's political style as Mayor is that the longstanding drives of his political personality were the sources of his political and administrative success. His identification with the Have Nots and his antipathy to the Haves supplied his goals and his burning, driving zeal. His need to be in the spotlight, to exhibit himself and the skills he had developed to serve that need supplied his dramatizing tactics. And his desire for power over others, and power for action, provided the fuel for his domineering, combative, dynamic style of attack upon the problems of the city and obstacles in his path. It almost seemed as if he had been shaped for the job of Mayor and in training for it all of his life.

The Reverse Side

Just as La Guardia's personality drives were responsible for his success as a politician, so these very same drives contained sources of great weakness, both for the man and the politician. Warren Moscow, a reporter for the *New York Times*, went so far as to say that if La Guardia "missed real greatness, of which he was capable, it was because of his emotional instability."[6]

One symptom of this emotional instability was his low threshold for criticism of himself. His relationships with reporters, editors and publishers were seldom good. His temper tantrums at press conferences when a question got too hot were legion.

He had only been Mayor two months in 1934 when he wrote Arthur Sulzberger, publisher of the *New York Times*, in protest against an editorial which had criticized him for sending health inspectors to hotels during a strike of hotel workers:

> You do me a great injustice when you say I acted impulsively. The writer of your editorial did not have the facts when he wrote that I acted "without acquainting himself with all the facts." . . . that is exactly when I did.[7]

Notice that it was the personal slap at him that he resented, more than the disapproval of the content of his action. In 1939 *Fortune* magazine published an issue on the La Guardia administration which was highly favorable in tone, but included one item that infuriated the Mayor. It was reported that Polly Adler was running a place of prostitution on the West Side. La Guardia wrote Henry Luce as follows:

> Personally I think the article was lousy. It surely was not in accordance with the galley proof I read. There is a great deal of poison throughout the various articles. I think the writers were all right but someone got in the dirty work which proves my contention that the oldest profession in the world is not limited to one sex.[8]

La Guardia then wrote his Police Commissioner saying how "humiliating to me" it was to read that *Fortune* knew Polly Adler's whereabouts, and he, the Mayor, did not. He identified everything that went on in the city with his own ego, as if he should have personally known the address.

In 1943 Secretary of War Henry Stimson announced to the press that La Guardia's long-standing request for an Army commission would probably not be granted. The Mayor was too useful in New York, he said. La Guardia's behind-the-scenes wise man C. C. Burlingham sent the Mayor a letter that Felix Frankfurter had written to him about La Guardia:

> I should think the Little Flower would offer a prayer of Thanksgiving to Stimson for not letting him go off soldiering and keeping him on his job in New York considering the potential danger of race riots in New York. Wouldn't it have been lovely for Fiorello to be prancing around somewhere in Africa? Why he should have ever thought he would be of more use in Sardinia than in New York, I cannot for the life of me understand except that romantic temperaments are notoriously restless.[9]

La Guardia's response to this not unfriendly letter was seen in his reply to Burlingham:

> I am very sorry you sent me the letter. I have not always admired Felix but have had a very warm affection for him. All of that has been killed. I will never talk to him as long as I live.
>
> As to Stimson, well, what he did to me was just plain rotten. The sneaking out of the information with dirty innuendos, when the Presidential directive was confidential, and throwing me to such dogs as Patterson of the News and McCormick of the Tribune and some of the anti-New Deal columnists, was not only unethical, unfriendly and pretty low, but borders on the dishonorable. . . .
>
> However, we have something to thank God for and that is that our fighting force in the field is as glorious and gallant and courageous as our civilians in the War Department are rotters and stink.[10]

His own ambition for fame and power was harmful to him in his last term as Mayor. As his response to the Frankfurter letter indicates he wanted very badly to duplicate his performance of the first World War by becoming a military personality. He hoped to become a military governor in North Africa and Italy. This would have been a convenient escape for him. His crusade for reform had run down by 1941 and the war had shifted attention to other kinds of problems in New York City. He lost many of his best commissioners to the war. But, more than this, he saw his political career in New York coming to a close and was reaching out for a new beginning. An Army career would have permitted this. La Guardia was beginning to think along these lines even before the war.

Rex Tugwell remembered that in 1938 he was getting restless and ready to move on:

> At that time he was a man driven as by whips. In my first year with him, before his hopes were diminished, he talked with me by the hour about national affairs, political grand strategy, and his own chances of moving up.
>
> La Guardia's climactic end was not, in his estimation, the New York mayoralty. That was now preliminary, a trial run, which now he judged had been wholly successful. But it had gone on too long. There must be a way out and up. Every waking moment of every day his sensitive feelers were out, groping for the situation that could be taken advantage of, the man who could be persuaded to help, the thing he could invent or do that would contribute. His body might be in New York or on the road, but his heart was in the capital.[11]

Even though he ran for a third term in 1941 La Guardia was hopeful at the time of escaping to the Army. Harry Hopkins and President Roosevelt seem to have given him tacit assurances that he would receive a commission, but for reasons that have never been completely explained the offer did not materialize. The evidence is compelling that this disappointment had an embittering effect on him. Many of his commissioners felt that toward the end of his third term he sometimes did things which bordered on the "psychopathic."[12]

In the 1941 mayoral election he made a bitter, vitriolic attack upon Herbert Lehman because Lehman was supporting La Guardia's Democratic opponent. La Guardia had supported Lehman against Dewey in 1938 but Lehman did not reciprocate, and La Guardia could not forgive him. The uproar from this attack was great but the Mayor refused to apologize and it is estimated that he lost a quarter of a million votes by his action.[13]

Also in 1941 the Mayor fell out with his Commissioner of Markets over an appointment. When the Commissioner resigned as a result the Mayor praised him to reporters. However, a few days later, La Guardia announced a discovery of "irregularities" in the Department of Markets and might have pursued the matter had not the *New York Times* attacked his attempted slur.

The most important outburst came out of La Guardia's fight with the city Board of Education, and the National Education Association. In principle the Board was independent of the city administration but La Guardia regarded it as a city department. In 1943 he fell out publicly with the Board and Superintendent of Schools over two relatively minor matters, a question of purchasing supplies and an appointment of a director of adult education. La Guardia attempted to force his will on the Board and they balked. His response was one of fury. He made a blistering attack upon the President of the Board and refused to reappoint one member of the Board, cut another out of the budget altogether, and kept a third on a day-to-day basis instead of reappointing him or appointing a successor. In addition, he cut an assistant superintendent of schools from the budget and held up the salary checks of three people who were newly appointed to administrative posts in the school system.

These acts raised a storm of protest from civic groups and the National Education Association issued a report in 1944 accusing the Mayor of undue interference with the Board of Education. La Guardia's response was to charge that "no one on the board has the mental capacity to grasp the magnitude of the school system of New York." He was unforgiving in the matter. In 1945 Comptroller McGoldrick cast the deciding vote in the Board of estimate in favor of a teachers' bonus. La Guardia, who had opposed the bonus, was so incensed that he broke off his friendship with McGoldrick. The NEA slap still rankled the Mayor.[14]

These and other outbursts of this nature undoubtedly hurt him badly with the public. In June, 1941, a Gallup Poll found that 59 per cent of the voters favored La Guardia for a third term. In 1937 he had been re-elected with 60 per cent of the vote. His attack on Lehman in 1941 caused him to win with a reduced 53 per cent of the vote. Then, during his third term, his disputes within the city government, his increased disputes with the press, and his seeming lack of interest in city affairs, caused his public stock to go down. In the spring of 1945 the New York *Daily News* ran a straw poll on mayoral candidates and found former mayor Jimmy Walker leading the field with 40 per cent, then William O'Dwyer with 30 per cent and La Guardia at the bottom with 25 per cent. La Guardia perhaps hastened the end of his own career by his responses to the fear of a political decline.[15]

NOTES

1. *New York Daily News*, September 27, 1937.

2. Charles Garrett, *The La Guardia Years: Machine and Reform Politics in New York City* (New Brunswick, New Jersey: Rutgers University Press, 1961) p. 363, footnote 10.

3. La Guardia memorandum to Department Heads, February 26, 1934. La Guardia Papers (Municipal Archives and Records Center, 238 Williams Street, New York, New York).

4. *New York Daily News*, March 24, 1935.

5. Rexford G. Tugwell, *The Art of Politics* (Garden City, New York: Doubleday, 1953), p. 221.

6. Warren Moscow, *Politics in the Empire State* (New York: Alfred A. Knopf, 1948), p. 24.

7. La Guardia to Arthur Sulzberger, February 25, 1934. *La Guardia Papers*.

8. La Guardia to Henry Luce, July 18, 1939. *La Guardia Papers*.

9. Frankfurter to C. C. Burlingham, June 25, 1943. *La Guardia Papers*.

10. La Guardia to C. C. Burlingham, July 17, 1943. *La Guardia Papers*.

11. Tugwell, *The Art of Politics*, p. 93.

12. Garrett, *The La Guardia Years*, p. 284.

13. Moscow, *Politics in the Empire State*, p. 235.

14. Garrett, *The La Guardia Years*, pp. 201–203, 120.

15. Ibid., pp. 284–285.

3.

Retailing Development

ALLAN R. TALBOT

URBAN RENEWAL, WITH ITS LARGE-SCALE DISRUPTIONS AND TECHNICAL complexities, is political dynamite and must be handled carefully. The desired results take years to achieve. Meanwhile problems can crop up—problems such as poorly rehoused families or idle vacant land—which call attention to themselves by picket lines or an unwanted crop of ragweed. Lee's answer to these problems, aside from trying to avoid them in the first place, was burning optimism and the "hard sell." Where else in America has a mayor stood before a group of citizens who have seen the center of town flattened for years and quip, "Well, we have no new construction yet, but at least the Russians have taken us off their primary target list." Of course, not everyone was amused, but enough laughed to indicate that, besides his sense of salesmanship and not really as a result of it, Lee enjoyed widespread community confidence and popularity. His ability to sustain both, even in hard times, was a remarkable testimony to the successful marriage of his naturally warm personality with the cold, complicated program he stood for.

Lee usually stayed out of his office as much as possible, traveling a circuit of bar mitzvahs, church suppers, communion breakfasts, P.T.A. meetings, and League of Women Voters teas. He charmed his hosts with jokes and stories, and by remembering their first names. He was, or soon became, the center of attraction at any gathering. When it came time for him to speak, he would hold his audience with extemporaneous statements of lofty and suitably vague goals, such as, "We're not only going to lift New Haven into the twentieth century, we'll push it forth into the twenty-first," or "New Haven will become the first slumless city, a truly *new* New Haven." These were never the culmination of long harangues about city problems, but crisp statements of purpose, designed to inspire or shock and devoid of the details that might get him into trouble. Lee extended the circuit usually followed by New Haven mayors to include formerly isolated sectors such as school classrooms, neighborhood stores, housing projects, and places of employment, where he would disrupt routine by mingling with the people, soliciting their problems, and jotting down notes in his little black book. At the end of the day the book would provide material for angry memos to department heads and reassuring notes to his constituents. He personified active local government.

Lee soon became known not only as a hard-working mayor with big ideas but as a regular fellow, too. He made it a point to be around when people were in trouble, and the best way for this friend of 152,048 people to be around when they needed him was to study the obituary notices. By projecting the number of funerals attended by Lee in a month in 1965, one of Lee's secretaries has estimated that he had attended more than 7,000 wakes. In a city with a high proportion of Italian and Irish families, which are usually large and close, Lee's attendance at funerals has put him in direct contact with much of the city's population at times when a visit by the Mayor leaves a deep personal impression. The practice has also required an efficiency of operation which Lee's chauffeurs—and he has worn out five of them—call the "wake stop." The wake stop involves dropping the Mayor off in front of a funeral home, slowly pulling the car up the driveway to the rear of the home, and idling for approximately two minutes. Meanwhile, the Mayor is wending his way through the groups of mourners inside, with gentle smiles and firm handshakes—stopping at the bier for a brief prayer and a quick inspection of the quality of work downstairs—then through the remainder of the crowd to a rear exit and back into the waiting car. To be sure, the practice is somewhat morbid and political, but it is also based on genuine concern. No one around City Hall will forget the time that Lee completely supervised, partly financed, and fully attended every step of a funeral for an obscure employee who died with no close friends or relatives, because "That was the least I could do for the poor devil." It was a memorable scene to watch Lee slip quietly into the church service, attended by only ten others, and pray alone in a rear pew while a priest celebrated the Mass.

As soon as his renewal program made a physical imprint on the town, Lee began matching his person with his program through carefully created devices designed to make renewal interesting, understandable, and exciting. The interest was aroused through the use of models and drawings which showed what he was trying to achieve. Renewal was made comprehensible by portraying it in homey terms. The opening of a neighborhood playground or a school, or even the installation of a traffic light, would be the subject for a full-blown dedication ceremony, and Lee would dramatically proclaim the improvement "another step in our city-wide renewal program." The excitement was generated by the hoopla that accompanied any achievement of his administration. When a new animal shelter was opened, Lee appeared on television to find homes for dogs and cats. When the first of the slums was to be razed, Lee manned the crane to swing the wrecking ball, and although he almost killed several observers, the excitement of it all led to the practice of inviting visiting dignitaries to join him in crushing a slum. For a few years Lee had his own television show during which he presented models and drawings of redevelopment proposals, and the Sunday Bridgeport *Herald* gave him a column in which he wrote about everything, from his plans for New Haven to comments on international affairs.

Aside from establishing himself and his programs in the minds of the people, Lee also took steps to enhance the post of mayor. He remodeled the office he inherited, which included a roll-top desk, asphalt-tile floors, a crumbling ceiling, and a huge, abandoned vault used for storing furniture. He modernized the facilities with a rug, draperies, furniture, renovation of the vault into added office space, and the installation of a private hot line to key aides. He held daily press conferences in the office, and conducted as many meetings as possible there. All major news from city departments was issued by his office under his name. Top city staff people even cleared their speeches with Lee. Ralph Taylor remembers, for instance, that for an out-of-town speech he sent his prepared remarks to Lee for clearance. Lee called him to his office, complimented him on the text, and then added, "Just remember, Ralph, it's spelled 'L-E-E.' "

The only regular forum most mayors have for delivering their message to the people is the press, including radio and television. This was an area of Lee's job which he complained about bitterly, but which he secretly enjoyed most. He enjoyed it not only because he was by experience and inclination a newsman but because there were few supporters of Lee's programs among the New Haven fourth estate. Getting the reporters to broadcast his message was therefore a test of his guile and cunning. New Haven has one television station, five radio stations, and two daily newspapers. Only one of the stations was a strong supporter of the Lee administration. The other five were unenthusiastic about administration programs and equated urban renewal with such topics as public safety or National Brotherhood Week. The two newspapers, which were jointly owned, were in basic opposition to the philosophy of urban renewal with its large expenditures of public money and its acquisition of private property. Both papers remain whipping posts for New Haven liberals, and some of Lee's staff have regarded them as biased, vindictive, second rate, and rigidly conservative. The two papers provided the main formal link between the administration and the public, and for that reason their roles will be emphasized here.

The morning paper, the *Journal Courier*, has a circulation of about 30,000, a small staff, and an editorial page which rarely touches on anything more controversial than the beauties of spring or the duty to vote. One suspects that it is subsidized by the publishers mainly to discourage competition for its afternoon paper, the *Register*. The *Register*, with its circulation of over 100,000, has a professional staff at least three times as large as that of the *Courier*, and its editorial page reflects the view of the management. That view is conservative if one considers support of Barry Goldwater to be indicative of conservatism; the *Register* endorsed Coldwater in the 1964 presidential campaign. The two papers are heavy with wire-service material, but on most state and local news they provide on-the-spot coverage, and many of their reporters write under by-lines.

For most of this century the papers were owned and managed by one man, the late John Day Jackson. It is difficult to describe Jackson accurately, for he was a man whose rugged independence seems to have polarized community attitudes on his papers and person. Most politicians in New Haven, regardless of party, characterize him in tyrannical terms. Old-line business leaders talk of him cautiously. There are few alive in New Haven today who knew him well and there are few who speak of him kindly, but this could be because he outlived his generation. It was not until his ninety-second year that he died; he stood virtually alone in a world of changing needs and conditions, and he was not a flexible sort.

It is clear that Jackson regarded both the *Courier* and the *Register*, from their pressrooms to their news columns, as his personal property. It is also clear that he was never blinded by party label in condemning those who violated his idea of what was right. He shocked many in New Haven with his support of President Truman, whom he always regarded as something of a fool, against General MacArthur over the conduct of the Korean War. The reason for his stand was given by one of his sons, Richard Jackson, who is now Co-Publisher of the *Register*:

"Of course, John Day had no time for Truman, but he felt strongly that the boss's word was law, and Truman, not MacArthur, was the boss. The editorial also had some family meaning. He was telling his sons that he, like Truman, was the boss to be listened to." The elder Jackson did not like Lee, his bravado, or his liberalism. Lee disliked Jackson and felt that their relations were permanently poisoned by an incident in the 1951 campaign. Jackson had refused to run a Lee political ad and story that accused Mayor Celentano of having an interest in a trucking firm which was doing business with the city. After a meeting between Lee and the publisher failed to achieve a compromise, Lee took to television to proclaim, "During this campaign, I have been fighting not only an opposing candidate but a biased, slanted, inequitable, and prejudiced press." According to Lee, Jackson saw this performance in his gardener's cottage, and there was born in that humble setting a grudge which he carried to his grave. Richard Jackson has minimized this incident and suggested the problem was more deep-seated.

"Although John Day and Dick differed deeply on issues, the two men were much alike. They were strong-willed, stubborn, and very proud. I have always told Dick that he made one serious mistake with John Day. He never came to him other than to tell him what he wanted or was going to do. He never swallowed his pride to ask for John Day's opinion or advice. Most mayors and even governors had done this, although they would often turn around and do precisely the opposite. Dick could never do it, and John Day never forgot. The two men were just too different politically and much too alike personally to ever get along."

It is ironic that despite his dislike of Lee, John Day Jackson's method of operating inadvertently helped Lee. By refusing to turn over control of the paper to his two sons, Richard and Lionel, and by instituting instead a gradual five-year shift of responsibility, the elder Jackson created a managerial hiatus, so that for the first few years of the Lee administration there was no one person in charge of the papers; as late as 1958 Jackson, at eighty-nine, was still butting into the decisions of his sons and the staff, and this practice naturally created problems, including an indecisive editorial page.

This and other internal problems at the city's two newspapers played a critical role in Lee's efforts to get his message across to the citizens. He was not really dealing with a strong publisher who opposed him and had a monopoly on community news, as Lee, his friends and staff, and at least one observer would suggest.* Rather he was dealing with an organization which was going through a difficult transition from one-man rule to the two-man management by sons who were bent on overcoming the problems of the past and, judging by their subsequent actions, democratizing decision-making for the future. The paper has not undergone any major change in its conservatism, but it has slowly improved in professional and technical quality.

While Lee encouraged the notion that he was being victimized by a monolithic, tyrannical newspaper, he was very much aware of the actual

*Robert A. Dahl, *Who Governs?* (New Haven: Yale University Press, 1961), pp. 256–67.

conditions at the papers. He had many sources—including the boys in the shipping department, who still give him a free copy of the *Register* as soon as it comes off the press. While the problems of transition went on at the top, Lee dealt almost exclusively with the men in the middle, the editors and reporters, who were getting the papers out. The two chief editorial men at the *Register* were Charles McQueeney, the Managing Editor, and Robert Leeney, the Executive Editor. Neither man shared Lee's politics, but they liked him personally and seemed to respect him professionally, if not always as a mayor, as an ex-newsman. Both men got daily calls from Lee to share gossip, to find out what was being printed, and to plug stories. Quite often Lee would offer unsolicited but professional advice on how all stories should be handled.

For his own stories, Lee would first call the newsman he had sent it to and suggest the way it should be written and provide any additional information that might be required. As soon as he hung up, he would call McQueeney to make a case for where the story should be placed. The case would never be made in vague layman's language, but would be couched in such terms as "Charlie, this one needs at least a two-column head, preferably above the fold. What do you think, Charlie?" If the story was big enough, Lee would invariably call up Leeney, who wrote most of the major editorials, begin with a polite suggestion, continue with a stern lecture on editorial responsibility, and often conclude with an angry note, such as one of these:

DEAR BOB [Leeney]:
    . . . Do you think the day will ever come when the *Register* can support anything in an unqualified fashion—anything constructive and good, that is, like Church Street?

Regards,
DICK

DEAR BOB:
    . . . With all this pioneering in New Haven, these great achievements in New Haven, don't you think there is something to be proud of editorially in our program . . . not lukewarm but enthusiastic?

Regards,
DICK

Sometimes a blast at Leeney was not enough for Lee, so to get things fully of his chest, he would shoot a wrathful note to the top:

DEAR DICK [Jackson]:
    I thought you would like to compare this editorial in the New York *Times* last Saturday with your editorial the preceding day on funds for

urban renewal. It was quite a contrast! Some day, I am sure, we are going to have an editorial page in New Haven which will properly reflect a progressive and enlightened attitude. . . . When that day will come, of course, I do not know, but I do hope I will live to see it.

Sincerely,
Dick

Jackson's reply infuriated Lee:

Dear Dick:

In connection with your letter to me . . . "I disapprove of what you say, but I will defend to the death your right to say it."—*Attributed to Voltaire.*

Sincerely,
Dick

However, such volleys fired privately at the editors were the exception. Normally Lee would court them. He would often call Leeney to seek advice on policy matters in conversations that would go like this: "Hello, Bob. Dick. How are you, Bob? . . . Tell me, Bob, what do you think I should do about this ———— matter? . . . Damn it, Bob, that's an interesting idea. . . . Do you mind if I borrow that phrase, Bob? . . . Thanks, Bob. Tell me, Bob, if I approached it in that way, how do you think the *Register* would treat it? . . . Well, think it over, Bob, and give me a call."

It would be an injustice to suggest the editors were taken in by such antics; they were capable of some cunning of their own. This was indicated whenever Lee organized a letter-writing campaign, called up Leeney to ask innocently if there had been any response, and Leeney, with equal innocence, claimed that he had received nothing at all. One *Register* reporter has described Lee's dealing with the editors in these terms:

"I don't think you can minimize Leeney's and McQueeney's role as a buffer between the publishers and Dick. A key part of that role is that both guys, like Dick, are Irish Catholics, and there is a subtle ethnic thing going. Dick's problem with the two has never been personal as it was with the old man. It's mainly a question of orientation. While I don't agree with everything Dick's done, I understand it, like some other reporters, because I've seen or covered the problems. Leeney and McQueeney really don't. They spend most of their time in the office and they live in the suburbs, and they just really don't appreciate the problems Dick has dealt with, so it's little wonder they don't usually approve or even understand his actions."

This comment not only summarizes the dynamics of Lee's relations with the *Register* editorial staff but also indicates one reason Lee found the reporters were least intractable when it came to ways for him to get the coverage he wanted. They would often sympathize with him because they were eyewitnesses to what he was doing, although the sympathy might be nothing more than the kind an umpire gives when he calls a batter out. Lee made the reporters feel important because he genuinely believed they were. He would walk out of any meeting to talk to a newsman, and he would make sure they got a briefing on a big story immediately before it broke. On major stories he would arrange a news conference which he personally directed with the flamboyance and extravagance of a Cecil B. deMille filming the Bible. Carefully multilithed press kits, enclosed in handsome blue covers and detailing every possible aspect of a story, were hand-delivered to reporters. The principals were herded to New Haven and propped up in the Mayor's Office along with drawings of the proposed improvements. Lee would solemnly enter the room and make his announcement. New Haven had never seen anything quite like these performances.

The reporters did not always respond to these inducements, so Lee employed some other tactics based on his control of what the reporters needed—the release of administration news. It was a relatively easy step to freeze out a hostile reporter by issuing stories on his day off or by giving it as an exclusive to another reporter who was more friendly. He would also play to their egos ("Damn it, why don't you come to work for me? I'll pay you twice as much as the *Register*"), their personal sympathies ("I'm just flesh and blood. I can't be beat around in the press every day and not be hurt by it"), or their insecurities ("McQueeney tells me there may be a shift in the beat soon"). Two things frequently irritated the reporters. One was based on the skepticism that reporters can develop on any beat when they get to know the personalities and problems and learn that the world is not quite as rosy as it appears in a handout. The other was peculiar to New Haven, where Lee and Logue's young staff clashed regularly with the newsmen. The reporters felt that "the whiz kids" were overpaid, which was understandable because the reporters were sometimes underpaid; that they were highhanded, which was a natural conclusion because some of the staff were considerably smarter than a few of the reporters and delighted in proving it; and that they were just plain arrogant, which a number of them were.

One of the redevelopment staff, Harold Grabino, was high on all the reporters' lists. Grabino, who was the Agency's counsel and later Executive Director, was proud of his ability to give one-word replies to any newsman's queries and, for some strange reason, insisted on calling some of them "Daddy-o." He was openly contemptuous of the newspapermen and would go out of his way to taunt them. One of his favorite tricks was to call *Courier* reporters at their homes early in the morning, waking them up to complain about a story written the night before.

The biggest complaint of the newspaper establishment was the secrecy which cloaked the administration plans and programs. On the surface, the complaint looks valid, for a lid was placed on specific project plans, negotiations with private developers, and proposed public improvements. Public announcements were held up until details were completed or were timed for the greatest dramatic impact, with the emphasis often placed on the impact. But the nature of redevelopment negotiations and the hostility of Jackson had a lot to do with it, too. Lee would often say, "Businessmen don't like to negotiate on a card table on the New Haven Green," and Logue, in lecturing his staff on staying away from the local press, would say, "You can't play square with the Jacksons because they are out to get you at every turn."

Lee was one of the first politicians to employ the full use of polling, techniques to provide him with some reading on the results of his varied devices for shaping public opinion. In fact, it seems to have been Lee who introduced John F. Kennedy to the work of Louis Harris, who was Kennedy's pollster in the 1960 presidential campaign and was Lee's personal pollster or "witch doctor," as the staff called him, during the fifties. Harris and, later, Oliver Quayle studied the city several times during an election year, and their assessments of voter attitudes were amazingly accurate, although their predictions of voter conduct could be quite fallible. Their work was helpful mainly in shaping campaign themes and cheering Lee up, for they were likable, intelligent men whose company the Mayor enjoyed. Sometimes Lee twisted their survey results to square with his impressions of citizen opinion which he claimed he received "through the antenna down here in my gut."

Lee's record of interpreting these impressions was not perfect, but it was accurate enough for one to marvel at his ability to pick up subtle shifts of opinion and to adjust his words and actions accordingly. His ability to speak when it was time to speak, to say what people felt, to act when there was impatience with talk, or to remain silent for fear that official words and action might tip the delicate balance when opposing community forces converged represented an eloquence—the finest of the political arts—of which Lee remains a true master. This Lee mastery was precisely what Harris, Quayle, and other studies of voter attitudes uncovered, for there was a significant voter identification with the Mayor. A Quayle survey in 1963 summarized this identification in these terms:

As always has been the case, Lee shows greatest strength as a person. His personal profile remains rich and warm. . . . The voters like him very much. He is a friendly and warm man who is honest and deeply dedicated to a better New Haven. . . .*

Anyone who has worked for Lee has his favorite pollster finding which dramatized Lee's attraction—the political-science poll in 1959 which showed that more schoolchildren in the city knew who the Mayor was than who the President of the United States was; an earlier finding which showed that 50 per cent of the sample not only liked Lee personally but regarded him as a close friend of the family.

But while the voters liked Lee, they often disagreed with him sharply, particularly on sensitive issues like civil rights. One cannot detect in any of the polls any great ground swell of community liberalism. Rather typically, New Haven voters took a somewhat limited view of what their local government should be doing, and their chief concerns were usually on the rapidity of snow removal, the efficiency of garbage collection, the availability of downtown parking, or the level of taxes. Their attitude on urban renewal was either problem-oriented ("Too much business displacement," "Not enough new housing") or very personal ("What's in it for me?").

In the face of urban renewal disruptions and problems, Lee would exude confidence and optimism sometimes to the point of self-delusion. And for the voter who sought a personal spot in renewal, Lee found one. Under his administration urban renewal became as comforting as a new home, as useful as a handsome new school, as liberal as an anti-poverty program, as commercial as a department store, as economic as a new industrial park, as convenient as a new expressway, and as understandable as a neighborhood playground. In the beginning it was a matter of public-relations imagery, but soon it became program policy. Urban renewal in New Haven was no two-step process of tearing down and rebuilding; it became an umbrella for new programs and services dealing with many areas of physical and human need.

It was the popular support that Lee enjoyed which sustained his coalition of other forces in the community—Yale, the businessmen, the politicians, and the bureaucrats. "Group dynamics" is what he would call it, but whatever it was, the careful courting of the voters, the personal link with Yale, the creation of a proadministration business organization, the accommodation with the politicians, and the control of the bureauc-

---

*A skeptic might properly suggest that such a glowing review is to be taken lightly since it was written by someone on the payroll; i.e., a pollster paid by the Mayor. However, I can remember both Harris and Quayle remarking in meetings not attended by Lee that Lee's personal tie with the voters was extraordinary compared to that of most other public officials they had served.

racy had the practical effect of immobilizing his opposition, giving him the support he needed, and creating apparent consensus. From afar the Lee coalition seemed to have the order, body, and unity of a symphony. But in many ways it was a one-man act with Lee assuming the combined role of composer, arranger, conductor, and performer.

No event better portrayed the character of the coalition than Lee's birthday party, which over the years developed into a pilgrimage of those connected with the administration to pay homage to the chief. The parties were usually held in the fading ballroom of the Hotel Taft and attended by about three hundred key persons. Up the small, cramped hotel elevators they would silently ascend, eyeball to neck, then alight and move into the ballroom to find the table where their group was sitting. There was never enough room, so the overflows created unlikely table partners. One could find a fire marshal next to a law professor, a bank president seated next to a ward heeler, a League of Women Voters member next to Arthur Barbieri, or a *Register* reporter next to a young Redevelopment Agency staff man. The three-man string ensemble would play "Marching Along Together," which was suffered in grim silence. Subjects of conversation might be the heavy layer of fried fat on the chicken legs or the appearance of Mayor Lee, beaming, at the head table. After dessert, discomfort would turn to boredom as the master of ceremonies told stale jokes. Finally Lee would be introduced, to accept, with suitable expressions of surprise and gratitude, the gift he had selected two weeks earlier. The ensemble would render "For He's a Jolly Good Fellow" as a conclusion, and the members of the Lee coalition would quickly leave and return to their separate occupations and areas of the city, not to reconvene until Lee was a year older. The remarkable thing about these otherwise routinely dull affairs was that Lee was usually the one most bored by them. The annual convocation of the coalition to honor his birthday was a bit of symbolism to be endured, not an end in itself. He was happy to get his lawnmower or a set of books, but there in the Taft ballroom the coalition was out of place and function. Its members belonged in their natural community setting linked only by Lee, and their purpose was not to bestow gifts on the leader but to play the Mayor's game.

4.

A Mayor Tours the Ghetto

NAT HENTOFF

I NEXT SAW THE MAYOR [JOHN V. LINDSAY OF NEW YORK CITY], unexpectedly, in front of a grocery store on the lower East Side one hot afternoon shortly after the summer's series of ghetto explosions had reached East Harlem. In comparison with Detroit and Newark, New York's explosion had been mild. But tension remained, and a middle-aged Puerto Rican who runs a store I sometimes patronize on Second Avenue near Third Street had just told me, "If it starts down here, I'm ready. It gets dark, I stay at home with my gun. I don't care who comes, they get it." We were standing on the sidewalk in front of his store, and his eyes left mine when a car stopped at the curb a few yards up Second Avenue and four men, including the Mayor, in his shirtsleeves, got out. The grocer gaped at the Mayor for a few seconds, and then broke into a smile.

The Mayor, seeing me, waved, and I walked over. I asked him about East Harlem. His face suddenly hardened. "We weren't getting to the kids," he said. "The agencies, the organizations weren't reaching them. Nobody's been talking to them. So we're trying to find ways to do that ourselves. The hell with the organizations. We're getting street people involved in setting up programs for the kids, and the kids are having a say in how they're run."

While we were talking a small crowd had gathered, and now people began complaining to the Mayor about their landlords or simply confirmed their actual nearness to the man they had seen on television by shaking his hand. A very old Puerto Rican woman tugged at the Mayor's sleeve. He bent down, accepted her good wishes, and was still smiling as he turned away. Then he caught sight of an ugly mound of debris in front of an empty store a few doors away. Two small children were playing in the filth, and Lindsay's face hardened again. He told an aide to have the Sanitation Department clean it up.

"You looked angry just then, but you must see that sort of thing all the time," I said.

He shook his head. "Each time, it's a fresh experience," he said.

The tension in the city continued, and a few weeks later I made plans to accompany the Mayor on one of his neighborhood tours. It was to begin at a public swimming pool in the Red Hook district of South Brooklyn. The Mayor was due by helicopter at 6 P.M., but he was late. A small, restless group of Puerto Rican boys, some in wet bathing suits, waited in a park near the swimming pool for the Mayor's descent. Also present were four policemen, several newspaper reporters, a photographer from the News, and a C.B.S. man with a hand-held television camera.

Four Negroes in their late teens arrived, wearing neat blue jackets that identified them as members of the South Brooklyn Youth Council. I asked them what sort of work they were doing, and one of them, a tall, slight boy, said, "We work with the kids, you know. Recreation, keeping them quiet, stopping fights. It's city money, you know. But it don't make it. I mean, we just got started in July and we're through in September. You know, this should be year-round. It's too hard trying to cool things just for a couple of months. It ain't easy, man. We got no protection. We can't carry nothing but our mouth."

At six-thirty, some of the children in the park shouted, and we all looked up to see a blue-and-white police helicopter heading toward us. It appeared to be overshooting the park, but it swiftly banked and came to earth not far from where we were gathered. The Mayor, in gray trousers and a short-sleeved white shirt with no tie, jumped out. He saw the cameramen and grimaced. In what seemed an instant, the small reception party expanded into a swarm of children, teen-agers, and adults, and the Mayor moved at the center of a bulging parade toward the swimming pool. Suddenly, though, he turned, found an opening in the crowd, and sprinted back to where the helicopter had landed. He shook hands with each of the four policemen who had been waiting for him. Just as he was about to be engulfed by the crowd again, I heard him say to his press secretary, Harry O'Donnell, "Ask C.B.S. to cool it—this is getting to be too much of a show."

"The point of these trips," O'Donnell said to me as the Mayor moved away, "is for him to find out what's happening in the neighborhoods. If there's too much press, they get in the way of his finding out."

As the parade resumed, the Mayor, while almost automatically shaking hands and signing autographs, listened attentively to an account of the neighborhood and its problems that was being given by a tall Negro, who was later identified for me as a senior staff member of the South Brooklyn Youth Council. At the pool, Buster Crabbe had just presented the first of what was to be a series of swimming demonstrations in ghetto neighborhoods throughout the city. Sidney Davidoff, who had recently become an assistant to the Mayor, was explaining Crabbe's function to several women of the community. "He says he can teach any kid to swim in a few minutes—at least give him a few strokes," Davidoff said. "You see, Crabbe believes you can get a lot of inhibitions and frustrations out through athletics."

A blond young man in his mid-twenties had for some minutes been trying without success to elbow his way through to talk to the Mayor. Acknowledging his defeat, he delivered his message to Davidoff. "I'm Peter Hughes, of the South Brooklyn Community Progress Center. Look, it's very clear to us that because there have been no disturbances here yet, Red Hook has been put at the bottom of the list for this summer. But you have to realize this is a worse ghetto than Harlem in some respects. We have practically none of the recreation or entertainment facilities Harlem has. And the people here—ask anybody—have to walk half a mile to get to the subway. There's only one good bus route, and that just skirts the area. We've got only four working traffic lights, and there's a terrible sanitation problem with some of the houses—toilets backing up. The streets aren't cleaned nearly as often as they ought to be, and we even have electricity lines running overground."

Davidoff promised to see what could be done, and I asked Hughes whether the neighborhood had been organizing itself to protest. "That's just the problem," he said. "It's hard to get any kind of organization going. These people don't know how to organize around a problem. They don't know how to bitch, and that's why they're at the bottom of this list."

I worked my way back into the crowd and caught up with the Mayor as he was leaving the pool. Looking up from a conversation with a teenager, he saw the News camera pointed straight at him. "Damn those cameras," he muttered.

With his arm around the shoulders of the tall Negro who had been assigned to brief him, the Mayor walked on to a nearby housing project, listening to a list of the neighborhood's needs, including more sprinklers for hydrants and more measures to combat drug addiction. Meanwhile, I got a briefing of my own from one of the other representatives of the Youth Council, who told me, "Since they built the Brooklyn-Queens Expressway, this neighborhood has been cut off from the rest of Brooklyn.

No movies, no market to speak of. I tell you, the community feels that nobody thinks about it anymore, that it wouldn't matter what happened to us here. Him coming in here, that's a good thing. It gives them a little hope."

I asked how long he thought the hope would last.

He shrugged. "Well, now, that's another thing," he said.

From the Negro and Puerto Rican section of Red Hook, the Mayor and his party moved on by car to Park Slope, a largely Italian enclave, consisting in the main of well-kept stores and two- and three-family houses. The Mayor got out, and in the first three blocks of his walk there he was noticed by only one man, who stopped, did a double take, and just managed to say "Hello" before the Mayor's party had passed.

"There are Negro kids who come to school here," the Youth Council official told Lindsay. "They always come into this neighborhood in a group. They have to. To protect themselves."

"What are the churches doing?" the Mayor asked.

"They try different things to bring the different elements together, but somehow they don't do too good a job."

By now, the Mayor was at the center of another parade. Park Slope had awakened to the presence of the city's chief executive. People yelled greetings from cars, others stepped into doorways and had their hands shaken, and children skipped alongside the swelling procession. Seeing a park, the Mayor strode in, and was guided by a group of elderly men to the area in which they play boccie. "The dirt is no good. It's too dusty," one of them complained. "And we need lights, for at night." At a glance from the Mayor, an aide made a note about dirt and lights.

I was standing next to the Mayor's Negro adviser from the South Brooklyn Youth Council, and I asked him, "Is this park kind of exclusive?"

He looked at me and smiled coldly. "I wouldn't come in here all by myself," he said.

As the Mayor moved back out to the street, a short, swarthy young man with dark glasses and long hair, carrying a half-full quart of beer, stepped in front of him. Lindsay grinned. "A Brooklyn hippie!" he exclaimed.

"Yeah. The difference between us and them Greenwich Village hippies is they smoke pot and we drink beer," the young man said. "Have some of my beer, Mr. Mayor."

Lindsay took the bottle. He saw the News photographer, looked hard at him, and said, "No shot—O.K.?" The photographer nodded, and the Mayor of New York took a swig from the Brooklyn hippie's bottle.

As the Mayor stopped to shake hands and talk with a group of middle-aged men in front of a bar, I told Davidoff about Lindsay's comment a few weeks before that East Harlem had erupted at least partly because no meaningful contact had been made with many of the young people in the streets. "That's right," Davidoff said briskly. "The official anti-poverty groups—and not only in East Harlem—had not been in touch with the most rootless of the young, for the simple reason that these kids are not part of the community structure. For that reason, we've been focussing this summer on sixteen satellite centers around the city. They're satellites of Youth Board offices, but they work pretty much on their own. The money comes from the federal Office of Economic Opportunity and some private corporations, but the policy is made by the neighborhood young people themselves, under the guidance of supervisors who also live there, or used to. The supervisors don't necessarily have social-work degrees. In fact, most don't. The mistake we made in East Harlem was that we'd figured any trouble would come in border areas. Therefore, the satellite center there was at a Hundred and Nineteenth Street, where Puerto Ricans and Negroes come together. But the disturbance was entirely within the Puerto Rican area. Two days after it happened, we had an emergency satellite center on a Hundred and Twelfth Street. Through that, we're reaching a much broader base among the kids."

"How long do the centers operate?" I asked.

"Well, we didn't get any of them going until July 10th. Bureaucratic procedures—the courier between Washington and New York seemed to have got lost. I don't know where we'll get the money after the summer, but somehow we'll keep at least some of the centers open through the winter. We've got to."

I caught up with the Mayor again. As he strode along amid a crowd of youngsters, he was stopped by an old woman, who grabbed his hand. A young woman with her said, "You really turn the kids on, Mr. Lindsay."

"They're the brightest of the crowd," the Mayor said. "They really know what's going on."

A newspaper reporter broke in to ask, "Mr. Mayor, do you really think these walks will continue to keep the city cool?"

Lindsay sighed. "I don't know," he said. "I really don't know. I'd have to be a bigger fool than I usually am to make predictions about that. Obviously, the thing to do is to rebuild the city the way it ought to be rebuilt."

"Hey!" A storekeeper rushed out into the street, shouting. "Hey, it's the Mayor! How about that?"

PART VII

The Mayor Speaks on Questions

of Policy and Resources

H OW LONG CAN THE METROPOLIS SURVIVE? IN THE FACE OF MOUNTING social and technological probems, this question is being asked with increasing frequency in all levels of society. More specifically, such conditions as blight, high welfare costs, unemployment, crime, pollution, depreciating tax resources, and traffic congestion, among others, have become standard features of the urban community and illustrate what is meant by the "urban crisis."

In this section we go directly to the mayors for their commentary on the particular cities they represent. What are the problems and what are the solutions, if any, as they see it? Before a United States Senate subcommittee investigating urban affairs, Mayor John Lindsay of New York City explains the kinds of reforms that he believes to be necessary, both at city hall and in Washington, if there is to be an effective treatment of urban needs. While his testimony ("On the Plight of New York City") is essentially informational, the second reading ("The Mayor of Los Angeles Cross-Examined"), which is a transcript from the same set of hearings, has a special sting to it. Here we witness a sparring session between Senators Abraham Ribicoff and Robert Kennedy on one side and Mayor Samuel Yorty on the other. In the give and take of debate, the reader is able to see at first hand the many limitations to mayoralty leadership as it attempts to meet the unrelenting pressures of community upheaval.

In the last selection, "On Racial Rioting in Detroit," Mayor Jerome P. Cavanagh relates his impressions of one of the worst race riots in the twentieth century. In treating the question "What went wrong?," the Mayor manages to convey something of the despair and frustration likely to be felt by anyone who must deal with the consequences of violence and social disintegration.

1.

On the Plight of New York City

JOHN V. LINDSAY

MAYOR LINDSAY. MR. CHAIRMAN, AND MEMBERS OF THE SUBCOMMIT-
tee, first, let me express my appreciation to you, Senator Ribicoff, for the
invitation to appear here today, and my gratification at appearing here before the two Senators from the Empire State, the senior Senator, Senator
Javits, and Senator Kennedy.

While my length of service as mayor of the Nation's largest city has
not been very long, New York has a certain intensity about it which, I
think, gives one a long view in a short time.

Mr. Chairman, I should like to commend you and the members of
your subcommittee for undertaking this inquiry. Committees of this Congress have in the past conducted important hearings concerning specific
local problems and specific national programs. But this is the first time
that an attempt has been made to assess the total crisis of our cities, to
measure it honestly against our present efforts, and to look toward an
overall strategy for rebuilding urban America.

Over the next few weeks, this subcommittee is scheduled to hear the
testimony of mayors from all over the country. I suspect that although
none of their communities is as large as mine, many of their problems are
like many of mine. I should think, therefore, that what lies before you is
a fairly grim business. Indeed, when I seek a comparison for what has been
happening in New York over the last few years, I find myself having to
go back some 3,000 years to the Old Testament and the ten plagues which
were visited upon the Egyptians. Unlike the children of Israel, however,
the people of our cities are not likely to be saved by a miracle.

In appearing before you today it is not my purpose to propose compre-

From a hearing before the Subcommittee on Executive Reorganization, *Federal
Role in Urban Affairs*, Part 3, August 22, 1966, pp. 550–561. Published by the U.S.
Government Printing Office.

hensive solutions to our urban problems. Nor do I believe it would be very helpful for me to enter into a numbers game over just how much Federal aid should be provided by any particular program or by all programs. The challenge to a mayor in these hearings is to set forth his own perceptions of the urban crisis and to relate to the Federal effort what the cities themselves can do.

Importance of Effective Action at Local Level

We all know that there are no panaceas for the problems of people in cities. There are, however, some important beginnings and some new directions being taken in cities across the Nation.

It is crucial in these inquiries to take note of what is happening at the local level of government. First, there are few exceptions to the rule that laws are only passed in Washington, not administered here. The finest act of Congress means little to an angry teenage Negro in the slums unless local government provides the resources, staff, and commitment to bring it to the streets of the city. Secondly, there is the matter of confidence and credibility. The Congress is being asked to appropriate sizable amounts of taxpayers' money to deal with urban problems. A central theme of these hearings must be that Congress will have to appropriate many times more than at present. But I do not think we can—nor should we—realistically expect the Congress to make available these vast amounts of money unless our cities demonstrate the willingness and the ability to modernize and streamline their administrative machinery to use Federal resources efficiently and to make the maximum effort from their own resources.

The challenge of gearing up local government is nowhere greater than in New York. New York City has a budget that is exceeded in the United States only by that of the Federal Government. Its population is larger than 67 of the 117 members of the United Nations. Its police force of 28,000 men is larger than many national armies. New York City is the equivalent of more than two Chicagos and four Philadelphias. The fact is that if each of the five boroughs that compose New York were treated as a separate city, we would have four of the eight largest cities in the country.

In a community of this size we have all of the urban problems that exist in other cities; but what is more, it would seem that as the size of the city goes up, the complexity of urban problems increases in geometric progression.

Changing Character of New York City Population

The dominant development in American urban life over the past two decades has been the changing composition of our urban population. In New York City, 2 million white inhabitants mostly in the middle- and high-income groups, have moved away and 750,000 Negroes and Puerto Ricans, mostly poor, have moved in. In 1945 Negroes and Puerto Ricans accounted for less than 10 per cent of the city's population. Today their proportion exceeds 25 per cent. This socioeconomic shift has leveled off here in New York relative to many of our smaller cities and the suburbs where these population changes are just beginning.

Problems of Minority Groups

These new residents have frequently suffered from the serious handicaps of inadequate education and job training, and they have continued to struggle under the burden of a color-conscious society.

For the Negro and the Puerto Rican, the result has been a high rate of unemployment, marginal low wage jobs for those who are employed, and a standard of living that, on the whole, is considerably lower than for the rest of the population.

In social terms we reap a harvest of broken families, illegitimate children, school dropouts, and disease.

For local government, this means that a large segment of the populace draws much more in services than it contributes in revenues. In New York City today nearly 2 million people live in poverty. Our welfare budget alone amounts to over $650 million, or 14 per cent of the entire budget, and this does not take into account the $571 million spent for municipal hospitals and health services, the $102 million spent in the war on poverty, or the additional costs of education, police, and sanitation generated by this situation.

Deterioration of City

This growing pressure on our city services has been exacerbated by the deterioration and obsolescence of our city's physical plant. As American cities go, ours is very old, and many of our schools, our hospitals, our apartment houses, and our commercial buildings are no longer either attractive or efficient. In the case of public buildings, their deterioration has been hastened by the chronic unavailability of city funds for all but the most imperative uses. In the case of multiple dwelling units, many reflect the economic dilemma of rent control. By 1970, almost 70 per cent of the housing units in New York City will be more than forty years old. About 350,000 units are in buildings built before 1900. We estimate that 800,000 dwelling units, representing over one-fourth of the total housing supply, are substandard and need either replacement or major rehabilitation.

One in four of our schools is more than 50 years old and is generally located among other scarred and broken buildings.

The condition of many of our 21 municipal hospitals is disgraceful. It is estimated that the city must spend a minimum of $400 million to renovate or rebuild obsolete hospital facilities.

Each working day 3½ million people crowd into the nine square miles of Manhattan south of Central Park. They insist on arriving at about the same time and in leaving at about the same time. This is tantamount to transporting every man, woman, and child in Connecticut into Bridgeport and taking them home again at night. The key to this massive movement is our rapid transit system. But it has responded neither technologically nor geographically to the changing patterns of city life and needs. Despite a recent fare increase, it is wholly dependent on public subsidy for maintenance, depreciation, debt service, and capital improvements. A program of subway modernization is likely to cost about $4 billion over the next ten years, roughly 40 per cent of New York City's capital budget for the period.

The depth and intensity of these needs, as I have said, cannot be exaggerated. The need is obvious that there be a vastly increased commitment of resources in New York City and in all the great urban centers of America. But the complex problems of urban America cannot be answered simply by appeals for more Federal funds badly needed as those funds are. Too often, in the past, local officials have used the argument of inadequate resources to pass the buck to Washington and thus escape hard decisions at home. The fact is the buck can't be passed anywhere because it stops both at city hall and in Washington. It is at city hall, as well as in Washington, that basic reforms are required which will permit us to respond effectively to the urban challenge. And it is only at city hall that local leadership can build effective coalitions behind controversial change.

I. GOVERNMENTAL STRUCTURE

City government, like all institutions, must reshape itself to the demands of rapid and complex change. But, unfortunately, government in many cities has been allowed to stagnate. That stagnation presents as great an obstacle to the goal of better services as does inadequate resources. In New York City, for example, we found well over fifty separate departments and agencies, each directly responsible to the mayor, with many having overlapping or competing jurisdiction.

There were more than a dozen federally funded manpower programs, with no overall coordination or central authority, and with no city official responsible for following their related activities. Five different agencies had jurisdiction over our roadways, again with no coordination. Over seven separate bodies made policy in the area of housing.

New York City Reorganization

To assure more effective administration, we are reorganizing our entire governmental structure so that the city's multitudinous agencies will be grouped into ten major administrations, organized along functional lines. For the first time, all agencies operating housing and urban development programs will be grouped into a single coordinated structure. The city's transportation agencies are scheduled to be assigned to a streamlined transportation administration. All of the city's programs concerned with health and hospitals are now the responsibility of a single administrator who oversees the newly created health services administration.

Last week we took a major step forward with the establishment of a human resources administration for New York. It will include the existing welfare department and youth board, as well as two new departments: one for community development which replaces the old and faulty municipal antipoverty structure; and one for manpower training and career development, which will organize all the separate, diffuse programs in manpower and employment into a single coherent system.

This reorganization will do a good deal more than rationalize the structure of government. For the first time, we have begun to redefine, simply and directly, the major goals of our city in the human resources area. These are:

First, manpower training and career development leading to useful employment;

Second, an education program with special emphasis on early childhood development;

Third, increased participation of the poor in planning and running programs for their benefit; and

Fourth, a social service system that operates in support of the first three objectives.

The new Human Resources Administration will permit us to measure the city's goals in the field of human resources development against the programs and funds needed to meet these goals, irrespective of departmental and agency boundaries.

This major governmental reform was not effected overnight. It is the result of an unusual four-month study, funded by the Ford Foundation and headed by Mr. Mitchell Sviridoff of New Haven. We estimate that it will take another six months to be put fully into effect. But only with such a streamlined agency can we hope to handle efficiently and effectively the vast amounts of funds necessary to develop the human resources of our city.

Other Efforts by City to Improve Governmental Structure

Another innovation is the recent creation of a policy planning council, bringing together on a formal basis for the first time the representatives of the three agencies concerned with program and fiscal planning. The council is chaired by the mayor and includes the city administrator, the budget director and the chairman of the city planning commission. One of its first and most critical tasks will be the initiation of a program planning budget system for the entire city. Such a system will provide us with long-range, comprehensive planning for the economic, social, and political development of New York. And because this planning council is chaired by the mayor, it will be exposed, as city planning rarely is, to political realities and tied into the governmental decisionmaking process at every point.

We have taken a number of other steps to increase efficiency and eliminate redtape. By executive order, I have created the Office of Narcotics Coordinator with responsibility for all city programs affecting addiction. Also by executive order, I have created a one-stop service to aid businessmen and industry in their dealings with all city departments. In a somewhat different vein, we recently terminated and altered 113 city-connected committees with an annual saving to the taxpayer of $200,000.

Need for Federal Coordination of Programs

Our effort to design comprehensive programs which link together all available resources will be stymied if a similar linkage does not exist in Washington. Cities must be able to combine separate Federal programs into effective services at the street level. Much can be done in Washington to make this possible. Effective coordination of all housing and physical development programs in New York will be impossible unless the Department of Housing and Urban Development has the authority and the effective working relationships to perform the same function in Washington. Similarly, the Office of Economic Opportunity's ability to coordinate all Federal programs related to the antipoverty program will intimately affect local efforts to mount a comprehensive attack on poverty.

More specifically, with the establishment of a manpower department in New York City, we will be formulating a citywide plan for a comprehensive manpower system. But we will be seriously hampered in this endeavor in our dealings with Federal funding sources. The artificial distinctions between Federal manpower programs, with different statutory requirements and agency regulations, will limit our ability to design a single manpower program. To resolve this, the Congress should consolidate into an Omnibus Manpower Act the various existing programs, such as the Manpower Development and Training Act, the Neighborhood Youth Corps, adult basic education, work experience, and the Nelson amendment.

It might also be appropriate to enact an Omnibus Low-Rent Housing Act, which would permit local communities to obtain a block-grant for a comprehensive plan to house low-income residents. This would make possible a choice of program components—public housing, rent supplements, or subsidized rehabilitation.

Better Information Needed on Urban Conditions

One area in which we need increased Federal assistance is information. Part of the difficulty of responding to urban change stems from the unprecedented rate of that change. We simply do not have the tools to measure or to describe accurately what is happening in our cities. For example, estimates of the number of unemployed high school dropouts in New York City range from 77,000 to 125,000. No one knows for sure—census data is 1959 data and employment data is collected for large regional districts.

Local government needs access to the latest and best data available. Federal data banks, contiguous data collection districts for all related Federal programs, a mid-decade census, and increased technical assistance to local governments' efforts to create their own information systems are ways in which this goal might be attained.

Two Innovations in Welfare Program

Administrative reforms, at both the local and Federal levels, are at least as critical as structural reorganizations. We have attempted bold new approaches in a number of programs, perhaps none so important as those in the welfare department. Two major demonstration projects have been designed. One would substitute a "declaration" procedure for establishing eligibility for public assistance in place of the present rigorous investigation. This would parallel the affidavit and spot-check system used by the Internal Revenue Service and would free caseworkers from the tedium of investigations, enabling them to devote more time to the fundamental problems of welfare recipients. The second proposal is for an employment "incentive" demonstration to enable welfare recipients to retain a larger portion of earned income. This program could make a major change in the patterns of dependency by encouraging the welfare recipient to seek employment and training that will lead to increasing self-support.

Unfortunately, the creativity of the welfare department and the support of the city administration are insufficient to try out these concepts. The necessary approvals at the State and Federal levels have not yet been granted. This inaction is not only frustrating to those who would confront the welfare problem with new approaches, but it has the effect of confirming the widespread belief that the problem itself is hopeless.

Give Local Government More Scope for Initiative

The difficulties we have encountered in initiating these two projects raise a more fundamental question. Every detail of every innovation or change in welfare procedure must be approved by State and Federal officials. Mere inaction at the State and Federal levels has blocked our efforts to achieve significant procedural improvements. We find this unreasonable and unnecessary. A more rational approach would be to grant to the city broad powers of procedural innovation subject to a veto by either the State or Federal Governments. The burden of action should be placed on those who would seek to restrict experimentation and innovation.

One final thought: Federal public assistance programs, although often singled out, are actually only one of several important ways in which Congress has sought to provide economic security for our citizens. Others include social security, medicare, minimum wages, and unemployment and workmen's compensation. It seems appropriate now that these various programs, developed independently, be rationalized into a coherent national program for economic security. I suggest that such a study be undertaken either by the Congress or in the executive branch.

II. PERSONNEL

Sound organization provides the framework for effective government, but the motivating force is people. For much too long, local government has been viewed as the backwater of government service. The glamour, the prestige, and the rewards were to be earned in the Federal service; to a lesser extent, at the State level but not in local government. Local government has traditionally been thought of as the province of the politicians.

This must change. Even with the limited expansion of urban programs that has taken place thus far, we are experiencing a personnel crisis. Improved governmental structures and better qualified personnel are closely related. Clear lines of authority and grants of responsibility will attract better people without whom new procedures will never reach their full potential.

To meet the personnel needs of New York City we have aggressively sought out the best talent we could find wherever we could find it—in the

Federal Government, in other cities and States, and in private industry. Often, to get the right man for the right job, we had to increase the level of compensation, and even then we were frustrated by the freezing in of pension systems. Federal legislation to produce pension mobility for persons transferring between Federal and local government would significantly reduce this problem, and I can't emphasize that enough.

City Urban Programs

Since January, we have brought together in New York a group of outstanding professionals, whom I like to call urbanists, from across the Nation. We were no more interested in their politics than in their religions. I believe that in New York City we are well on the way to fostering a new breed of top-level executive—forward-looking professionals with outstanding administrative experience and with a perspective that goes beyond the borders of any particular city.

But we must look to the future as well as the present and we must be concerned with getting the best people at all levels of local government, not only for the top executive positions, important though they are.

This summer we established, with substantial Federal assistance, a program to bring able young people into city government. The New York City urban corps program brought us more than 1,000 college students from across the country to work at useful tasks in city government. It is our hope that this exposure will induce many of them to return on a permanent basis after graduation.

Older retired citizens provide another source of talent for our city governments. There are many able men and women who, although they have completed one career, can still make a valuable contribution to society. We propose to tap this source by the creation of a senior citizens service corps which would provide part-time employment in city agencies.

We also propose to bring university faculty members into government through a faculty residency program. As with the senior citizens service corps, we are hopeful that Federal assistance can be obtained to support these projects. Both will serve to seed our local government with people who have somewhat different but very valuable perspectives from those of the career service.

Another program which we think can make an important contribution is already in operation in New York. It is an executive volunteer corps which is to consist of about 100 retired business executives, who will make available their expertise to small businessmen throughout the city.

While programs such as the urban corps will produce dividends over the long pull, we cannot wait. The magnitude and complexity of city responsibilities make it imperative for us to secure a massive infusion of talent now. One possible way of dealing with the problem is contained in the proposed Intergovernmental Personnel Act, S. 3408, introduced by Senator Muskie. This bill would make it possible, through the grant of Federal funds, for the city to improve its recruitment, selection, classification, training, and supervision of vital personnel. The inadequacies in these areas were highlighted a few years ago by a Brookings Institution study of professional, managerial, and technical personnel in New York. Aware as the city has been of its failings in these matters, budget considerations have precluded remedying them.

The Muskie bill would also authorize the Federal Government to share its personnel programs with States and localities, and it promotes a much-needed mobility of personnel between Federal and State and local governments. In short, it creates a climate and a means for joint efforts by all levels of government to solve increasingly difficult manpower problems.

III. CITIZEN PARTICIPATION

In the midst of our new sense of urgency about the material needs of our cities, we must never lose sight of an intangible which profoundly affects our urban future—the quality of the relationship between the citizens of our cities and their government. All that we can do to rebuild our cities will have limited effect unless we are able at the same time to rebuild a sense of participation in determining the fate of the city among all its citizens.

Nowhere has this goal become more important than in New York City. The scale of the daily tasks of government in so large a city has led to the centralization of decisionmaking in a massive bureaucracy. Too often that centralization means government which is remote, insensitive, invisible, and unresponsive to the needs of the people. A government with 300,000 employees, 800 schools, 76 police precincts, and 21 municipal hospitals is a government which must learn the art of creative decentralization at the same time it uses new technology to centralize its operations. Resolving this tension between the two simultaneous directions of modern government—centralization and decentralization—represents one of the greatest challenges facing city government today.

City Efforts to Improve Delivery of Services

In New York we have begun to take some deliberate steps toward improving the delivery of services to our citizens. To provide prompt response to housing complaints, the building department has begun to locate its inspectors in local offices and has equipped them with an instant communication system. Under the OEO grant, we have also opened five trailer offices in slum areas as part of our emergency repair program. The welfare department has opened its first satellite welfare center. Seven community progress centers are now operating in target areas under the antipoverty program. The Health Services Administration is designing comprehensive neighborhood health clinics for low-income areas. As a first priority, the newly created Department of Manpower and Career Development of the Human Resources Administration will establish a system of neighborhood employment centers which will undertake a door-to-door, household-by-household survey to find out precisely who needs and wants training and a job.

All of this will be made more effective by the creation of neighborhood city halls, the first of which opened last week in east New York. These will bring to each neighborhood in our vast city a complete municipal information and referral system as well as a full-time staff to deal with local problems when and where they occur.

Importance of Citizen Participation

But placing city services in neighborhoods where they are needed will not, in itself, end city dwellers' pervasive feelings that they have no way to influence their government. This sense of fundamental powerlessness in the face of invisible uncaring government is the greatest disease of urban culture today. At its worst, the gnawing frustration of powerlessness explodes in senseless acts of individual or mob violence. No mere appropriation or reorganization will touch this disease. It will take a basic commitment on the part of local and Federal Governments to provide new channels of participation in urban government for those who now feel they have no relationship to the agencies which touch their lives.

In New York this goal underlies the commitment my administration has made to the creation of a civilian review board for the police department.* Similarly, the creation of welfare-recipient advisory groups and community corporations to coordinate and operate neighborhood antipoverty programs grows out of our recognition that those who receive services must shape those services. Only thus will they gain a true sense of influencing their own destiny in their own neighborhoods. In this same effort, over 200 grassroots organizations are now operating their own summer antipoverty programs in 26 target neighborhoods across the city.

Let me be clear. What is needed to cure the disease of powerlessness in our great cities is neither black nor white power. What is crucial is a new sense of citizen power—power to influence city governments' efforts to improve the quality of life in our cities. Without citizen power, we will still be pouring our resources into programs which may fail because they do not reflect the needs and aspirations of those who are most deeply affected by the decay of our cities.

---

*After a heated campaign, the civilian review board proposal was defeated in a public referendum in November 1966—Ed.

I have described some of the things that we in New York City are doing to meet the urban crisis—streamlining local government, rethinking our goals and aspirations, a new emphasis on searching out top-rate professionals, and a new emphasis on creating an aura of excitement and participation in local government. However, our financial ability to do these things is severely limited. And this does not begin to take into account the funding of the very large programs of capital improvements and social and economic development which are indispensable if we are to make our cities livable. Let me give you an idea of the deepening financial plight in which we find ourselves.

Financial Plight of City

When I took office last January New York City was preparing its budget for its coming fiscal year. It amounted to over $4.5 billion* and included a deficit of well over $500 million. This deficit could not be attributed to an overly ambitious approach to the city's problems for even with this deficit the city planned only to engage in a holding operation. Nor could it be attributed to any reluctance to tax ourselves. The mainstay of the city's revenue, its property tax, while not the highest in the country, is at $4.96 per $100 of assessed valuation—certainly on the high side.

The second major source of tax revenue is the sales tax, which at a combined State-city rate of 5 per cent is higher than it is anywhere else in the United States, except Pennsylvania, which also has a 5 per cent sales tax.

The city's business tax structure, which produced about $250 million annually, was built around a gross receipts tax of four-tenths of 1 per cent. For the many businesses with low profit margins, this tax was equivalent to anywhere from an 8 per cent to 20 per cent net income tax. All of this was on top of a State tax structure with a personal income tax that rises quickly from 2 per cent to 10 per cent.

As you see there was not very much flexibility. Yet without additional tax revenues, the city's financial condition was fast deteriorating. We had no choice, therefore, but to ask the State legislature for authority to levy a city personal income tax, applicable to both commuters and residents; to increase the stock transfer tax, to double water charges, and to increase utility taxes and the premium tax on life insurance companies. In addition, primarily for reasons of equity, we rewrote the city's business tax law eliminating the old gross receipts tax and substituting a more equitable net profits tax. The revenue from this package plus additional aid from

*The expense of running New York City has continued to grow rapidly. The budget for the fiscal year 1969–70 was projected at over $6.5 billion—Ed.

the State, plus a job freeze and other economies will enable us to get through the current fiscal year in the black.

But what of next year and the year after, and what of the mountain of problems which we cannot touch on this budget? The Temporary Commission on City Finances—a nonpartisan citizens group appointed by Mayor Wagner—estimates a deficit for the city's next fiscal year of some $400 million, even taking into account the revenue growth factor. I hope that we can, by prudent management and by economies, substantially reduce that figure. But I know that the result will not be a budget that will allow us to wage all-out war on the economic and social problems of the disadvantaged, on dreadful housing, on traffic strangulation, and on filth in our streets, in the air we breathe, and in the water around us.

Solving the Financial Problem

The answer is not additional local taxes. On Monday Senator Clark said he thought business was blackmailing local governments into low taxes by threats to relocate. While I would not describe this situation in precisely those terms, the mobility of people and industry is a substantial deterrent to the reliance which State and local governments can place upon income taxation. If a company's operations can be carried on in a low-tax area as well as a high-tax area, the company may be induced to settle where taxes are lower. Similarly, individuals are tempted to move to areas of lower taxation. These are facts of life which result from the autonomy and diversity of a Federal system, for in this country, it is only the Federal tax which has the advantage of being ubiquitous.

The limitations which this situation places upon the efforts of the States and localities to solve their fiscal problems through increasing their taxes is a forceful argument for some form of Federal tax sharing. Whether that tax sharing is accomplished by a limited credit against Federal taxes for State and local taxes or whether it is derived through the so-called Heller plan is less important than that something of the sort be done.

This then is the fiscal crisis which confronts us in New York. With taxes already at a level which causes daily complaints by both business and individuals, we are barely able to meet our essential needs. New taxes, higher taxes, are no solution in New York, and to a greater or lesser degree, I expect that the same is true for our other cities. The money must come from Federal revenues. Without very large amounts of Federal money, the plain fact is that the crisis of our cities will continue and worsen. This is a malignancy that this great Nation cannot afford to ignore.

Thank you very much.

Senator RIBICOFF. Thank you very much, Mayor Lindsay. We appreciate your coming here to testify.

2.

The Mayor of Los Angeles Cross-Examined

United States Senators Question SAMUEL YORTY

SENATOR RIBICOFF. I AM JUST CURIOUS HOW A CITY IN A YEAR GOES about trying to handle some of its problems once it is called to their attention. I have before me the original McCone report. I do not know what you think of the McCone report. I think I might have read about your feeling on it. I do not know whether you thought it was good or bad.

MAYOR YORTY. No; I think they tried very hard to do a good job. They had a difficult problem because they were trying to reach unanimity, which is not easy when you have a group of people that bring various viewpoints to a problem like this.

Senator RIBICOFF. Let us go over together some of the recommendations as to what they think should have happened, and I am just curious as to what you people in Los Angeles have done with these recommendations during the past year.

To implement its conclusions on law enforcement the McCone Commission recommended that:

> The Board of Police Commissioners should be strengthened.

Did you do anything there?

Mayor YORTY. Yes, although not as a result of the McCone Commission report. I told the commission before that report that they should

From a hearing before the Subcommittee on Executive Reorganization, *Federal Role in Urban Affairs*, Part 3, August 23, 1966, pp. 750–764, 774–779. Published by the U.S. Government Printing Office. The "McCone Report" referred to is more formally entitled, "A Report of the Governor's Commission on the Los Angeles Riots" [in Watts]. The Commission Chairman was John A. McCone, California businessman and former director of the Central Intelligence Agency—Ed.

start holding hearings if there were any cases where people felt that the department had not taken proper disciplinary action against an officer, and so they were prepared to do that. As a matter of fact, the first hearing that was scheduled, they complained and asked us to call it off because it was not a factual complaint. Now I might say, Senator, if you do not mind, that the president of the police commission today is a Negro attorney.

Senator RIBICOFF. When was he appointed?

Mayor YORTY. He was appointed several years ago. He is not my first Negro commissioner on the police commission. I appointed another attorney, Mr. Porter, in 1961, but he became a referee over in the court and left. So I appointed Mr. Hudson, and he is currently the president of the commission.

Senator RIBICOFF. The Commission also recommended that:

> Investigations of all citizen complaints should be conducted by an independent Inspector General under the authority of the Chief of Police in the implementation of procedures established by the Board of Police Commissioners.

Mayor YORTY. We are doing that.

Senator RIBICOFF. You are doing that?

Mayor YORTY. Yes. There was some criticism the other day. They felt that we had not implemented it as much as we could. But we are doing that.

Senator RIBICOFF. Now may I say this to you, I am not trying to entrap you or anything.

Mayor YORTY. I know that.

Appraisal of City Actions in Second McCone Report

Senator RIBICOFF. I am asking these questions to get your answers. I have with me the second McCone report issued on August 17. It is a staff report of actions taken to implement the recommendations in the original report.

Mayor YORTY. That is the one I was referring to that they had some criticism of our implementation of the inspector general.

Senator RIBICOFF. I just read these back and forth. I do not think the second McCone report has ever been made public.

Mayor YORTY. Yes, the press has it.

Senator RIBICOFF. Parts of it? On page 4 it states:

> The Police Department, with the approval of the City Council, has established an Inspector in Charge of Citizen Complaints, as recommended by our Commission. However, our recommendation that the "Inspector

General" be "properly staffed with sworn officers and civilian personnel" so that civilian complaints could be investigated independently and outside the chain of command has not been followed. If the failure to provide the Inspector General with the recommended staff assistants is an economy move, as we have heard suggested, we think it is a false economy.

Would you want to comment on that? We will make this entire report a part of the record.

Mayor YORTY. It is not an economy move, and we do not accept all their fiindings as gospel. We think that with a minority controlling the police department, the head of it, three minority out of the five members, and sitting patiently and listening to, they told me the other day, about twenty complaints a week, they would tend themselves to answer that part of the McCone latest report.

Senator RIBICOFF. In other words, the police department replied to that?

Mayor YORTY. The president of the police commission I think intends to reply.

Senator RIBICOFF. The original report recommended that:

The Police Department should institute expanded community relations programs.

Mayor YORTY. You have a whole list in one of the exhibits there of the very large number of things that we are doing.

Senator RIBICOFF. Has the police department been doing that?

Mayor YORTY. Yes, they have.

Senator RIBICOFF. The police department itself?

Mayor YORTY. The police department and some of my staff. We are holding police team meetings, for instance, all day conferences. We are holding meetings at the police stations in the curfew area, with citizens, Negro citizens, business people and others, and the Westminster project, which is an OEO project, has done quite a good job of talking to citizens about the need to maintain law and order in their area. Actually in a little flareup not too far back, they were very useful.

Employment Programs Have Been Started

Senator RIBICOFF. You make the point that hard-core [un]employment is the No. 1 problem in these areas. I read from the original McCone report page 47:

There should immediately be developed in the affected area a job training and placement center through the combined efforts of Negroes, employers, labor unions and government.

I will read the whole thing.

Mayor YORTY. You do not need to. Much of this has been done. Among other things we have developed this "Opportunities industrialization center," based upon the Philadelphia model, and of course you will find one of the exhibits there where the employment group of private employers feel that they themselves have created about 12,000 jobs in about a year for people in this area. I tried to point out in my statement that there is no way that the city itself, with our limited jurisdiction, can just hire all these people.

Senator RIBICOFF. Another recommendation was that:

> Federal and state governments should seek to insure, through the development of new facilities and additional means of communication, that maximum advantage is taken of government and private training programs and employment opportunities in our disadvantaged communities.

Is there anything being done on a cooperative basis here between the city, the State, and the Federal Government?

Mayor YORTY. Well, our board at present does not have the State represented on it, but the city and county and the city and county schools, our OEO screening board, and the State is working, yes, on some training programs, and some in cooperation with private industry. This is not under my jurisdiction. I have nothing to do with it.

Senator RIBICOFF. You have nothing to do with it at all?

Mayor YORTY. No, but the State is doing——

Senator RIBICOFF. Some of these training programs and placement centers, where are they located? Are they located in the so-called disadvantaged areas where the Spanish-speaking and the Negroes live, or do you have to go downtown to get to them?

Mayor YORTY. No, we have them in the area. As a matter of fact, before OEO was ever developed, we had some youth training in employment areas under the old "Youth Opportunities Board." Now the opportunities industrialization center is just really getting started. We hope it is going to be a big success.

Is City Locating Community Facilities in Disadvantaged Areas?

Senator RIBICOFF. Are you in the process in Los Angeles of building or constructing any new municipal facilities?

Mayor YORTY. We are building—of course, we are always building lots of municipal facilities. I think you are probably referring to a county hospital.

Senator RIBICOFF. No, I am just talking generally. I am not talking about the rate of——

Mayor Yorty. We have plans. Do we have our grant approved yet?

Mr. Goe.* We have two grants that are nearing approval which would supply community facilities in both the Watts area specifically, the 2.5 square mile area, and community facilities in another area of south central, which is more near the heart of the curfew area.

Senator Ribicoff. These are Federal grants?

Mr. Goe. These are Federal matching grants.

Senator Ribicoff. How about the city itself placing some of its facilities in these areas?

Mr. Goe. The city is pretty well represented in that respect. We have thirteen administrative centers throughout the city. It is very well decentralized as far as availability of service. Police stations, building and safety locations, most of the major departments who serve great numbers of people are located in the area. We have no major capital projects programed because there is no need to multiply the services that already exist.

Mayor Yorty. This is not an area like an eastern slum. If you wanted to take a look at the curfew area you would probably be a little bit surprised if you have not seen it.

Senator Ribicoff. I have seen pictures and I have a general idea that it does not look like what we conceive of as the average urban slum. But in Watts itself there is no hospital; is that correct?

Mr. Goe. Correct.

Mayor Yorty. No; and as I have pointed out to you, the health department is under the county. The county put a bond issue on the ballot for a hospital. It was narrowly defeated, and we hope the county will go ahead and build it anyway. In the meantime, we have worked with the University of Southern California on a health center, which is being put up as a prefab, and this working with OEO, and we hope that this will be a one-stop, real effective service center. So that is under construction.

McCone Report Recommendation on Education

Senator Ribicoff. With regard to education, the original McCone report recommended that:

> Elementary and junior high schools in the disadvantaged areas which
> have achievement levels substantially below the city average should be
> designated as "Emergency Schools." In each of these schools, an "Emergency Literacy Program" should be established consisting of a drastic
> reduction in class size to a maximum of twenty-two students and additional

*At the time of the hearing, Robert Goe was the Mayor's Executive Assistant and Director of Community Development in Los Angeles.

supportive personnel to provide special services. It is estimated that this program will cost at least $250 per year per student in addition to present per student costs and exclusive of capital expenditures, and that it must be continued for a minimum of six years for the elementary schools and three years for junior high schools.

It was also recommended that:

A permanent preschool program should be established throughout the school year to provide education beginning at age three. Efforts should be focused on the development of language skills essential to prepare children to learn to read and write.

You mentioned the fact that these youngsters move in at the high rate of some 1,000 a week and that many of them are way behind in education, causing great problems. They cannot develop their educational skills and get good jobs. Now, what has happened in Los Angeles with this particular recommendation?

City Has No Jurisdiction over Schools

Mayor YORTY. I think I must remind you again, Senator, I have no jurisdiction whatever over the city schools. I can['t] answer your question.

Senator RIBICOFF. You may not have jurisdiction, but if someone else is responsible, I think it ought to be known.

Mayor YORTY. Well, it is. It is an elected school board in the city of Los Angeles. I noticed this newspaper clipping the other day from Dr. Crowther, the head of our schools, who says that he needs money for 150 projects from the Federal Government for these local schools, but the Federal Government has been helping the local schools some under your new acts, but, primarily, I think the problem has been the lack of State aid at the elementary, secondary, and junior college level. It has been going down on a percentage basis. Half of the tax bill of the city of Los Angeles on the homeowner is for the schools, and the schools in that area are good schools and they have good teachers. I think the one thing that is the most difficult for them is overcrowding.

Senator RIBICOFF. Do I understand you correctly that you, as the mayor and the city council, have no jurisdiction at all over any phase of education?

Mayor YORTY. Absolutely none, and that is why I tried to make that clear at the start of my talk, so you would understand how different the cities are, and how sometimes limited the mayor can be. Primarily in all these areas you are talking about, the one thing I have is law enforcement.

Senator RIBICOFF. I think it is tragic, and I think it ought to be known where the responsibility is, and it should be placed upon the shoulders of those responsible. I would like to read from the August 17, 1966, followup by the McCone committee, the following:

> The "Emergency Schools" program which we believed last December, as we do now, to be absolutely essential for areas of substandard educational achievement, has not been adopted, although the 1966 California State Legislature provided assistance for reduction of class size and for supplemental reading programs. The problem of attracting teachers to the South Central area, which has been aggravated in the last eight months, adds to the urgency of adopting an "Emergency Schools" program . . . The absence of greater achievement on the Commission's education recommendations does not stem from any lack of agreement regarding their merit; indeed, there seems to have been no serious dissent from the Commission's analysis of the problem or from the validity of the recommendations. Rather, budgetary considerations have kept the Federal, State, and local governments from further implementation of the recommendations.

What was the damage, what was the overall property damage as a result of the Watts riots?

Mr. GOE. There were 744 structures damaged. The total——

Mayor YORTY. The city school system has been very pressed for funds. They have a ceiling on the amount of taxes they can levy on the homeowner. Fifty per cent of the property tax bill in the city of Los Angeles is for support of the schools, and the taxes on the homeowner are extremely high, and this is where I say the lack of State aid is hurting, and the Federal programs are relatively new that are beginning to help. But, certainly, Dr. Crowther and the board of education would like to have the money to do the things that they know need to be done. They have even considered and have cut out some like musical training and been faced with the problem of maybe cutting out some of the physical education program. They have had to cut corners in many directions just trying to keep the standards that we have today, which are quite high. But the people in the area you are talking about need no larger classes than other areas. They, some of them, actually need almost tutoring, and it is expensive, and the money cannot come out of the homeowners.

Tax Rate in Los Angeles

Senator RIBICOFF. But Los Angeles is not considered a poor city; is it?

Mayor YORTY. No; we are not a poor city, but that does not mean that you can tax too heavily on any one group. A city does not have the authority to levy a myriad of taxes. This is preempted by the State. At some levels the taxes are so heavy we could not add a local levy onto them.

Senator RIBICOFF. What is the tax rate in Los Angeles?

Mayor YORTY. Over $9 per $100 of assessed valuation.

Senator RIBICOFF. How do you assess it?

Mayor YORTY. We assess it 25 per cent.

Senator RIBICOFF. That is pretty cheap if you assess at 25 per cent. You get $9.00, so basically that is $2.25 and 22 mills. I am just thinking back in my own State of Connecticut, I do not know of a town of the 169 that has a rate as low as that.

Mayor YORTY. We have found that these comparisons are usually pretty invalid. We do not know how some other people assess.

Los Angeles Not Meeting Its Obligations to Citizens

Senator RIBICOFF. I know. But let us say that if you have 100 per cent or 80 or 90 per cent, if you have a 25 per cent valuation, the chances are that there are probably some very unrealistic appraisals in the first place. In the second place, the rate then would go very, very low to actual valuation, and there must be a fantastic increase of property values in Los Angeles as the population keeps growing and the new construction takes place. Los Angeles is a rich town. I think one of the great tragedies is to expect or to fail to expect the general community to share its burden.

Now here is the McCone report mentioning the turmoil and tragedy of Watts and explosive situation in Los Angeles and talking about the need for an emergency school program. You talk, yourself, as mayor of the great responsibility and the lack of education, hard-core unemployment, and bringing people up to date, and the 1966 California State Legislature makes provision for assistance for reduction of class size.

Mayor YORTY. That was very small.

Senator RIBICOFF. Very small what?

Mayor YORTY. Very minor assistance. The bill that failed at the legislature that should have passed was the 1 per cent increase in the sales tax, with all of the money subvened back for local education. It did not pass.

Senator RIBICOFF. Mayor Yorty, what is the responsibility of a town, what is the responsibility of the people? Basically you have got a 22-mill rate, and you have got great problems in Los Angeles, one of the glittering capitals of the entire world, population growing, real estate values going up.

Mayor YORTY. Senator, assessed values are also going up. We reassess all the time. I would venture to say that I could take your State of Connecticut and probably we would come out with a very good comparison with you. I would not be surprised but what our taxes may be higher on the whole. I do not accept anyone's word at face value on the basis of how assessments are made, because I have seen too many variations in the system, and whether they actually figure the real value or not, it is a very complicated way of doing business. But I can tell you this, that property taxes in Los Angeles are very high.

Senator RIBICOFF. What tax would a person pay on a home that sells for $25,000? What would be his tax bill?

Mayor YORTY. Probably about $600.

Senator RIBICOFF. And the people who live in the $25,000 home, do they feel a sense of responsibility for the other people?

Mayor YORTY. Well, they not only do but they show that all the time.

Senator RIBICOFF. How do they show it if there is a reluctance to pay for educational needs?

Mayor YORTY. We are paying very well for educational needs. Our schools probably have as high standards as you have any place in the Nation and perhaps higher.

Senator RIBICOFF. But yet you do not have them high enough to take care of the children who need education the most.

Mayor YORTY. Yes we do, but you have to distribute your educational dollar, and these people need very special training. We think they should have it, and we feel that the State has been remiss in forcing more of a load onto the local community instead of keeping up the percentage that they are supposed to subvene back, which would be about 50 per cent.

When the sales tax was passed in California, it was passed on the promise that the State would pay a major share of the cost of local schools. The State is now keeping the sales tax and not subvening back their proper share.

Senator RIBICOFF. I am not aware of the local situation between the State and Los Angeles, but evidently if a policy was adopted, it is a policy that applies for education throughout the State equally, is that right? You get so much per pupil in grants from the State.

Mayor YORTY. We have that, but as the cost has gone up, the State has remained the same, and percentagewise it has gone down. Besides that, they have different formulas for different districts, too.

Role of Mayor in Supporting Education

Senator RIBICOFF. I am just curious. What happens? You do not control education. Separate elected boards of education do. You know as a leader of the community that education is an absolute essential. You have before you the McCone report. Do you go out in the forefront and beat the drums and campaign for higher taxes?

Mayor YORTY. Yes.

Senator RIBICOFF. And more aid to education?

Mayor YORTY. I even ran for Governor to try and correct the situation, to get where I could do something about it at the State level.

Senator RIBICOFF. On the State level. But how about mayor on the local level?

Mayor YORTY. There is nothing I can do to help defray the cost of the schools in my position. The taxing power of the local school board is limited to property taxation, and they have reached their legal limit.

Senator RIBICOFF. Have you told the school board that they are wrong?

Mayor YORTY. Senator, nobody can tell them that they are wrong. They have reached the legal limit.

Tax Rate Limit Prevents Obtaining More Funds for Education

Senator RIBICOFF. We can sit here and say the President of the United States can be wrong or a member of the Cabinet. They may not like it. In other words, I am talking about the responsibility of one elected official who does not take for granted the problem that exists and say he cannot do something about it.

Mayor YORTY. The school board has a legal limit and they have reached it and we have tried to get an override and we have failed, so they are right up against so many dollars in trying to do this job with them.

Senator RIBICOFF. A legal limit in what respect? How is the school board limited, by State or local law?

Mayor YORTY. By State.

Senator RIBICOFF. Limited to what?

Mayor YORTY. To the amount that they can tax. They have a legal limit.

Senator RIBICOFF. They are legally limited to a mill rate or assessed rate or what?

Mayor YORTY. It is $2.65 per $100 of assessed valuation.

Senator RIBICOFF. That is a maximum of the school board.

Mayor YORTY. Without getting a vote to override and we have not been able to do it.

Senator RIBICOFF. A vote to override by who? By referendum?

Mayor YORTY. Yes.

Senator RIBICOFF. Has this type of referendum been tried in Los Angeles?

Mayor YORTY. We have tried and we have failed. Besides that there is tremendous resistance to increasing taxes on the homeowner. As I pointed out to you, I think the State is wrong in forcing us to classify all property whether it is income-producing or not for taxation on the same basis. I think that there should be a difference where you can pass the tax on commercial or income property. But the State limits us to 25 per cent of the assessed valuation as the State law, and all properties are classified the same. The taxes on homes in Los Angeles are very high, particularly as you get up in the homes that are worth a little more than the one that you used as an example.

Senator RIBICOFF. How about the complex of large office buildings and industry? What is the tax rate on those?

Mayor YORTY. The same.

Senator RIBICOFF. Twenty-five per cent of assessed valuation.

Mayor YORTY. That is right and the taxes are the same. The State has the law on the subject. I just got a new ruling from my city attorney the other day, to make sure that we could not do anything about it, and he said we cannot. This is one of the problems I did not think that you were interested in discussing here, but the preemption by the State of jurisdiction from local communities is extremely serious in our State. I do not know whether it is in others or not.

Transportation Problem in Los Angeles

Senator RIBICOFF. Going to the McCone report recommendations on transportation:

> A public subsidy in one form or another to give SCRTD* financial ability to provide an adequate and reasonable bus transportation system throughout the metropolitan area. The acquisition by SCRTD of the existing small transportation companies which now complicate and increase the cost of transportation in the Los Angeles area. The establishment of transfer privileges in order to minimize transportation costs. With respect to the Watts area in particular, immediate establishment of an adequate east-west cross town service as well as increasing the north-south service to permit efficient transportation to and from the area.

What has been done about these four recommendations?

Mayor YORTY. Some of this is being accomplished, but our transportation system is far from adequate. At my suggestion we recently got $4 million from the State legislature out of tidelands funds to complete the planning for a mass transit system. I do not mean by that we do not have good transportation by other modes in Los Angeles because our freeway system, I think, is used as an example pretty much around the world, but our mass transportation is not good.

We have improved the transportation in and out of the curfew area, however. But this again is not under my jurisdiction. It is under a State agency. Southern California Rapid Transit District is a State agency.

*Southern California Rapid Transit District—Ed.

Senator RIBICOFF. So what you have here is a breakdown not so much of the Federal-city relationship but the State and city relationship.

Mayor YORTY. That is true. The State, until I was able to get them to give us $4 million out of the tidelands funds to complete planning, had never contributed 1 cent to their own instrument, the State transit system.

Health Problem in Watts

Senator RIBICOFF. How about health? Infant mortality, for example is about 1½ times greater in Watts than the citywide average, according to the McCone report. The number of doctors in the southeastern part of Los Angeles is grossly inadequate as compared with other parts of the city. The report says there are 106 physicians for some 252,000 people, whereas the county ratio is three times higher. The hospitals readily accessible to citizens in southeast Los Angeles are also grossly inadequate in quality and number of beds, according to the report.

Is the hospital system municipal, county, State, or private?

Mayor YORTY. It is county and private.

Senator RIBICOFF. You have no municipal hospital?

Mayor YORTY. No, we have no municipal hospital except emergency hospital, which is primarily for our police and fire, but we are building this USC health center in that area. The city is not, but it is being built, and we hope the county will go ahead with the so-called Watts Hospital.

Federal Spending in Los Angeles

Senator RIBICOFF. How much in the way of funds does Los Angeles get from the Federal Government; do you know?

Mayor YORTY. Mr. Goe made a compilation, and we figured over ten years we have had $58 million.

Senator RIBICOFF. Over ten years. What did you get last year?

Mayor YORTY. Do you have the figure for last year?

Mr. GOE. The last year would be——

Mayor YORTY. If you are going to try to relate this like to New York, Detroit, and Chicago, again you will not get a valid comparison, because our city has such limited jurisdiction. We are not in the field of welfare, health, or any of these areas where you would make grants. Our grants, for instance, are to our harbor department or even to the airport department. These are the areas in which we deal and have jurisdiction at the city.

Mr. GOE. It was about $4 million last year, Senator.

Mayor YORTY. You say we had $4 million?

Mr. GOE. Total. This includes grants to the airport, a disaster grant after the Bel Aire fire, and it is very small. The city has not been a great participant in Federal funding up to now. We have $38 million so far going through the poverty program——

Mayor YORTY. But that is not the city either, $38 million. That is the whole county.

Senator KENNEDY. Could I ask how much money does the city of Los Angeles receive from the Federal Government, the people that live in the city of Los Angeles?

Mr. GOE. $58 million in ten years, Senator, and it breaks down like this.

Mayor YORTY. But that really would not be anything that you could compare with the other figures you have used.

Senator KENNEDY. Just on the question that I have asked, it might go through private organizations, it might go through the poverty program, it might go through the State government, but how much money do the people of the city of Los Angeles——

Mayor YORTY. We do not have the figures where you have gone through like the county welfare department because I do not think they even break it down that way. They take the whole county. So we do not have that figure here.

We are talking about grants to the city of Los Angeles only.

Senator KENNEDY. The figure that we have been asking for from other cities is how much money is received from the Federal Government.

Mayor YORTY. You were not here when I made my opening statement, Senator.

Senator KENNEDY. I was here for some of it.

Mayor YORTY. I know. I tried to explain how very different Los Angeles is and how split up the jurisdiction of these various areas is.

For instance, the health and the welfare being with the county and the schools under separate school boards, and so forth. So some of the figures you are asking for we would have to get from them.

Senator KENNEDY. Yes.

Mayor YORTY. If they have it.

Senator KENNEDY. I understand.

Mayor YORTY. If they have it.

Senator KENNEDY. But are you not mayor of all of the people in Los Angeles?

Mayor YORTY. In the city of Los Angeles only.

Senator KENNEDY. But are you not mayor of them?

Mayor YORTY. Of the people of the city of Los Angeles, yes.

Limited Power of Mayor in Los Angeles

Senator KENNEDY. Then if they have a problem, do they not look to you for some leadership?

Mayor YORTY. Yes. They get the leadership, too, evidenced by the last election. But whether or not I can solve a problem may depend on my jurisdiction. You cannot always solve a problem down in some borough in New York, even though you are U.S. Senator, and I cannot solve some of the local school problems, for instance, myself. I can only help to do it, and I do. But I have no jurisdiction to order anybody to do it.

Children in Headstart Program in Los Angeles

Senator KENNEDY. For instance, let me ask you how many children are in the Headstart program at the present time in Los Angeles.

Mayor YORTY. In the county?

Senator KENNEDY. Well, in the Los Angeles area.

Mr. GOE. About 10,000.

Mayor YORTY. We figure about 10,000.

Mr. GOE. About 10,000 at this point.

Senator KENNEDY. How many would qualify to be included in the Headstart program?

Mayor YORTY. What criteria are you going to use, because they have changed it on us?

Senator KENNEDY. Whatever you use to get the 10,000.

Mr. GOE. Under the new criteria, with the 10,000 there are probably another 3,000 that would qualify. We have 100 locations within the city limits, Headstart locations.

Senator KENNEDY. You have only 3,000 children that would qualify for Headstart, 3,000 more that are not included?

Mr. GOE. Under the criteria.

Mayor YORTY. Under the existing criteria. The criteria was just changed. It is 4,000 down to 3,000, which had the effect of cutting the program down, because of evidently lack of funds at this level, the Federal level.

Senator KENNEDY. What is being done about those 3,000 children to include them in Headstart?

Mayor YORTY. We hope to get the funds to include them.

Senator KENNEDY. What have you done about that?

Mayor YORTY. There is not anything as mayor I can do about that. I have absolutely no jurisdiction. I can only help the school system to get the funds, and this is one of the reasons that I have tried at the State level to get them to subvene back a fair share of the costs of local schools. They are not doing it.

Unemployment Rate in Watts

Senator KENNEDY. What is the unemployment rate in Watts?

Mr. GOE. Fifteen per cent would be an accurate figure.

Senator KENNEDY. I am addressing the question, if I may, to the mayor.

Mayor YORTY. Well, Mr. Goe is our representative on the OEO and I would hope he can answer some of these questions.

Senator KENNEDY. I know Mr. Goe.

Mayor YORTY. Probably 15 per cent, but I doubt if a really accurate figure is available. We know it is too high, and this is one of the reasons.

Senator KENNEDY. How many unemployed are there, whether you call it the curfew area or the Watts area?

Mayor YORTY. The curfew area has eleven square miles not even in the city of Los Angeles.

Senator KENNEDY. What is the unemployment rate for Watts; what is the percentage of unemployment?

Mayor YORTY. Mr. Goe thinks 15 per cent. We have three Negro councilmen, two of them representing Negro areas, and they estimate to me, at least they think that they have as much as 25 to 27 per cent unemployment in their areas. That is why you will find the sheaf of correspondence between me and the Federal departments asking that an area of the city be made eligible for some of the Federal programs, even though the whole area might not have over 6 per cent unemployment on a chronic basis. We feel we should break these areas down.

Senator KENNEDY. Some of the figures that I have seen that have been used, and used earlier by Mr. McCone, were up to 35 per cent. Would you say that was inaccurate?

Mayor YORTY. Well, it is his estimate, that commission. It may be accurate. It depends on the area you take.

Senator KENNEDY. Are not the people entitled in the Watts area to know, to have the feeling that their mayor knows whether there is 15 per cent unemployed or 35 per cent unemployed?

Mayor YORTY. Well, I think that the man unemployed knows that we know and that we would like some kind of program to get him a job. This would not be anything new with me, Senator. I have been trying to do that for thirty years.

Senator KENNEDY. It is an entirely different kind of a problem if you have 3 or 4 per cent unemployed, Mr. Mayor. It seems to me, I am not mayor of the city but it seems to me it would be a different problem if you have 6 per cent unemployed in a particular area or 10 per cent unemployed.

Mayor YORTY. Certainly——

Senator KENNEDY. Could I just finish?

If you have thirty-five, or one out of every three men is unemployed in that part of the city, I would think it is——

Mayor Yorty. What is the unemployment say in the Harlem area?

Senator Kennedy. Well, among what group? It is 26.5 per cent——

Mayor Yorty. What are you doing to get them jobs?

Senator Kennedy. I am establishing youth programs.

Mayor Yorty. So are we. We are trying to do all these things too, but we are much more limited than the Federal Government.

We do not have the amount of money, and I do not even have jurisdiction. I cannot hire people except under civil service.

City Employment Program in Watts

Senator Kennedy. Mr. Mayor, you are the mayor of all the people, as I say, of the city of Los Angeles, the head of all the people of Watts. What kind of programs have you begun down in Watts to try to improve the employment situation?

Mayor Yorty. Well, we have to work with other groups, as I have told you. I cannot just employ all these people. We never have the funds nor jurisdiction. I would have to have them under civil service. So we are working with the private sector, Mr. McClellan. We think we have got about 12,000 jobs in the year for people, not in Watts but in the curfew area. We are working with other jurisdictions on the poverty program. We also have this opportunities industrialization center starting, and I helped do that.

The State of course has the department of employment, and they are working now on some training programs along with private industry.

So you have to understand, as I tried to explain here, that we have an entirely different situation in our area from some of the areas where you have a strong mayor-type of government and where the services are centralized under the city.

I remember when I asked Bob Wagner [a former Mayor of New York] the size of his budget one time, I could hardly believe it, but then he explained to me that he makes up the school budget and all of these other budgets that are not under the jurisdiction of the mayor of Los Angeles. I would like them to be but they are not. Unfortunately, we have a very bad charter, and jurisdiction is very diffused and as the former mayor of Los Angeles said, the mayor of Los Angeles has all of the responsibility and no authority.

Senator Kennedy. You talk about the budget. The budget of the city of New York is under the city, but the school authority is independent of the city, and yet the mayor traditionally of the city of New York has taken some leadership and given some directions as to what should be done in the field of education in the city of New York as well as in many of these other cities.

Mayor YORTY. I do not think you could very well criticize the Los Angeles educational system. It is one of the best in the Nation.

Senator KENNEDY. That is not the direction I am going in, Mr. Mayor.

Mayor YORTY. It is one of the best in the Nation.

How Many Children in Watts Could Benefit from Headstart?

Senator KENNEDY. How many children, what is the need for Headstart in the Watts area, for instance? How many children that could use preschool education?

Mayor YORTY. As far as I am concerned, I think every child should have preschool education irrespective of whether or not it is a matter of being disadvantaged. I once myself saved the child-care program in California in a budget fight, because I feel that we should start the children learning a little bit younger, for many reasons, primarily of course to get the challenge of other youngsters and stimulation of the intellect. I think that we should make preschool, as we call it now, training a part of our permanent educational system.

Senator KENNEDY. How many are there in Watts that would come under such a program?

Mayor YORTY. In that little two-and-a-half-mile area I would not know exactly how many.

How Many Youngsters Are Out of School and Have No Work?

Senator KENNEDY. Do you know how many children are out of school and out of work in Watts?

Mayor YORTY. I cannot give you figures for a little two-and-a-half-mile area of the city.

It is pretty high. We do not have any permanent census to know exactly what that figure would be. Now the State department of employment would have the number of people registered, seeking employment with them.

Senator KENNEDY. Just the question, I understand there was a good deal of difficulty there. There is still some dissension and alienation in that area.

Again, I understand that as mayor of the city you would be very interested in what the problems are.

Mayor YORTY. I am very interested.

Senator KENNEDY. One of the problems is school youth who are out of school and out of work. Do you have that figure?

Mayor YORTY. It is one of our problems. I do not know as we have that figure, but we have a lot of projects in cooperation with the other jurisdictions that are trying to solve it. We gave you this exhibit that Mr. Goe says has all these figures that you are asking about.

Senator KENNEDY. Do you know yourself?

Mayor YORTY. I do not think anybody could sit down and reel off all the statistics that one would have to keep in mind without referring either to notes or to staff.

How Many Are on Welfare in Watts?

Senator KENNEDY. How many are on welfare in Watts?

Mayor YORTY. The exact number? I do not know.

Senator KENNEDY. Approximately.

Mayor YORTY. You are being extremely unfair in asking some of these questions when I would have to refer to the ones who have jurisdiction, and I do not know as they would know about Watts, because they do not break it down that way.

Need for Mayor to Know Facts About City

Senator KENNEDY. Mr. Mayor, I do not think really, if I may say so, I do not think it is unfair because I think this is the heart of the problem that is facing the United States at the present time, and in your city of Los Angeles it happens to be in Watts. I would think that to try to determine what steps need to be taken to remedy some of these problems, that you would have to know what the problems are.

Mayor YORTY. Well, we certainly——

Senator KENNEDY. Could I just finish?

What the problems are, the number of Negro youth out of school and out of work, how many children need the Headstart program, what the unemployment rate is. You cannot talk about the unemployment rate in this area and in a very inflammatory situation and say it is somewhere between 15 and 35 per cent. You might not have the responsibility in each one of these fields, but you certainly are mayor of the city and therefore we need some leadership.

Mayor YORTY. I do not need a lecture from you on how to run my city. I think you should confine your questions to things that are possible for me to answer without bringing a computer.

Watts is a two-and-a-half-mile section of the city. We do not break down our city like that.

Senator KENNEDY. I think Watts is a very important area and I think for us to understand what needs to be done in the city we have to understand what the mayor is doing.

Mayor YORTY. The people of Watts, as I said when you were not here, are very unhappy about having Watts designated as the trouble area because it is only two and a half miles.

Senator KENNEDY. Are they unhappy about the unemployment rate?

Mayor YORTY. We prefer the curfew area. We are all very unhappy about the unemployment rate. It is too bad you did not hear what I said about taking these people out of the competitive system if possible and giving them jobs even though they cannot compete for jobs. This I think should be done, should have been done a long time ago. I think at some point it is going to have to be done......

Senator RIBICOFF. As I listened to your testimony, Mayor Yorty, I made some notes. This morning you have really waived authority and responsibility in the following areas: schools, welfare, transportation, employment, health, and housing, which leaves you as the head of the city basically with a ceremonial function, police and recreation.

Mayor YORTY. That is right, and fire.

Senator RIBICOFF. And fire.

Mayor YORTY. Yes.

Senator RIBICOFF. Collecting sewage?

Mayor YORTY. Sanitation; that is right.

Senator RIBICOFF. In other words, basically you lack jurisdiction, authority, responsibility for what makes a city move?

Mayor YORTY. That is exactly it.

Senator RIBICOFF. What makes a city go around.

Mayor Has Tried to Obtain Authority over These Functions

Mayor YORTY. That is exactly right, Senator, and, of course, for five years I have been trying to get charter amendments. Some of the cities of the country have modernized their city government, and we badly need to do it but, unfortunately, under our form of government the city council has all the power. It is, I think, the only one in the nation that meets every day the year round, and charter amendments have to be put on the ballot by them. Any reform would strengthen the mayor, and to some extent at the hands of the council. So they do not want to put those things on the ballot.

Then, on the other hand, even if the city charter were better and the mayor was stronger, this still would not give the mayor jurisdiction over these areas that we are talking about. This is one reason that I gave up the health department and consolidated it—agreed to a consolidation with the county—so as to get one place at least in the county where all the health problems could be worked out.

Los Angeles Does Not Stand for a Damn Thing

Senator RIBICOFF. I would think the people of Los Angeles have an awful lot of soul searching to do of their own. They brag all over the country what a great city they are and how big they are and what they achieve and what they stand for.

I would say that the city of Los Angeles right now, from your testimony, does not stand for a damn thing.

Mayor YORTY. Well, it stands for a lot. We are a great city.

Senator RIBICOFF. Oh, yes; you are a great city.

Mayor YORTY. In many of the areas.

Senator RIBICOFF. But you do not have any jurisdiction over the basic throb of life of a city from early morning until late at night.

Senator KENNEDY. I think, Mr. Chairman, if I may say so, your statement was based on the testimony of the mayor, not what you personally feel.

Mayor YORTY. Also, you see, there is another——

Senator KENNEDY. I want you to be able to get in and out of Los Angeles.

Los Angeles Government Should Be Organized on County Basis

Mayor YORTY. There is another factor in this, that is the problems that you are talking about there, they are under a jurisdiction, though not under mine, and I think, as I said at the start, I think in the East sometimes they tend to look at cities as all the same, and they forget that the structures of the cities may be entirely different and the jurisdictions different.

Now in many ways, for instance welfare, it is better that the county handles it, because the county can handle it countywide, and this includes over seventy-five cities, and it is much more efficient to do it that way. Probably in time we will consolidate more city services with the county.

The late Chief Parker felt that we should have one law enforcement agency for the whole county, and I would agree with him on that, if we could work it out. But in this way we could achieve the kind of unity and jurisdiction that you already have in the East, where a large area, with all the problems will be under the city, where we have this big county structure.

Los Angeles Needs Better Organization to Take Advantage of Federal Programs

Senator RIBICOFF. But I would predict that we are going to move toward doing something about the cities of America. I think that there is a realization that the future of our country depends upon solving the crisis of the American city. I believe that there will be Federal programs that will be initiated in the next two years and that will really put America on the road to start doing something about the cities of America.

That means the cities are going to have to be in position to take advantage of these programs. I would say, as I have listened to you, and if it is the charter it is no reflection on you personally, that the one city that won't be able to take advantage of any of these programs will be Los Angeles, because you are not organized to do so.

Mayor YORTY. The only way we can organize is the way we did with as I explained to you about the Youth Opportunities Board, and the way we are working with our present OEO Board. We do it by a joint powers agreement with the other jurisdictions that are involved, so at that point we can work together. When you get to solving the problems of the cities, in our community we probably have to work countywide.

Senator RIBICOFF. I understand that Mr. Shriver has been trying to get a new poverty director in Los Angeles for some time, but is having difficulty in getting one, because no one will be assured that if a poverty man has to take on some controversial programs, that he has got anybody in Los Angeles that will back him up in the tough decisions.

Now, we know this. That if these programs are going to work, you have to have someone in authority, if he is the mayor, or whoever, to really stand back of a man to make some really unpopular, tough decisions. Now, in Los Angeles apparently there is nobody to back a man up who wants to make a tough decision.

Mayor YORTY. Well, I don't think that is a correct statement, as I have backed the war on poverty since the very start.

Senator RIBICOFF. In other words, you are getting——

Mayor YORTY. Well, we have more poverty funds than anybody in the Nation, according to Mr. Shriver.

Senator RIBICOFF. That is the trouble. Next to New York you have——

Mayor YORTY. We have more than New York, he said.

Poverty Funds Are Not Helping Those in Need in Los Angeles

Senator RIBICOFF. $33 million, but basically I think what is happening as I listen to this testimony, and the questioning of Senator Kennedy, instead of that $33 million really helping the people in Watts, and the Mexican-Americans, the Negroes, and the poor white—there must be plenty of white poor in Los Angeles—that money is being used basically to prop up your school system because the people in Los Angeles and the State of California are unwilling to pay the bill to educate their kids.

Now if they are not using their money to educate their kids, I think it is unfair to use the general tax funds of this country through the poverty program for the educational system of Los Angeles. I am willing to do it with our eyes wide open on Federal education programs.

Mayor YORTY. But, Senator, you have to take into consideration the fact that we have one of the best educational systems in the Nation and we are supporting it, including free higher education.

Senator RIBICOFF. That is absolutely correct. In other words, this is a great thing for the middle class, and it is. I think that the higher education system in California is the most far reaching, I think it is the best in the entire United States. There is no question about this. I noticed this when I was Secretary and I have said it publicly. I think the middle class get a very good education financed free. But as I listened to you today, you are giving short shrift and you are shortchanging a few generations by doing absolutely nothing for the disadvantaged groups, the people on the bottom of the ladder, the group of people that the McCone report says something should be done for.

With $250 a year being spent for these youngsters in smaller classes and, illiteracies, to bring them up, and here you are in the Los Angeles area doing absolutely nothing for the people who need it the most.

Programs and Projects Must be Translated into
Effective Assistance to People

Mayor YORTY. Have you looked at this list of projects that we have going and what we are doing?

Senator RIBICOFF. I am very unimpressed with a list of projects if they are not translated into doing something for the people.

Mayor YORTY. There are all kinds of things being done for these people through all these projects.

Senator RIBICOFF. And yet the McCone report—

Mayor YORTY. By your own director more than any in the Nation. I would like to see one of your cities dissected as McCone did ours, and point out the faults.

Senator RIBICOFF. Well, I will tell you this. All right.

Mayor YORTY. We will do the same.

Senator RIBICOFF. The mayor of New Haven will be here on Thursday. Of course, he is a friend of mine so I won't dissect him, but will you do that, Senator Kennedy.

Senator KENNEDY. He is a very good friend of mine.

Mayor YORTY. He is a very good mayor. It is a very unfair statement to say that nothing is being done in our city.

Senator KENNEDY. The mayor of Los Angeles I would like to have stay here through all of these hearings, and I think he could safely do so, because as I understand from your testimony you have nothing to get back to.

Mayor Yorty. That is sort of a ridiculous statement but I think—

Senator KENNEDY. That is what you have to gather from the testimony you have given to this committee.

Mayor YORTY. I think that I have explained, and I said when I came back here that I thought in the East they tend to look at the whole Nation, look at the cities and think they are all the same. They are all different, and they have to be handled differently, and ours certainly has to be handled in a different way, because of the various jurisdictions that are involved in the various problems.

Senator RIBICOFF. I bring this up not because it happens to refer to my own State of Connecticut, but the McCone report states, and this gets to another phase:

Moreover, unlike cities such as New Haven, Connecticut, private groups have not taken full advantage of the numerous federally supported programs designed to assist the construction of low-cost housing.

In other words, you have a rich city. You have a powerful city, with people and industries who parade themselves across the world as standing for something positive. Now there is much that can be done in the private sector. Someone has to bring them together. I think that, really, the people of Los Angeles, both official and private, have an awful lot of soul searching to do. They can wring their hands and view with alarm what happened in Watts, and then go home and pray that it doesn't happen again. But it would seem to me that the people of Los Angeles aren't doing very much to prevent another Watts by helping themselves. They are closing their eyes to the grave problems of public and personal responsibility that I think a city like Los Angeles, if it is to be worthy of its name, should undertake.

Mayor YORTY. I don't think that that is a fair conclusion. As a matter of fact, if you look at the housing in Los Angeles, you can hardly compare it with some of the cities you are talking about. Our public housing at the moment we have vacancies in it. Mainly we lack the larger units that we could use, but we like the rent supplement program, and we are one of the cities using that, and we hope that it can be expanded, but there isn't enough money to do the whole job now.

Again you get back to this matter. I could sit here and blame the Federal Government as many are doing for not appropriating enough, if I wanted to, but I just don't believe in that.

McCone Report Points the Way to Improvement of Conditions

Senator KENNEDY. Mr. Chairman, could I just add a qualification to what you just said? I think it has to be impressed on the rest of the country the fact that John McCone, Warren Christopher, and others made this kind of study. The initial report—I know there is a great deal of controversy about it, but in my judgment it was a major step forward and highlighted some of the needs not only in Watts but elsewhere across the country, and the fact that this was supplemented by this second report.

Also, I think that the effort that has been made by the newspapers and particularly the *Los Angeles Times* in pointing out some of the matters that need to have attention has been also extremely impressive. Budd Schulberg [author and screenwriter] made an effort in Watts, and there have been a number of others. I went there a year or so ago, but I was terribly impressed by the fact that there were a number of people in private companies and corporations, private individuals who went into Watts and went into the more deprived areas to try to help the people, and I am sure it could be improved and could be expanded, but I think that in a lot of other places of the country even that much hasn't been done.

Mayor YORTY. Well, there is lots being done in that area.

Los Angeles Needs Leadership to Give Direction

Senator KENNEDY. I think what is lacking, if I may say so, Mr. Mayor, is just one authority who speaks out and gives some direction and says "This is what we have to do and this is what we have to face up to."

I think the impression that you have, we had Mayor Cavanagh earlier, Mayor Lindsay yesterday, who is of a different political affiliation from me, but at least saying "This is what we are going to try to do and this is the direction I would like to have my city move in" instead of always saying "This is a problem I really haven't got the background on, I don't really have the jurisdiction to do anything about it."

Mayor YORTY. No, I think it is only fair to say when I don't have the jurisdiction, so I can only tell the others what I think they should do and what they ought to do, and we do. But if you try to tell them too much, then they think you are demagoging on them. They say "We can't do it," and so forth. So I tried to explain to you what we are up against, and how we try to work together with the other jurisdictions, and we can work with them and we are. But one of the best projects we had was broken up, the Youth Opportunities Board, with a good structure, by I think the failure at the Federal level to understand that our area was different, when they tried to give us the same criteria for the OEO Board as for everybody else.

Mayor's Actions During Riot

Senator KENNEDY. Mr. Mayor, is it true or correct that you left the city the night that they began to have riots in Watts?

Mayor YORTY. That is not true.

Senator KENNEDY. Were you in the city all the time?

Mayor YORTY. I was in the city all but two hours; yes.

Senator KENNEDY. Did you leave the city at all during that time?

Mayor YORTY. Yes; for two hours.

Senator KENNEDY. Is that when you went to make a speech?

Mayor YORTY. I went to make a prescheduled speech, but the riot had stopped. This was a very peculiar stop-and-start riot. The chief of police thought that it would not start again, and there were 700 people waiting an hour away in San Francisco at the Commonwealth Club, and I had to decide whether I could keep that commitment, although I would only be a minute away by telephone, or not, and so I went up and made it and came right back. Later that night it started again.

Senator KENNEDY. Were there disorders while you were away?

Mayor YORTY. No. During that time—the chief and I decided that morning on the big decision that was made before I left that we would call out the National Guard just in case. But Chief Parker was of the opinion that it wouldn't start again. But this riot would——

Senator KENNEDY. Were there any disorders while you were away?

Mayor YORTY. Well, some, but not a big problem. What would happen is that this thing would be late into the night and then it would stop, and you couldn't tell which night it was going to end. But, then, of course, we had a long delay in getting out the Guard. They didn't get in until late at night with the disorders raging.

Besides that, the first night the police department made a mistake in their tactics, which we frankly admit.

Senator RIBICOFF. Thank you, Mayor Yorty.

3.

On Racial Rioting in Detroit

An Interview with J E R O M E   P .   C A V A N A G H

MR. NEWMAN: OUR GUEST TODAY ON *Meet the Press* IS THE MAYOR of Detroit, Jerome P. Cavanagh, whose city has just experienced its worst racial violence in modern history. Mayor Cavanagh, elected in 1961, is one of the nation's leading spokesmen on urban affairs and is the only Mayor to have served simultaneously as President of both the United States Conference of Mayors and the National League of Cities.

We will have the first questions now from Mr. Bill Matney of NBC News.

MR. MATNEY: Mr. Cavanagh, President Johnson has asked this question, and people across the nation are asking this question: Why? Why Detroit? You have had seven days to study this situation. Do you have any answers now?

MAYOR CAVANAGH: Mr. Matney, I think that really it is sort of a geographic happenstance that this broke out in Detroit. By that I mean that it is a national malady—that which occurred in Detroit—and could just as easily have happened in any major American city or any other city even smaller than Detroit, anyplace in the United States.

That may sound sort of defensive, but really it isn't. I think Detroit by anyone's standards had done at least all the textbook things in relation to dealing with some of these urban problems, and still it broke out. So it indicates to me that it was more than just a local problem. There

From *Meet the Press* telecast by NBC Television Network, July 30, 1967. Transcript published by Merkle Press, Inc., Washington, D. C. The panel included Martin Hayden, *Detroit News*; Haynes Johnson, Washington Star Syndicate; Bill Matney, NBC News; and John Steele, Time-Life. The moderator was Edwin Newman, NBC News—Ed.

were all sorts of reasons. We could sit here all afternoon probably and talk about them. Basically we were confronted with thousands of people that felt alienated from our society, that proposed to take the law into their own hands and violate that law, that weren't bound by any of the precepts that you and I understand, which constitute regular law and order in this country.

MR. MATNEY: Of all the big city Mayors, your ties in communication with the Negro community were considered just about as good as anybody could get, and yet this happened. What broke down? What went wrong?

MAYOR CAVANAGH: I think the ties which the city government had and still has certainly with much of the Negro community, the vast percentage of the members of the Negro community in this city, are still good. But still there are people in this as well as every city in the country that are outside of our society—not just the white society, but the society in which most of the Negroes and most of the whites belong. And, given the slightest provocation—in many instances even no provocation is needed—the law is taken into their own hands. You can characterize it as protest or you can characterize it as resentment. They have been popularly fashioned as the "have-nots." I think all of those things are probably apt characterizations, and certainly I don't know of any government in America, local government, state government or national government, or any institution for that matter, that is communicating in any way or carrying on any kind of a dialogue with the so-called have-nots.

MR. MATNEY: Let's get a bit more specific, Mr. Cavanagh, there has been strong criticism and a great deal of it coming from the Negro community, that the riot could have been avoided had your police department moved in early Sunday morning and squashed the thing—when the atmosphere was pretty much fun and games, and people were standing around laughing and so forth.

MAYOR CAVANAGH: I know that there is a great deal of criticism both here and around the country. I really don't lend any substance to it, and I will tell you why. I don't think it deserves any substance. The tactics which were used this year by our police department last Sunday morning were the same tactics that were used by our police department a year ago in this community when we had a potential riot. We had some very serious incidents with which I am sure you are familiar out on the east side. Our police department moved with speed, but restraint, and with what we thought was reason and order, and this series of incidents didn't balloon into a riot. Everyone around the country credited the moderation or the restraint or the order which the police department exercised that morning. The same tactics were used last Sunday. It is not and has not been our position in this city, nor has it been really in most of the major cities, I think, the position, to move in bristling with a lot of hardware and weaponry when you have mobs out on the street, because it has been proven time and time again that generally this just incites people into further violence and further rioting.

Frankly, what happened was the fact that our police department, when it moved in—and incidentally Sunday morning in any big city is almost like Pearl Harbor on Sunday morning, at least like it was back in 1941. We are at our weakest; there are fewer men on the streets at that period of time. When our police department moved in, the crowd just overwhelmed them. We were attempting to protect firemen when they were fighting fires, and our primary concern at that point— and these were field decisions which were made, by the way. There was no order which came down from on high, from me or from the Commissioner of Police: "Do not shoot." At no time during the week did I issue any order of that kind or any other kind in relation to police procedure to the police department, but the police department has been instructed in this city over the years by its professional police leaders that they are to use such force as they deem necessary and as the circumstances deem necessary. If they can apprehend a criminal without the use of force, then that is what they should attempt to do. It was their judgment out on the street that morning that these rioters and looters were just going to overwhelm them if they shot into the crowd, so they refrained initially from shooting in many instances.

MR. HAYDEN: Mr. Mayor, going back to the subject that Bill Matney raised about action at the time the riot started, one of the ranking officers in the field was an Inspector Paul Donnelly, who yesterday retired from the department—this had already been arranged. He was in charge of two squads of commandoes who were at Fourteenth and Euclid Street, kept there idle, then finally moved farther away to the Tenth Precinct station because they were attracting crowds. On the eve of his retirement, without naming anybody, he said the politicians held the police back from effective control and said specifically, "If we had been permitted to go after the looters and troublemakers on Twelfth right from the start, we might have stopped it."

What about it; do you agree with the Inspector?

MAYOR CAVANAGH: No, I certainly do not agree with the Inspector. I don't know of any politicians downtown or anyplace else that gave any kind of instructions to our police officers, especially in those early morning hours about which you are speaking, in relation to their conduct. As a matter of fact, Inspector Donnelly, when he was questioned by our Police Commissioner about that specific reference, which he made in your newspaper, indicated he wasn't talking about the politicians in Detroit. He was talking about politicians sort of as a euphemism, I suppose, for people who have handcuffed police officers generally speaking. He was one of the commanders out there, and we had given the field commanders—as they always do in situations like that certainly—broad authority to use whatever force, whatever tactics, whatever means are necessary to contain the situation or deal with it as they see best.

I wasn't then nor all during that day, for that matter, familiar with the exact tactics that were being used in the field because these are police matters, professional police matters. It has always been my policy in the five years which I have served as Mayor to allow the professionals in the police agencies or any others of those agencies to do those things, particularly in times of stress, which they knew better than anyone else.

Mr. Hayden: Mr. Mayor, in retrospect, now that it is over and not knowing why it started here, if it starts next Sunday again, would we be doing things differently right at the start?

Mayor Cavanagh: I think in all candor that I would have to say to you that the role of the police officer and the definition of his authority and his authority to act out on that street should be more clearly defined. We assumed that it was clearly defined in the minds of the men, in the minds of certainly their sergeants and their lieutenants and their inspectors. I think it was, generally speaking, but obviously in the minds of some, as evidenced by the remark made by Inspector Donnelly and evidenced by remarks made by other police officers, they were, if not unsure, at least a little dubious at times about exactly what role they should be taking and what role they should be playing.

I talked to a number of police officers, and if I might just quickly bring my answer to a conclusion on that one, that were out on the scene that morning. One, a patrolman, very interestingly told me just the other day—he said he was one of a squad guarding a fire company that was fighting a fire early on Twelfth Street, early that Sunday morning, and the mob was all around them, looting down the street. The sergeant in command of that squad ordered them not to fire at those looters, many of the looters being mothers and fathers with seven- and eight-year-old children, walking along in, as Mr. Matney said, sort of a carnival-like spirit, garnering up groceries and shoes and things like that. They said their primary function at that point was to guard the firemen, to guard the lives of the firemen, guard the lives of the people out in the neighborhood. This policeman said to me—he is a veteran police officer and no particular friend of mine, I had never met him before—he said as far as he was concerned, had any man in the squadron fired at that crowd, that whole squad of police officers probably would have been wiped out by that mob, and certainly he agreed with that field decision which was made at that point.

MR. JOHNSON: In response to Mr. Matney's question a few minutes ago about why the riots struck Detroit, you said it was a geographic happenstance, a national malady and that it is more than a local problem.

MAYOR CAVANAGH: Yes.

MR. JOHNSON: My question is, what can the nation do to get back on the track. To be more specific about it in a larger framework, just going back three years ago, President Johnson was traveling the country, declaring war on poverty, promising to lead Americans toward a Great Society, and today he is asking Americans to pray for the violence that afflicts us.

MAYOR CAVANAGH: Yes.

MR. JOHNSON: What can we do about this?

MAYOR CAVANAGH: I think the first thing that has to be done is the indifference which is expressed in the Congress almost daily.

We have, gentlemen, in my judgment at least, a highly reactionary Congress in the broadest sense of that term, and this is reflected, unfortunately, at times, even in the administration.

But there is no question about the fact that the administration has proposed program after program to the Congress, and the Congress just seems to ignore it. They laugh and holler and rail when they vote down a minor rat-control bill for the cities and yet pay two or three or four times that amount of money just for the storage of cotton in any one year.

We have great difficulty even getting through the Congress a $75 million appropriation for summer programs, and yet, compare that to the $70 billion that this country has committed for defense.

There is a madness in the country, and the Congress reacts by being indifferent, sometimes not just indifferent, just by being completely negative about it.

So, I think there are a lot of things that can be done, one of the first things certainly is a change on the part of the attitude of the people in this country, and hopefully it will be reflected in the Congress. I am sure we will have an opportunity to develop this as we go on. I don't want to take up too much of your time.

Mr. Johnson: When you say there is a madness in the country and you refer to the billions of dollars for defense, are you alluding there also to the war in Vietnam which many critics this week—Senator Fulbright among them—linked, again, as a direct relationship between the urban violence and our commitment overseas?

Mayor Cavanagh: All I know is that I have yet really to convince myself in my own mind that—what will it profit this country if we, say, put our man on the moon by 1970, and at the same time you can't walk down Woodward Avenue in this city without some fear of violence or fear as to your own safety and security?

And we may be able to pacify every village in Vietnam, over a period of years, but what good does it do if we can't pacify the American cities. And the American cities aren't pacified, there is no question about it.

What I am saying, really, Mr. Johnson, is that our priorities in this country are all out of balance. There is no question about it. I am not too sure what we have to do to change these priorities, but maybe Detroit was a watershed this week in American history, and it might well be that out of the ashes of this city comes the national resolve to do far more than anything we have done in the past. Because what we have done has been proven to be not only inadequate, but certainly I think we have to take some whole new directions and new looks in this country at our dealings with the urban affairs.

Mr. Steele: Mr. Mayor, you have already said that the rioters were somehow outside of society. Do you really believe that increased federal funds, say, for education and housing and other city problems would have made any difference in these riots of this summer, not only in Detroit but elsewhere as well; would they have been avoided? Is it a matter of money, in other words?

Mayor Cavanagh: I think much of the answer does boil down to money. I know that may sound like a very simple response to a very difficult question, but there is no doubt about it. Expectations have been built up not by just federal officials but local officials about what those programs, those federal city programs would do, and then when the programs are cut back and sniped at, really, they only nibble at the real periphery of the problem. They never really get at the heart of it.

What we have to do in this country—and long ago we declared a commitment to do it, but we have never really done it—and that is, provide full employment in this country. And the government, I think, the United States Government, should be the employer of the last resort —that if, through the public or private sectors, it is impossible to obtain employment, the United States Government should guarantee the opportunity for employment, maybe not guarantee a job but at least the opportunity for a job.

This isn't a new concept. I think President Roosevelt back in 1944 first suggested it. But we need jobs, and certainly we need a far greater involvement on the part of the private sector. There are a lot of government people in this country, both federal, state and local, that like to talk about the need to involve the private sector, and yet government as yet in this country has not defined very clearly, if at all, the areas into which the private sector should be moving.

MR. STEELE: Mr. Mayor, not only in Detroit but elsewhere in the country, in the civil disturbances, there has been almost no dialogue so far, as I have been able to find out, concerning problems which you have mentioned, concerning jobs, housing, health, and welfare.

Do you think that those subjects are really the answer to looting and insurrection? These are not riots over better education. The people rioting don't even talk about them. They are looting stores.

How do you square that with education?

MAYOR CAVANAGH: Mr. Steele, the fact that—and I am sure we could demonstrate it by examining the records of the four or five thousand people that have been arrested, that they just have not been very significantly, I am sure, in most instances, involved in our educational process in this city, and the same would be true in most cities of the country, Newark or any other city that had a riot. So education certainly speaks and addresses itself, or the lack of educational opportunities, to the causes of riots. So does the provision of jobs. So does housing. Our housing situation in this country is a national disgrace. No one seems to be talking about it. It is estimated we need about 2 million new housing starts a year in this country.

Last year we had, as I am sure you gentlemen know, less than 800,000 housing starts in the whole country. That is the lowest since 1946. And most of those housing starts were in middle and upper middle income areas.

Why aren't we building low-income housing, either publicly or privately? Publicly we know the reasons, because this Congress seems to think that the country shouldn't have it. But privately we are not building it, because there is no incentive or no profit that has been developed by the government for the private developer.

MR. MATNEY: Mr. Cavanagh, you have said this rioting was not racial in the traditional confrontation of white and black, such as occurred here in 1943. But nevertheless it was racial—you and I both know this——

MAYOR CAVANAGH: I won't dispute it.

MR. MATNEY: —in the sense there was almost pinpoint accuracy in the fire bombing throughout this city. It was very obvious that the vengeance and the wrath was directed at the white businessman. In walking the streets of the riot area, I have been told time and time again that "Whitey, don't come back. We don't want you in here."

If this is true and if this is widespread, then what about your plans for the redevelopment of this city? What sort of voice do you plan to give these people in the ghetto who are being so vocal about this?

MAYOR CAVANAGH: Let me first preface my answer by saying that the usual and the classic kind of race riots that we have been led to believe exist in this country, the white mob against the Negro mob, did not happen in this city, as you know. But I agree with you, and let's be frank about it, that underneath the surface, this in fact was a race riot and a race revolution. It did involve the race, the races, particularly the Negro race.

It is our plan to involve as best we can—and we are making every effort just in the last week or so, to involve some kind of participation, as full as we can get it, from the residents of the neighborhoods involved. We have been trying to do this in the poverty program; we have been trying to do it in some of the other programs. We haven't succeeded completely, but we have succeeded to a better degree than a lot of people would give us credit for.

Let me just say in relation to the poverty program—I am sure all of you gentlemen would be interested in this—we have done some fast analysis—of the 5,000 young people who are in your neighborhood Youth Corps and other youth programs connected with the poverty program here, only three of those 5,000 were involved in any kind of illegal activity. I'd hesitate to contemplate how many more people would have been involved in this riot this week had we not had a poverty program.

MR. NEWMAN: Less than four minutes, gentlemen.

MR. HAYDEN: Mr. Mayor, do I understand you to say that this is going to keep up—I mean for you as the Mayor of the fifth biggest city —to say that this is going to keep up until Congress passes legislation and gets these long-range programs into effect and builds housing and gets job equality and education, all of which is a matter of years?

MAYOR CAVANAGH: It shouldn't be a matter of years, and I don't think that we can wait, but I am saying that when the National Guard and the Federal troops leave here and when law and order is restored, as it just about is in our city today, there is no assurance that I can give to you, nor can anyone really give to you, that a week from now or two weeks from now or a year from now that the same thing won't happen, it won't happen here or won't happen in some other city, because until we get at these root causes and until we start to provide things like that great American Pat Moynihan has suggested, I think, a children's allowance—he makes the point that we are the only industrial democracy in the world that doesn't have a children or a family allowance, and yet we seem to be the only industrial democracy that every summer has race riots in all of our cities—until we start to do these things, provide some guarantee of money or income for all of our people in this country, and until the Congress begins to realistically deal with the problems of the cities, we are going to have not just a continuation, but I'd say—and it is terrible to contemplate—we are going to have some things far, far worse. It may well be that Washington, D. C.—and I hate to think of this, and I would pray that it would never happen, but if what happened in Detroit this week happened in Washington, D. C., this might lift the veil off the eyes of the Members of Congress.

MR. JOHNSON: Let's hope it doesn't happen in that city.

MAYOR CAVANAGH: No, I hope so.

MR. JOHNSON: I would like to ask you whether you had any advance warning of the riots? I understand—and correct me if I am wrong about this—that you had some sort of intelligence system set up to try to find out, detect trouble in the Negro community and this apparently failed. Is that correct?

MAYOR CAVANAGH: Yes. I would have to be candid and say we had such a system set up, a Mayor's Summer Task Force that worked out of my office twenty-four hours a day ever since the summer began—not just for informational purposes, but also to coordinate our summer programs—and even though we had plenty of—we could fairly well pinpoint it, if trouble was to happen that it would happen probably in the Twelfth Street area, I cannot in honesty say to you that we had advance knowledge or notice or information that on that day this was going to happen.

MR. STEELE: Mr. Mayor, now you have said that politicians, which presumably includes yourself—and I use that in the most respectful sense —I happen to like politicians——

MAYOR CAVANAGH: Thank you.

MR. STEELE: —had no responsibility for the handling of the police force in the field.

You have indicated the chief problems of meeting the city's needs are in Washington.

What as Mayor and President of the council of Mayors, do you anticipate cities to do?

MAYOR CAVANAGH: Cities are really swimming upstream. Cities are doing more than any other agency of government in dealing with the problems. They have all the problems. They have the fewest resources, and as Professor Galbraith once said, you couldn't structure a worse design than we have in America. The cities and the local governments, the mayors, have all the problems of crime, delinquency—we can tick them all off—the states traditionally have ignored their responsibility in this area, and the federal government deals almost semi-apologetically with them.

MR. MATNEY: Where do we go now, Mr. Mayor, immediately?

MAYOR CAVANAGH: I think there are a lot of things that could be done. One thing, by the way, rather than——

MR. NEWMAN: Just one.

MAYOR CAVANAGH: Rather than strengthen the riot-control training of the National Guard, I think—I think it would be appropriate if the federal government undertook, for example, to——

MR. NEWMAN: I have to interrupt you, Mr. Mayor. I am sorry. Our time is up. Thank you, Mayor Cavanagh, for being with us on *Meet the Press*.

PART VIII

Conclusions: Mayoralty Power

Where the mayor is excessively limited in authority and influence, the city is also limited in what it can do for itself, for it is the chief executive who is in the best position to provide over-all direction and coordination without which the metropolis must remain fragmented.

This final section of readings looks ahead to inquire into the likelihood of an effective mayoralty. Our two concluding articles offer little room for optimism. The first selection by Edward C. Banfield and James Q. Wilson weighs the effects of the spread of middle-class values on city politics ("The Trend of City Politics"). They argue that the exit of "self-regarding" politics and the continued development of the "public-regarding" style will in many ways accentuate the mayor's ordeal. Such a trend makes the governing process more difficult by adding new and more subtle dimensions to decision-making and leadership.

Of special value in Robert H. Salisbury's article is his treatment of urban leadership and the mayoralty in relationship to urban power structures. He traces the historical development of basic power patterns and highlights the present-day significance of the "executive-centered coalition," which in most big cities consists of the mayor, local economic interests, and the professional city workers. His careful analysis of this coalition of leadership makes plain how greatly the metropolis lacks, not only economic and social resources, but also the power required to cope with its needs.

1.

The Trend of City Politics

EDWARD C. BANFIELD *and*
JAMES Q. WILSON

OUR ACCOUNT OF CITY POLITICS HAS FOLLOWED THREE MAIN LINES OF analysis. One of them concerns the distribution of authority within the city, especially the effects of increases and decreases in the centralization of authority. A second concerns the various mechanisms by which power is accumulated and an informal centralization of influence established. And a third concerns the political ethos and emphasizes the fundamental cleavage between the public-regarding, Anglo-Saxon Protestant, middle-class ethos and the private-regarding, lower-class, immigrant ethos. In looking ahead at the changes that may be expected to occur in city politics over the next decade or two, these same lines of analysis appear to be relevant. What we have to say in this chapter will therefore carry forward some of the main implications of the analysis in the preceding ones.

The General Trend

All three of these factors—distribution of authority, mechanism for centralizing influence, and political ethos—are of course changing in response to a variety of pressures. In our view, the changes that are occurring in political ethos are the most important. These to a large extent determine the nature of the changes in the distribution of authority and in the mechanisms by which influence is centralized.

The changes in political ethos are the product of changes in the class composition of the urban electorate. The immigrant lower class has been, and is still being, absorbed into the middle class at a rapid rate. This has profoundly affected the outlook of the electorate, for the middle class has always held to the Anglo-Saxon Protestant political ideal and those who have joined it have accepted this ideal along with others. The "new immigrant" (as Samuel Lubell has called these newcomers to the middle class) prefers political candidates who like himself have passed along the "tenement trail."[1] But increasingly the "new immigrant" has come to demand candidates who, whatever their origins, have the community-serving ethos and the public virtues that have long been associated with the Protestant elite.

The reader . . . . . will see that this shift from a predominantly lower-class to a predominantly middle-class political style is of pervasive importance. The middle-class ideal sees local politics as a cooperative search for the concrete implications of a more or less objective public interest, an interest of the community "as a whole." The logic of the middle-class ideal requires that authority be exercised by those who are "best qualified," that is, technical experts and statesmen, not "politicians." The logic of the middle-class ideal implies also certain institutional arrangements (nonpartisanship, at-large election, the council-manager form, master planning, and metropolitan area organization); particular regard for the public virtues of honesty, efficiency, and impartiality; and a disposition to encourage the consumption of "public goods" like schools, parks, museums, libraries, and, by extension, urban renewal. In general, the tendency is toward what Benjamin DeMott has called "an apolitical politics, partyless and problemless."[2]

To be sure, middle-class families are moving toward the outskirts of metropolitan areas, and the populations of the larger, older cities are still heavily lower-class. Indeed, they may become somewhat more so in the next decade. The old-style politics of the boss and machine is, and no doubt will remain, highly congenial to the lower class. However, the nationally growing middle class has shown that it will use its control of state and federal governments—and particularly of law enforcement agencies and of special districts within the metropolitan areas—to withhold the patronage, protection, and other political resources that are indispensable to the growth of political machines in the central cities. This means that the lower class will have to play politics of a kind that is tolerable to the middle class or not play it at all.

Some Particular Trends

The general trend toward local government in accordance with the middle-class ideal implies a great many particular trends, only a few of which can be mentioned here.

One is a spreading and deepening popular hostility toward everything that has about it the odor of the smoke-filled room—toward such bosses and remnants of machines as still exist, toward all forms of professionalism in politics, and even toward politics itself. In many cities politicians find it easier to stir the electorate with charges of "bossism" and corruption, however little the grounds for such charges, than with discussion of matters that are more substantial and more pertinent. For example, in New York City, where many things of real and pressing importance need discussion, Governor Rockefeller and Mayor Wagner found it profitable to carry on their warfare mainly by exchanging charges and counter-charges of "machine politics" and "bossism."

To regard politics as contrary to the public interest is consistent with the middle-class ideal; reformers have always taken this view. That the "new immigrants," once they have been assimilated into the middle class, should be contemptuous of politics is to be expected. There are indications, however, that their contempt for it is stronger than can be accounted for on these grounds alone. Perhaps it is in part symbolic—a gesture meant to repudiate not the style of politics alone but also, and perhaps mainly, the inferior class and ethnic status from which it sprang.

The old style of politics was not at all concerned with principles or ideology, and characteristically it took account of policy issues only as they promised to afford some private advantages. The new style, although highly principled and the expression of an ideology of sorts, is much more concerned with *how* things are done than with *what* is done. By an altogether different route, then, it arrives at a politics which is almost, if not quite, as problemless as the politics of the machine and the boss. In this, perhaps, is to be found another reason for the growing popular dissatisfaction with local politics in general. The tendency of the new style is to produce cynicism and boredom—cynicism because its procedural principles can never be fully lived up to and boredom because, when self-interest is excluded and the public interest is understood in procedural rather than substantive terms, nothing of much importance remains. Politics was more exciting as a "game" than it is as "service" to the community.

The ascendancy of the middle-class ideal will have an effect on what kinds of people enter local politics and rise through it. Without "gravy" with which to build machines and large followings, opportunities for political entrepreneurs to appear from within the lower class and to rise in the world through local politics will be few. The present lower class in many of the central cities and older suburbs is largely Negro, and the disappearance of this time-tested route of social mobility will doubtless have importance for the status of the race. If able and ambitious young men cannot get ahead through local politics (and therefore not through illicit enterprises either, since these enterprises cannot prosper in the atmosphere of the middle-class ideal), the assimilation of the whole minority may be retarded. Doubtless the most able and ambitious individuals will find other routes by which to climb; even so, the total amount of mobility—the number who rise multiplied by the distance that they rise—will be reduced.

Another effect of denying to the lower class the opportunity to play the only kind of politics that it knows how to play, or wants to play, will be to slow down the rate at which it acquires political interests and skills. The old style of politics gave the European immigrant a sense of belonging to a political community. The most recent immigrants to the cities, rural Negroes mainly, are unfortunate in having come just after the earlier immigrant groups, having learned their first lessons, have declared the old elementary school of politics—the ward-based machine —obsolete and anachronistic. To some extent, the Negro's segregated position may exempt him from this effect. Just as segregation and the alleged inferiority of the Negro make it possible for "policy" and other illicit activities that would not be so easily tolerated among whites to flourish in the Negro community, so the same causes may allow the old style of politics to continue there after it has been proscribed elsewhere. This is likely to happen only insofar as the Negro political world does not intrude upon the white one, however, and this, because of forces operating in both the Negro and the white political worlds, is not likely to be very far. Where the white majority has something to gain or lose from the existence of lower-class Negro organization, it may be expected to intervene and, ultimately, to set the rules within which Negro politics must be carried on. Moreover, even where Negroes are permitted to play the old style of politics, those of them who are most successful at it will not be permitted, as quite a few of the last generation were, to become respectable and to move into (predominantly middle-class) state and national politics. Such Negroes as manage to enter state and national politics will almost certainly have to do so by some route less offensive to the middle class than the old-style, necessarily corrupt machine.

If the middle-class ideal will exclude some types from politics, it will bring others into it. There will be a constant demand for "fresh faces" —for candidates who at least *seem* free from the taint of professionalism and who have the technical qualifications and the disinterestedness that the new style of politics calls for. The ideal, of course, is government without politics or politicians—real nonpartisanship. Even where partisan forms are retained, politicians will find it increasingly necessary to pretend to be nonpartisan—to play "party apolitics" as DeMott calls it.

Mayor Daley of Chicago, for example, makes no mention of his party affiliation in his campaign literature; he presents himself as an efficient, impartial, and expert administrator. As the political weight of the middle class grows, politicians will try to look more and more like city managers.

The same forces that push the politician in this direction will draw professional administrators into politics. Here the example from Chicago can be balanced by one from New York. Paul R. Screvane, a career civil servant in the sanitation department who was elected to public office for the first time in 1962, was written about in the spring of 1963 as a likely successor to Mayor Wagner.[3] A professional administrator like Screvane who wishes to pass for a politician needs some disguise, just as the politician who wishes to pass for a city manager needs some, for there are still many in the party and in the electorate who would not be satisfied with an administrator pure and simple. In general, however, it will probably be easier for the administrator than for the professional politician to acquire the right "image."

To an increasing extent, the issues of city politics will be connected with the larger, ideological ones of national politics. Urban renewal projects, for example, are very likely to raise the national and ideological issue of race. Because of this close connection with larger issues, local politics will be of increasing interest to those people whom Robert K. Merton has described as cosmopolitans rather than locals. It is altogether unlikely, however, that the locals will lose their near monopoly on city politics. City government will always be mainly a matter of finding concrete solutions for practical problems, a task not congenial to the cosmopolitan. If here and there ideologues acquire power, they will have to find ways of coping with real problems; and that . . . . . will not be easy.

The circumstances that give an advantage to "fresh faces" (whether faces of politicians made up to look like city managers or of city managers made up to look like politicians) will tend also to increase the influence of the press, the civic associations, and lay civic leadership in general. These institutions speak (or claim to speak) from expertise and with regard to "objective facts," and to represent a conception of the public interest. To the extent that they supplant the parties in the management of the local electoral process, candidates will have to take their cues from them.

Much of this gain in influence will accrue to the paid executives who run the larger civic associations. Newspaper editors may have the final say about what candidates and issues are to be "pushed," but they will make their decisions largely on the advice of the civic association executives. Most editors do not follow civic affairs closely enough to have a basis for independent judgment. Apart from the professional politician, the civic association executive is the only one in the city who does.

There is a tendency also for the activists in local government—especially civic association executives, but many bureaucrats and some newspaper editors as well—to take their general policy lines from the executives of the national foundations, from federal agencies, and from such national bodies as the International City Managers' Association, the National Municipal League, the National Association of Housing and Redevelopment Officials, and the American Institute of Planners. The agenda of city government is being determined more and more by professionals within such bodies and less and less by the needs and problems of the particular city. This is not to say that cities are likely to do all, or even very much, of what the national "experts" say they should do. It is the subjects to be discussed, not the actions to be taken, that will be decided nationally. If the national "experts" stress the need for, say, metropolitan area organization, this need—whether real or imaginary— will preoccupy local civic associations and editorial writers; but it may not lead to acceptance of any plan for reorganization. When considered concretely, such matters are likely to be decided in the light of particular needs and interests, not of general principles.

The changes that *are* produced by the orthodoxy of the national "experts" may be more symbolic than real. The immediate purposes of the executives in the national organizations may sometimes be served as well by nominal changes as by real ones. If, for example, the officials of federal agencies are keen to have the cities engage in master planning because it gives them (the federal officials) grounds on which to claim that federal assistance is being used wisely, it matters little that the plans have no real validity; it is enough that they exist on paper. And if master planning can be accepted by the cities in principle and rejected by them in practice, other reforms prescribed by the national orthodoxy probably can too.

The tendency toward centralization of authority in the hands of the executive (mayor or manager) will doubtless be more marked in the next decade as the demand for more and better city services mounts. Independent and semi-independent boards and commissions (civil service agencies, for example) will be brought under the authority of the executive, and the amount and quality of technical aids and staff services available to the executive will be increased. All the recommendations of the national "experts," it is safe to say, will tend in this direction.[4]

The decay of the old style of politics will hasten the process of centralization. When there were many jobs and favors to be dispensed and much money and power to be acquired by dispensing them, a horde of local politicians had a powerful incentive to maintain the decentralization of authority that gave each his bailiwick.[5] As the number and value of jobs and favors has declined, so has the number of old-style politicians. The relatively few who remain will resist losing their bailiwicks, no doubt, but their resistance will not be as strenuous or effective as it was when there was more at stake.

The middle-class ideal favors centralization of authority in an ever-wider sphere. In order to treat all elements of a situation in a coordinated way—"as a single whole"—the city manager, planner, or other administrator must cross over any jurisdictional boundary. For example, a housing program for a central city cannot be planned apart from related facilities like schools, transportation lines, and parks. These, it will then appear, cannot be planned on a purely central-city basis; if the situation is to be treated "as a whole," the planning must be as broad as the metropolitan area. But even this is not enough; there are always some features of the situation which can be treated only on a state, regional, or national, indeed a world, basis.

Although the centralizing tendency has been at work in most cities for a long time, it has not gone far enough to offset the loss of power occasioned by the decay of the machines and, more generally, the decay of the style of politics based upon specific, and usually material, inducements. A mayor or party boss who had plenty of "gravy" to pass out could get along with little *authority* or (in the case of those bosses who did not hold office) none at all. As reform slashed the number of jobs, favors, and other rewards at the politician's disposal, it reduced his power. It compensated for this to some extent by increasing his authority. But, because the increase in authority was usually not enough to make up entirely for the loss of power, the politician's total influence declined. While this was happening, more and more accomplishment was being expected of public officials (i.e., politicians in office); both the quantity and the quality of public services being demanded increased. This left elected officials in a difficult position: as their need for influence increased, their supply of it declined.

Persistent as are the forces tending toward centralization of authority, it may be doubted that in the next decade or two they will produce city governments as strong as were those run by the old machines. The American people seem to have a deeply ingrained reluctance to centralize authority, as contrasted with power. In this respect, at least, the logic of the Anglo-Saxon Protestant political ideal has not prevailed. It seems unlikely that measures to strengthen the authority of the executive, numerous and extensive as they will probably be, will catch up with the need for greater influence that is being generated by the new demands for service. New York City is perhaps the paradigm of what may be expected. The authority of the mayor of New York is relatively great; but his power is small, and the city government, measured against the tasks that are given it, is weak.

The shift from "ward politics" to "city administration" will be a cause, as well as an effect, of ambitious and expensive public programs. The old-style politician had no incentive to try to confer benefits on the public at large. So long as he gave jobs and favors to the right people he could maintain his organization and get the votes he needed. The new-style, "good government" politician must employ other means. Insofar as he cannot persuade people to vote for him on purely rational grounds, he must use charm and salesmanship or else offer inducements to large classes of people or to the whole public. This will cause him to think of big undertakings—generous welfare and housing programs, civil rights campaigns, transportation subsidies, and the like—which he can offer to the mass of voters in place of the "friendship" that they used to get from precinct workers. In the nature of the case, these undertakings are likely to be costly and to entail many large and unintended consequences for the life of the city. In the nature of the case, too, "general" inducements will prove less reliable in their operation than did the "specific" ones of the machine. The new-style politician's position will therefore be relatively unstable. Whereas the old-style politician could withstand almost anything except an organization stronger than his, the new-style one may disappear from the scene the moment his charm ceases to work or his general inducements cease to appeal.

Insofar as he must rely upon general inducements, there will be sharp limits on the amount of power that the new-style politician can acquire. If the benefits of a public project will be accompanied by a perceptible increase in the tax bill, the voter may decide to forgo them. The politician is then in difficulty. He may get out of the difficulty by offering programs which will confer benefits on some people while putting the costs on others. He may, for example, offer the voters of his city a new sewage disposal plant which is to be paid for by the federal government—that is, by taxpayers who cannot vote against him. The need of most local politicians to offer inducements of this kind accounts in large measure for the steady enlargement of the federal, and to a lesser extent the state, government's role in local affairs.

The politician's difficulty in finding inducements to offer his constituents is increased because a program which confers a net benefit on a large majority may nevertheless decrease his vote. This is likely to happen if the benefit to the average member of the majority is rather small or intangible and if the cost imposed on the average member of a minority—even a very small minority—is large. Suppose, for example, that hundreds of thousands of voters mildly favor fluoridation of the city's water supply ("it would be a good thing on the whole") and that a few hundred are strongly opposed to it ("it is a menace to health"). In such a case, a politician may decide that supporting fluoridation will bring him no votes, since no one will vote for him for that reason alone, and will lose him some, since a few will vote *against* him for that reason alone.

In several cities mayors have set up special "citizens' relations" bureaus to help them evaluate the intensity of voters' feelings on neighborhood issues. Thus they have incorporated into the formal governmental structure mechanisms for gathering and evaluating information that used to be part of the precinct and ward organizations of the party. Some mayors have tried to encourage the growth of neighborhood associations by tacitly giving them power to modify, or veto, policies that affect their neighborhoods in return for support at election time. It is too early to judge how well these arrangements will serve the purposes of the voters or the politicians. Obviously the fundamental difficulty cannot be got around altogether. The more aware city hall is of intensely moved voters, the better it can pick its steps around the danger spots; but it must step somewhere, and so it is bound to suffer the wrath of some of the intensely moved.

The reason why city hall must step somewhere is, of course, that inducements must continually be offered to the mass of voters. It might possibly "pay" a politician to favor an intense minority over a not-intense majority on every issue if issues are considered separately. But it will not "pay" him to favor the intense minorities on all issues if issues are considered—as they must be—for the aggregate effect that they will produce. Unless a politician has "accomplishments" to point to, the majority will forsake him. If a mayor has his eyes too much on the intensely moved minorities and not enough on the not intensely moved majority, a sudden groundswell of opinion is likely to sweep him out of office in favor of an unknown who has promised to "get the city moving again."

Something fairly close to the style of politics toward which the cities are tending is to be seen in the case of Washington, D.C., a city which carries "nonpartisan apolitics" to its logical extreme, there being no local electorate and the conduct of affairs being largely in the hands of professional managers. The peculiarities of Washington's governmental structure have led, according to Martha Derthick, to a characteristic style of politics: one which encourages debate on issues rather than competition for public jobs or ethnic recognition or personal publicity, and is therefore "biased in favor of both 'liberals' and 'conservatives' at the expense of people who are neither." Ideologues and representatives of organized interest groups (the latter often in association with bureaucratic allies), Miss Derthick says, are especially important in the politics of Washington because the system tends to exclude from it those who would seek patronage and public recognition. Where there is no competition for election to office, programmatic—or at least ostensibly programmatic—goals become more important.[6]

The Significance of the Changes

If one asks whether on the whole these changes are for the better, the answer is by no means obvious. Perhaps the safest statement that can be made is that the routine business of the cities will be better administered. The old-style politician got his power in part by deliberately sacrificing the efficiency and integrity of city services. He could ignore intensely moved minorities because he used jobs, favors, and protection to maintain his organization and get the vote. This, of course, made for bad administration. The new-style politician, whose power—such as it is—arises from other sources, is not under the necessity to interfere with the processes of administration. On the contrary, he wants the approval of middle-class voters who regard good government and good administration as practically synonymous, and therefore he has the strongest incentive to search out and eliminate inefficiency and corruption.

It does not necessarily follow, however, that the new style of administration will be much better—or indeed any better—than the old. Its virtues have their corresponding defects, and these, although very different in kind from the defects of the old style of administration, may—even if the quality of government services is better than before—produce a ratio of costs to benefits that is every bit as bad and perhaps even worse. If in the old days there was waste and lack of coordination for want of technically trained supervisory personnel, now there is waste and lack of coordination because of the very profusion of such personnel. If in the old days city administration was biased in favor of the tastes of the lower class as made known by ward politicians, now it is biased in favor of the tastes of the middle class as made known by newspapers, civic associations, and, especially, professionals in various bureaucracies. If in the old days authority was overly decentralized because great numbers of politicians clung to their separate scraps of it, now it is too decentralized because great numbers of bureaucrats cling to their separate scraps of it. If in the old days specific material inducements were illegally given as bribes to favored individuals, now much bigger ones are legally given to a different class of favored individuals, and, in addition, general inducements are proffered in packages to every large group in the electorate and to tiny but intensely moved minorities as well.

The difference seems to be not so much in the effect produced as in the motives leading to the production of it. The motives that produced the faults of the old-style administration were reprehensible, and this made the faults readily identifiable as such, not only by the press and public but even by those who committed them. The faults of the new style of administration arise from motives that are respectable, often even admirable, and therefore they are not usually regarded as faults at all. If by zealously protecting the tenure of city employees an independent civil service commission fills the bureaucracy with hacks, the effect of its actions, although objectively no different from that which was produced by a machine politician, escapes notice because the intentions of the civil service commissioners were good. Similarly, if a downtown merchant, by promising election support to a mayor who "does things for the city," initiates a vast urban renewal project, he may enrich himself and impoverish others more than any businessman ever did by carrying a black bag to a boss's back room; but urban renewal rarely shocks anyone's sensibilities, for the intention of the merchant is good ("in the public interest," as he would say) even though the economic consequences of his actions may be no different, except in the larger dollar values usually involved nowadays, from those of the actions of the "boodlers" whom Lincoln Steffens excoriated.

It will be understood, of course, that this evaluation says little about the authors' own preferences in the matter. Speaking for ourselves, we would prefer (other things being equal) to live in a "good government" community where the service function is honestly and efficiently performed, provided this does not prevent the government from attending to more important matters.

One might expect a city with a nonpartisan, council-manager form of government and a long "good government" tradition to provide more and better services, and to provide them at lower unit cost, than a city which has long been governed by a corrupt machine. Although this may actually be the case, there is no evidence to prove it. Measurements of governmental efficiency are seldom possible, because the services supplied by different cities are never identical and because the tastes of taxpayer-consumers differ from city to city.[7] If the people of city "A" want their rubbish collected once a week and those of city "B" want theirs collected once in two weeks, any statement about the relative efficiency of the two sanitation departments must be extremely hazardous.

Although the spread of the middle-class ideal may reduce local government's ability to manage conflict, it will also reduce the amount of conflict requiring management and make easier the management of such conflict as there is.[8] Where the electorate is divided along class lines into two camps of approximately equal size, the political problem is severe: whatever one camp favors the other opposes and neither is strong enough to have its way. This has been the situation in many cities for two or three generations. The assimilation of the lower class to the middle is upsetting the balance, however, and as the middle class achieves a large majority the old lines of conflict will disappear because the middle class will be under no necessity of making concessions. There will still be conflicts, but they will tend to be within the majority rather than between the majority and the minority. They will be relatively easy to manage, too, because they will concern the merits of concrete issues, not generalized class antagonisms. What is more, the content of the middle-class ideal is such as to make the management of conflict easier, for the ideal includes willingness to settle matters on the basis of reasonable discussion and to make sacrifices of immediate and private interest for the sake of the longer-run "larger good of the community as a whole."

It does not follow from this, however, that as the cities become "less political" they will deal more effectively with their larger problems. It is not without significance that Washington, D.C., the voteless and preeminently apolitical city, has not been notably more successful in coping with its major problems than have other large cities. Indeed, according to Martha Derthick, it is the *style* of politics ("the way in which competition proceeds") and not the *substance* of it ("the outcome of political action") that is chiefly affected by Washington's special governmental structure.[9]

One might expect that the character of a city's government would be reflected in the scope of its activities and ultimately in the income, education, and living standards of its people. Actually such fragmentary evidence as exists suggests that the more middle-class a city the less likely it is to carry out what are generally considered to be progressive undertakings. Amos H. Hawley, for example, has shown that the higher the proportion of managers, proprietors, and officials in the employed labor force of a city, the *less* likely the city is to have undertaken an urban renewal project or, if it has undertaken one, to have carried it to the execution stage. Hawley found that this correlation persists even when one holds constant such variables as region, city size, age of housing, extent of dilapidation, size of planning budget, central city or suburban character, and form of city government.[10] Similarly, Maurice Pinard has found that the higher the proportion of employed males in managerial or professional occupations in a city, the *less* likely the city is to have voted favorably on the question of fluoridation of its water supplies.[11] Our explanation of these anomalies is that the political and governmental arrangements to which the middle-class ideal gives rise tend to emphasize procedural matters (honesty, efficiency, and impartiality) at the expense of substantive ones, and are in fact often incapable of assembling the amounts of influence necessary to carry out a large undertaking. Perhaps this is because their preoccupation with procedural proprieties makes it impossible for them to offer specific inducements in the right kinds and amounts. (Pinard, it is interesting to note, remarks that middle-class *individuals* tend to be more favorable to fluoridation than lower-class ones, whereas middle-class *communities* tend to be less favorable to it than lower-class ones. This, he thinks, may be explained "by different structural arrangements within the elites and between the social classes.")[12] Whatever may be the effect of city politics on the scope and character of local government activities, it seems to make little or no difference in the general standard of living. If one compares a few notably "good government" cities with a few notably "not good government" ones (eliminating from consideration all those that differ greatly in size, racial composition, and geographical location), the differences in median education, in median income, and in median rents will be found to be greater among cities in the same category ("good government" or "not good government") than among those in different categories.

It is our impression that the character of a city's politics affects the amount and manner of law enforcement more than it does anything else in the city. "Good government" cities are never "wide open," and their policemen and courts are relatively honest and impartial. So far as we know, the police forces with national reputations for competence and integrity are all in cities dominated by the middle-class ideal. Beyond this, however, it is very difficult to generalize. Cities with similar political styles differ greatly in their treatment of the various forms of vice. We suspect that cities which are markedly new-style in their politics, although in general much less tolerant of vice than other cities, are nevertheless relatively tolerant of those forms of it—obscenity, for example—that are peculiar to the middle class. Moreover, among the cities that retain the old style of politics, some are much less tolerant of vice—or in some cases of certain vices—than others. The notorious Hague machine, for example, was puritanical in its enforcement of laws against prostitution and dope peddling, and it kept the Prohibition mobs and later the Syndicate out of Jersey City.

It would be easy to overestimate what even strong city governments could do about the most important problems of the cities nowadays. The city, it should not be forgotten, is legally and in fact the creature of the state. In some places, to be sure, "home rule" has lengthened the leading strings on which the city is held; nevertheless the critical decisions will be made mostly by governors and legislatures, not mayors and city councils. If the control over the cities is taken from the states, it will be taken by the federal government, not the cities.

The most fundamental problem of the central cities and of the older suburbs—one that constitutes a life-and-death crisis for them—is of such a nature that it cannot be "solved," or even much relieved, by government action at any level—local, state, or national. A large part of the housing in these cities, although built not very long ago and still structurally sound, has become obsolete by the rising standards of the middle class. It is cheaper to build new communities on farm lands beyond the city's borders than to remodel, or to tear down and rebuild, the old housing in the cities. (Even in the most congested metropolitan areas, including the one centering on New York City, there is enough vacant suburban land to meet the probable demand for another generation at least.) The middle class steadily moves out of the unpromising "gray areas" lying between the central business district and the suburbs. Therefore it is to be expected that the lower-class people—many of them Negro—who have been living in the high-density slums will spread out into those "gray areas" and will convert them into low-density slums. With few exceptions (such as midtown and lower Manhattan, Chicago's Loop and lakefront, and San Francisco) the downtown districts of the older cities will decline as centers of commerce, entertainment, and culture. There is little that government can do about this. The forces that are at work—especially changes in technology, in location of industry and population, and in consumer tastes and incomes—are all largely beyond the control of government in a free society. Given these constraints, the future of the cities is probably beyond the reach of policy.[13]

If trends in city politics do not make as much difference as one would expect in some matters, they may make far *more* difference than one would expect in others. Changes in the city's politics may have profound consequences for the national parties and thus indirectly for the whole governmental system. To the extent that national leaders—the President above all—cannot draw upon reservoirs of political power that are created out of, and maintained as adjuncts of, local politics, they must either make up for the loss by appealing directly to the electorate or else be weaker in consequence. President Roosevelt depended heavily for support at crucial times on Boss Kelly, Boss Flynn, Boss Crump, Boss Hague, and, for a time, Boss Pendergast. No President will ever again find such support in city politicians. Now that a national leader cannot expect to have large blocs of votes "delivered" by city bosses, he must get them for himself; to do this he may have to pay a higher price than was paid before, and a higher one, perhaps, than the nation can afford. To the extent that he cannot count on the "delivery" of votes, he is less free to disregard public opinion at crucial moments when public opinion, or intensely moved parts of it, is out of line with long-term national interests. He is under a greater necessity to offer extravagant bribes to large classes of voters—farmers, homeowners, manufacturers, and so on. And he is more dependent on the arts of charm, salesmanship, and rhetoric, and on the appeal of ideology. As the sources of power change, so will the kinds of men who are adept at getting power and so also will the uses to which power is put.[14]

The changes that are occurring in city politics will have an effect upon character also. From Aristotle through Tocqueville, theorists have explained that the individual is formed in and by the local community and that his attachment to it influences profoundly his outlook and morality. In the long run, this effect upon character may be the most important of all. It does not follow from this, however, that we can judge what the nature of the effect is likely to be; relations between cause and effect in these matters are far from straightforward. Machine politics, although corrupt and selfish, may not have had a generally detrimental effect upon character. (Machine politics "left no moral scars on my generation," writes Thomas J. Fleming, a novelist whose father was one of Mayor Frank Hague's ward leaders in Jersey City. "Instead, we all nourished respectable nonpolitical ambitions, and most of us have realized them. My block has produced two engineers, a Harvard Law School graduate, two stock brokers, a college professor.")[15] Similarly, it cannot be assumed that the more democratic and community-regarding new style of local politics will have a generally ennobling effect upon character. Important long-run effects there will undoubtedly be, but about their nature we can say nothing even in retrospect.

What is true about effects on individual character is true about other effects as well. Probably all of the effects of changes in city politics that make the most difference in the long run will occur in ways so indirect as to make their identification unlikely or impossible. Some ultimate effects will occur because of intermediate changes that are brought about in the functioning of political institutions; conceivably, for example, changes in the style of city politics, by affecting the national party system and thus the Presidency, may affect the peace of the world and the future of mankind. Other ultimate effects may be produced in ways that are remote from government and politics; if, for example, the new style of politics is less able than the old to contain and give controlled release to popular restlessness, energy, and emotion, these may break out at unexpected times and places and in forms—fads and fashions, religious revivals, or new social movements—that are as remote from politics as it is possible to imagine. Among these indirect effects there may be some that are more dangerous to the well-being of the society than any of the ills that municipal reformers have ever contemplated. There is, of course, nothing to be gained from speculating about these matters since in the nature of the case nothing much can be known about them. It is well to recognize, however, that the common-sense view of things is probably wrong both in attributing to city politics an importance that it does not have in matters that seem to be obviously connected with it and also—perhaps especially —in failing to attribute to it a much larger, although unspecifiable, importance that it has in matters that seem to bear no relation to it whatever.

N O T E S

1. Samuel Lubell, *The Future of American Politics* (Garden City, N.Y.: Doubleday, 1952), chap. iv.

2. Benjamin DeMott, "Party Apolitics," *The American Scholar*, Autumn 1962, p. 597.

3. See Marion K. Sanders, "The Next Mayor of New York?" *Harper's*, February 1963. Screvane is described as "a kind of one-man balanced ticket— half Italian, half Irish, and he speaks Yiddish." But the writer attaches great importance to the "vigorous public commitments" he has made to "good government" goals. [Screvane was eliminated in the Democratic primary by Abraham Beame, who, in turn, was defeated by Republican John Lindsay— the epitome of the professional administrator—Ed.]

4. For example, these changes are recommended by the Municipal Manpower Commission, which was created by the Ford Foundation through the vehicle of the American Muncipal Association, the American Society of Planning Officials, and the American Institute of Planners. The Commission is a good example of the kind of body that produces the orthodoxy referred to in the text; it describes its recommendations as "An Agenda for Metropolis," incidentally. See Municipal Manpower Commission, *Governmental Manpower for Tomorrow's Cities* (New York: McGraw-Hill, 1962), chap. iv.

5. The Municipal Manpower Commission quotes an administrator as saying that "cities are too hemmed in by checks and balances to make it possible to deal effectively with the types of problems which now confront cities." Ibid., p. 48.

6. Martha Derthick, "Politics in Voteless Washington," *Journal of Politics*, vol. XXV (1963), pp. 101–2.

7. See Alice Vandermeulen, "Guideposts for Measuring the Efficiency of Governmental Expenditure," *Public Administration Review*, Winter 1950, pp. 7–12.

8. This argument is developed by Banfield, "The Political Implications of Metropolitan Growth," in Lloyd Rodwin (ed.), *The Future Metropolis* (New York: George Braziller, 1960).

9. Martha Derthick, "Politics in Voteless Washington," p. 100.

10. Amos H. Hawley, "Community Power and Urban Renewal Success," *American Journal of Sociology*, January 1963, pp. 422–31. See also the evidence that variations in the form of city government make no difference in the likelihood of a city's having a successful renewal program, in George S. Duggar, "The Relation of Local Government Structure to Urban Renewal," *Law and Contemporary Problems*, vol. XXVI (1961), pp. 49–69.

11. Maurice Pinard, "Structural Attachments and Political Support in Urban Politics: The Case of Fluoridation Referendums," *American Journal of Sociology*, March 1963, pp. 513–26.

12. Ibid., p. 525.

13. This seems to us to be the clear implication of the position taken by Raymond Vernon in *The Myth and Reality of Our Urban Problems* (Cambridge, Mass.: Joint Center for Urban Studies, 1962). Anthony Downs takes a contrary view in "The Future Structure of American Cities," a paper presented at the Conference on Transportation of the National Academy of Sciences at Woods Hole, Massachusetts, August 1960 (mimeo).

14. For a fuller discussion of these matters see Edward C. Banfield, "In Defense of the American Party System," a paper appearing in a symposium edited by Robert C. Goldwin and to be published by Rand-McNally.

15. Thomas J. Fleming, "City in the Shadow," *Saturday Evening Post*, Jan. 6, 1962, p. 82.

2.

The New Convergence of Power

R O B E R T   H .   S A L I S B U R Y

I

Economically, culturally, and in many ways even politically, the United States has become a thoroughly urban nation.[1] One aspect of this urbanization is that scholars have increasingly paid attention to phenomena occurring in the cities. Sociologists, political scientists, economists, geographers, and historians have all developed urban subfields of specialization; and in recent years the sub-fields have been infused with the great enthusiasm of virtual armies of researchers. When these efforts are combined with those of architects, planners, social workers, administrative managers, and all the other urbanists asking questions about life in the city, the resulting stack of data, reports, proposals, admonitions, and manifestos is truly staggering. Inevitably, perhaps, concern for the substance of city life gets mixed with concern for the methods of inquiry. Both, of course, are legitimate and important areas of concern, each helps illuminate and is illuminated by the other. Specifically, the study of power structure—a basic issue for all political inquiry—has come to focus very largely on the city. In the process, both the substantive and methodological issues surrounding this generic political question—the question, as Dahl puts it, Who Governs?—have been involved in virtually every discussion of urban affairs in recent years.[2]

Yet despite, or perhaps because of, this special ferment some important gaps on this question— who governs the city?—have remained. Many of these relate to the basic criticism to be made of almost all urban studies,

From "Urban Politics: The New Convergence of Power" by Robert H. Salisbury, *The Journal of Politics*, Vol. 26 (November 1964), pp. 775–797. Reprinted by permission. An earlier version of this paper was presented to the 59th Annual Meeting of the American Political Science Association, New York City, September 5, 1963.

the absence of comparative dimensions. Serious, theoretically sophisticated social and political analysis of urban data is relatively new on the scholarly scene, however. It is perhaps not so surprising therefore that so little genuine comparative work has been undertaken. . . . . .[3] One who is interested in general patterns of big city politics must deal with a series of case studies, each study dealing with a single community. Each study then serves its author as the empirical foundation for a series of generalizations about politics (or society—the sociologists have been firmly in the tradition since the days of the Lynds). Some of these are brilliant. At best, however, they are sophisticated insights and theoretical conjectures built upon descriptions of a single case which, one hopes intuitively, may fit a larger number of cases.

The limitations of the data are compounded by variations in conceptual apparatus and/or data-gathering technique. One wishes that there were a clear basis for determining that Atlanta was or was not a pyramid-shaped monolith; the Springdale was "really" controlled by a caucus, and that New Haven actually conforms to Dahl's analysis.[4] None of these three was studied in a manner which permits accurate comparisons with the other two (or twenty more which might be named), and hence no generalizations about either of two central points is possible. First, what is (are) the structure(s) of power in American cities? Second, what are the principal independent variables affecting the shape, scope and operation of these putative structures? It may turn out that each city is unique and no useful generalizations can be made using the city as the unit of analysis. Or the city may really be the most useful microcosm of the political system in which all essential processes, structures, and relationships can be found. The professional conclusion probably lies somewhere between. We will not know without systematic comparative study.

One major effort at synthesis of exciting materials about city, principally big city, politics is that of Edward C. Banfield and James Q. Wilson.[5] To a large extent they draw upon the same materials as this essay, and there are many areas of agreement. There are important differences, too, however, both in conclusions and approach. Thus Banfield and Wilson give only passing attention to the historical dimension of urban politics. I propose to examine the question of the structure of power and do so over time. By viewing the city historically a number of critical elements, particularly those which have changed, can be seen more clearly than if a more strictly contemporaneous study were made. My discussion focuses upon the big cities in the United States that experienced major growth prior to World War I. The pattern I shall describe may apply to other communities as well, but my model city in what follows is heterogeneous in ethnic and racial terms, contains considerable industry and a suburban ring, is experiencing core city decay, and is, in short, what those who wrote about urban problems generally have in mind when they refer to "the city."

Anyone who talks about urban structures of power must take a stand on two related questions: what is meant by power and how does one go about trying to establish its empirical dimensions. By "structure of power" I mean the set of relationships among community roles, durable over time, through which relationships scarce resources are allocated in a community. I am primarily concerned with those allocations which involve decisions by governmental agencies. We should recognize, however, the shifting importance over time of public allocations to the total of allocations made in the community, and remember, too, that public and private actions are always mixed together, nowhere more than in the city. I shall not give attention to the allocation of all those resources that might be deemed scarce, but only those that are of substantial volume or scope. I recognize the difficulty of drawing clear distinctions between "important" and "unimportant" decisions, but there *is* a difference, and it is recognized by decision-makers in a city. Thus the structure of power affecting a primary fight over the nomination for recorder of deeds may bear no relationship to the structure within which the city's urban renewal program is determined. In such a case it is only the latter that is of much interest; the decisions involve much more substantial resource allocations and the structure of power involved is therefore a more important one.

In short, we shall examine the most crucial structures of policy-relevant power in the large American city and attempt partly to identify and partly to postulate a pattern of development that seems warranted by the histories and present circumstances of several such cities. In doing so we must necessarily make comparisons among fragments of data drawn from sources that are widely diverse in concept and method. The result must obviously fall short of definitive status, but hopefully it may at least provide some stimulus to systematic comparative research in urban data.

II

Two systematic historical studies of urban power structure are those of New Haven by Dahl and Cibola by Schulze.[6] Both identify patterns of change that, despite considerable differences between the communities, are roughly similar. Much of the other published material on American urban history can be read as confirming this general pattern.[7]

Dahl finds that political office in New Haven was dominated first by the "patricians," then by the "entrepreneurs," and finally by the "explebes." Patrician dominance rested upon oligarchic control of all of the major resources from which influence could be fashioned. "[S]ocial status, education, wealth, and political influence were united in the same hands."[8] The entrepreneur's prominence emerged as wealth and social standing were separated, and the new men of business displaced the patricians in controlling economic resources. The entrepreneurs, moreover, were popular as the crabbed patricians were not. But the increasing immigrant labor force led to changing standards of popularity, and by about 1900 "[P]opularity had been split off from both wealth and social standing. Popularity meant votes; votes meant office; office meant influence."[9] The resulting pattern Dahl refers to as one of "dispersed inequalities." Many actors possess politically relevant resources but none possesses enough to dominate a broad range of actions. Particular actors exercise influence over particular policy decisions depending on the resources relevant to that decision, and several types of coalitions may aggregate the influentials concerned with specific problems, but no continuous structure of influence is operative for the broad range of public decision.

Robert Schulze describes a similar historical pattern in Cibola except that Cibola, a much younger community, had no patrician era. Instead it experienced two stages, local capitalism and non-local or absentee capitalism. In the former stage, until 1900, the economic dominants were also the political dominants. They held public office as well as controlling local economic resources and their preeminent social standing reinforced their hegemony. After 1900 Cibola increasingly became an economic satellite and local economic resources came increasingly under the control of national firms. Local officials of these firms did not involve themselves in the active influence structure of the community, much less hold office. Rather, there developed a separate category of influentials, the public leaders, whose influence rested primarily upon such factors as popularity and commitment to the locality. Schulze describes this as a bifurcation of power, but it may not be amiss to suggest that Schulze's data permit the inference that Cibola is more polylithic—influence is widely dispersed and discontinuous—than the bifurcation image implies.

Both Dahl and Schulze give support to the general view that roughly from the end of the Civil War until 1900 American cities were dominated by the merchantry. Where the community had long existed as a substantial population center, notably in the East, the entrepreneurs were likely, as Dahl describes, to have displaced the patricians. Where there hardly had been a city in the ante-bellum years, there were no patricians to displace, and the commercial elite, relatively open to talents and money, but an elite nonetheless, dominated all the major institutions of the community. Political offices were typically held for short terms with each important merchant expected to contribute some time to the marginal activity of public office-holding.

Although the economic elite of the mercantile city dominated political institutions as well, it is unlikely that much additional influence accrued to them as a result. Public authority did relatively little in this stage of urban development. Only gradually were such elemental functions as water supply and sewage disposal, street construction and maintenance, police and fire protection undertaken. In many cases, too, the initial phases of service were provided by a mixture of public and private effort that mirrored the mixture of public and private position held by influentials. Public improvements were undertaken not only to make life possible in the increasingly crowded and extended city, but also as "booster activities." "Let's put good old —— on the map!" was an oft-repeated watchword of civic promotion. As McKelvey notes, chambers of commerce were formed to promote economic development in a number of post-Civil War cities,[10] and the promotion of canals, railroads, exhibition halls, and—the classic booster gimmick—the World's Fair, all were part of the merchantry's effort to sell their particular community to the nation. Boosterism, even for the one-shot, short-run promotion, almost invariably involved a complex intermixture of public and private efforts and rested, therefore, on an elite which dominated both public and private office.

The gradual expansion of public services, however, had a significance for the structure of influence that booster gimmicks did not. Water and sewer systems, schools, streets, parks, police and fire were functions that required continuous operation by larger and larger corps of public employees. With the industrial growth of the city, the object for which boosterism strove, more and more people, requiring near-geometric increases in services, came to the city. Further, the new immigrants came to work in the new industries. Whereas the mercantile city had been as nearly classless as the frontier itself, the industrial city was the site of a differentiated class structure; differentiated by income and life chances, by ethnic origins, by religion, and by political potential.

At the same time, the industrial economic giant viewed the city very differently from the merchant. He was far less dependent on local sales or real estate values and thus less concerned with growth itself. His was a contingent investment in the community—gradually in the several communities housing his several branches—and his civil liability was therefore limited just as the corporate form limited his legal liability. His participation in the allocation of community resources, while potentially great, was infrequent and discontinuous. He was concerned only to protect his relatively narrowly defined corporate interests, not a generalized pattern of influence.

The merchantry had been deeply committed to the city in an economic and emotional way that was missing from the industrial manager. In the industrial city the modes by which civic obligations were discharged became more diverse and more specialized. Service on special boards or committees for libraries or schools, or parks, or slum dwellers was increasingly the way that the local notables— and their wives!— made their community contributions. These were likely to be structurally separated from the main body of governmental institutions and something of a preserve for "the best people," insulated from "politics." In addition, the slowly growing concern for planning the City Beautiful and reforming inefficient or corrupt government provided larger and larger amounts of "program material" for the luncheon clubs and merchants' association.[11] That occasionally reform campaigns would actually elect a mayor or effect a change in governmental operation did not cancel the fact that economic and social influence had been separated from political influence, and that each now (ca. 1900) rested on a different social base.

An autonomous political elite was, of course, a function of expanded governmental activity and a growing working class population that altered the numerical balance of the city. As Dahl points out, not only were the political entrepreneurs now more popular than the economic entrepreneurs but the criteria of political popularity changed. Effective representation of the Booster spirit and promotion of industrial growth gave way to effective representation of the needs of the poor for elemental services and the promotion of the political organization itself. The boss and his machine we now recognize to have been functional for the newly industrial city; a growing army of public job-holders was recruited, a vast immigration was socialized and provided means of advancement in the urban society, welfare needs were at least minimally provided for, further extensions of public improvement programs were constructed, albeit expensively, and specific services were rendered to the economic elites as well. Railroad spurs, street car franchises, assessment adjustments, police protection of imported labor and a variety of other benefits could be conferred upon business by governmental agencies, even though the latter were no longer controlled by the businessmen themselves. Although businessmen were often appalled and sometimes intimidated by the "new men" of city politics, they rarely intervened or even protested against the system in any continuous way.

Surely a portion of the reason that the boss remained in power was that although government was far more formidable in this period than formerly, the major decisions allocating resources in the city were still made by private interests. Governmental functions were no doubt of crucial importance to the machine itself and to its followers, but, for the most part, they were of marginal importance to the private sector of the economy. It therefore made relatively little difference whether they were done well or not. This is the obverse of the point that economic notables tended to withdraw from civic involvement after about 1900. Not only did the changing city pretty well force them out of office; it was quite rational for them to tend their private gardens and only enter the political arena on behalf of specific policy questions with an immediate payoff to their specialized economic concerns.

What Schulze describes as the bifurcation of power between economic and political elites was thus a function of a changing industrial and social order in the city supported by the enlarged opportunities for political entrepreneurs in the growth of governmental activity. At the same time, the economic and social notables were fragmented by the split between absentee and local capital, the diffusion of energies in a myriad of specialized civic but largely nonpolitical enterprises, and finally by the exodus from the city's corporate limits of the middle class. The efforts of the Progressive WASPs to reform local government, to cleanse the stables of municipal corruption, were in the main doomed by the inexorable movements of people. The middle class moved to suburbia and put political popularity—the ability to get elected—permanently on a working class basis.

The final seal on the bifurcation was effected by the shift of the voting habits of the urban working class to overwhelming Democracy. From the beginning of the New Deal more and more of the large cities became safely Democratic. The metropolitan middle class maintained its Republican loyalties with respect to the national scene, but in local matters a modus vivendi on a business-like basis with the Democratic leadership— a matter of necessity for those with local interests at stake—was often achieved.

Yet the Democratic partisan hegemony provided a kind of cover by which middle class values could reappear in the public decisions of a working class city. By the end of the 1940's the machines were fading. The disciplined delivery of votes was rarely possible, at least on a citywide basis, and the professionalization of the city bureaucracy was well along. Political office still went to those who mustered majorities from a predominantly working class city electorate but the circular pattern that characterized the era of "Politics for Profit"—votes gave power, power provided favors, favors provided votes—was increasingly broken. It is significant that a move toward "Good Government"—meaning rational policy making—came from within the political stratum itself in these years in Chicago, St. Louis, Pittsburgh, and New Orleans. This move coincided with a change in the agenda of urban resource allocation, and this change in turn has led to a change in the structure of influence.

III

I propose to designate the contemporary structure of urban power as the "new convergence." It is similar in many ways to what Dahl calls the executive-centered coalition. It is headed, and sometimes led, by the elected chief executive of the city, the mayor. Included in the coalition are two principal active groupings, locally-oriented economic interests and the professional workers in technical city-related programs. Both these groupings are sources of initiative for programs that involve major allocations of resources, both public and private. Associated with the coalition, also, are whatever groups constitute the popular vote-base of the mayor's electoral success. Their association is more distant and permissive, however. Their power to direct specific policy choices is severely limited. In the following pages I shall examine each element in the coalition as well as some of the groups in the city that largely lack power. In all cases I am concerned with power that is relevant to key resource allocation decisions.

In the period roughly centered on the turn of the century business leadership was transformed from local to absentee capital, from merchantry to corporate managers. Accompanying this shift in economic organization was a shift in community political commitment and orientations, and this shift, in the direction of reduced interest, concided with and reinforced the burgeoning autonomous political organization. Now, however, I am saying that business plays an important role in the structure of city affairs. The apparent contradiction points to some complexities in the notion of "business."

First, some kinds of business never experienced the nationalizing effects of industrial reorganization. These often remained intimately associated with politics throughout the era of the bosses. Real estate dealers, building suppy firms, insurance agents, and corner confectioneries were always likely to have an iron or two in the political fire. They still do, but these interests are not part of the coalition we are examining. Their interests are small with respect to resource allocations, and they deal in channels that are peripheral to the main body of decisions. Their politics is a kind of eternal process which goes on in many different kinds of worlds without affecting them. Petty business and petty politics are thus handmaidens but irrelevant to the larger issues of power.

The large international corporation continues to regard the local scene with the same investment calculus described earlier. In general, the branch plant will do only as much about the community as is required to develop and maintain an image of good corporate citizenship, and this is far less than is necessary for power or even concern about community resource allocation.[12] Occasionally, the needs of the firm may require it to intrude into the community political system, but such intrusions would be very much on an *ad hoc* basis. The same is likely to be true of large, nationally-oriented unions.[13] The exception occurs when the union or the firm has a large home office or plant in the city or has grown large from a base in a particular community. Then "good citizenship" may require more than charitable work and involve the company or union leadership in larger urban policy issues.

The most active business firms in the new convergence, however, are those with major investments in the community, and which are dependent on the growth of a particular community, and which have come to recognize that all the major issues and decisions of the city affect their interests.[14] Furthermore, they all share a growing concern with that congeries of problems labeled "core city decay." They include the major banks, utilities, railroads, department stores, large real estate firms, and metropolitan newspapers. Functionally, the list is remarkably similar from city to city. Also similar is the fact that active concern with community affairs is relatively recent, largely post-World War II, and coincides with the perception of threat to tangible "downtown" economic values. Finally, the re-entry of these groups into the active quest for power coincides with the weakening of the party-political dominance of the governmental arena. This permitted the numerically inferior business groups to assert their claims on a more continuous basis than formerly had been the case. In Chicago, where the machine did not weaken so much, the loop businessmen continued to operate a largely *ad hoc* basis.[15] Elsewhere, however, the downtown business interests articulated their concerns more forcefully and organized their community-centered energies more efficiently than ever before. Insted of boosterism, business-centered groups helped to trigger a variety of problem-solving programs such as redevelopment and traffic revision and provided continuing support for efforts at solving other problems such as delinquency and crime. Much of the lay leadership of public campaigns for bonds, for example; much of the stimulus to action itself; and much of the private portion of new investment necessary to redevelopment came from this newly organized group. It is important to recognize, however, that, although the support and stimulus of downtown business was and is an essential element in the coalition that dominates decisions in the city, downtown business does not constitute a power elite. It does not run the city, or call the shots for its puppets.

The second element in the coalition—one would be tempted to call it the Civic Establishment except that the term may connote more tradition-based power than this coalition possesses—is composed of the technician, the professional, the expert. As Barry Karl has pointed out, the innovative function of the Progressive reform groups has largely been taken over by the professional.[16] The social worker has replaced Jane Addams. The social scientist in a Charles Merriam has replaced the amateur politician/reformer. Police administration, comprehensive budgeting and capital programming, systematic traffic control, land use planning, and renewal and rehabilitation have all become, in one degree or another, the domains of the expert. Technical criteria play a far greater role than before in determining choices, and the specification of alternatives is likewise largely a function of the technician who, often alone, knows what is possible.[17]

Perhaps the policy area most obviously dominated by the expert is that of public education. Teachers and school administrators not only set the agenda for action. They provide most of the arguments and evidence relevant to the choices that can be made and constitute the most active and powerful interests participating in the decision-making process. If non-professionals protest against certain policies—Negroes denouncing *de facto* segregation, for example—the professional educators cite technical educational criteria as a sufficient justification for their decisions and frequently carry the day.

The existence of professional skills relevant to city problems is, of course, a relatively new feature on the urban scene. Even now we are a long way from a technocracy, for the skills fall far short of the problems. Nevertheless, the growth of what broadly may be called applied social science has added a significant number of new people in new roles to the urban system, and these people help articulate and specify the problems and alternative courses of action for the other interests in the coalition. In this way the technician exercises power over resource allocation that is every bit as real as that of the economic interests or authority-wielders.

Let us turn to the peak of the loose coalition of interests that dominate today's urban scene, the mayor. He presides over the "new convergence," and, if the coalition is to succeed, he must lead it. More than anyone else he determines the direction of urban development; yet his sanctions are few, his base of support insecure. The mayor is both the most visible person in the community and, on questions of public policy, probably the most influential. Yet his is a classic example of the separation of influence and power.[18] Few big-city mayors have significant patronage resources. Even fewer use their appointments to give themselves direct leverage over policy. Although the mayor in a partisan city is necessarily elected through processes that involve the ward organizations, no big-city mayor, not even Daley, can be regarded as the creature of the machine. Rather the mayor is an individual who has 1) sufficient mass appeal and/or organizational support to win election, 2) enough awareness of the complexity of urban problems to rely heavily on a professional staff for advice and counsel, and 3) the ability to negotiate successfully with the economic notables in the city to mobilize both public and private resources in efforts to solve core city economic and social problems.

Successful electioneering in the city requires that the candidate be palatable to a lower income constituency, especially to Negroes. Where there remain vestiges of party organization with vote-delivering capabilities the successful candidate must have some appeal for them, too. An ethnic background or family association that evokes support from the delivery wards is often helpful. At the same time, however, the successful mayoral candidate is likely to appeal to that portion of the urban electorate which historically has been reformist or mugwumpish in orientation. He personifies good government by his espousal of professionalism in local administration. Frequently his personal style, despite his name or political forebears, is thoroughly white-collar and middle class. He is relatively articulate on local television, and his campaigns are likely to stress his competence at communal problem-solving rather than the particular group benefits that may accrue following his election. Nor is this mere campaign talk. His administration concentrates on solving or alleviating particular problems rather than building memorials or dramatizing the city's commercial prospects. Again, this posture requires collaboration with those possessing the relevant resources, the experts and the businessmen.

Obviously, there are variations in the way the mayoral role is played. From city to city and mayor to mayor many differences may appear. The main lines of demarcation may be twofold, however. Some mayors, possessing the gifts of self-dramatization, may more fully personify the programs of the city than others. This has little effect on the content of the decisions but may have consequences in terms of support. Mayors may also differ in the degree to which they actively seek out problems and solutions. Banfield describes Daley waiting for things to come to a head; other mayors more actively seek either to forestall the problem entirely or to structure the whole process through which the issue develops. The latter distinction may be related to the structure of the city; the larger and more diverse the city, the less effectively can the mayor actively shape the problem-solving process.

Of what is mayoral influence composed? Much of it is contained in the office itself. Of all the roles in the community none is so well situated with respect to the flow of information concerning the city's problems. This alone gives the occupant of the office a great advantage over other influentials. He knows more about more things than anyone else. Although his patronage power may be relatively slight, his budgetary authority is typically substantial. Insofar as he, by himself or in a board or commission, presents the budget to the council, he is determining much of the agenda for the discussion of public affairs, and no one else in the city can compete with him. Third, his ability to co-opt persons into *ad hoc* committees is unmatched in the city. As the only official with formal authority to speak for the entire city, he can confer legitimacy on co-opted leaders as no one else can. Thus, if he chooses to, a shrewd mayor may have a good deal to say about who shall be regarded as leaders and who shall not. Negotiations on civil rights issues in a number of cities illustrate the point well. Finally, as noted earlier, the mayor is, or soon becomes, far better known in the community than anyone else, and is far better able to command and structure public attention.

A considerable factor in the mayor's ability to structure public debate is his superior access to and influence over the press. City hall reporters not only cover his office closely but their view of city problems is very largely gained through their daily contacts with the official city fathers. The latter, in turn, are cordial and by being helpful can be reasonably assured that most of the news stories out of city hall will reflect mayoral interpretation. The newspapers as major businesses with their economic future tied to the local community and its elites are likely to favor editorially a mayor whose style embraces their interests. Thus even though the editors may differ with some specific recommendation of the mayor, they give him general support, while through them the mayor communicates his conceptions of city problems and program. One result, of course, is to make it difficult for others to challenge successfully the incumbent mayor for re-election.[19] Thus despite the unstable character of the coalition's base—predominantly low income voters and downtown businessmen—the mayor, once elected, may serve a good many terms. No outsider can find a sufficiently sharp wedge of controversy to drive between the disparate elements, or sufficient visibility to exploit whatever gaps develop.

Nevertheless, the mayor is influential only relative to other groups in the city. He is not powerful relative to the problems he tries to solve. The mayor cannot determine by fiat or, apparently, any other way that the economic resources of the city shall increase, that crime and poverty shall decline, that traffic shall move efficiently. He only has rather more directly to say about how the problems shall be approached than anyone else.

This discussions omits those cities which have adopted the council-manager form of government. In Kansas City or Cincinnati, for example, the aggregative and legitimating functions are less likely to be performed by the mayor who is seldom more than the ceremonial head of the city. The manager can rarely perform these functions either, since they are largely incompatible with his professional role. The result may be that the functions are not performed at all. On the other hand, the manager does possess some of the elements of leadership, especially information. As Banfield and Wilson note, the manager "sits at the center of things, where all communication lines converge. In the nature of the case, then, the councilmen must depend on him for their information. Whether he likes it or not, this gives him a large measure of control over them."[20]

IV

The "new convergence" we have described actively seeks out solutions to certain problems it regards as critical to the city's growth. This activist posture may be viewed as somewhat at variance with the approaches to decision-making described by Dahl and by Banfield. Dahl suggests that in New Haven the coalition led by Mayor Lee has actively sought to resolve certain major issues with Lee serving as the principal negotiator among the contending forces. But, says Dahl, Lee selected issues with a view towards their effect upon his chances for re-election. Permanently conditioning the mayor's strategy was the fact that "the mayor and his political opponents were constantly engaged in a battle for votes at the next election, which was always just around the corner."[21] So far as most large cities are concerned, this may greatly overstate the impact of the necessity for re-election on the specific choices made by the mayor and his allies. We shall try to suggest both the role of the electorate and some of the more immediate restraints upon mayoral choice-making in a moment.

Banfield's analysis of Chicago leads to the conclusion that issues are raised primarily by large formal organizations, some of which are governmental and some of which are not.[22] As the maintenance or enhancement needs of the organization require governmental decisions they enter the political arena and usually seek the support of Mayor Daley. Daley himself, however, operates in primarily a reflexive fashion. Although he desires to "do big things," he must move slowly and cautiously, fearful of generating further controversies, and aware that the ponderous and intricate structure of power he heads can be disrupted and his influence capital used up if he moves too soon or too often. But Banfield selects issues that illustrate this argument. His cases fall far short of representing the range of major resource allocation decisions for Chicago. It may still be true, therefore, that Daley initiates or actively participates in the process involved in making other decisions. Certainly it seems that other big-city mayors do.[23]

I focused originally on the processes of allocating scarce resources. These processes may sometimes involve bitter conflict among rival interests. They may sometimes be resolved, however, in a highly consensual way. Particularly is this likely to be the case when the technical experts play a large role in shaping the decision. Much of the time such major areas of public policy as expressway planning, zoning, and budget-making are determined in ways that evoke little complaint or dispute. The fact that no one in the city effectively objects to the decision makes the decision no less important in terms of resource allocation.

A closely related aspect of urban decision-making is that a great many decisions are made in a fashion that may best be described as habitual. The pressures on the time and attention of decision-makers are such that many decisions must continue to be made (or avoided) as they have been in the past. No continuing calculation can be made of the costs and benefits for each area of possible choice. Much is done routinely. Much is left undone in the same way. Control of the routine is largely in the hands of the technicians with the mayor in the best position to alter it at the margins.

Some issues are forced "from the outside," of course. Things which city leaders would prefer not to have to deal with may be pressed in the fashion Banfield describes. Race relations issues generally come under this category. Almost every large city mayor has been compelled to take action, not because he or his coalition particularly wanted to, but because they were forced to by external pressure.

The recent demands of militant Negro groups have often been concentrated on city hall, however, even when the substance of the demands dealt with jobs in private employment. Negro leaders have correctly identified the mayor as the appropriate figure to convene local elites in order to negotiate agreements that will open job opportunities to Negroes. Militant Negroes have often greatly over-estimated the power of the mayor to effect a satisfactory solution, however. For while he is in a stronger position than any other person or group or functioning organization, his resources and those of his allies may fall far short of the requirements.

Pressure from the constituency would not be the usual way for policy to be initiated, however. The bulk of the city's working agenda is made up of proposals drawn up by the city's own technicians to meet problems identified by them or by their allies in the problem-oriented sectors of the community. The need for new revenue sources, for example, is perceived by the mayor and his staff long before public pressure is exerted, and it is the mayoral coalition which seeks a viable solution to the problem.

Not all mayors, not all corps of technicians, and not all downtown business groups are equal in ability to perceive problems, devise solutions, or negotiate settlements. One of the significant variables that distinguishes one city's political system from another is the energy and imagination of its newly convergent elites. In some cities solutions may be found that escape the leaders of another. It is probably true, however, that these differences have been narrowed somewhat by the collaboration among urban elites throughout the nation. The American Municipal Association and the U.S. Conference of Mayors provide organized communication networks that link the political executives. So does HHFA* in its field. So do the various associations of urban technicians in their respective specialties. The metropolitan press facilitates a certain amount of interchange with respect to both problems and solutions in urban areas. Thus there has developed some degree of consensus as to what should be done and some uniformity in the structure of power by which action may be accomplished.

Cities vary with respect not only to energy and skill of leadership but in tangible resources, public and private that may be mobilized for reallocation. In Pittsburgh, for example, there was probably no available substitute for the Mellon cash. In St. Louis the scarcity or stodginess or both of local private capital has made the redevelopment task more difficult. These are variables involved in the power structure of a community. That there are also variations in the range and severity of the problems cities face is obvious and complicates further the task of comparative analysis.

v

I have suggested that a large portion of the content of urban public policy is provided directly by one or more of the three main elements of the governing coalition; the mayor, the technical experts, and the downtown business community. They identify the problems, they articulate the alternative actions that might be taken, and they themselves take most of the relevant actions. This structure of decision-making provides no immediate role for the community-at-large, the voters; and, although Dahl may overstate the significance of their role in limiting New Haven's

---

*The U.S. Housing and Home Finance Agency, predecessor to the present Department of Housing and Urban Development—Ed.

executive-centered coalition, they do play a role in resource allocations, and so do the organized groups that represent segments of the electorate that are outside the dominant coalition.

Dahl's attribution of "weight" to the electorate seems to be based on the relatively intense partisan competition in New Haven, and it may be reinforced by the need to run every two years. But in many cities the direct competition for office is neither so sharp nor so frequent. The tenure in office of prominent mayors such as Tucker, Daley, or Wagner suggests that survival in office may not always require the close attention to voter desires that Dahl suggests. Particularly is this likely in a city where elections are partisan, for the safety of the Democratic ticket is not often in question in many of these cities. The primary may occasionally present peril to the incumbent, and in both partisan and nonpartisan cities incumbents sometimes lose. But there is little evidence to show that mayors, or other elected executives for that matter, have any reliable way of perceiving voter needs very accurately or consciously building support for himself among them. The new mayor may say, with Richard Daley, that "good government is good politics," in part because he doesn't have the option to engage in any other kind.

Nevertheless, generalized constituency sentiment remains a factor that affects policy-making, albeit in a secondary, boundary-setting way. It works primarily in three ways. First, the technician as social scientist often takes into account the interests and needs of the public he hopes to serve when making his plans and recommendations. If he proposes an enlarged staff of case workers for the Welfare Department, he does so partly because in some sense he expects the public to benefit. It is rarely, however, because any public demand for the larger staff is expressed. Rather, the technician believed the proposal would be "good" for the constituents. Secondly, the electorate must make certain broad choices directly. Bond issues and tax rates must often be voted upon; other types of referenda must be approved; key policy-making officials must be elected. Very often this involves "selling the public" on the desirability of the proposal. They have not demanded it. They often have no strong predispositions one way or another except perhaps for a class-related bias on public expenditures in general. But this approval is required, and in anticipation of the limits of tolerance the key decision-makers must tailor their proposals. This is influence, of course, but of a general and largely negative kind. Thirdly, there is the active demand stemming directly from the constituents to which policy-makers respond, but which response would not have been made in the absence of the public demand. Some of these demands go counter to the policies espoused by the coalition; spot zoning, for example, or construction unions' demands on the building code. In some instances the coalition may have the power to block the demands; in other cases, not. Some demands, however, are more difficult to deal with because, if they arise, they cannot be blocked by the exercise of power, but at the same time they are so controversial that almost any solution is likely to damage the overall position of the leaders. As we have noted, many of the issues of race relations are in this category. The city fathers have not agitated these issues, but once raised they must be met.

As we assign "the public" to a largely secondary role, we must also relegate those officials most closely associated with immediate constituency relationships to a similarly secondary position. Councilmen or aldermen, ward leaders, and other local party leaders are likely to play only supportive or obstructive roles in the community's decision-making process. The demands for action do not come from or through them, they are not privy to the councils either of the notables or the experts. They may well play out their traditional roles of precinct or ward politician, but, unlike the machine leader of yore, these roles are separated quite completely from those of policy-making. Even in Chicago, where the mayor's position in part depends on his vote-getting strength through the party organization, very little participation in policy-making filters down to the ward leaders. Similarly, William Green's rise to power in the party organization in Philadelphia had little effect on the content of public policy. It is essential to see that the difference between the policy-making leadership and the "politicians" is more than rhetorical. It carries a substantial impact on the content of policy.[24]

Even though neither the party professionals nor the electorate generally are active participants in the process of resource allocation, is not the top political leadership, specifically the mayor, constrained by his desire for re-election? In part, of course, the answer is yes. In partisan cities the mayor must be nominated and elected on the party ticket, and, particularly in the primary, this may involve getting party organization support. In a non-partisan community too, the mayor must get enough votes to win. It does not follow, however, that there is much connection between what is needed to gain votes and the specific decisions made once in office. Dahl emphasizes the vote-getting popularity of Richard Lee's program in New Haven, especially of urban renewal. Yet that popularity was not really evident in advance of the decisions and was largely dissipated within a very few years. Doubtless Mayor Collins has increased his popularity in Boston by rationalizing and reducing the fiscal burden, but, if Levin is at all correct, his election was not a mandate for *any* particular decisions he has made.[25] The same, I think, could be argued for Dilworth, Tucker, and others of the "new mayors." Certainly the limits of public understanding and acceptance constitute restraints upon the decision-making system, but these are broad restraints, rarely specific in directing choices, and operating largely as almost subconscious limits to the kinds of choices that may be made.[26]

VI

It may not be amiss to conclude this discussion by juxtaposing three quite different strands of thought concerning the urban scene. On the one hand, Dahl and his associates have generally denied the existence of a single structure of power in the city. We have argued, not contradicting Dahl but changing the emphasis, that on a substantial set of key issues such a structure may be discerned. Hunter, et al., have stressed an essentially monolithic structure heavily weighted in behalf of the economic elites. We have stressed the central role of elected political leadership. Finally, such writers as Lewis Mumford and Jane Jacobs, less interested in the problems of power, have doubted the capacity of the urban community to serve man's essential needs at all. In a sense, we are suggesting that each may be partly correct, partly wrong. The coalition of interests headed by the mayor may indeed lack the resources, public and private, separately or combined, to solve the communal problems now dominating the civic agenda. This is the irony that lies behind the convergence of power elements in the modern city. Where once there seemed to be ample resources to keep what were regarded as the major problems of urban life within quite tolerable limits, now, with far more self-conscious collaboration of governmental and private economic power than ever before, and with those structures of power themselves larger and more extensive than ever, the capacity to cope with the recognized problems of the environment seems almost pathetically inadequate. Partly, this may be because the problems have changed in magnitude, and, partly, that we perceive their magnitude in more sophisticated fashion. In any case, it makes the notion of an elite with ample power to deal with the urban community if ever it chooses to, seem a romance, a utopian dream. Like other municipal utopias—Progressive-era reform or today's metropolitan reorganization—it may be yearned for but largely unrealized.

N O T E S

1. For a most comprehensive and thoughtful history of urban growth in America see Blake McKelvey, *The Urbanization of America* (New Brunswick, New Jersey: Rutgers University Press, 1963).

2. Robert A. Dahl's study of New Haven was a classic of political science almost before it was published. See *Who Governs?* (New Haven: Yale University Press, 1961). Dahl chose not to integrate his findings with those avail-

able concerning other communities, and in a number of respects one may argue that his conclusions are limited to the New Haven context. One cannot deny, however, that the larger question of how to approach the study of power has been given theoretically sophisticated stimulus from the work of Dahl and his associates. See Nelson W. Polsby, *Community Power and Political Theory* (New Haven: Yale University Press, 1963). For a convenient summary of many of the items in the large monographic literature on community power structure, see Charles Press, *Main Street Politics* (East Lansing: Michigan State University Institute for Community Development, 1962).

3. Recent attempts to engage in genuinely comparative analysis include Oliver P. Williams and Charles Adrian, *Four Cities* (Philadelphia: University of Pennsylvania Press, 1963); Amos H. Hawley, "Community Power and Urban Renewal Success," *American Journal of Sociology*, VIII (1963), pp. 422–31; Leo F. Schnore and Robert R. Alford, "Forms of Government and Socio-economic Characteristics of Suburbs," *Administrative Science Quarterly*, VIII (1963), pp. 1–17.

4. See the categorization suggested by Peter Rossi, "Power and Community Structure," *Midwest Journal of Political Science*, IV (1960), p. 398.

5. *City Politics* (Cambridge: Harvard University Press, 1963). See the excerpt from this work on page 332.

6. Robert Schulze, "The Bifurcation of Power in a Satellite City," in M. Janowitz, ed., *Community Political Systems* (Glencoe, Illinois: The Free Press of Glencoe, Illinois, 1961), pp. 19–81.

7. The volume of historical work dealing with American cities is immense but often disappointing when it comes to the questions of greatest interest to political scientists. McKelvey's work is masterful both as a summary and as an introduction to the literature. Op. cit., passim.

8. Dahl, op. cit., p. 24.

9. Ibid., p. 51.

10. McKelvey, p. 43.

11. The suggestion that civic reform issues provide "program material" and sometimes little else is developed in Edward Banfield, *Political Influence* (New York: The Free Press of Glencoe, 1961), pp. 298, ff. See the excerpt on page 247 of this volume.

12. See the provocative essay by Norton Long, "The Corporation and the Local Community," in Charles Press, ed., *The Polity* (Chicago: Rand McNally & Co., 1962), pp. 122–36.

13. See Banfield and Wilson, op. cit., pp. 277–80.

14. See ibid., Ch. 18.

15. See Banfield, *Political Influence*, pp. 291, ff. Banfield himself emphasizes the tangible conflicts of interest which divide Chicago business interests. Even so, however, one may suspect that without the Daley machine Loop business interests would have developed more commonality of interests.

16. See *Executive Reorganization and Reform in the New Deal* (Cambridge: Harvard University Press, 1963), Ch. 1.

17. Banfield and Wilson note that the city manager often acquires power by virtue of "his virtual monopoly of technical and other detailed information." op. cit., p. 175. They pay little attention to the possibility that other technicians in the city bureaucracy may acquire power over limited segments of policy in the same manner. Banfield and Wilson do note that in many cities it is the bureaucracy which can initiate and implement change but do not concede increasing significance to this group. See pp. 218–23.

18. Banfield and Wilson suggest that as the mayor's machine-based power has declined his formal authority has increased, by virtue of reformers' efforts to achieve greater centralization. They recognize, of course, that the increased authority does not compensate for the loss of power. Moreover, in the contemporary city the scope of the perceived problems and needs is often so broad that the strongest political machine could have done little about it from its own resources. Providing investment capital to rebuild downtown or opening employment opportunities for Negroes must be negotiated in the broader community. The mayor is likely to be the chief negotiator and neither formal authority nor political clout is as effective as bargaining skills. Ibid., p. 336, ff.

19. Banfield and Wilson note that the city hall reporter "is likely to be in a symbiotic relationship with the politicians and bureaucrats whose activities he reports." op. cit., p. 316. They do not conclude, however, that this relationship strengthens the elected leadership. Indeed, they imply the opposite. See, e.g. p. 325. This difference in judgment calls for more systematic empirical analysis than is presently available.

20. Ibid., p. 175. Banfield and Wilson, however, do not make this point concerning the position of the mayor in non-manager cities.

21. *Political Influence*, p. 214.

22. Ibid., p. 263, ff.

23. In addition to Dahl's discussion of Mayor Lee's active role, one may cite as particularly pertinent the discussions of Philadelphia, Detroit, Nashville and Seattle reported in the appropriate volumes of Edward Banfield, ed., *City Politics Reports* (Cambridge: Joint Center for Urban Studies, mimeo). My own research in St. Louis, the initial foundation for much of the argument in this essay, certainly leads to this conclusion.

24. For an illustration, see Robert H. Salisbury, "St. Louis: Relationships among Interests, Parties and Governmental Structure," *Western Political Quarterly*, XIII (1960), pp. 498–507.

25. See *The Alienated* Voter (New York: Holt, Rinehart and Winston, 1960), excerpted on page 62 of this volume.

26. Banfield and Wilson also discuss a shift in the contemporary city, at least in political style, from working class to middle class. They conclude that the new style politician, reflecting middle class values in a working class city, will be compelled to offer broad inducements to the electorate in the form of major civic accomplishments if he wishes reelection. Op. cit., p. 329 ff. This argument, like Dahl's, seems to me to assume that the urban electorate "shops" more actively than I think it does. It also assumes that political leaders in the urban community are more acutely conscious of their reelection problems than I think they are.

Selected References on Mayors and Urban Politics

BANFIELD, EDWARD C. *Big City Politics*. New York: Random House, 1965.

————. *Political Influence*. New York: Free Press, 1961. An analysis of Chicago politics.

————, ed. *Urban Government*. New York: Free Press, 1961.

————, and James Q. Wilson. *City Politics*. Cambridge, Mass.: Harvard University Press and M.I.T. Press, 1963.

BEAN, WALTON. *Boss Ruef's San Francisco*. Berkeley: University of California Press, 1952.

BUCKLEY, WILLIAM F., JR. *The Unmaking of a Mayor*. New York: Viking, 1966. An account by the Conservative party candidate of the 1965 New York City mayoralty campaign.

CARTER, BARBARA. *The Road to City Hall*. Englewood Cliffs, N.J.: Prentice Hall, 1967. How John V. Lindsay was elected Mayor of New York City.

COSTIKYAN, EDWARD N. *Behind Closed Doors*. New York: Harcourt, Brace & World, 1966. A treatment of New York City politics by a former leader of Tammany Hall.

CROUCH, WINSTON W., and Beatrice Dinerman. *Southern California Metropolis: A Study in Development of Government for a Metropolitan Area*. Berkeley: University of California Press, 1963. Los Angeles government and politics.

CURLEY, JAMES M. *I'd Do It Again*. Englewood Cliffs, N. J.: Prentice Hall, 1957. Autobiography of the former mayor of Boston.

DAHL, ROBERT A. *Who Governs?* New Haven: Yale University Press, 1961. Analysis of power relationships in New Haven.

FOWLER, GENE. *Beau James*. New York: Viking, 1949. Biography of Jimmy Walker, former mayor of New York City.

369

GARRETT, CHARLES. *The La Guardia Years.* New Brunswick, N.J.: Rutgers University Press, 1961.

GLAZER, NATHAN, AND DANIEL P. MOYNIHAN. *Beyond the Melting Pot.* Cambridge, Mass.: M.I.T. Press, 1963. Ethnic politics in New York City.

GOSNELL, HAROLD F. *Machine Politics: Chicago Model.* Chicago: University of Chicago Press, 1937.

GOTTFRIED, ALEX. *Boss Cermak of Chicago.* Seattle: University of Washington Press, 1962. Psychological study of a former mayor of Chicago.

GREER, SCOTT. *Governing the Metropolis.* New York: John Wiley, 1962.

HUNTER, FLOYD. *Community Power Structure.* Chapel Hill: University of North Carolina Press, 1953. The power structure of Atlanta.

JENNINGS, M. KENT. *Community Influentials: The Elites of Atlanta.* New York: Macmillan, 1964.

LEVIN, MURRAY B. *The Alienated Voter: Politics in Boston.* New York: Holt, Rinehart & Winston, 1960.

LEVINE, EDWARD M. *The Irish and Irish Politicians.* Notre Dame, Ind.: University of Notre Dame Press, 1967. Focuses on Chicago.

LINDSAY, JOHN V. *Journey into Politics.* New York: Dodd, Mead, 1967. Informal observations by the Mayor of New York City.

LOWI, THEODORE J. *At the Pleasure of the Mayor.* New York: Free Press, 1964. An analysis of office-holders appointed by the mayor in New York City.

MAIER, HENRY W. *Challenge to the Cities.* New York: Random House, 1966. An approach to a theory of urban leadership by the Mayor of Milwaukee.

MANN, ARTHUR. *La Guardia Comes to Power: 1933.* Philadelphia and New York: Lippincott, 1965. Analysis of New York City's 1933 mayoralty election.

McKEAN, DAYTON D. *The Boss: The Hague Machine in Action.* Boston: Houghton Mifflin, 1940.

MERRIAM, CHARLES E. *Chicago: A More Intimate View of Urban Politics.* New York: Macmillan, 1929.

MEYERSON, MARTIN, AND EDWARD C. BANFIELD. *Politics, Planning, and the Public Interest.* Glencoe, Ill.: Free Press, 1955. Case study of public housing in Chicago during a weak mayor administration.

MOWITZ, ROBERT J., AND DEIL S. WRIGHT. *Profile of a Metropolis.* Detroit: Wayne State University Press, 1962. Decision-making in Detroit.

PILAT, OLIVER. *Lindsay's Campaign.* Boston: Beacon Press, 1968. Behind-the-scenes during the 1965 mayoralty campaign in New York City.

POLSBY, NELSON. *Community Power and Political Theory.* New Haven: Yale University Press, 1963. An examination of the literature of community power structure.

REICHLEY, JAMES. *The Art of Government: Reform and Organization Politics in Philadelphia.* New York: Fund for the Republic, 1959.

SAYRE, WALLACE S., AND HERBERT KAUFMAN. *Governing New York City.* New York: Russell Sage Foundation, 1960.

TALBOT, ALLAN R. *The Mayor's Game.* New York: Harper & Row, 1967. The story of Richard Lee, Mayor of New Haven.

WENDT, LLOYD, AND HERMAN KOGAN. *Big Bill of Chicago.* Indianapolis: Bobbs-Merrill, 1953. The story of William H. Thompson, a former mayor of Chicago.

WHITLOCK, BRAND. *Forty Years of It.* New York: Appleton-Century-Crofts, 1925. By a reform mayor of Toledo, Ohio.

WILLIAMS, OLIVER P., AND CHARLES PRESS, eds. *Democracy in Urban America.* Chicago: Rand McNally, 1961.

WILSON, JAMES Q. *The Amateur Democrat: Club Politics in Three Cities.* Chicago: University of Chicago Press, 1962. Comparison of New York City, Chicago, and Los Angeles.

————. *Negro Politics: The Search for Leadership.* New York: Free Press, 1960. Comparison of New York City and Chicago.